The Administration of Justice in Medieval Egypt

Edinburgh Studies in Classical Islamic History and Culture
Series Editor: Carole Hillenbrand

A particular feature of medieval Islamic civilisation was its wide horizons. The Muslims fell heir not only to the Graeco-Roman world of the Mediterranean, but also to that of the ancient Near East, to the empires of Assyria, Babylon and the Persians; and beyond that, they were in frequent contact with India and China to the east and with black Africa to the south. This intellectual openness can be sensed in many interrelated fields of Muslim thought, and it impacted powerfully on trade and on the networks that made it possible. Books in this series reflect this openness and cover a wide range of topics, periods and geographical areas.

Titles in the series include:
Arabian Drugs in Early Medieval Mediterranean Medicine
Zohar Amar and Efraim Lev

The Abbasid Caliphate of Cairo, 1261–1517: Out of the Shadows
Mustafa Banister

The Medieval Western Maghrib: Cities, Patronage and Power
Amira K. Bennison

Keeping the Peace in Premodern Islam: Diplomacy under the Mamluk Sultanate, 1250–1517
Malika Dekkiche

Queens, Concubines and Eunuchs in Medieval Islam
Taef El-Azhari

The Kharijites in Early Islamic Historical Tradition: Heroes and Villains
Hannah-Lena Hagemann

Medieval Damascus: Plurality and Diversity in an Arabic Library – The Ashrafiya Library Catalogue
Konrad Hirschler

A Monument to Medieval Syrian Book Culture: The Library of Ibn ʿAbd al-Hādī
Konrad Hirschler

The Popularisation of Sufism in Ayyubid and Mamluk Egypt: State and Society, 1173–1325
Nathan Hofer

Defining Anthropomorphism: The Challenge of Islamic Traditionalism
Livnat Holtzman

Making Mongol History: Rashid al-Din and the Jamiʿ al-Tawarikh
Stefan Kamola

Lyrics of Life: Saʿdi on Love, Cosmopolitanism and Care of the Self
Fatemeh Keshavarz

Art, Allegory and The Rise of Shiism In Iran, 1487–1565
Chad Kia

The Adminstration of Justice in Medieval Egypt: From the Seventh to the Twelfth Century
Yaacov Lev

A History of the True Balsam of Matarea
Marcus Milwright

Ruling from a Red Canopy: Political Authority in the Medieval Islamic World, From Anatolia to South Asia
Colin P. Mitchell

Islam, Christianity and the Realms of the Miraculous: A Comparative Exploration
Ian Richard Netton

Conquered Populations in Early Islam: Non-Arabs, Slaves and the Sons of Slave Mothers
Elizabeth Urban

edinburghuniversitypress.com/series/escihc

The Administration of Justice in Medieval Egypt

From the Seventh to the Twelfth Century

Yaacov Lev

EDINBURGH
University Press

Edinburgh University Press is one of the leading university presses in the UK. We publish academic books and journals in our selected subject areas across the humanities and social sciences, combining cutting-edge scholarship with high editorial and production values to produce academic works of lasting importance. For more information visit our website: edinburghuniversitypress.com

Edinburgh University Press Ltd
The Tun – Holyrood Road
12 (2f) Jackson's Entry
Edinburgh EH8 8PJ

First published in hardback by Edinburgh University Press 2020

Typeset in 11/15 Adobe Garamond by
Servis Filmsetting Ltd, Stockport, Cheshire

A CIP record for this book is available from the British Library

ISBN 978 1 4744 5923 5 (hardback)
ISBN 978 1 4744 5924 2 (paperback)
ISBN 978 1 4744 5926 6 (webready PDF)
ISBN 978 1 4744 5925 9 (epub)

Contents

Acknowledgements vi

Introduction: Issues and Methodology 1

PART ONE The Cadi: Judge and Administrator

1 The Cadi's Jurisdiction: Evolution and Consolidation 37

2 Sunnī Rulers and their Cadis 83

3 Ismāʿīlī Rulers and the Judicial System 111

PART TWO Judicial Institutions outside the Pale of Islamic Law

4 Criminal Justice and the Police 161

5 The Law of the Market 184

6 The Ruler's Justice: The Maẓālim Institution 202

PART THREE The Administration of Justice in Non-Muslim Communities

7 Judicial Autonomy: Medieval Realities and Modern Discourse 231

8 The Administration of Justice in a Broader Perspective 259

Bibliography 265

Index 296

Acknowledgements

I owe a great debt of gratitude to Petra M. Sijpesteijn and the Leiden Institute for Area Studies for their warm hospitality during my sabbatical at Leiden University in 2012–13. I became aware of the significance of papyrology, and Arabic papyrology in particular, through many conversations with Petra and Khaled Younes and Jelle Bruning, then Ph.D. students at the research project 'The Formation of Islam: The View from Below'. The year in Leiden was formative for my understanding of how early Muslim history should be approached and studied. I owe an equally great debt of gratitude to Mathieu Tillier of the Sorbonne University, who read the first draft of the Introduction and Chapters 1–3 and offered many valuable corrections and thoughtful remarks. My colleagues Miriam Frenkel and Oded Zinger of the Hebrew University generously shared with me their knowledge of Jewish history and Geniza studies, and offered many useful comments on Chapter 7.

It was a great pleasure, and a great intellectual experience, to participate in and contribute to the 'Histoire et archéologie de l'Islam et de la Méditerranée médiévale' seminar at the Sorbonne University in October–December 2014. I am grateful to Anne-Marie Eddé, Annliese Nef and Sylvie Denoix for their welcome in Paris, and to Christophe Picard and David Bramoullé for their hospitality in Toulouse during a short visit to Le Miral University.

The peer-review system has its imperfections, but I had the privilege of benefiting from corrections, suggestions and bibliographical references to sources and literature made by two anonymous readers on behalf of Edinburgh University Press.

During the course of my research I received generous assistance from numerous libraries and librarians. I am much obliged to Marlis J. Saleh, who kindly introduced me to the vast resources of the Joseph Regenstein Library,

University of Chicago in the summer of 2016. Geula Elimelekh, who vastly expanded the Arabic collection at the Bar Ilan University Library, helped me in procuring sources and literature, while Dina Baum's expertise with electronic resources proved invaluable. My thanks to all of them.

Introduction: Issues and Methodology

At the heart of the book lies the largely ignored question of to what extent Muslim law (*sharīʿa*) was applied in medieval Islamic states and whether its precepts indeed governed the life of individuals and the conduct of society. This book, however, is not about the formation of Islamic law, but rather about judicial institutions which preceded and paralleled the formation of the law and remained in place unaffected by that formation. The book is also about the political-administrative history that shaped the way justice was administrated, and what the spheres of competence were of the various bodies that made up the system.

Four judicial institutions were involved in the administration of justice in medieval Islam: the cadi, the chief of police (*shurṭa/ṣāḥib al-shurṭa*), the market inspector (*ḥisba/muḥtasib*) and the ruler (the *maẓālim* institution). There are ample sources and a considerable body of literature on the way the cadi operated and how justice was dispensed by the ruler. To what extent, however, the *maẓālim* court – not to say criminal justice dispensed by the chief of the police – adhered to and was congruent with the *sharīʿa* remains little-discussed. What is known about the chiefs of police in early Islam and the Fatimid period casts doubt as to whether *sharīʿ* law was applied in the cases adjudicated by them, and how the police gained a monopoly on the administration of criminal justice is another obscure question. The same set of questions is applicable to the *ḥisba* law and the post of market inspector; both became Islamised and perceived as the embodiment of the Koranic dictum of 'commanding right and forbidding wrong'. Early *ḥisba* manuals, however, are texts with no religious connotations, and the core of the *ḥisba* regulations remained beyond the pale of the *sharīʿa*.

Modern literature on medieval Islam perceives the *sharīʿa* as an embodiment of Islam as a system of beliefs and civilisation. Joseph Schacht, for example, has stated:

> Islamic law is the epitome of the Islamic spirit, the most typical manifestation of the Islamic way of life, the kernel of Islam itself.
>
> For the majority of the Muslims, the law has always been and still is of much greater practical importance than the dogma.[1]

I would argue that medieval realities were complex, and that within the system of the administration of justice *sharīʿa* played a well-defined but narrow place since full congruence between the two obtained only at the cadi's court. Medieval people and authors were well aware of the situation, which is implicitly reflected in their writings. As a means of realising that my observation is a fair and balanced reflection of medieval realities, one can begin with the famous *Aḥkām al-Sulṭāniyya* by Māwardī (974–1058). The topic of the 'administration of justice' is not dealt with as such by Māwardī, but the various components of the system are extensively discussed in several chapters. Māwardī's account of the cadi institution is long and complex, and the discussion begins with the question of who is qualified for the appointment: that is, a mature free-born Muslim male who is in full control of his faculties and endowed with proper moral qualities (*ʿadāla*) and knowledge of the law.[2] According to Māwardī, a cadi's jurisdiction, or fields of competence (*aḥkām*), involves ten cases, which include resolution of disputes (*munāzaʿāt*), the securing of rights for those who legally possess them (*istifāʾ al-ḥuqūq*), establishing guardianship (*wilāya*), conducting marriages and divorces, disposing of legacies, supervision of pious endowments, and implementation of the punishments laid down by God (*ḥadd*, pl. *ḥudūd*). Under the heading of the cadi's *aḥkām* Māwardī also discusses procedural aspects of how the cadi's court is run and the moral principles that must guide his conduct. The cadi has the right to examine the probity of the court's witnesses and trustees

[1] See 'Pre-Islamic Background and Early Development of Jurisprudence', 28.

[2] Māwardī, 199–203. These sections of Māwardī's text have been discussed in three articles by Amedroz: see 'The Office of Kadi', 761–9, 'The Hisba Jurisdiction', 287–314 and 'The Mazalim Jurisdiction', 635–74. The two first articles contain very brief discussion of Māwardī's text, while most of the references are to cadis and *ḥisba* in the Abbasid caliphate and pre-Fatimid and Fatimid Egypt. There are two lucid English translations of Māwardī's text, by Wafaa H. Wahba and Asadullah Yate. Inevitably, both have sacrificed precision for readability.

and to appoint and dismiss them. He is also reminded that he must treat the powerful and weak equally, and the same applies to the treatment of a noble descendant of the Prophet's family (*sharīf*) and an ordinary respected commoner (*mashrūf*).[3]

Other institutions that were involved in the administration of justice, such as *ḥisba* and *maẓālim*, are also discussed. Māwardī's discussion of the *ḥisba* reflects its full Islamisation under the motto of commanding right and forbidding wrong. From Māwardī's account one can argue that the *ḥisba* institution represented a fusion of the Islamic principles of commanding right and forbidding wrong, which were drafted onto the existing laws of the market. Māwardī enumerates nine distinctions between the institutional role of the person in charge of the *ḥisba* (*wālī al-ḥisba*) in implementing 'commanding right and forbidding wrong' and an individual involved in doing this. From the point of view of the current discussion, the most significant aspect of Māwardī's account of the *ḥisba* is the attempt to explain the differences between the *ḥisba* and the cadi. Māwardī states that the *ḥisba* is an institution placed between the jurisdiction of the cadi and *maẓālim*. He also states that in two respects the *ḥisba* is analogous to the cadi, but also inferior in two respects and superior in two other respects. Perhaps Māwardī's most important observation concerns the different approach of the *muḥtasib* and cadi towards stemming the spread of morally reprehensible practices (*munkarāt*). He states: '*Ḥisba* involves [the striking of] fear and the *muḥtasib*'s use of fear and harsh conduct [*salāṭa* and *ghilẓa*] should not be considered as oppression [*jawr*] and violation of rights [*kharq*], while cadi's jurisdiction is about implementation of justice [by means of] leniency and reverence.'[4] Following these illuminating remarks, the subsequent sections of Māwardī's discussion are dedicated to the 'commanding right and forbidding wrong' aspect of the *ḥisba* institution. If an anachronistic approach can be pardoned here, it can be argued that Māwardī perceives the *muḥtasib* as belonging to the executive branch of the government and as an official exercising of legitimate coercive powers.

From the point of view of my argument, the most significant aspect of Māwardī's discussion of the *ḥisba* has been noted by Emile Tyan, and

[3] Māwardī, 215–16; Amedroz, 'The Office of Kadi', 762–4.
[4] Māwardī, 606.

the key sentence in his translation is as follows: 'la jurisprudence *lato sensu* du *muḥtasib* est une jurisprudence *coutumière* et non une jurisprudence *légale*.'[5] Tyan's sentence is taken from the section of Māwardī's text which offers a brief description of the practical matters which should concern the *muḥtasib*. He also offers a general observation, saying that the *muḥtasib* is concerned with the distinction between what is harmful and what is not. His decision-making process is described as involving independent reasoning (*ijtihād*) based on customary law. Māwardī also asserts that there is a difference between independent reasoning based on customary and *sharī*ʿ law, and vaguely implies that the *muḥtasib* is prevented from exercising *ijtihād* within the framework of the *sharīʿa*.[6]

The Islamisation of the *ḥisba* under the motto 'commanding right and forbidding wrong' did not alter its substance as *ʿurfī* law (jurisprudence *coutumière*) outside the pale of the *sharīʿa* (jurisprudence *légale*). Although not explicitly stated, the recognition of the tension between *ʿurfī* and *sharʿī* elements in the way the *ḥisba* functioned also characterises János Jany's discussion of the institution.[7]

Māwardī's list of the qualities required of a person appointed *maẓālim* involves an almost impossible combination of projecting power and religious scrupulousness. The nominee should be *ʿaẓīm al-hayba* (most awe-inspiring) and *kathīr al-waraʿ* (most religiously strict, or pious). Māwardī provides an extensive account of how the *maẓālim* sessions should be conducted and specifies ten spheres of the *maẓālim*'s jurisdiction, which also includes supervision of pious endowments. This statement can be perceived as an encroachment on the cadi's domain, but actually it reflects the superior nature of the *maẓālim* institution.[8] Unhesitatingly, Māwardī states that the person

5 See *Histoire de l'organisation judiciaire*, 648 (emphasis in the original text). This quotation stems from the undated Cairo edition of the text published by al-Maḥmūdiyya al-Tijāriyya Press, which was not available to me.

6 Māwardī, 639.

7 See *Judging in the Islamic, Jewish and Zoroastrian Legal Traditions*, 107–9.

8 Māwardī, 243; Amedroz, 'The Mazalim Jurisdiction', 635–46. The *maẓālim* institution is also discussed in another eleventh-century *Aḥkām al-Sulṭāniyya* text by Abū Yaʿlā ibn al-Farrāʾ. For a comparison between the two texts see Hurvitz, 'Competing Texts', 1–53, esp. 21–6; Melchert, 'Māwardī, Abū Yaʿlā, and the Sunnī Revival', 37–61, which concludes that Ibn al-Farrāʾ preceded Māwardī in writing the *Aḥkām al-Sulṭāniyya*. I owe the last reference to the kindness of Mathieu Tillier.

in charge of the *maẓālim* (*wālī al-maẓālim*) is more awe-inspiring, has a stronger hand and is more powerful than the cadi. The *maẓālim* institution is perceived as an institution superior to that of the cadi and the *ḥisba*. Māwardī states:

> it is permitted to a person in charge of the *maẓālim* to examine the affairs of both the cadi and the market inspector while it is not permitted to the cadi to examine the affairs of the *wālī al-maẓālim* but it is permitted to him to examine the affairs of the market supervisor. The market inspector is neither allowed to examine the affairs of the cadi nor those of the *wālī al-maẓālim*.[9]

Tyan's discussion of the *maẓālim* institution is very extensive and goes beyond Māwardī's text. It combines topical and chronological approaches and gives attention to both the Muslim East and West. Jany's discussion is focused more on Māwardī's text, and he lists the ten areas of competence ascribed to the *maẓālim* institution. Both perceive the procedural aspects of the *maẓalim* as marking the main difference between it and the cadi's court.[10] Reading the sources and the literature, we draw the unavoidable conclusion that the *maẓālim* institution was mostly, if not completely, outside the pale of the Islamic law.

The police are not mentioned as an institution involved in the administration of justice, but a long chapter is devoted to the dispensing of criminal justice (*aḥkām al-jarā'im*). Māwardī's discussion commences with the unequivocal statement that 'crimes are things forbidden by the *sharīʿa* which God has restrained by *ḥadd* and *taʿzīr* [discretionary punishments]'. The sections that immediately follow this statement, however, envisage the *amīr* (the person who wields power [*amr*]), not the cadi, as the state official who renders criminal justice. Subsequently, the chapter specifies ten situations in which he has a role to play.[11]

The role of the cadi in the implementation of the *ḥudūd* is alluded to but not detailed. The different perspectives of the *umarā'* (pl. form of *amīr*) and the cadis when examining the guilt or innocence of the accused are

[9] Māwardī, 606.
[10] Tyan, *Histoire de l'organisation judiciaire*, 445; Jany, *Judging in the Islamic, Jewish and Zoroastrian Legal Traditions*, 110.
[11] Māwardī, 555–8.

emphasized, and Māwardī states that the *umarā'* are more concerned with the political (*siyāsa*) aspects of the case while the cadis are more concerned with the legal norms (*aḥkām*). Once guilt was established there was, however, no difference between the *umarā'* and the cadis in the implementation of God's laid-down punishments.

Māwardī's description of the administration of justice as a hierarchical system created by the state which involved the *maẓālim*, cadi, *ḥisba* and *aḥkām al-jarā'im* is a reflection of medieval realities with which a student of medieval Islamic history and society is quite familiar. In order to see how limited the role of the cadi was within this system one has to read Māwardī's chapter dealing with the *niqāba* institution (the headship of the ʿAlid family) which investigated, supervised and took care of people who claimed the Prophet's lineage.[12] The institution involved two officials (*naqīb*, pl. *nuqabā'*): one was responsible for people claiming lineage through ʿAlī (the Prophet's son-in-law) and one for those claiming lineage through ʿAbbās (the Prophet's uncle). The rationale behind the institution's existence was to prevent people of lower status, having no lineage to the Prophet, from exercising authority over the Prophet's descendants. The institution's spheres of responsibility involved *niqāba al-khaṣṣa* and *niqāba al-ʿāmma*. The *naqīb* entrusted with the *niqāba al-khaṣṣa* was responsible for maintaining the purity of the lineage of people claiming to be the Prophet's descendants and for rendering them various services. The *naqīb* entrusted with *niqāba al-ʿāmma* had judicial authority over the people claiming both lines of descent, but his appointment did not necessarily curtail the involvement of the cadi in their judicial affairs.[13]

The value of Māwardī's discussion of the various state institutions that played a role in the administration of justice goes beyond the light it sheds on the role of the cadi within the system. The text provides insights into two issues of which we always must be aware when medieval legal and judicial realities are discussed: frequently, the spheres of administrative and judicial

[12] I have adopted Teresa Bernheimer's terminology. See *The ʿAlids*, 51. I owe this reference to the kindness of Mathieu Tillier.

[13] Māwardī, 273. For the full range of duties of both *naqībs*, see Bernheimer, *The ʿAlids*, 54–5. For other aspects of this institution, see her discussion at 55–70. For the post of *naqīb* during the Fatimid period, see Musabbiḥī, 9, 46; Maqrīzī, *Kitāb al-Muqaffā*, III, 465–6; *Ittiʿāẓ*, II, 133; III, 148.

responsibilities were blurred (see the *niqāba* institution) and the system had ingrained biases and preferences. Although the notion of equity before the law is firmly stated in medieval Arabic texts dealing with the cadi institution, the system (in the modern perception) was biased against women and exhibited strong class/social preferences. The cadi, like any other official involved in the administration of justice, operated within these parameters and the system must be evaluated on its strengths and weaknesses, not by modern notions of justice.

Setting the Stage: The Contemporary Historiography of Early Islam

The aim of the following three sections is to provide a unifying framework for the book and to present topics which are directly relevant to the discussion of the administration of justice. A diachronic approach has been adopted as the methodology for discussing the question of to what extent Muslim law was applied in medieval Islamic states and societies. The inquiry is also heavily influenced and informed by the progress that has been made in recent decades in the study of early Islam.

The contemporary historiography of early Islam is dominated by two paradigms: 'From *Jāhiliyya* to Islam', and 'From Late Antiquity to Early Islam'. These are complementary approaches that emphasise dynamic processes of transition and change while depicting the emerging Muslim civilisation as firmly rooted in both its Arab pre-Islamic past and the world of Late Antiquity. Medieval Muslim discourse on the formation of Islam is structured more along the lines of the 'From *Jāhiliyya* to Islam' paradigm, and emphasises a break with the Arab pagan past (*jāhiliyya*) and a transition to monotheism (*tawḥīd*).[14] This break supposedly involved a total reorientation

[14] While I use the terms 'Arab', 'Muslims' and 'Islamic conquest', I am aware that the validity of this terminology is questioned. Some would say that these terms lack precision and others that they are erroneous. For an eloquent explanation of the problems involved, see Hoyland, *In God's Path*, 5–6; 'Reflections on the Identity', 113–40, where he offers an extensive critical review of recent literature on the subject. For a nuanced discussion of the terms 'believers', 'emigrants' and 'Muslims' see Lindstedt, 'Muhājirūn as a Name', 67–73. For the late perception of the expansion of the 'intruders coming from the desert' as conquest and other suggestions concerning terminology, see Donner, 'Arabic Fatḥ as 'Conquest', 1–14; 'Talking about Islam's Origins', 1–23, esp. 15, 22–3. For the notion that 'the comprehensive construction of Arabness' took place 'in the early Muslim period', see Webb, *Imagining the Arabs*, chs 4–5. I owe this reference to the kindness of one of the anonymous readers on behalf of EUP. When this line of inquiry is pursued

of beliefs and social practices and included, for example, changing female or male first names. When we turn to literature, we find that discussion about the acceptance of Islam at the time of the Prophet is surprisingly sparse and hampered by the late date of the sources and the question as to what extent they retain the early sense of the phenomenon.[15] Islamic discourse also emphasises the formation of a separate and unique Muslim identity that differed from those of Christianity and Judaism. The various themes of this internal discourse are illustrated by Ibn Ḥabīb's account of the reforms of the Umayyad caliph ʿAbd al-Malik (685–705), which involved the replacement of pre-Islamic weights by Islamic ones and the decision to mint coins bearing exclusively Koranic inscriptions which, Ibn Ḥabīb (d. 852) asserts, was a unique Islamic practice.[16] Glimpses and insights into how a separate Islamic identity (vis-à-vis Christianity) was formed are also provided by non-Muslim sources, which emphasise the killing of pigs in 693–4 in Syria and the destruction of icons in 723–4.[17]

Recently, the study of early Islam has been more and more influenced by a third paradigm, which emphasises processes taking place from below as playing a decisive role in shaping of Islam as a religion and socio-political entity. This approach is encapsulated by the heading of the Leiden University research project, 'The Formation of Islam: The View from Below', and is characterised by reliance on documentary sources, the papyri, relegating literary sources to second place.[18] Like any other historiographical method it has its problems, and Frank E. Peters, for example, alludes to some of these in stating 'the view from below is random, scattered and occasional' and poses the question of whether it is typical or eccentric.[19] Although papyri

one must not forget Drory's 'The Abbasid Construction of Jāhiliyya', 33–49. For the evolution of the Coptic identity during the seventh to ninth centuries, see Chapter 8.

15 Abū Zurʿa, II, 764–5; Quḍāʿī, *ʿUyūn al-Maʿārif*, 129. For literature see, for example, Stern, 'Muḥammad's Bond with the Women', 185–97; Calasso, 'Récits de conversion', 19–47.

16 See *Kitāb al-Taʾrīkh*, 133. There is extensive literature discussing ʿAbd al-Malik's all-epigraphic gold and silver coinage minted from 696–7 and its success and consequences. See, for example, Bacharach, 'Signs of Sovereignty', 1–30; Heidemann, 'The Evolving Representation', 149–95; Duggan, 'Some Reasons for the Currency Reform of A.H. 77/696–7 A.D.', 1–24.

17 Theophanes Confessor, *The Chronicle*, 512; Theophilus of Edessa, *Chronicle*, 189; *The Chronicle of Zuqnīn*, 155.

18 See the project's website (accessed 24 April 2017). For this and other research projects, see Reinfandt, 'Arabic Papyrology and Early Islamic Egypt', 229–35.

19 See 'The Roman Near East', 187.

have been found in a number of places in the Middle East, the greatest and most significant finds come from several sites in Upper Egypt and the Fayyūm. The problems involved in interpreting papyri in general, and in the Egyptian context in particular, have been discussed by Petra M. Sijpesteijn, who points out that most of the Egyptian population lived in the Delta, and the question of whether the realities of Upper Egypt also apply to the Delta is largely unanswered.[20] As Marie Legendre's work clearly bears out, the question of how to interpret papyrological evidence pertaining to a certain topic or region in the absence of parallel documentation is always relevant whether in the context of broad study or a case study.[21] Furthermore, as has been noted by Maged S. A. Mikhail, papyri mostly reflect local daily life and the policies of the provincial government (mostly taxation), while policies at the state level largely fall outside the scope of these documents.[22] The same can be said about other institutions which are scarcely referred to in the papyrological record. Sijpesteijn has noted, for example, that 'The Muslim army has left us a surprisingly meagre paper trail, at least in the papyri that have come to light so far'. The contradiction between the central role of the army and military affairs in political and social life, which is amply attested in the literary sources, and the documentary record is explained by the lack of correlation between the location of Muslim armies in Egypt and the places where papyri were discovered.[23]

The inverse correlation between the papyrological record and certain state institutions also applies to the judiciary and has a direct bearing on the present discussion. Mathieu Tillier, Lucian Reinfandt and Jelle Bruning have discussed the administration of justice in Egypt's provinces and have pointed out that state officials at the local level and the governor in Fusṭāṭ played a significant role in the provincial system. When approaching the matter in the context of the paradigm of continuity and rupture – or, to put it differently, 'from Late Antiquity to Early Islam' – one must note Bruning's observation that from the 710s onward the governor of Egypt dealt with legal disputes among the country's non-Muslim population in the provinces. According

[20] See *Shaping a Muslim State*, 2–4.
[21] See for example 'Hiérarchie administrative', 105.
[22] See *From Byzantine to Islamic Egypt*, 8.
[23] See 'Army Economics', 246.

to Bruning, the first indisputable reference (in documentary sources) to a provincial cadi dates from 811.[24] Significant changes took place along the eighth century, and Tillier has noted:

> Ce n'est qu'au second âge Abbasside, alors que l'Égypte s'engageait dans la voie de l'autonomie provinciale, que le modèle classique de la judicature cadiale finit par s'imposer en Haute-Égypte.[25]

Meanwhile Reinfandt has pointed out:

> Documentary sources never mention *qāḍī-s* earlier than the middle of the 2nd/8th century and confirm that under Umayyad rule judicial tasks and practical legal matters were dealt with by state authorities and officials of the public executive, such as provincial governors, heads of districts, and village headmen.[26]

The remarks made by them are presented in the context of a study of provincial judicial authorities in Umayyad Egypt and apply to this context only. The situation in Fusṭāṭ was different, and the difference between what was happening in the capital and the provinces is not only a reflection of the inverse correlation between institutional presence and papyri finds, but also reflects Arab-Muslim demography and patterns of settlement in Egypt. In other words, the cadi was a Muslim institution that served the Muslim population mainly concentrated in Fusṭāṭ. Ninth- to tenth-century Arab-Muslim historiography was written in Fusṭāṭ and reflects its realities; however, as the Islamisation process progressed the cadi institution also spread to the provinces. Different types of sources reflect different segments of population and different types of interaction between these populations and the state and its institutions. The cadi, as a marker of sizeable Muslim populations in provincial towns, is, for example, clearly attested in Ibn Ḥawqal's tenth-century description of the Delta. This argument tallies with that of Tillier: the study of the role of the cadi as a dispenser of justice must be undertaken in the context of the Islamisation of Egypt.[27] I am fully aware that correlation between

[24] See *The Rise of a Capital*, 136, 139.
[25] See 'Du pagarque au cadi', 20.
[26] See 'Local Judicial Authorities', 131.
[27] Tillier, 'Du pagarque au cadi', 31; Lev, 'Coptic Rebellions', 331–7.

the two issues is difficult, if not impossible. The study of Fusṭāṭ and other garrison towns is easier because of the settlement of Arab-Muslim population there and the fact that the cadi institution evolved there. It reached Egypt's provincial towns when the spread of Arab-Muslim population accelerated and Islamisation advanced. The office of the cadi was a Muslim urban institution, and one cannot expect to find it in small and insignificant settlements with no, or a small, Muslim population.

When the administration of justice is discussed in a wider context, the topic transcends the three paradigmatic approaches outlined above and also touches upon two other interwoven issues: the formation of Islamic identity and the Islamic state. Any discussion about the existence of the early Islamic state seems somewhat artificial, especially in view of the vast Muslim military and naval activity that took place during 630–750, which was sustained through state political authority and institutions that marshalled the necessary resources. Nonetheless, the notion that there was an Umayyad state that was characterised by institutions and a legitimising ideology has been convincingly demonstrated in Fred M. Donner's 1986 seminal study, in which he relied on non-literary sources in support of the argument. Another approach has been suggested by Legendre, who perceives the formation of the Islamic state as an interplay between the conquerors and the conquered.[28]

Whatever the methodological problems involved with the study of the papyri, the contribution of papyri and epigraphy to the study of early Islam is immense. When the methodology of relying on non-literary sources is adopted, the epigraphic evidence can be perceived as showing the emergence of an Islamic identity during ʿAbd al-Malik's rule. For example, a funerary stela from Aswān in Upper Egypt dated to 652 implores God to forgive the deceased, reflecting typical monotheistic piety which lacks any particular Islamic character. Forty years after the 652 stela was engraved, another funerary stela from the same place is couched in typical Islamic terminology which invokes God's mercy on the Prophet Muḥammad His messenger and states

[28] Donner, 'The Formation of the Islamic State', 283–94. For updates and new findings, see Donner, 'Introduction', XIII–XXXIII; Legendre, 'Neither Byzantine nor Islamic?', 3–18. See also Hoyland, 'New Documentary Texts', 395–416.

that there is no God but the One God, who has no associates.[29] Allusions to Islamic identity pre-date the 652 Aswān stela and include references to the *Hijrī* calendar and historical events associated with the rise of Islam. The death of the caliph ʿUmar ibn al-Khaṭṭāb (ʿUmar I 634–44), referred to simply by his name with no titles, is recorded in a graffito/commemorative inscription on the Syrian pilgrimage road south of Medina. The inscription, which refers to the year 24/644–5, indicates the use and diffusion of the *Hijrī* calendar and is in line with similar off-hand references made in other early inscriptions.[30] Recent years have seen great progress in the study of graffiti, and more references to early caliphs and political events such as the killing of the caliph ʿUthmān (644–58) have come to light. One of the most interesting allusions is to an Umayyad prince referred to as *walī ʿahd al-muslimīn wa-l-muslimāt* (heir apparent of Muslim men and women), which, eventually, was simplified to *walī ʿahd al-muslimīn* (heir apparent of Muslims).[31] Equally fascinating is the Greek inscription commemorating the rebuilding of the hot baths of Ḥammat Gader, on the Golan Heights, for the use of the sick (5 December 662). It begins with the name of Muʿāwiya, referred to as the Commander of the Faithful, mentions the name of the person responsible for the project and alludes to both the local dating system and the *Hijrī* one.[32]

When the scope of the investigation is expanded to also include documentary evidence, the introduction of the *Hijrī* calendar is alluded to in bilingual Greek–Arabic papyri of a fiscal nature which refer to the Egyptian calendar with a cycle of fifteen indiction years and the Muslim calendar. The first known papyrus of this kind, using both the calendar of the indiction cycle and the Muslim dating system (Jumādā II 22), is from 25 April 643.[33] The use of *Hijrī* dating can be interpreted as indicating the existence of a basic Islamic identity that is concurrent with the caliphs of Medina (the Rāshidūn,

[29] El-Hawary, 'The Most Ancient', 321–33; 'The Second Oldest', 289–93; Halevi, 'The Paradox of Islamization', 121–2.

[30] Ghabban and Hoyland, 'The Inscription of Zuhayr', 210–37; Rāġib, 'Un papyrus arab de l'an 22 de l'hégire', 363–72.

[31] Imbert, 'Califes, princes et compagnons dans les graffiti du debut de l'Islam', 59–78, esp. 64–5, 67, 69–70.

[32] Hirschfeld and Solar, 'The Roman Thermae', 203–4; Green and Tsafrir, 'Greek Inscriptions', 95–6. For pre-Islamic Arab calendars, see Masʿūdī, 202; Meimaris, 'The Arab (*Hijra*) Era', 183–4.

[33] Worp, 'Hegira Years', 107–15, esp. 109.

632–60) and the beginning of Muʿāwiya's rule. The notion that a strong state had already existed during the rule of Muʿāwiya has recently been put forward by Clive Foss, who considers the caliph to be 'the most important secular ruler of the entire 7th century', while Robert Hoyland discerns a gradual institutional and ideological evolution throughout the Umayyad period.[34]

Many aspects of Umayyad state activity, such as public building and road improvements, are attested in inscriptions and papyri. The Umayyads also sponsored the building of mosques in Damascus, Jerusalem and the holy cities of Arabia, while the development of a legitimising ideology is clearly borne out by coinage and literary sources.[35] On the political level, the Umayyad state sponsored theological dogmas, fought rebels of diverse political and religious backgrounds, and persecuted and executed those branded as heretics.[36]

The contribution of literary sources to the debate about the formation of an Islamic identity must not be overlooked, since these sources indicate that the process was also inspired from above, with the governors playing an important role in the development of Islamic religious rituals. In 673 in Fusṭāṭ, for instance, the governor Maslama ibn Mukhallad ordered that the call to prayer should be made simultaneously in all the city's mosques, while in 690–1 another governor was the first to introduce the supplication prayers on 9 Dhū l-Ḥijja, to coincide with the *wuqūf* performed in ʿArafa during the pilgrimage.[37] In addition, the governors of Egypt were responsible for the building and rebuilding of the congregational Ancient Mosque in Fusṭāṭ, also

[34] Foss, 'Egypt under Muʿāwiya Part II', 75; Hoyland, 'New Documentary Texts', 401, 410–11; Robinson, *ʿAbd al-Malik*, 9, 118.

[35] For Muʿāwiya's public works, see Miles, 'Early Islamic Inscriptions Near Ṭāʾif', 237. For ʿAbd al-Malik's building of new roads and construction of milestones, see Sharon, 'An Arabic Inscription', 367–72; Elad, 'The Southern Golan', 33–46; Cytryn-Silverman, 'The Fifth Mīl from Jerusalem', 603–10. For other Umayyad construction projects, see Bacharach, 'Marwanid Umayyad Building Activities', 27–44; Khamis, 'Two Wall Mosaic Inscriptions', 159–76. For the development of the governmental postal service during the Umayyad period, see Silverstein, *Postal Systems*, Ch. 2.

[36] For state-sponsored dogmas and persecution of heretics, see Anthony, 'The Prophecy and Passion of al-Ḥāriṯ b. Saʿīd', 1–29; Marsham, 'Public Execution', 101–36; Judd, 'Muslim Persecution of the Heretics', 1–14.

[37] Kindī, 39, 50. For prayer rituals attributed to ʿUmar I, see Sijpesteijn, 'A Ḥadīth Fragment on Papyrus', 321–31.

known as the mosque of ʿAmr ibn al-ʿĀṣ. In these works politics and religion intervened, as the architectural shaping of a common sacred public space conveyed political authority. In 664–5, for example, Maslama ibn Mukhallad enlarged the Ancient Mosque and pulled down sections built by ʿAmr ibn al-ʿĀṣ in 656–7 (for ʿAmr's complex relations with the Umayyads see the next section). He also added minarets to other mosques. In 696–7, the entire mosque was razed and rebuilt on the orders of ʿAbd al-ʿAzīz, the governor of Egypt and the son of the caliph Marwān. Nonetheless, even such high-ranking patronage did not ensure the future of the new edifice. In 710–11, the governor Qurra ibn Sharīk, acting on the instructions of the caliph, pulled down the mosque built by the governor ʿAbd al-ʿAzīz in 696–7. In this case, the rebuilding of the mosque reflected an intra-Umayyad power struggle. In 705–6, the caliph ʿAbd al-Malik appointed his son ʿAbd Allāh governor of Egypt and ordered him to dismiss the people appointed by his uncle ʿAbd al-ʿAzīz. It seems that the ultimate undoing of ʿAbd al-ʿAzīz's policies was the destruction of the mosque he had built.

The rulers' interest in mosques was not limited to the congregational mosque in Fusṭāṭ, and in 749–50 an order was issued to install pulpits in provincial mosques.[38] This deed, like the appearance of the institution of cadi in the provincial context, might be considered as indicating the spread of Muslim population and Islamisation. In the broader Islamic context, what happened with the Ancient Mosque in Fusṭāṭ happened with the Kaaba sanctuary, which was pulled down and rebuilt by the anti-Umayyad rebel Ibn Zubayr and, following the Umayyad suppression of the rebellion, reconstructed in its original form.[39] While the state was responsible for the shap-

[38] Kindī, 38, 51, 58, 65. The different phases of construction, destruction and rebuilding of the Ancient Mosque are recorded in Arabic non-Muslim sources. See Saʿīd ibn Baṭrīq, 40, 51. For the remodelling of the Ancient Mosque in Fusṭāṭ and other provincial mosques, see Kindī, 60, 65, 94, 134. Donald Whitcomb has suggested that the destruction of the mosque by Qurra ibn Sharīk was perhaps motivated by the need to change the southern (*qibla*) orientation of the mosque towards Mecca to tally with the calculation of the *qibla* by the astronomers. See 'An Umayyad Legacy', 406–7.

[39] Yaʿqūbī, II, 260–1; Quḍāʿī, *ʿUyūn al-Maʿārif*, 159–60, 168; Ibn Ḥabīb, 132–3. In 707, the mosque of the Prophet in Medina was pulled down by the Umayyad caliph al-Walīd and built anew and embellished with mosaics supplied by the Byzantine emperor. See Yaʿqūbī, II, 284; Ibn Ḥabīb, 139. For broader textual and historical discussion, see Gibb, 'Arab–Byzantine Relations', 52–7. For the Abbasid caliphs sponsoring the extension of mosques in Medina, Mecca and Basra in 778 and 784, and the rebuilding of the Zamzam well in Mecca in 834, see Fasawī, I, 149, 156, 203.

ing of the architectural form of mosques, it also took responsibility for the performance of the *ḥājj*. An Arabic papyrus dated to 705–17 indicates that the caliph called people to perform the *ḥājj* and state dignitaries echoed the call, while non-Muslim literary sources date the state patronage of the *ḥājj* to Muʿāwiya.[40]

In the literary sources Muʿāwiya is described as playing a crucial role in the shaping of religious rites, court etiquette and governing institutions. The geographer and historian Yaqūbī (fl. second half of the ninth century), for example, provides a long list of things that Muʿāwiya did first, referring to the installation of pulpits and *maqṣūras* (the area in a mosque near the prayer niche [*miḥrāb*], preserved for the ruler) in mosques and, in the court context, the use of the throne and the establishment of a bodyguard (*ḥaras*). Muʿāwiya was also the first to employ Christian clerks in the administration and to set up the office of the seal.[41] When approached from the perspective of state formation and the crystallisation of Islamic identity, the contribution made by judicial institutions, especially the cadi, to the shaping of medieval Islamic civilisation and its modes of life is clearly discernible. The institutionalisation of the administration of justice was a complex process that took place both top down and bottom up. The cadi's pivotal role within this system and in social life in general was achieved through the actions of individual cadis, some of whom introduced new judicial procedures while others assumed extra-judicial responsibilities and extended the scope of the cadi's jurisdiction (see Chapter 1).

The Outlines of Egypt's Political History (642–1171)

While the hallmarks of Egypt's political history from the Arab conquest up until the rise to power of Saladin (642–1171) are well-known and need little elaboration, the aim of this section is to introduce events, people, issues and terms that will be constantly referred to in the subsequent chapters, and to set the topic in its broader contextual and conceptual framework.

The political life of the nascent Muslim community in Medina was marked by an intense personal and ideological clash between the pre-Islamic

40 Sijpesteijn, 'An Early Umayyad Papyrus', 179–90. For literary sources, see the tenth-century writings of Agapius, *Kitāb al-ʿUnwān*, 350.

41 Yaʿqūbī, II, 223, 232–3. For the formation of Muslim cults and rituals during the Umayyad period, see Donner, 'Umayyad Efforts at Legitimization', 193–201.

Arab past and its ethos and the changes associated with the rise of Islam and its new religious belief system. These conflicts are illustrated by the personal and political vicissitudes of ʿAmr ibn al-ʿĀṣ, the conqueror of Egypt, whose career has been discussed by Nabia Abbott, Michael Lecker and Andrew Marsham. Ibn Isḥāq (d. 767) depicts ʿAmr ibn al-ʿĀṣ's career in Islam as having been dominated by a factor beyond his control: his mother's humble status as a captive woman who claimed that ʿĀṣ ibn Wāʾil was his father. Another factor to be considered was the late conversion of members of ʿAmr ibn al-ʿĀṣ's family to Islam (in 628 or 629). According to Ibn Isḥāq, both blemishes on the family line were thrown at ʿAmr ibn al-ʿĀṣ' when the succession of ʿUmar I was discussed at his deathbed in Medina.[42] Our perception of this stage of Muslim history should not be unduly influenced by Ibn Isḥāq's views that humble origins and a late conversion to Islam hindered the careers of people during the transition period from paganism to Islam. This phase of early Islamic history was dynamic, deeds and personal achievements mattered, and people rose through the ranks, especially since late converts among the Quraysh had not been ostracised by the Prophet. ʿAmr ibn al-ʿĀṣ, for example, served as governor and military commander during the life of the Prophet and participated in the conquests both of Palestine and, later, Egypt. The conquest of Egypt has recently been re-examined by Phil Booth, who argues that it involved two Muslim armies, moving in different directions under the command of ʿAmr, who served as governor of the country under ʿUmar I and during the early years of ʿUthmān's rule (644–56). It seems, however, that in 648–9 he was dismissed and even banned from Medina.[43]

ʿAmr ibn al-ʿĀṣ's re-emergence onto the political scene and his return as governor of Egypt in 658–9 was the result of what has been described by Abbott as a deal made between him, his sons ʿAbd Allāh and Muḥammad and Wardān, the family's protégé and confidant, and Muʿāwiya in which

[42] See *Taʾrīkh al-Khulafāʾ*, 81–2. One may doubt whether ʿAmr ibn al-ʿĀṣ was at that time in Medina at all; most likely he was in Egypt. For his conversion, see Lecker, 'The Estates of ʿAmr ibn al-ʿĀṣ', 27. For Ibn al-Isḥāq's version of Egypt's surrender to the Arabs, as reproduced by Ṭabarī, see Butler, *The Treaty of Miṣr*, 49–64.

[43] Booth, 'The Muslim Conquest of Egypt Reconsidered', 639–71; Hoyland, In *God's Path*, 69–76; Lecker, 'The Estates of ʿAmr ibn al-ʿĀṣ ', 28–30. For two different interpretations of Muslim historiography about the conquest of Egypt, see Noth, *The Early Arabic Historical Tradition*, esp. Introduction; Donner, 'ʿUmar ibn al-Khaṭṭāb', 67–85.

military and political support was traded for the governorship and revenues of Egypt. How the co-operation between Muʿāwiya and ʿAmr ibn al-ʿĀṣ evolved after the killing of ʿUthmān (June 655) has been elucidated by Marsham. ʿAmr ibn al-ʿĀṣ served Muʿāwiya during the arbitration following the Battle of Ṣiffīn (in early July 657) and made a formal pact with him in 658–9. The text of the pact, as reproduced by Ibn Saʿd (d. 845), is considered to be genuine (to the extent that these texts can be perceived as such), and it promises the governorship of Egypt to ʿAmr ibn al-ʿĀṣ upon the conquest of the province from the hands of Muʿāwiya's opponents.[44] Indeed, after heavy fighting, ʿAmr ibn al-ʿĀṣ conquered Egypt with troops drafted in Syria and held the governorship of Egypt. Muḥammad ibn Yusūf al-Kindī (hereafter referred to as Kindī, 897–961) writes that Egypt became ʿAmr ibn al-ʿĀṣ's personal source of income (*ṭuʿma*) and that he kept the revenues for himself after paying the troops and covering other expenses involved with ruling the country.[45] ʿAmr ibn al-ʿĀṣ governed Egypt until his death in 663–4 and was briefly succeeded by his son ʿAbd Allāh, whom Muʿāwiya immediately dismissed and replaced with his brother ʿUtba ibn Abī Sufyān, a move that marked the return of Egypt from private patrimonial rule to the direct control of the ruling family and, perhaps, one should say, state control.

The political culture and social fabric of the Umayyad and early Abbasid period were marked by familial ties, bonds of personal loyalty and patronage. Brothers, for instance, shared appointments or, more accurately, a person who received an appointment took advantage of the opportunity to appoint a brother to a key post. The regime regarded this conduct as normative since both familial and forged bonds constituted the basic building blocks of society and social life. On the political level bonds of personal loyalty and patronage involving provincial elites, administrators and rulers were maintained and regularly reinforced through the *wafd* (delegation) institution. The most notable example of a *wafd* is perhaps the one performed by ʿUtba ibn Abī Sufyān, who, immediately after his arrival in Egypt, returned to Damascus

[44] For detailed linguistic and historical discussion of the text, see Marsham, 'The Pact', 69–96.

[45] Kindī, 28–9, 31, 34. Other reports claim that, in addition to covering all of Egypt's expenses, ʿAmr ibn al-ʿĀṣ used to send 600,000 *dīnārs* to Muʿāwiya in Damascus. The reliability of this account is questionable, since the same figure is quoted as the poll tax collected by ʿAmr ibn al-ʿĀṣ at the rate of two *dīnārs* per person.

leading a delegation of local notables (*ashrāf ahl Miṣr*). His knowledge of the local scene in Fusṭāṭ was, however, inadequate since the nomination of his deputy was much resented. Upon his return to Egypt, he made a public appearance at a mosque and reportedly reminded the people that the oath of allegiance they swore to the caliph involved obedience, while what they could expect in return was justice.[46] To what extent Kindī's text contains echoes of political concepts prevalent during the 660s is an open question, but, if we take a long-term view of medieval Islamic political scene, justice as an obligation of the rulers towards their subjects became a common trope.[47]

The very personal character of the *wafd* in establishing, or re-enforcing, bonds of loyalty between the reigning caliph, the governor and provincial notables is exemplified by the events of 723–4. In 720–1, Bishr ibn Ṣafwān, who served as governor of Egypt, was also nominated as governor of Ifrīqiya (modern Tunisia), and when he took his new post he left his brother as deputy on his behalf in Egypt. In 105/723–4 Bishr returned to Egypt leading a *wafd* from Ifrīqiya to Damascus, but when the news about the death of the caliph reached him he returned to Ifrīqiya. The *wafd* institution also reflected an attempt to project an image of good government and just rule. A shipment of tax money sent to Damascus from the garrison towns was accompanied by a delegation of trustworthy people chosen from among the inhabitants and the military who had to swear that the money had been justly collected and constituted a surplus left after the troops and their families had been paid.[48] The *wafd* institution also served the caliph al-Manṣūr (754–75) to consolidate his rule, and the newly appointed governor of Egypt sent a delegation to deliver the oath of allegiance of the Arab population of Egypt (*ahl Miṣr*) to the caliph. One can assume that the *wafd* institution became irrelevant during the political breakdown of the Abbasid caliphate, but, in 799 and again in 801, Egypt's governor Layth ibn Faḍl went twice to Baghdad to deliver money and gifts, leaving his brother as deputy in Egypt.[49]

At the provincial level, the state military payroll, or the *dīwān* system,

46 Another *wafd* took place in 710–11. Kindī, 35, 65.
47 Lev, 'Charity and Justice', 1–17.
48 Fasawī, III, 345, 346; Kindī, 71, 72; Maqrīzī, *Kitāb al-Muqaffā*, II, 125.
49 Kindī, 97–8, 139.

was the most important institution. It had a twofold impact on the Arab population of Egypt, making the recipients of the *dīwān*'s payments a highly privileged group while intensifying intra-Arab rivalries over the inclusion in the system. The creation of the *dīwān* system is attributed to ʿUmar I and the registration was done according to tribal affiliation (*nasab*), but the payments were determined according to seniority in Islam, the *sābiqa* principle.[50] Throughout its long history, however, the seniority principle was much eroded and the local and central authorities used the system to maintain Arab and non-Arab military groups. People affiliated with Arab tribes (*mawālī*, clients) were also added to the state payroll and, occasionally, received the highest payments. *Mawālī* also served as a fighting force and it is reasonable to assume that they were registered on the military payroll under the names of their Arab patrons.[51]

In Egypt, the first payroll was drawn up shortly after the conquest of the country and, up until 721, it was redrawn four times. The people on the payroll received payments (*ʿatāʾ*) and allocations of wheat (*arzāq*), which made them largely independent of the wheat market. It seems that the annual wheat allocation per family was twelve *irddabs*, which was considered sufficient for the yearly consumption of a middle-class family.[52] Our understanding of the system and how it functioned is marred by many difficulties. The main question is whether the system supported the Arab and *mawālī* population of a province or the local military only. Other problems concern the shifts in policy on two crucial questions: whether families continue to receive payments for deceased beneficiaries and whether new-born babies and young children were entitled to payments from the *dīwān*.[53]

The tribal and social composition of the army in Egypt saw many changes during the Rāshidūn, Umayyad and Abbasid periods and the *dīwān* system

[50] Puin, *Der Dīwān*, 89–92; Savant, *The New Muslims*, 97–101.

[51] Ibn Yūnus, I, 224, 273, 297, 317, 411, 419, 513; Mikhail, 'Notes on the Ahl al-Dīwān', 283. The military role of the *mawālī* is illustrated by the events of 720–1, when they fought under the command of the governor of Tinnīs against a Byzantine naval raid. See Kindī, 70

[52] These figures are given for the year 742. Kindī, 82. For wheat consumption, see Goitein, *Med. Soc.*, IV, 235.

[53] These questions have been discussed in detail by Al-Qāḍī, 'A Documentary Report on Umayyad Stipends Registers', 7–44, with ample references to literary and documentary sources and most recent literature (Kennedy and Sijpesteijn).

was modified accordingly. These changes involved the arrival of new Arab troops in Egypt, the recruitment of non-Arab troops in Egypt and, during the Abbasid period, the arrival of non-Arab caliphal troops. Although the core of the army that conquered Egypt was made up of Arab troops, other groups of diverse ethnic and geographical origin also participated in the campaign and settled in Fusṭāṭ.[54] Moreover, because of the political struggles during early Islam and the Umayyad period, new Arab armies came to Egypt and settled in the country. This certainly was the case with the Syrian Arab troops with whom ʿAmr ibn al-ʿĀṣ reconquered Egypt for Muʿāwiya. According to Ibn ʿAbd al-Ḥakam (772–829), during Mu'āwiya's reign there were 40,000 names on the *dīwān*'s payroll and 4,000 people received the highest remuneration. The lists of the *dīwān* were updated regularly with births and deaths recorded on a daily basis.[55] A second Umayyad reconquest of Egypt took place during Ibn Zubayr's rebellion and saw the arrival of fresh troops from Syria. A detailed examination of the socio-military situation in Egypt is beyond the scope of the present discussion, but the system must have been a burden on the local government and, in 809, a radical change in the way payments were rendered to the recipients was attempted. It was suggested that payments be divided into three parts, cash, grain and textiles, but in face of violent opposition the proposal had to be shelved. The use of textiles as a means of payment is interesting and might indicate government control over Egypt's flourishing textile industry and the accumulation of surpluses. Eventually, in 834, as a result of the new socio-military policy of the caliph al-Muʿtaṣim, who removed the Arabs from the state military payroll, the system was abolished.[56]

Except for the frequent references to the *dīwān* system, broader social policies, whether at the state level or at local Egyptian level, are rarely attested in literary sources. Among the Umayyad caliphs only ʿUmar ibn ʿAbd al-ʿAzīz (ʿUmar II, 717–20) captured the attention of historians. Ibn ʿAbd al-Ḥakam, for example, depicts him as a benevolent ruler who was also

[54] Ibn ʿAbd al-Ḥakam, *Futūḥ*, 129; Al-Qāḍī, 'Non-Muslims in the Muslim Conquest', 95–6; Kubiak, *Al-Fusṭāṭ*, 88–174, accompanied by illuminating maps.

[55] Ibn ʿAbd al-Ḥakam, *Futūḥ*, 102; Kindī, 29–31; Mikhail, 'Notes on the Ahl al-Dīwān', 274–80; Al-Qāḍī, 'Death Dates in Umayyad Stipends Registers', 59–83.

[56] Kindī, 146, 193.

painfully aware of the difficulties involved in implementing a comprehensive welfare policy. He is described as a ruler who provided slaves to the crippled, chronically ill and blind to help them with their daily needs. These slaves (known as *al-akhmās*) consisted of the share of war spoils (*khums*) to which he was entitled as ruler of the state and reflected Koranic teachings concerning how booty should be divided. He is also described as handing out *ṣadaqāt*, meaning either voluntary charities or alms tax money. Yaḥyā ibn Saʿid, the cadi of Medina, for example, stated that he was sent to Ifrīqiya on behalf of the caliph to distribute *ṣadaqāt* among the poor, but that he found no poor people in the province since ʿUmar II's polices had enriched everybody.[57] On the other hand, the caliph was very suspicious of Sulaymān ʿAbd al-Malik, who had distributed vast sums of money in Medina and expected to be praised, but ʿUmar II snapped at him saying: 'You have enriched the rich and the left the poor impoverished.'[58]

The fiscal directives sent by ʿUmar II to Egypt can be described as a mixed bag of financial largesse and pietistic demands. The caliph ordered an overall increase of the payments rendered to Arabs in Egypt and the enlistment of fresh troops. In line with Koranic teachings, he ordered that the debts of the debtors should be paid and money be given to the righteous (*al-ṣāliḥāt*) and those living in seclusion (*ahl al-buyūtāt*). The caliph's payment of debts reflects the spirit of Koran 9:60, which states that debtors are entitled to charitable giving. The caliph's payments also went to people who were not on the military payroll. Adherence to Koranic morals and values can explain the ban on the consumption of wine and the closure of wine stores, but why women were forbidden to visit bathhouses remains vague. ʿUmar II's military policies and payments did not endure. Because of wider financial and social considerations state policies were constantly changing, and in 720–1 the pay increases introduced by ʿUmar II were revoked.[59]

The Abbasid revolution enjoyed widespread support in Egypt, and the

[57] Ibn ʿAbd al-Ḥakam, *Sīrat ʿUmar ibn ʿAbd al-ʿAzīz*, 65, 78. For *al-akhmās* in the Ḥaram of Jerusalem during the Umayyad period, see Elad, *Medieval Jerusalem*, 51–2. The question of whether the text referring to ʿUmar II's fiscal directives sent to his governor is genuine must be reconsidered. H. A. R. Gibb has argued that the text 'carries every indication of genuineness in its content and linguistic style' (see 'The Fiscal Rescript', 2).

[58] Ibn ʿAbd al-Ḥakam, *Sīrat ʿUmar ibn ʿAbd al-ʿAzīz*, 134.

[59] Kindī, 68–71.

Umayyad caliph Marwān, who had fled to Fusṭāṭ, found no local support there and fought his last battle against the Abbasid pursuers with only a handful of followers. The consolidation of Abbasid power in Egypt involved the execution of local opponents and rewarding Arab supporters and their families with generous distributions of *ʿaṭā'* and *ṣadaqāt* payments to the orphans and the poor. [60]

If we take a broad perspective on the years 750–868, during which Egypt was directly ruled by the Abbasids, one is struck by the financial importance of the province and by the regime's failure to govern it properly.[61] The Abbasid misgovernment of Egypt was multifold and was marked by repeated Arab and Coptic rebellions and the failure to maintain a reliable local military force. Twice during the 830s large Abbasid armies were dispatched to Egypt to quell rebellions. The first was led by the future caliph al-Muʿtaṣim and the second by the reigning caliph al-Ma'mūn. This direct intervention brought three decades of stability but failed to address the problems that were besetting the country, and, in 866, a widescale Arab–Coptic rebellion that focused on Alexandria and the western Delta was put down by the governor after heavy fighting. The entire pattern of Abbasid rule over Egypt and the local socio-political scene was, however, dramatically altered with the arrival of Aḥmad ibn Ṭūlūn in 868.

Aḥmad ibn Ṭūlūn belonged to the first generation of Muslims born to Turkish military slaves of the Abbasids, and from his youth he was deeply involved in Abbasid court politics. As ruler of Egypt he succeeded in establishing a short-lived quasi-independent local dynasty recognised by the Abbasids. Aḥmad ibn Ṭūlūn and the other Tulunid rulers also ruled Palestine and Syria and were involved in Abbasid dynastic politics. In Egypt they created a large army and built a new government centre of which only the mosque of Aḥmad ibn Ṭūlūn in Cairo has survived. The Abbasids loathed the Tulunids and, in 905, launched a massive land and sea invasion to topple the dynasty and brought Egypt back under direct Abbasid rule. This, however, brought little comfort to the country, which was threatened

[60] Kindī, 94–7, 99–100.

[61] For financial and military aspects of Abbasid Egypt, see Kennedy, 'Central Government and Provincial Élites', 31–7.

by the Fatimids in Ifrīqiya and needed the military assistance of the caliphate to stave off Fatimid invasions.

In 935, Muḥammad ibn Ṭughj al-Ikhshīd succeeded in establishing a second quasi-independent local dynasty recognised by the Abbasids. He belonged to the same milieu as Aḥmad ibn Ṭūlūn, being a scion of Persian mercenaries in the service of the Abbasids. Egypt's de facto independence during the Tulunid and Ikhshidid periods saw the expansion of the local administration and the rise of an assertive civilian elite. The Ikhshidid dynasty barely survived the death of its founder Muḥammad ibn Ṭughj in 946, and only the involvement of the civilian elite in Fusṭāṭ, which included members of three prominent administrative families, Shīʿī notables and cadis, ensured the smooth transfer of rule to Unjūr, Muḥammad ibn Ṭughj's twelve-year-old son, and the appointment of his uncle as regent. Other groups that were involved in this political pact (*ʿaqd*) were people of the court, administrators and the military. The cadis mentioned as involved in the pact were the cadis of Mecca and of Fusṭāṭ, who also served as cadi of the towns of Ramla and Tiberias in Palestine. These cadis remained in Fusṭāṭ and sent their representatives to the towns under their jurisdiction. Several prominent members of the corps of witnesses associated with the cadi's court in Fusṭāṭ are also mentioned as being involved in some way with the *ʿaqd*. The integration of the judicial system into the state structure was a typical medieval phenomenon and, by that time, the post of cadi had acquired respectability and a religious aura that was instrumental in bestowing legitimacy on the pact that preserved the political status quo and the vested interests of the groups and people involved in it.[62]

Following Unjūr's death in 961 the rule was usurped by the black eunuch Kāfūr, who enjoyed the co-operation of many but mostly relied on his private army. Upon Kāfūr's death in 968 a new succession of rule and disposition of power was arranged and formulated in a document devised by the vizier Jaʿfar ibn Faḍl ibn al-Furāt and the Shīʿī notable Abū Jaʿfar Musallam and also signed by Kāfūr's leading military commanders. The document specified a division of responsibilities among the people involved and made allusion to an exchange of oaths invoking obedience to God, to His messenger and to the Koranic dictum of commanding right and forbidding wrong. The

[62] Maqrīzī, *Kitāb al-Muqaffā*, II, 313–14.

document also proclaimed a political programme that promised to uphold justice, to help the oppressed against the oppressor, to care for the holy cities in Arabia and frontier towns and to conduct the holy war. This elaborate disposition of power failed to win wide approval and members of the Ikhshsdid ruling family, the administrators and the military factions remained suspicious of each other. The situation quickly deteriorated into chaos and many welcomed the Fatimid conquest of the country in 969.[63]

The Fatimids were an Ismāʿīlī-Shiʿī splinter group and bitter rivals of the Abbasids for hegemony in the Muslim world. They saw themselves as divinely chosen guided rulers (*imāms*) whose role was to instruct the Ismāʿīlī believers towards the right path, and under their absolute rule no group had a political role, making the political blossoming of the civilian elite of Fusṭāṭ a short-lived phenomenon. The enduring Fatimid legacy is the establishment of Cairo and, in the broader medieval context, the integration of Egypt's Mediterranean trade with the Indian Ocean commercial network. In terms of administrative and military organisation the Fatimid state represented the pinnacle of the political achievements of medieval Islam, but the Fatimids failed to win over the population to Ismailism. Although Ismāʿīlī Islam became the state religion of the country, Sunnī Islam and learning continued to flourish under the Fatimids.[64] The position of Ismailism was progressively eroded following the civil war (1060s–early 1070s) and the emergence of military dictators in the Fatimid state. The political fortunes of the ruling dynasty had direct repercussions on the way justice was administrated in Fatimid Egypt and one must distinguish between the periods prior to and after the civil war.

Egypt, The Country: Resources and Geopolitics

Egypt's political history is also a reflection of the country's uniqueness, and this section focuses on geography and resources. It is difficult to provide a

[63] Maqrīzī, *Kitāb al-Muqaffā*, I, 537–8; Bianquis, 'L'act de succession de Kāfūr', 263–9, including French translation of the document. For sarcastic remarks on the disposition of power promulgated after Kāfūr's death and satirical depiction of the people involved, see the remarks of the contemporary 'holy fool' Sībawayhi. Ibn Zūlāq, *Kitāb Akhbār Sībawayhi*, 52–3; Bianquis, 'La prise du pouvoir', 55–6.

[64] Cortese, 'Voices of the Silent Majority', 345–67.

comprehensive picture of Egypt's demography and agriculture on the eve of the Arab conquest since the impact of the Justinianic plague (541–2) and its recurrent outbreaks on Egypt's population and agriculture is unclear. Josiah C. Russell, for example, believes that Egypt's seventh-century population was 2.6 million, while Walter E. Kaegi states that by 600 the population of Egypt was 3 million. A much higher estimate is offered by Jean Gascou, who argues that in the 650s the population of Upper Egypt was 2 million.[65] Medieval authors were more generous in their estimate of Egypt's population, with ʿUthmān ibn Ṣāliḥ (761–834) claiming that at the time of the Arab conquest Egypt's population was 6 million.[66] Two tenth-century authors, ʿUmar al-Kindī (the son of Muḥammad ibn Yūsuf al-Kindī) and Ibn Zūlāq (919–98), who wrote treaties on *Faḍā'il Miṣr* (the *Excellences of Egypt*), state that a census of the population was taken during the governorship of al-Walīd ibn Rafāʿ (727–35), in which 10,000 villages were counted and the population was 5 million. The estimate of Egypt's mid-eighth-century villages is, however, questionable since much lower figures are quoted for the second half of the tenth century. It has also been claimed that on the eve of the Fatimid conquest there were 2,395 villages of which 1,439 were in the Delta. Medieval demography, however, is an elusive topic and the reliability of cadastral surveys problematic. Nonetheless, one can argue that whatever the real situation in Egypt was, for the conquerors coming from the deserts and semi-deserts of Arabia and the Middle East it was a country of plenty and could easily provide for them and their needs.

More significant than the figures quoted by ʿUmar al-Kindī and Ibn Zūlāq is their perception of what constituted a good government able to preserve and perpetuate Egypt's agricultural wealth. This concept, expressed by the term *ʿimāra*, was retrospectively projected back onto the Pharaonic

65 Russell estimates Egypt's population during the eighth to ninth centuries to be 2.2–2.6 million and perceives a drop to 1.5 million during the tenth to eleventh centuries. See 'The Population of Medieval Egypt', 73, 75; Kaegi, 'Egypt on the Eve of the Muslim Conquest', 34; Gascou, 'Arabic Taxation', 674. For the 541–2 plague's outbreak in Egypt, see Morony, 'For Whom Does the Writer Write', 72–3; McCormick, 'Toward a Molecular History', 303.

66 For ʿUthmān ibn Ṣāliḥ's reports embedded in the writings of the Patriarch Saʿīd ibn Baṭrīq (Eutychius of Alexandria, 935–40), see Breydy, 'La conquête arabe de l'Égypte', 390, 391. For extensive discussion of epidemics and demography in Byzantine and early Arab Egypt, see Sijpesteijn, *Shaping a Muslim State*, 44–5; Al-Qāḍī, 'Population Census', 349–52.

period, which is described as being marked by exceptionally high tax yields and concern for Egypt's irrigation infrastructure. Furthermore, the Pharaohs distributed payments to widows and orphans and *ṣadaqāt* to people who had suffered because of disasters. In another version of the *ʿimāra* concept, ʿAmr ibn al-ʿĀṣ is portrayed as asking the Patriarch how to ensure Egypt's prosperity and was advised to take good care of the irrigation canals and dams, to collect taxes according to accepted rules and to abolish certain impositions levied on the peasantry.[67]

Seventh-century conquerors of Egypt both the Persians and Arabs were quick to successfully exploit the agricultural and financial resources of the country for their needs while relying on local administration and its personnel.[68] Whatever the advice that ʿAmr ibn al-ʿĀṣ received, if he asked for any, it is clear that Muslim rulers showed ingenuity in creating and imposing new taxes and mobilising resources to maintain their armies, navies, building activities and feeding the holy cities of Arabia.[69] According to Muslim and non-Muslim literary sources, the exploitation of Egypt's surplus grain took place immediately after the conquest of the country. During the sixth century Egypt's grain had been shipped to feed Constantinople, with 160,000 metric tons being transported annually by a fleet of over 1,200 ships. This system was gravely affected by the plague in 541 and its recurrent outbreaks and came to an end in 618 because of the Persian conquest of Egypt.[70] On the request of the caliph ʿUmar I, Egypt's grain was shipped to Arabia to feed Mecca and Medina. The Coptic chronicler John the Bishop of Nikiu (fl. second half of the eighth century) recounts that the Arabs using Coptic corvée labour re-dug the Trajan canal which linked the Nile valley with the Red Sea. Archaeological finds in Fusṭāṭ support the claim that the canal was re-dug and connected the Nile through natural depressions to the Red Sea. The canal is explicitly mentioned in the correspondence of the governor Qurra ibn Sharīk (709–15) and was usable when the water level of the Nile

[67] Ibn Zūlāq, *Faḍā'il Miṣr*, MS Paris, 205a–206b, 207a; MS Dublin, 16b, 26a–b, 27a–b; ʿUmar (ed.), 86–7, 90–1 (relying on two Cairo manuscripts: Dār al-Kutub and the Azhar Library); ʿUmar al-Kindī, *Faḍā'il Miṣr*, 55, 57.

[68] Sänger, 'The Administration of Sasanian Egypt', 653–65.

[69] Legendre, 'Islamic Conquest', 237–8, referring to the 640s documents from the archive of Senouthios published by Federico Morelli (2010).

[70] McCormick, *Origins of the European Economy*, 104–5, 108–10.

was high. The canal probably functioned as late as 775 when it either fell into disuse or was deliberately blocked.[71]

In the case of Egypt's grain economy we can truly speak about *longue durée* trends, and the shipment of grain to Arabia became deeply ingrained in the policies of medieval and Ottoman rulers of the country. Evidently, even when operational, the canal had its limitations and other means of transporting grain to Mecca and Medina had to be devised. In 727, on the initiative of Ibn al- Ḥabḥāb, Qaysī Arabs were settled in the eastern Delta in apparently depopulated administrative districts (*kūra*). They were given money to buy camels to transport food (most likely grain) to Qulzum (on the tip of the Gulf of Suez), apparently for shipment to Arabia. This proved to be a lucrative business and they were also instructed to breed horses and, owing to the rich local pasture, they had no expenses for fodder to feed their camels and horses. This migration was a success story that encouraged a further influx of Qaysī tribesmen to the area.[72]

Qulzum maintained its position as a hub for overland shipments of grain to Arabia during the tenth century prior to and after the Fatimid rule.[73] For the Fatimids, receiving political recognition from the local rulers of Mecca and Medina was an important asset which bolstered their overall legitimacy and was an issue in the political struggle against the Abbasids. In addition to grain, the Fatimids sent expensive high-quality inscribed textiles (*ṭirāz*) for external and internal use in the Kaaba sanctuary.[74] Tenth-century Egypt was an important producer of *ṭirāz* fabrics and textile-producing centres were spread all over the country. The Fatimid rulers harnessed both the agricultural

[71] John Coptic Bishop of Nikiu, *The Chronicle*, 195. For the history of the Trajan canal, see Redmount, 'The Wadi Tumilat', 127, 135; Mayerson, 'The Port of Clysma', 125–6. For archaeological finds in Fusṭāṭ pertaining to the canal, see Sheehan, *Babylon of Egypt*, 39–40, 42–50. According to Balādhurī (d. 892), ʿUmar I's order to ʿAmr ibn al-ʿĀṣ to ship supplies to the holy cities of Arabia was issued in 642. See *Kitāb Futūḥ al-Buldān*, 216. The geography of the canal is vaguely alluded to in the sources. See Ibn ʿAbd al-Ḥakam, *Futūḥ*, 163–4; Maqrīzī, *Kitāb al-Muqaffā*, II, 410.

[72] Kindī, 76–7; Lev, 'Coptic Rebellions', 310–11.

[73] Muqaddasī, 195–6.

[74] Yaʿqūbī claims that Muʿāwiya was the first to cover the Kaaba sanctuary with silk and that he installed a corps of slave servants at the shrine. Other Umayyad caliphs embellished the sanctuary, while the Abbasid caliph al-Mahdī (775–85) covered the Kaaba by a fabric made in Egypt. He financed his works in Mecca and Medina by money sent from Egypt and, in 777, made the pilgrimage to Arabia. See *Ta'rīkh*, II, 238, 284, 395–6.

and industrial resources of Egypt to enhance and manifest their predominance in Arabia.

When the overall impact of the Arab conquest of Egypt is examined, there is considerable agreement among papyrologists that the first fifty years were characterised by a subtle process involving both continuity and change. The issue of continuity is extensively dealt with by Sijpesteijn, who points out that there is evidence neither for massive confiscations of land nor for the population fleeing the land following the conquest of the country. Gladys Frantz-Murphy has emphasised the continued role of the Coptic Church in the agrarian fiscal administration, while papyri dating from the 670s from Edfu in Upper Egypt reveal that the new rulers worked through the traditional local administration. Foss points out that although the Arab rulers were remote from the local provincial level their presence was felt and their orders, though frequently delayed, were eventually obeyed.[75]

Continuity should not obscure the fact that Arab exploitation of Egypt began early on and took place through requisitions and tax innovations. Immediately after the conquest building materials were requested from Egypt's provinces and were shipped to Fusṭāṭ to sustain building activities in the new Arab garrison town. By the time of Qurra ibn Sharīk's governorship the requisition system was in full swing with local resources and a local workforce being used for building projects in Fusṭāṭ (a granary) and palaces and mosques in Damascus and Jerusalem. The requisition orders issued by the governor of Egypt demonstrate the Umayyad capability in amassing resources and reflect both the administrative practices and the economic mindset of the rulers. The responsibility for fleets and building projects was entrusted to Arab-Muslim overseers, while these enterprises were financed through the allocation of specific sources of income to cover the required materials, workforce and costs of each project. One can doubt whether projects had well-defined budgets, and it seems that the state and the overseer in charge of a project usually had only a general idea of the costs involved and devised ways to meet them through the allocation of various regional resources. In

[75] Sijpesteijn, 'New Rule over Old Structures', 183, 194–5; *Shaping a Muslim State*, 81–4; Frantz-Murphy, 'The Economics of State Formation', 101–4; Foss, 'Egypt under Muʿāwiya Part I', 9–11.

any case, Qurra ibn Sharīk's correspondence reveals the full integration of Egypt within the broader structure of the Umayyad state.[76]

The requisition system became embedded in Egypt's tax structure, but fiscal tax innovations were also quickly introduced. Sijpesteijn has pointed out that the levy of the poll tax began within one generation of the Arab conquest of Egypt, while Gascou has argued that the imposition of differential poll tax on the non-Muslim male population of Egypt above the age of fourteen dates to January 653.[77] Only later was the poll tax endowed with religious meanings and justifications and came to define the legal status of non-Muslims. In other cases of tax innovations, Koranic teachings were invoked from the very beginning to justify taxes imposed on Muslims. During the 730s to 750s an alms tax (*ṣadaqa*) collected in cash and kind (animals) was imposed on the Muslim rural population of the Fayyūm. The collection of these taxes was announced in a letter sent by Nājid ibn Muslim, the chief tax collector of the province. The format and wording of the letter, which employs Koranic terminology referring to injunctions to pray and pay *zakāt*, are understood by Sijpesteijn as indicating state attempts to provide a religious aura and legitimisation for this tax innovation.[78]

The implementation of another aspect of Koranic teachings (i.e. the exhortations to distribute charity to the poor and needy) is attested by an undated seventh- to eighth-century document published by Geoffrey Khan. The document includes a list of villages in the Bahnasā region (Upper Egypt) and the sums of money to be paid in each place to the poor and needy, referred to by the Koranic expression *masākīn wa-l-fuqarā'*. The sums are low, not to say trifling, but their economic impact in the rural context cannot be properly estimated.[79] The impression is that this distribution, whether sporadic or permanent, was more about ethics than economics. Nonetheless, it can be argued that throughout the seventh century both aspects of the Koranic teachings (i.e. the collection and distribution of charitable payments)

[76] Legendre, 'Islamic Conquest', 237–8. For the range of foodstuffs and other products demanded under the requisition system, see Trombley, 'Fiscal Documents from the Muslim Conquest of Egypt', 5–38, relying on both literary sources and Greek papyri.

[77] Sijpesteijn, *Shaping a Muslim State*, 72–4; Gascou, 'Arabic Taxation', 674–7.

[78] See *Shaping a Muslim State*, doc. 8, discussion, 181–99. Ya'qūbī claims that Mu'āwiya was the first to collect *zakāt* from the payments that the state paid to the Muslims. See II, 232.

[79] See *Bills, Letters and Deeds*, doc. 2.

were translated into an administrative practice that consequently was constantly developed and reshaped.

Changes that began taking place at the end of the seventh century intensified throughout the eighth century, and gradually the Coptic Church lost its intermediary role between Arab ruling officials and the peasantry. This led to a tightening of the grip over tax assessment, taxation and land, especially uncultivated land. The Islamisation of the administration meant the appointment of Muslim officials and the process of Arabisation had profound long-term effects on the administrative and social life of the country. The cumulative impact of these changes affected the tenor of life of the average Copt.[80] One thing that strikes the reader of the published corpus of Egyptian papyri and the growing literature that discusses these findings is how wide this impact was, an aspect completely unattested in Muslim historiography but prevalent in Coptic historiography. Three examples illustrate how papyrology expanded our understanding of the social realities of early Muslim Egypt: (1) the imposition of angaria and the concomitant problem of fugitives; (2) the conscription of the Copts into the navy and the tax burden involved in the Umayyad naval build-up; and (3) the acquisition of land by the Arabs and the early emergence of an Arab landholding elite.[81]

When one goes beyond tax innovations and the exploitation of Egypt's resources, one sees that the country's geopolitical position can be characterised as being interlocked within three settings: the local, the regional (Middle Eastern) and the broader Mediterranean world. The embroilment of local, regional and Mediterranean settings touched the lives of contemporary people and can be followed through Ibn Yūnus (894–958)'s biographical dictionary, which refers to the Arabs who conquered Egypt and settled in Fusṭāṭ. Many of them, like ʿAbd Allāh ibn Ḥudāfa, were early converts to

[80] Frantz-Murphy, 'The Economics of State Formation', 104–13; *The Agrarian Administration*, 67–8; Sijpesteijn, *Shaping a Muslim State*, 91–105.

[81] For the link between angaria and the fugitive problem, see Legendre, 'Islamic Conquest', 242–5; Sijpesteijn, *Shaping a Muslim State*, 100–11, discusses the settlement of Arab Muslims in the countryside. For Umayyad naval build-up, see Trombley, 'Sawīrus Ibn al-Muqaffaʿ and the Christians of Umayyad Egypt', 199–226. For the Arab settlement in Kharibtā, on the desert edge in the western Delta, see Gascoigne, *The Impact of the Arab Conquest*, I, ch. 4, which combines archaeological work and textual study. A large Arab population settled, or stayed, there immediately after the Arab conquest. See Kindī, 21.

Islam and participated in the wars of conquest under the caliphs of Medina, but eventually fell into oblivion. Others became involved, on different levels, in the affairs of the emerging Muslim state and its politics. ʿUqba ibn ʿĀmir, for example, was a companion of the Prophet and a veteran Muslim (his seniority is expressed by the terms *sābika* and *hijra*), who participated in the conquest of Egypt and, after settling in Fusṭāṭ, asked Muʿāwiya for a grant of land. During Muʿāwiya's reign he served as commander of the army and navy in Egypt and died in 677–8. He is praised, rather anachronistically, for his learning in the Koranic law of inheritances.[82] Khālid ibn Thābit, another member of the early Muslim community, was also involved in the naval affairs of Egypt and was appointed in 671 to command the *baḥr Miṣr*, meaning Egypt's fleet or the Mediterranean coast. Prior to that appointment he had been sent to conquer Jerusalem, but the glory for this achievement went to ʿUmar I. His naval appointment, however, must have been short-lived, since in 674 he was campaigning in North Africa. Other people of similar background were involved in and consumed by the internal wars of early Islam. ʿAbd al-Raḥmān ibn ʿUdays, for example, who participated in the conquest of Egypt, was killed in 651–2 in Palestine while serving as commander of the cavalry force that went to fight ʿUthmān in Medina.[83]

Within the regional Middle Eastern context Egypt served as a springboard for the conquest of North Africa. Although both regions evolved into distinctive entities, the links between them were many on both personal and political levels. Incursions into North Africa, led by veterans of the Muslim conquest of Egypt, took place in 647–8, 657–8 and 676–7 and enriched the participants. At least three of the participants of the 647–8 campaign were people of some fame, including ʿAmr ibn al-ʿĀṣ's son ʿAbd Allāh, ʿAbd Allāh ibn al-ʿAbbās ibn ʿAbd al-Muṭṭalib, who was responsible for the division of the spoils, and ʿAbd Allāh ibn Saʿd ibn Abī Sarḥ, who was a military man in the full sense of the word. In 651–2, he campaigned in Nubia and, in 654, fought at the Battle of the Masts against the Byzantine navy. The future Umayyad caliph Marwān ibn al-Ḥakam also participated in the

[82] Ibn Yūnus, I, 346–7, who claims that he saw a Koranic codex written by ʿUqba ibn ʿĀmir.
[83] Ibn Yūnus, I, 146, 147, 264, 308, 317.

657–8 military expedition to Ifrīqiya.[84] Egypt's fiscal and human resources were tapped to sustain state policies in Ifrīqiya. During the reign of al-Walīd I (705–15), for example, 1,000 Coptic families were sent to establish the arsenal in Tunis while, during the late eighth century, 100,000 *dīnārs* of Egypt's tax revenues were diverted to cover expenditures made in Ifrīqiya.[85]

On the eve of the Arab-Muslim conquest Byzantium was the main naval power in the Mediterranean while Muslim naval activity in the Mediterranean can be characterised as a corollary to the conquest of the Middle East. Ibn Yūnus's biographical dictionary, which alludes to several naval commanders, describes the scope of Muslim sea endeavours during the seventh and eighth centuries, but the terms he uses, such as the common phrases *baḥr Miṣr wa-Shām* and *baḥr Ifrīqiya*, lack precision. They can be understood as denoting the fleets of Syria, Egypt and Tunisia, but references are also made to the squadron of Damietta. The post of naval command must have been an assignment of trust and significance under Muʿāwiya since he appointed one of his staunch supporters, Ibn Abī Arṭāh, to the post. He fought with Muʿāwiya at the Battle of Ṣiffīn and later harshly persecuted ʿAlī's supporters in the Ḥijāz and Yemen. In later life, he became a pious man much concerned with ritual purity (*waswās*).[86]

The full extent of the Umayyad naval effort is revealed through the letters of Qurra ibn Sharīk. In Fusṭāṭ there was an active shipyard and the governor frequently demanded supplies of sailors, victuals and nails for Egypt's fleet. Sailors from Egypt were also sent to serve in the fleets of Syria and North Africa. With the exception of the 676–7 raid on Burullus (on a narrow stretch of land that separated Lake Burullus from the Mediterranean), Byzantine naval activity along the Egyptian coast is rarely mentioned during the Umayyad period. Following the fall of the Umayyads Muslim naval activity in the Eastern Mediterranean contracted and, in 853, a Byzantine fleet sacked Damietta. This event brought the Abbasid caliph al-Mutawakkil (846–61) to

[84] Ibn Yūnus, I, 269, 273, 277, 423, II, 230.

[85] Raqīq al-Qayrawānī, 50–1; Maqrīzī, *Kitāb al-Muqaffā*, I, 109; Muḥammad, 'The Role of the Copts in the Islamic Navigation', 4–5; Picard, 'La Méditerranée centrale', 40–1; Al-Qāḍī, 'Non-Muslims in the Muslim Conquest', 111–23.

[86] Ibn Yūnus, I, 62–3, 95, 135, 198, 223, 229, 255, 353, 385, II, 194. For extensive discussion of *waswās*, see Reid, *Law and Piety*, index. For broader discussion of Umayyad naval effort and policies, see Picard, *La mer des califes*, ch. 8.

fortify Egypt's coastal towns and rebuild Egypt's navy. Coptic historiography describes, in bleak terms, the plight of the Copts who were forcibly drafted to serve in the navy.[87] Ṭarsūs (on the Mercin Bay) was, in fact, the main Abbasid port but its powerful navy had been reduced to impotence by the caliph al-Muʿtaḍid (892–902), who ordered its destruction following a rebellion in the town in 900. Somehow the Ṭarsūs navy recovered from this blow and played a role in fighting the Fatimid attempt to conquer Egypt in 920.

Whatever were the fortunes of Muslim navies in the Eastern Mediterranean, maritime trade is poorly attested in early literary sources and is entirely missing from the papyri. Egypt was at the crossroads of Mediterranean and Indian Ocean commercial networks which never ceased to be active. Both networks flourished prior to and during the Fatimid period and are alluded to in the tenth-century *Faḍāʾil Miṣr* literature and eleventh-century Geniza documents. Egypt is described by ʿUmar al-Kindī as the entrepôt (*furḍa*) of the holy cities of Mecca and Medina, Ṣanʿa, Aden, Shīḥr (on Arabia's Indian Ocean's coast) and Oman as well as India, Ceylon and China. The port that served this commerce was Qulzum and the products traded were aromatics, gems and rare objects. Egypt's Mediterranean trade, which involved both the Muslim Mediterranean (North Africa, including the Western Sahara [Sijilmāsa], and Syria) and the Christian lands (*bilād al-rūm*), receives more attention and its scope is better-described. ʿUmar al-Kindī, however, clearly distinguishes between Byzantium (referred to as Constantinople) and Western Europe (referred to as Rome [*rūmiyya*] and the lands of the Franks, *ifranjiyya*). The goods imported from these regions included male and female slaves, brocades, mastic gum, resin from the Storax tree (*mayʿa*), saffron, corals and amber. In Ibn Zūlāq's writings the role of Egypt as *furḍa* is amplified and he alludes to Egypt as a hub of world trade. The significance of Egypt's Mediterranean ports Tinnīs, Damietta and, especially, Alexandria is much emphasised and Upper Egypt is described as the entrepôt for trade with Africa (Beja and Ethiopia), Arabia and Yemen.[88]

[87] *History of the Patriarchs of the Egyptian Church*, II. pt. 1, 9–10 (Arabic), 13–14 (trans.); Vida, 'A Papyrus Reference', 212–21.

[88] ʿUmar al-Kindī, *Faḍāʾil Miṣr*, 70–1; Ibn Zūlāq, *Faḍāʾil Miṣr*, MS Paris, 195b; MS Dublin, 13a, For the significance of amber, mastic gum and corals in Egypt's Mediterranean trade, see Goitein, *Med. Soc.*, I, 47, 153, IV, 207–8. For geographical aspects of the account, see Cornu, *Atlas*, index.

Indian Ocean trade, alluded to in the *Fāʾḍil Miṣr* literature, expanded during the eleventh century, and Mordechai Akiva Friedman describes its pivotal role in the following terms:

> The India trade was the backbone of the international economy in the Middle Ages in general and within the Islamic world in particular. More than anything else, it stimulated inter-territorial traffic, furthered the rise of a flourishing merchant class and created close and fruitful links between the countries of Islam and the Far East on the one hand and Europe on the other.[89]

Important though long-distance maritime trade with India was, one must not forget the realities of medieval times, and Jessica L. Goldberg has noted that, in the eleventh century, 'Agriculture production determined business cycles, movements of credit and species, and even how merchants valued each other's service'. She continues: 'These activities created strong and intimate bonds between international merchants and local agriculturalists in the Islamic Mediterranean and injected coins directly into the countryside every year.'[90] The product responsible for the 'strong and intimate bonds between international merchants and local agriculturalists' was flax, whose history and significance in Tulunid Egypt and later periods has been studied by Frantz-Murphy, Abraham L. Udovitch and Goldberg.[91] The prosperity of the class that tapped Egypt's agricultural wealth through the tax collection system and the cultivation of flax is reflected in the cases adjudicated at the cadi's court in Fusṭāṭ during the Tulunid period (see Chapter 2). Taking a broad view of the judicial system, it can be said that it mirrors the changes that the country underwent, and its vicissitudes and history is the subject of the following chapters.

89 Goitein and Friedman, *India Traders of the Middle Ages*, 3.
90 See *Trade and Institutions*, 338.
91 Frantz-Murphy, 'A New Interpretation', 284–5, 288; Mayerson, 'The Role of Flax', 201–7. Udovitch, 'Fatimid Cairo', 687; 'International Trade', 271. For Latin, Hebrew and Arabic sources referring to the processing of flax, see Gil, 'The Flax Trade', 81–3.

PART ONE

THE CADI: JUDGE AND ADMINISTRATOR

1

The Cadi's Jurisdiction: Evolution and Consolidation

Definitions and Perspectives

Customarily, the nature of the cadi's jurisdiction has been approached through etymological inquiry into the meaning of the root *q.ḍ.y* in the Koran. Schacht, for example, has pointed out that in the Koran the verb *qaḍā* signifies God's, or the Prophet's, decrees, while when referring to the Prophet's judicial activities the terminology is derived from the root *ḥ.k.m.* As Arzina B. Lalani has pointed out in an illuminating entry in the *Encyclopaedia of the Qur'ān*, the Koran also includes many ethical injunctions concerning how justice should be dispensed.[1] Moving from the Koranic teachings to classical lexicography as studied by Tillier, we observe that the infinitive noun *qaḍā'* signifies judgment, and the primary function of the cadi (*qāḍī*) was to pronounce authoritative decisions regarding disputes brought before him. Tillier concludes the discussion with a powerful, neatly formulated statement:

> Étymologiquement, la racine '*q.ḍ.y*' est étrangère à l'idée de 'droit' ou de 'justice' et si le *qāḍī* peut être un juge, ses fonctions sont rarement réductibles à ce que recouvre le terme français, défini comme un 'magistrate chargé d'appliquer les lois et de rendre la justice'. Traduire '*qāḍī*' par 'juge', c'est attirer de force la cadi musulman dans un univers sémantique qui n'est pas le sien, plaquer sur lui un système référential anachronique.

[1] Schacht, *An Introduction*, 6; Lalani, 'Judgment', 65–6.

At the end of the discussion Tillier offers his readers the following explanation: 'C'est pourquoi le mot '*qāḍī*' sera exclusivement rendu par 'cadi' dans cet ouvrage [i.e. his book].'[2]

Although approached from a different angle, similar conclusions have been reached by students of the Ottoman system of the administration of justice. Gyula Káldy Nagy, writing about the Ottoman cadi, has stated: 'The authority of the *ḳāḍī* covered such a large area of responsibility that the full meaning of the title cannot be accurately rendered by the word "judge".'[3] Case studies on the Ottoman judicial system have corroborated Nagy's statement and depict the Ottoman cadi as a provincial administrator who was also vested with judicial authority, a duality reflected by the Ottoman court records.[4] When the broader context of the cadi's role in medieval and Ottoman Islam is considered, Max Weber's concept of Kadijustiz must be addressed. Weber has stated:

> The 'rational' interpretation of law on the basis of strictly formal concepts can be juxtaposed to a kind of adjudication that is primarily bound to hallowed tradition. Individual cases which cannot be unambiguously decided by tradition it either settles by concrete revelation . . . or . . . by informal judgments rendered in terms of concrete ethical or other practical concepts, by drawing on 'analogies' and by depending upon and interpreting concrete 'precedents'.
>
> Kadi-justice knows no rational 'rules of decision' (Urteilsgründe) whatever, nor does empirical justice of the pure type give any reason which in our sense could be rational.[5]

[2] Tillier, *Les cadis d'Iraq*, 79–83, esp. 82, 83.
[3] See 'Ḳāḍī, Ottoman Empire', 375b.
[4] Ergene, *Local Court, Provincial Society*, 33–6; Aykan, *Rendre la justice à Amid*, 46.
[5] See *Economy and Society*, II, 976. Although the term 'Kadijustiz' unmistakably invokes an Islamic context, most of Weber's examples illustrating this type of justice are taken from the European context. See II, 976–8, esp. 978. His only example referring to Islamic context alludes to French-occupied Tunisia, where, in his words, 'a very tangible handicap for capitalism remained in that the ecclesiastic court (the *Chara*) decided over land holdings "at discretion" as the Europeans put it' (II, 978). Although Weber was aware that the perspective he adopted was Europe-centric, the situation in colonial Maghreb was far more complex than he could possibly have known. These complexities are delineated in David S. Powers' seminal study, showing how French jurists reinterpreted Islamic legal history to justify attempts of transferring lands tied up in familial *waqfs* to French settlers. See 'Orientalism, Colonialism, and Legal History', 535–71. For inexplicable reasons Weber's other remarks about Islamic law still serve as a term of reference. See, for example, Zarinebaf, *Crime and Punishment in Istanbul*, 141–2, 152.

The Kadijustiz paradigm has been examined by David S. Powers in a case study that involved a paternity dispute in Marinid Morocco of the early 1310s. He also set out to explore the levels of familiarity with the law in Muslim society in general and in that of Marimid Morocco in particular. Powers argues against the stereotype of a cadi as an arbitrary judge unconstrained by the rulers of law.[6] When the scope of the discussion is extended, Powers' conclusions are reaffirmed. Stefan Knost, for example, has made the following observation:

> Judges in Ottoman Aleppo c. 1800 were neither automatons who applied procedural rules in a mechanical manner nor Weberian Kadis who decided cases arbitrarily without reference to any legal rules and principles. Judges were not required to follow a single doctrine. They decided each case according to its particularities, using all the legal tools at their disposal.[7]

While avoiding any reference to Weber's Kadijustiz paradigm, Lesile Peirce has drawn attention to the social dimension of the law, and implicitly she explains the main flaw in the paradigm:

> It was not an ideal of the premodern Ottoman legal system that its justice be blind. Not until the mid-nineteenth century was the idea entertained that the law should encounter the individual as notional entity rather than as a particular combination of social and civil attributes to be scrutinized and entered into the calculus of judgment.[8]

Peirce's observations are supported and corroborated by other evidence. Hülya Canbakal, for example, has characterised the Ottoman Ḥanafī law as 'status-sensitive' and the application of *ta'zīr* penalties was related to the social standing of the offender and the severity of the punishment increased as one went down the social ladder. Ḥanafī law of the Ottoman period preserved the classical legacy of its legal school and the cultural bias of al-Kāsānī (d. 1191), concerning how *ta'zīr* punishments should be applied.[9]

The medieval legal system (e.g. as portrayed in the writings of Māwardī)

6 See 'Kadijustiz or qāḍī-justice?', 365–6.
7 See 'The Waqf in Court', 444.
8 See *Morality Tales*, 143.
9 Canbakal, *Society and Politics*, 142–5; Schneider, 'Imprisonment', 163–4.

was not only sensitive to the social standing of the litigants; it was also patriarchal and gender-biased, and women's access to and use of the court were governed by social norms.[10] The congruence between anti-women bias and class preferences is discerned, for example, in the way Halfon ben Menasse, clerk of the Jewish court in Fusṭāṭ (1100–38), recorded two documents dealing with settlement of marriage disputes in 1118 and 1135. The document from 1118 is a transcript of the settlement of Sitt al-Nasab's marital strife which, although it never transmits her first-person speech, records almost verbatim the speech delivered by her uncle, who represented her at court. The people involved in this dispute belonged to well-off reputable families, while those involved in the 1135 dispute were of lower economic and social standing. The document from 1135 is a transcript of the settlement of the marital strife of Bat Shabbetay, who was unrepresented by any male relative at the court and remained under the full authority of her husband. David Marmer, who has published and discussed these two documents, assumes that Halfon ben Menasse's brief summary of the 1135 court proceedings reflects his class bias towards the people involved in this case.[11]

While the rendering of the term *qāḍī* as judge should be avoided and the complex calculus of judgment guiding the cadi taken into account, the otherness of medieval Muslim society and its legal system must not be exaggerated. The quest for justice and fairness is universal although its meaning varies and the institutional implementation of these values took many forms.[12] Ancient concepts and sayings about justice, both on an ethical level and as practical precepts for running the state, have permeated Islamic political writings.[13] The

[10] As Tillier's study has shown, women frequented the court for matters relating to issues of personal status, and the court, with the help of female assistance, handled these cases. The identification of a female plaintiff before the cadi was, however, a delicate issue and had to be handled sensitively. See 'Women before the Qāḍī', 280–301.

[11] Marmer, 'Patrilocal Residence and Jewish Court Documents', 76–83. The reliance on random documents is, however, problematic and offers imprecise glimpses into social realities. A confidant and assertive woman is revealed by a Coptic divorce document (probably seventh–eighth century, from Ashmūnayn), who declares that she will not sue her divorced husband if he remarries. See Balogh and Kahle, 'Two Coptic Documents', 331–41.

[12] The question of universal characteristic traits of mankind, on the one hand, and the otherness of ancient and medieval societies on the other can be expanded to include a myriad of topics. For violence and depictions of violence see, for example, Zimmermann's evocative essay 'Violence in Late Antiquity Reconsidered', esp. 351–2.

[13] For general discussion of justice in medieval Islam, see Sadan, 'A "Closed-Circuit" Saying',

standards which should guide the administration of justice are exemplified by the text known as Caliph ʿUmar I's instructions to a cadi. Although this attribution cannot be sustained and the text is more likely a product of the eighth to ninth centuries, it contains ancient elements too. It begins by asserting that jurisdiction (*qaḍāʾ*) is a duty and established practice (*sunna*) and demands that the cadi maintain equality between the powerful (*sharīf*) and the humble (*ḍaʿīf*) at his court, and emphasises the expectations of the humble for justice on the part of the cadi. The cadi is encouraged to find the spiritual strength to retract from previous judgment if he reached the conclusion that he had been wrong, since pursuit of justice (*ḥaqq*) is the ultimate goal.[14]

The text reflects a developed judicial system well aware of its potential pitfalls and is in line with other texts which emphasise the difficulties inherent in executing judicial duties. These difficulties are embodied in a Prophetic tradition (*ḥadīth*) transmitted on the authority of Ibn Hurayra (a renowned companion of the Prophet, d. 678), which says: 'A person appointed as a cadi is like one butchered without a knife.' Other traditions present the cadi as exposed to the danger that erroneous judgment might result in people's ruin and incur eternal punishment for him, while just and balanced judgment ensures prosperity for the people and the Hereafter for the cadi. Other traditions, however, powerfully convey the perception that most of the cadis end in Hell since brazen and unjust rulings bring God's punishment.[15] It is very difficult to put this rich *ḥadīth* literature into a specific historical context, but the notion of legal and social justice permeated the moral imagination of Muslims and became embedded in the vision of how the ideal state should function.[16] It is said that the Abbasid caliph al-Manṣūr (754–75) declared that the state, like the throne, rests on four buttresses: a righteous cadi, a chief

325–42; Darling, 'The Vicegerent of God, from Him We Expect Rain', 407–29. For justice as a guiding principle in the system of administration of justice and the cadi's accountability to God for his judgments, see Tillier, 'La société abbasside', 157–82; Lange, *Justice, Punishment*, 246–7.

14 Margoliouth, 'Omar's Instruction', 308–12; Serjeant, 'The Caliph ʿUmar's Letters', 65–72.

15 Ibn ʿAbd al-Ḥakam, *Futūḥ*, 226–8, Wakīʿ, I, 7–13, 14–34; Kindī, 470–1. For the perceptions of the cadi's accountability to God in social practice and the eschatological literature, see Tillier, 'The Qāḍī before the Judge', 260–75; Lange, *Justice, Punishment*, 157, 160.

16 Juynboll assumes that the *ḥadīth* originated in the middle of the eighth century and began circulating in Egypt during the first half of the ninth century. See *Muslim Tradition*, 81–2. I owe this reference to the kindness of one of the anonymous readers on behalf of EUP. For concepts of justice, see Lev, 'Charity and Justice', 1–16.

of police who provides justice to the weak in the face of the powerful, a tax collector who conducts himself justly and avoids oppression, and the chief of the secret police, who reliably informs the caliph.[17]

While literary sources can offer only a general outline of how Muslim concepts on impartiality and justice had evolved, the epigraphic evidence provides a datable basis for such a discussion and the inscription at the Prophet's Mosque in Medina (752–3) is a crucial piece of evidence. It is a by-product of Abbasid propaganda and proclaims the regime's political and socio-religious credo but, assuming that propaganda cannot be totally divorced from realities and from people's expectations, it can be used in the context of the present discussion. The inscription begins by restating the essence of the Abbasids' political message, or their *daʿwa*, which mobilised the people to the Book of God and the practice of the Prophet. It also states the need for just judgments, egalitarian distribution of booty (*fa'y*) and allocation of the tribute (*akhmās*), for relatives, orphans and the poor.[18] Going beyond the inscription and its message, on the political level the notion that justice is a duty permeated the state phraseology and had many manifestations.

Literary sources provide an insight into how cadis in real-life situations perceived their role in the administration of justice. Tawba ibn Namir, who served as cadi of Fusṭāṭ between 733 and 738, was very concerned that his wife's inquisitiveness about his work might imperil the integrity of the judicial process. On pain of divorce he forbade her to enquire about his work. This rather harsh conversation adversely affected their otherwise ideal marriage.[19] Other eighth- to ninth-century cadis were concerned that intercession (*shafāʿa*) might lead to perversion of justice and resisted any attempts by state officials to interfere in lawsuits adjudicated at their courts, even at the cost of being removed from their post, while other cadis adopted uncompromising attitude towards the rulers.[20] Ibrāhīm ibn Isḥāq, for example, who was

[17] Ibn Ḥajar, ed. Majīd, II, 371–2; Tillier, *Les cadis d'Iraq*, 105, quoting Ṭabarī. For Manṣūr's passion for reports, see Silverstein, *Postal Systems*, 72–3.

[18] *Répertoire*, I, no. 38. Both terms are Koranic and refer to division of spoils (*ghanima*, *fa'y*) among God and the Prophet (*khums*) and other beneficiaries such as relatives, orphans and the poor (See Koran, 8:41; 59:7).

[19] Kindī, 342–3; Coulson, *A History of Islamic Law*, 32; Tillier, *Histoire des cadis*, 98–9.

[20] For three such cases in the years 780s and 820s, see Kindī, 373, 384, 427; Tillier, *Histoire des cadis*, 136, 148, 196–7.

appointed by the governor al-Sarī ibn al-Ḥakam to the post of cadi and preacher in 819, used to reprove the authorities by saying: 'You punish for illicit sex while you yourself indulge in it, you execute a thief while you yourself steal, you put [people] to death because of wine while you yourself consume it.' He was a severe judge who relinquished his post because of al-Sarī ibn al-Ḥakam's attempt to influence his judicial decisions. The governor asked him to resume his duties, but he refused, saying 'no intercession [is allowed] in the judicial process'.[21]

Ibrāhīm ibn Isḥāq's criticism of the authorities was couched in moral terms and unfocused. The defiance of other cadis was overtly and unmistakably political, and the most remarkable example is, perhaps, the cadi al-Ḥārith ibn Miskīn's confrontation with the caliph al-Ma'mūn, who came to Egypt in 832 to suppress rural rebellions and to investigate their causes. The hearings took place in Fusṭāṭ at the Ancient Mosque, where the cadi referred to the two tax collectors in Egypt as oppressors, using the strong term *ẓulm*. The hearing broke into uproar and al-Ma'mūn, who was told that the cadi enjoyed popular support and that his view reflected that of the people, invited al-Ḥārith ibn Miskīn to a private session. The cadi was asked whether he had been in any way wronged by these two tax collectors and he said no. Then he was asked how he could accuse them of oppression. His answer touched at the very core of the debate about legitimisation of political power. Al-Ḥārith ibn Miskīn said that he had never met al-Ma'mūn, but he testifies that he is the caliph, and that although he did not participate in his raids (meaning apparently the summer raids on Byzantium), he bears witness that they took place. He was immediately detained, and later exiled to Baghdad.

Al-Ḥārith ibn Miskīn's response implies that when a regime presents itself as legitimate and pretends to rule properly it bears the burden of proof. Legitimacy is not accorded but won, and a regime must earn it for itself in order to be beyond reproach. In Baghdad he was subjected to the inquisition (*miḥna*) over whether the Koran was the 'created' or 'uncreated' word of God, and having failed to give the right answer he suffered lengthy imprisonment.[22]

[21] Ibn Ḥajar, ed. Majīd, I, 22.
[22] Ibn Ḥajar, ed. Guest, 502–3; Maqrīzī, *Kitāb al-Muqaffā*, III, 129–30; Tillier, *Vies des cadis*, 38–40.

In 851, the Abbasid caliph al-Mutawakkil re-appointed al-Ḥārith ibn Miskīn cadi in Fusṭāṭ. This appointment was part of a broader but gradual policy of dissociation of the regime from the *miḥna* and the doctrine that the Koran was the 'created' word of God. It must be pointed out that the imposition of the *miḥna* had grave consequences for the administration of justice since court witnesses who failed to acknowledge the doctrine of the 'createdness' of the Koran were barred from testifying at the cadi's court.[23] Although al-Ḥārith ibn Miskīn owed his re-appointment to the caliph, he demonstrated his independence vis-à-vis the regime in a very subtle way: while presiding at the court he wore a black woollen cloak (*kisā*). Black was the Abbasid regnal colour, but the cadi and the wider public understood well the symbolic messages conveyed by the cadi's choice of a woollen garment. In this case, a black silk cloak would be out of question since silk signified disputed, though not explicitly forbidden, luxury. A good-quality black linen cloak would be expected of a cadi, but al-Ḥārith ibn Miskīn chose wool, the fabric of the poor and the one preferred by the ascetics. At the visual-symbolic level his choice of colour proclaimed the legitimacy of the regime, while the choice of the fabric manifested his independence vis-à-vis state authority. The issue of al-Ḥārith ibn Miskīn's attire while serving as cadi was brought to the attention of the caliph, who was not satisfied with al-Ḥārith ibn Miskīn's choice of a black over-garment and insisted that he must wear the standard insignia of the cadi's office (*khilaʿ*). Eventually, at local level, a compromise was worked out between the cadi and the governor and al-Ḥārith ibn Miskīn settled for a Yemeni-made garment.[24]

Al-Ḥārith ibn Miskīn proved to be strict and unyielding as ever, even when the personal economic interests of the Abbasid family in Egypt were at stake. Eventually, he was dismissed for the second time, following his ruling against the agent of the caliph's mother, who had seized a house from its owner. The agent complained to Baghdad and in response a quite remarkable

[23] The implementation of the *miḥna* in Egypt was divisive and provoked strive within the religious class. See Maqrīzī, *Kitāb al-Muqaffā*, V, 515–16. For the caliphate, see Melchert, 'Religious Policies of the Caliphs', 316–42; Zaman, 'The Caliphs', 1–36; 'Death, Funeral Processions', 34–5.

[24] Kindī, 469, Tillier, *Histoire des cadis*, 245; Ibn Ḥajar, ed. Majīd, I, 172; Tillier, *Vies des cadis*, 42–3; Maqrīzī, *Kitāb al-Muqaffā*, III, 134, offers a fuller account of this incident.

letter was sent to the local government (3 September 854). The letter begins by stating that the cadi was, from the days of the caliph al-Ma'mūn, known for being ill-disposed towards the Abbasids, but the main point is the claim that the agents who managed the urban and rural properties of the caliph's family enjoyed legal immunity and the cadi must revoke his ruling. This is a rare example of Muslim ruling circles, whether caliphs or sultans, claiming ex-judicial status for their economic interests and the personnel responsible for them. On the textual level, the Abbasid claims are bolstered through the frequent use of Abbasid royal titles. The agents are referred to as agents of the Commander of the Faithful and the royal properties as the 'rights' (*ḥuqūq*) of the Commander of the Faithful.[25]

Al-Mutawakkil's nomination of al-Ḥārith ibn Miskīn reflected a permanent dilemma of rulers as to who should be appointed to the post of cadi. On the one hand, the rulers were interested in people of integrity who would be respected both personally and as representatives of the regime. An honest cadi meant an honest government, but such people were not easily manipulated. Important though al-Ḥārith ibn Miskīn's uncompromising integrity was, his ability to confront the rulers also reflected the long evolution of the judicial institution headed by the cadi. The beginnings were, however, quite different and the evolutionary process was slow and complex.

The First Cadis

When a diachronic approach is adopted, it is possible to follow the evolution of the judicial system from its early beginnings to its reconstruction under the Fatimids. The notion that ʿUmar I created the Muslim judicial system by appointing cadis permeates Arabic literary sources. Ibn al-Khayyāṭ (d. 844 or 854), for example, provides a list of cadis appointed by ʿUmar I, and Abū Zurʿa (d. 894), the historian of Damascus, writes in the same vein. He traces the beginning of Damascus's judicial system to ʿUmar I and elaborates upon the history of the judicial institutions in his native town under the Umayyads.[26] In line with these claims, Ibn ʿAbd al-Ḥakam's and

[25] Kindī, 472–3; Tillier, *Histoire des cadis*, 249–50; Ibn Ḥajar, ed. Majīd I, 177–8; Tillier, *Vies des cadis*, 47; Maqrīzī, *Kitāb al-Muqaffā*, III, 137–9.

[26] Ibn al-Khayyāt, I, 128, 184; Abū Zurʿa, I, 196–206.

Kindī's remarks about the beginnings of the administration of justice in early Muslim Egypt fall within a familiar pattern. According to them, the first cadi was nominated in 643 but he died after three months and the post was offered to Kaʿb ibn Ḍinna, who declined the appointment, explaining that his pagan past prevented him from accepting the nomination. Kaʿb ibn Ḍinna's pagan past involved two elements: occupational prestige and familial ties. In pre-Islamic times he had served as a *ḥakam* (arbitrator), and he was the son of the daughter of Khālid ibn Sinān al-ʿAbsī, who, allegedly, was a prophet in the Jāhiliyya. Kindī's text also refers rather enigmatically to Kaʿb ibn Ḍinna's close relations with the Berbers in Fusṭāṭ, who claimed that Khālid ibn Sinān al-ʿAbsī was sent to them (to preach?). Furthermore, in the Jāhiliyya, Khālid ibn Sinān al-ʿAbsī was in charge of a holy fire cult. According to another version of the events, Kaʿb ibn Ḍinna actually served for two months as cadi since his refusal to take the post was rejected by ʿAmr ibn al-ʿĀṣ, who claimed that one must obey ʿUmar I, the Commander of the Faithful, who being informed about Kaʿb ibn Ḍinna's reasons for turning down the post accepted his refusal, and allowed him to quit the post.[27]

These accounts can be considered as typifying themes that are common in literary sources which depict a total rupture between a pre-Islamic Arab pagan past and Islam and portray ʿUmar I as a strong centralist ruler who initiated a range of administrative policies. This historiographical tendency has brought some modern scholars to doubt whether the post of cadi existed in the first decades after the Prophet's death, pointing out that the sources are patchy and contradictory. The whole issue has been re-examined by Tillier, who concludes that the sources provide a rather coherent picture of the early judicial system and one must take into account that there were regional variations in the way cadis were appointed.[28]

To what extent the early beginnings of an Islamic judicial system can be reconstructed from documentary sources is a matter of debate, which focuses

[27] Kindī, 301–2; 304–5; Tillier, *Histoire des cadis*, 49–51, 54. For another example of a pagan arbitrator who became a cadi, see Simonsohn, *A Common Justice*, 73. In this particular case the term 'Berbers' could, or should, be understood as referring to people of East Africa facing Arabia. For this interpretation, see Rouighi, 'The Berbers of the Arabs', 70–1. For Sūq Barbar in ninth-century Fusṭāṭ, see Bruning, *The Rise of a Capital*, 60–1.

[28] Tillier, *Les cadis d'Iraq*, 71–3.

on documents of the *dhikr al-ḥaqq* type published recently by Yūsuf Rāġib and reinterpreted by Bruning. These documents are private contracts which record a claim (*ḥaqq*) held by one of the involved parties against the other. The nature of the claim can vary, but the legal phraseology which refers to the debtor and the amount of the debt is standard.[29] Rāġib has published such documents, which refer to obligations undertaken within an agricultural context, flooding of the basins, and contain the phrase *'sanat qaḍā' al-mu'minīn'* and refer to *Hijrī* years 42 and 57 (662–3 and 676–7). Rāġib's translation 'l'ère de la jurisdiction des croyants' is challenged by Bruning, who has suggested a different reading: *sunnat qaḍā al-mu'minīn*. He has also pointed out that there are also shorter versions of this formula, which should be understood as referring to the normative procedure of the believers, which he perceives as indicating 'a strong sense of legal community among Muslims in early Sufyanid Egypt'.[30]

Valuable and supportive as the papyri evidence indicating the existence of early legal practices is, for the nature of the cadi's jurisdiction one must go back to literary sources. Ibn ʿAbd al-Ḥakam's and Kindī's accounts of the judicial system in early Muslim Egypt are, however, marked by an inextricable interweaving of history and discourse. The discourse is Islamic and projected backward onto the seventh century in an attempt to give an Islamic aura to the fuzzy and amorphous beginnings of the administration of justice in Egypt. Therefore, one must be cautious about Kaʿb ibn Ḍinna's explanation that his pagan past hindered his involvement in the Islamic administration of justice, which implies that already in those early years a clear-cut division between Jāhiliyya and Islam existed and that some people were aware of the

[29] Thung, 'Written Obligations' 1–12, including extensive discussion of the structure of these documents and examples.

[30] Rāġib, 'Une ère inconnue', 197–8; Bruning, 'A Legal Sunna', 352–74, esp. 373. Bruning's reading has been challenged by Shaddel, 'The Year According to the Reckoning of the Believers', 293–7. The documents discussed by Rāġib, Bruning and Shaddel must be seen in a broader context of irrigation practices and Arab pre-Islamic legal tradition. For the way the basin irrigation system worked, see Borsch, *The Black Death in Egypt*, 34–5. Each basin in the system was watered for a period of about forty days and the flooding was regulated by an elaborated timing sequence, which had nothing to do with the *Hijrī* calendar (see Rāġib's remarks, 193–4). In a number of publications Geoffrey Khan has drawn the attention to the existence of Arab pre-Islamic legal tradition, going back to the ancient Semitic Near East (see 'The Pre-Islamic Background of Muslim Legal Formularies', 193–224; 'An Early Arabic Legal Papyrus', 227–37; 'Remarks on the Historical Background', 887–9, 891). This topic is also alluded to by Bruning (see 373–4).

fact that their pagan past impeded their ability to play a meaningful role in the social life of the new religion. The explanation put forward by Kaʿb ibn Ḍinna seems to be more a literary motif than a reflection of early seventh-century religious and social realities.[31]

The discourse covering the first cadis of Egypt in an Islamic aura is cohesive and consistent, and Sulaym ibn ʿItr (appointed cadi in 660 by the caliph Muʿāwiyya) is, in contrast to Kaʿb ibn Ḍinna, presented as the prototype of an Islamic cadi. He belonged to the class of a few thousand Arabs who took part in the monumental events associated with the establishment and consolidation of Muslim power in the Middle East. He is described as having been a cadi in the army of ʿAmr ibn al-ʿĀṣ (*qāḍī al-jund*) and participated in the conquest of Egypt. In addition, he is depicted as a pious Muslim who performed three complete recitations of the Koran each night and also reported on ʿUmar I's ritual and devotional practices.[32]

From the very beginning of the administration of justice the cadi was a paid official appointed by the state, and proclamation of judicial directives by early caliphs was considered normative conduct. Ninth-century writings depict how early caliphs shaped the scale of punishment which, eventually, came to be considered binding. Ibn Ḥabīb (d. 853), for example, claims that ʿUmar I whipped his son for storing alcohol, and ordered the stoning of a sorcerer and a woman for infringement of sexual mores.[33]

[31] A smooth transition of leading members of the Qyraysh clan from Arab paganism to Islam is widely attested. See, for example, Ibn Yūnus I, 339. No less instructive is Ibn Yūnus's account of Kaʿb ibn Ḍinna's service as a judge in pre-Islamic and Islamic times (I, 413–14).

[32] Kindī inserts a comment that could be understood as alluding to differences between how rituals were performed at that time and their performance in his time. The issue at question was how many prostrations should be performed during the recitation of the Koranic pilgrimage verses: two, as the caliph practised, or three, as was done in Kindī's lifetime. See Kindī, 304, 308; Tillier, *Histoire des cadis*, 53; Ibn Yūnus, I, 218–19.

[33] Ibn Ḥabīb, 108, 110, 111, 116. For different versions of this incident, see Maqrīzī, *Kitāb al-Muqaffā*, IV, 91–6. Similar reports in the form of *akhbār* and *ḥadīth* enjoyed wide circulation. The caliph ʿUthmān is depicted as ordering the flogging of his half-brother, the governor of Kūfa, for leading prayers in a state of drunkenness. And no less a personality than ʿAlī, the future caliph, was chosen to administer the punishment. See Hakim, 'Conflicting Images', 173–4. How the punishment for drinking wine had evolved is discussed by Opwis. See 'Shifting Legal Authority from the Ruler to ʿUlamā', 66–70. The involvement of caliphs in setting the severity of punishments is also noted by non-Muslim sources. In 724–5, Yazīd II introduced a new scale for punishing theft by amputating an arm instead of a hand. His order was met with discontent. See *The Chronicle of Zuqnīn*, 156.

When the motifs typical of the late Muslim discourse on the formation of Islam are put aside, the reports about Sulaym ibn ʿItr's term in office do reveal the social dimension of administration of justice in traditional medieval society. Caliphal authority and guidance were not enough, and the cadi searched for authoritative and socially acceptable endorsements for the way he conducted his judicial business. Sulaym ibn ʿItr is credited as being the first cadi who wrote down his rulings in inheritance cases, while military chiefs (*shuyūkh al-jund*) signed these documents.[34] The involvement of the officer class, or the tribal leadership, exemplifies both the tribal and the military character of the Arab-Muslim conqueror society, a trait also reflected by Muʿāwiya's instructions to Sulaym ibn ʿItr as to how to compensate injured victims of violent crimes. The cadi was supposed to apply the collective responsibility of the agnate solidarity group (*ʿāqila*) for paying blood money (*ḍiya*) to the victims. Sulaym ibn ʿItr was ordered to record the details of the injury suffered by a person and to notify in writing (*qiṣṣa*) the head of the office of payments (*ṣāḥib al-dīwān*) about the amount of the compensation he imposed on the perpetrator's *ʿaqila* group. When the office made payments to the Arab-Muslim population, the injured person was supposed to receive compensation in three yearly instalments from the kinsmen (*ʿashīra*) of the perpetrator.[35]

In 717, another case of blood-money involving group responsibility was brought to the attention of the caliph ʿUmar II by the cadi ʿIyāḍ ibn ʿUbayd Allāh. In this case, a protégé (*mawlā*) of an unspecified Arab group killed a woman when riding and his *mawālī* comrades refused to bear any responsibility as his *ʿāqila* group. The text explicitly states that the perpetrator was not on the payroll of the *dīwān* and reproves the *mawālī* for their duplicity since they would have demanded compensation had they suffered injury. The caliph, in the letter to the cadi, reminded him that the *mawālī* have no recollections of their genealogies (*ansāb*), alluding to the futility of the *ʿāqila* concept in this case. He ordered the cadi not to leave a case involving

[34] With the benefit of hindsight, Ibn Ḥajar (ed. Majīd, II, 254) emphasises Sulaym ibn ʿItr's innovation of recording judgments.

[35] Kindī, 309; Tillier, *Histoire des cadis*, 58; Schacht, *The Origins*, 207–8; Tsafrir, 'The ʿĀqila', 221–3. For military organisation in early Muslim Egypt, see Mikhail, 'Notes on the Ahl al-Dīwān', 273–84; Sipesteijn, 'Army Economics', 245–67.

blood-money owed to a Muslim unresolved and to pay the blood-money for the killed woman himself and to collect it from the reluctant *mawālīs*.[36]

The case illuminates a social process that by the first decades of the eighth century was in full swing: the incorporation of non-Arabs into Arab-Muslim society through patronage and, possibly, Islamisation. However, the application of Arab tribal concepts to people of diverse origins unrelated by blood relations proved to be difficult, if not impractical. In the long run, Islamisation and the growing number of *mawālīs* rendered the tribal structure of the early Arab-Muslim society obsolete and created a Muslim society in which the Arabs were just one of the ethnic groups that it contained and, in regions such as Persia and North Africa, a minority. The tempo and scope of this process are difficult to date, but, during the first half of the eighth century, Arab tribal structure in Fusṭāṭ was still pervasive and the cadi Tawba ibn Namir al-Ḥaḍramī (733–8) was very aware of Arab tribal sensitivities and their potential implications for the judicial process. He did not accept the testimony of an Arab belonging to the northern Arab tribal groups against one belonging to the southern tribal groups and vice versa. In such disputes he delegated the cases to the tribal leaders for arbitration.[37] Obviously, the cadi hesitated to grapple with tribal identities and solidarity, but this account also throws light on the evolution of Islamic law and court procedures. The notion that testimony is a legal requirement and an essential element in the cadi's court took root, and when the cadi felt unable to meet this standard he preferred other alternatives. Apparently, at that time, a dual (or parallel) system of administration of justice and conflict resolution existed and the arbitration option implemented by socially prestigious tribal notables was available. The cadi, as the caliph's/state's appointee, administrated the law, which was evolving and shaped through processes that were taking place both from above and in the ranks of the cadis.

During the first decades of the eighth century the guidance of the caliph in legal matters was constantly sought, and ʿIyāḍ ibn ʿUbayd Allāh frequently asked the caliph for advice (he served for nineteen months [717–19] under

36 Kindī, 333–4; Tillier, *Histoire des cadis*, 88–9; Tsafrir, 'The 'Āqila', 224. For a broader approach with references to sources and literature, see Hentati, 'Āqila', 203–19.

37 Kindī, 345–6; Tillier, *Histoire des cadis*, 102.

ʿUmar II). One of these cases involved a mother who had bequeathed one third of her property to her son, including slaves, and stipulated that they should be set free upon his death. One of these slaves injured a person, who was entitled to compensation (*ʿaql*) of 70 *dīnārs*, which the cadi tried to collect from the reluctant owner. ʿIyāḍ ibn ʿUbayd Allāh's wrote to ʿUmar II about the case and the caliph upheld cadi's decision to impose the payment on the owner and stipulated that otherwise the slave would be handed to the injured person as compensation. Eventually, a family member of the owner paid the money.[38]

The position of the cadi as a state official was probably enhanced by investing him with additional non-judicial responsibilities. Sulaym ibn ʿItr, for example, was also entrusted with the function of *qaṣaṣ*, which is usually understood as storytelling/preaching. From the beginning it was a political institution, and Ibn Ḥajar (1372–1449) traces its origin to the aftermath of the struggle between ʿAlī and Muʿāwiya. After the Battle of Ṣiffīn (July 657), ʿAlī prayed and vilified his opponents, while Muʿāwiya's response involved the introduction of the *qaṣaṣ*, which was delivered after dawn and sunset and contained a positive political message: preaching for Muʿāwiya and the Arab population of Syria. Ibn Ḥajar maintains that there were two form of *qaṣaṣ*: one intended for the common people and another for the elite. The *qaṣaṣ* for the commoners was more a storytelling affair, while the one for the elite was imbued with political messages and this reorientation of the *qaṣaṣ* was Muʿāwiya's innovation. The political form of the *qaṣaṣ* took place after the morning prayer and involved glorifying God and extolling the caliph and his family, his supporters and the army, and defamation of opponents. While placing the origin of the political form of *qaṣaṣ* in the context of the Battle of Ṣiffīn and its aftermath makes sense, the distinction between its supposed two forms seems doubtful. One would expect any regime to be interested in conveying its political messages to and galvanising support from the people and the elite alike.

The renowned Egyptian Shāfiʿī jurist and historian al-Quḍāʿī (d. 1062) stated that Sulaym ibn ʿItr served as cadi and *qāṣṣ* (storyteller/preacher) for 37 years, and that he used to lift his arms while performing. Other reports

[38] Kindī, 335–6; Tillier, *Histoire de cadis*, 90–1.

claim that he was the first preacher to have stood on his feet when delivering sermons and that he was criticised for deviating from the traditional sitting posture of the preacher.[39] Important though the post of preacher/storyteller might have been, during the Umayyad period the most frequent extension of judicial responsibilities was the dual appointment to the post of cadi and commander of the police.[40] The merging of these two posts goes back to the early years of Muʿāwiya's rule, when extensive administrative responsibilities were entrusted to officials. Maslama ibn Mukhallad, Egypt's governor in the early 660s, for example, was invested with political and fiscal responsibilities, and his area of authority also included North Africa.[41] Nevertheless, in the long term, the post of cadi acquired a separate judicial identity and the practice of investing him with additional functions became less common and, eventually, ceased. Actually, the process that truly shaped the nature of the cadi's post did not take place from above, but rather from the ranks of the cadis, and had enduring consequences: cadis extended the sphere of their authority by assuming new, extra-judicial financial supervisory responsibilities.

New Responsibilities

The expansion of the cadi's role beyond the judicial sphere was initiated by the cadi ʿAbd al-Raḥmān ibn Muʿāwiya (appointed in 705), who held the post in addition to that of commander of the police. He was the first cadi to have supervised the money belonging to orphans, and, like Sulaym ibn ʿItr, he worked via the existing social system. He co-opted the tribal chiefs to record the moneys belonging to the orphans of their tribes (*amwāl al-yatāmā*), while he kept these records and supervised the funds. How he manage to wrest powers from the tribal chiefs is not explained, but apparently the combination of military, or semi-military, powers and judicial authority

[39] Kindī, 304; Tillier, *Histoire de cadis*, 53; Ibn Ḥajar, ed. Majīd II, 253; for an English translation of Ibn Ḥajar's account, see Juynboll, *Muslim Tradition*, 14–15. For other references to storytellers/preachers, see Ibn Yūnus, I, 76–7, 97 (referring to a storyteller/preacher in Alexandria at the time of ʿUmar II), 369, 424, 490. For broader discussion of this institution and its origin and function, see Armstrong, *The Quṣṣāṣ of Early Islam*, 190–240, esp. 233–40.

[40] Ibn ʿAbd al-Ḥakam, *Futūḥ*, 236, 238 (referring to the 710s). The combination of judicial responsibility with supervision of the Treasury reoccurred in 715, while the addition of preaching to the cadi's responsibilities also took place in 738. Kindī, 313, 317, 332, 348; Bligh-Abramski, 'The Judiciary', 46, 49; Tillier, *Les cadis d'Iraq*, 75–7.

[41] Ibn ʿAbd al-Ḥakam, *Futūḥ*, 233; Ibn Yūnus, I, 199; Kindī, 38.

gave him the necessary leverage. In the context of the evolving role of the cadi, ʿAbd al-Raḥmān ibn Muʿāwiya's deeds had a far greater impact than those of his predecessor ʿĀbis ibn Saʿīd, who was involved in digging a canal and increasing the salaries paid by the office of payments. In the long term, the cadi's involvement in such activities became atypical.[42]

The newly established supervisory authority of the cadi went hand in hand with the slow formation of his judicial identity and growing expectations of justice and impartiality. The fusion of these two trends is illuminated by events that took place in 732 which involved the cadi Yaḥyā ibn Maymūn, who was notorious for being indifferent to the corrupt ways of his clerks, who demanded bribes for writing down his rulings. In line with standard practice since 705, he managed the property of an orphan, who upon maturity complained both to his tribal leader and to the cadi, but to no avail. People from his tribe provided testimony on the orphan's behalf stating that he had been harshly treated, but the cadi remained unmoved. The orphan, in an attempt to draw attention to his plight, sent the cadi some lines of poetry, for which he was imprisoned. The case somehow reached the attention of the caliph, who ordered the governor of Egypt to dismiss the cadi and also set clear guidelines for appointing cadis. The gist of the account can be found in the caliph's address to the governor: 'You should choose a cadi for your army who is virtuous, scrupulous, pious and blameless.'[43]

This example of an arrogant cadi unaware of the people's expectations of justice also offers us a glimpse into the social make-up of Arab-Muslim society in Fusṭāṭ, which still maintained its military character. Although the tribal structure was powerful and the cadi had co-operated with a tribal leader to appropriate the legacy of an orphan, the authority of the caliph is depicted as overriding, and he was attentive to local opinion and keen to preserve the integrity and image of the institutions for which the government was responsible. Eventually, in the early years of Abbasid rule, the state came to control orphans' moneys. In 750, on the orders of the caliph al-Manṣūr, these funds were transferred to the local treasury and each transaction was duly recorded.

[42] Kindī, 313, 325; Tillier, *Histoire des cadis*, 63, 78; Ibn Ḥajar, ed. Majīd, II, 348; Maqrīzī, *Kitāb al-Muqaffā*, III, 101–2.

[43] Kindī, 340–1; Tillier, *Histoire des cadis*, 96.

During the 790s, the cadi Muḥammad ibn Masrūq al-Kindī, who had come to Fusṭāṭ from Baghdad, was falsely accused of trying to transfer this money to Baghdad. He was greatly disliked by the local elite, who had a vested interest in dealing with funds of this sort and in keeping the money in Egypt.[44]

What really was at stake is revealed by the discussion of how these funds should be invested and profiteering avoided. The practice grew up of investing the orphans' moneys in urban and agricultural properties, but how payments to the orphans should be made was contested. The problem preoccupied the cadi ʿAbd al-Raḥmān ibn ʿAbd Allāh al-ʿUmarī (801–9), who came to Egypt from Iraq and is described as a Mālikī jurist. He entrusted the management of this type of money to a trustee, who rendered payments to orphans from the profits from his investments and deducted the sums from the capital sum (*aṣl al-māl/uṣūl*) under his management. Eventually, he claimed the capital for himself, saying that he had fulfilled his obligations towards the orphans through the payments he had made from the profits. The cadi punished him by publicly shaming him, but he did not yield up any of the money. Another account states that al-ʿUmarī was the first cadi to create a special deposit (*tābūt al-quḍā*, the cadis' coffer) within the Treasury for various types of funds: orphans' moneys, absent persons' moneys and legacies with no legal heirs. One is left to guess whether there was any connection between these two deeds of the cadi, who became disillusioned with the way these funds were handled and preferred to play things safe by depositing them in the Treasury. This prevented the skimming off of the profits, but in the long run depleted the capital because of a lack of investment.[45]

Problems relating to the management of the orphans' monies persisted, and the cadi Harūn ibn ʿAbd Allāh (appointed 833) invested great effort in stemming corruption and mismanagement. Vast sums of money were handled by court trustees, and many people were involved in dealing with this type of money, while the cadi had difficulties in even knowing these people, let alone effectively supervising them, especially if he was a foreigner whose term in office was short.[46]

[44] Kindī, 355, 390; Tillier, *Histoire des cadis*, 114, 155; Maqrīzī, *Kitāb al-Muqaffā*, VII, 233.

[45] Kindī, 405; Tillier, *Histoire des cadis*, 172; Ibn Ḥajar, ed. Majīd, II, 324.

[46] Kindī, 390. 404–5, 444, 450, Ibn Ḥajar, ed. Majīd, I, 39; Tillier, *Histoire des cadis*, 155, 171, 219, 225.

The cadis' involvement in supervising how orphans' monies were managed can be seen as a reflection of Koranic injunctions which emphasise honest dealings with this type of money and warn wrongdoers of God's punishment. To what extent orphanage was a serious social problem in pre-Islamic Arabia and Muslim society in Fusṭāṭ remains unknown. One must bear in mind that there was apparently a considerable age difference between men and women at the time of their first marriage.[47] Furthermore, orphanage was defined as absence of the father, and given the age difference at first marriage and the fact that men died on the battlefield and on business trips, or abandoned their families, the phenomenon of fatherless children may have been quite widespread. On the other hand, one can imagine that a widow with children from her first marriage remarried and that these children lived with her in the new family setting but were defined as orphans. One should also not rule out the fact that many divorcees or widows did not remarry and so the property of their minor children came under the cadi's control.[48] In any case, it can be argued that Koranic ethics were the driving force behind the attention paid to the welfare of orphans, but this line of argument is less applicable in explaining the cadi's involvement in the supervision of pious endowments (*waqf*, pl. *awqāf*/*ḥubs*, pl. *aḥbās*).

While charity is part and parcel of the Koranic teachings, the concept of endowment is not Koranic. Koranic notions of, and terminology surrounding, charity were, however, grafted onto the *waqf* institution. The current scholarly discussion of *waqf* is broad and diversified, and Benjamin Jokish, for example, characterises monotheistic religions as compatible in this respect, 'forming something like [a] spiritual alliance', and proving to be 'quite similar in structure'. According to this line of argument, the existence of a pious endowment system in Islam comes as no surprise. Jokish nevertheless perceives *waqf* as an institution that mirrors Byzantine precedents and

[47] This issue is marred by many methodological difficulties. See Krakowski's extensive discussion, *Coming of Age in Medieval Egypt*, 122–9.

[48] The topic of 'the absent husband' is extensively discussed by Goitein. See *Med. Soc.* III, 189–205. The argument about a high percentage of unmarried women in Mamlūk cities has been put forward by Rapoport, *Marriage, Money and Divorce*.

Byzantine imperial legislation.[49] The notion that *waqf* was influenced by the Byzantine system of endowment prevails in the literature and the Islamic institution of endowment is perceived as a marker of continuity between the world of Late Antiquity and Islam.[50]

Going beyond the parameters of monotheistic religions, the notion and practice of endowment were not alien to ancient Middle Eastern civilisations, the Graeco-Roman world or Sasanian Iran.[51] The human quest for eternal life, commemoration and charitable drive transcend the pagan/monotheistic divide, and the same is true for socio-judicial forms. Belief in an afterlife with a heaven and a hell was part of Zoroaster's teaching, and the performance of rites for the departed became central for Zoroastrians and manifested their piety. Charitable foundations established through bequests financed commemorative services for the dead, while others were set up for the maintenance of the sacred fires. Zoroastrian charitable foundations created for good and pious causes also served to commemorate the soul of the founder, who sought gratitude and acknowledgement for his deed from the beneficiaries of the foundation.[52]

Important though parallel notions of endowment in other civilisations are, direct influence of Persian or Byzantine concepts of endowment on Islam remains unclear. *Waqf*, therefore, must be studied within the parameters of Islam and evolving early Muslim society and law. Islamic tradition perceives the pious endowment institution as an internal development and attributes its origin to the Prophet and his Companions. Some reports claim that the properties of the Jews of Medina, who were expelled by the Prophet and killed, were dedicated by Muḥammad in favour of the Muslim community. 'Umar I is quoted as saying that, when he made his share of land in Khaybar (an oasis populated by Jews who had surrendered to Muḥammad in 628) a

[49] See *Islamic Imperial Law*, 17, 137–42. For the need to look at the Byzantine parallels, see Cahen, 'Réflexions sur le waqf ancien', 52–3. For a detailed examination of this question, see Barnes, *An Introduction to Religious Foundations in the Ottoman Empire*, 11–20.

[50] Pahlitzsch, 'Christian Pious Foundations', 125–52.

[51] For endowments in the ancient world, see Allam, 'Islamic Foundations', 105–13.

[52] Boyce, 'On the Sacred Fires of the Zoroastrians', 52–68; 'The Pious Foundations of the Zoroastrians', 270–89; Macuch, 'Pious Foundations in Byzantine and Sasanian Law', 181–96. The legal aspects of the endowments dedicated for the performance of rituals for the soul are discussed in a Sasanian law book compiled in the first half of the seventh century. See Perikhanian, *The Book of a Thousand Judgments*, 97, 99, 101.

waqf, he had acted on the advice of the Prophet himself. 'Umar I is also credited with the decision to declare most of the agricultural land in Iraq *waqf* for the benefit of Muslims, thereby turning the peasants into serfs. It was also he who finally rejected the claim of Fāṭima, Muḥammad's daughter, against her father's estate. In doing this he upheld the ruling of his predecessor, Abū Bakr (632–4). Both of them relied on a saying of 'Ā'isha, Muḥammad's wife, who had repeated the Prophet's words that no one would inherit anything from him and that what he had left would be *ṣadaqa* (meaning charity or *waqf*) for the Muslim community. ʿAlī is credited with turning his vast rural holdings in the Ḥijāz into endowments, and the origin of familial endowments, meaning an endowment in favour of the founder's family, supposedly goes back to the 690s.[53]

When one turns to legal literature a more coherent picture of the development of *waqf* emerges, but the beginnings nevertheless remain hazy. Schacht has noted a strong link between the pious endowment institution and the holy war embodied in the *ḥabs fī sabīl Allāh* (endowment for God) concept. Mālik and other early eighth-century Mālikī jurists, for example, permitted the endowment of movables, including horses, for the holy war, and such endowments were established in Ṭarsūs on the Muslim–Byzantine frontier (Adana district in modern Turkey) during the tenth century. The Mālikī school also permitted the establishment of temporary endowments that would revert to the owner or his heirs upon the death of the original beneficiary. These endowments for life were known as *ʿumrā*, and Norbert Oberauer argues that eighth-century sources indicate that the laws of *waqf* evolved as a fusion of

[53] The caliph ʿUthmān is credited with establishing a *waqf* (a water well) for the Muslims. See Ibn Ḥabīb, 117. For the caliph ʿAlī's supposed endowments in the vicinity of Medina, see Rabb, 'The Curious Case of Bughaybigha', 24, 27, 34. Whether the Islamic tradition on the origin of *waqf* can be trusted is a matter of opinion and controversial. Gil, for example, is very explicit on this issue: 'I find the general corpus of tradition – as preserved in the Arab sources – to be essentially genuine.' See 'The Earliest Waqf Foundations', 125. For the same methodological approach, see Lecker, 'A Pre-Islamic Endowment Deed in Arabic'. (The use of the term 'endowment' in this context is, however, somewhat problematic since the property in question was not endowed but given as a gift.) For pious endowments at the time of the Prophet and 'Umar, see Amin, *Al-Awqāf wa'l-Hayat al-Ijtima'iyya*, 18–21; Lecker, 'Glimpses of Muḥammad's Medinan Decade', 69; Forand, 'The Status of the Land and Inhabitants of the Sawad', 29–30; Abdullah, 'A New Definition of Waqf', 57–73; Haji Othman, 'Origin of the Institution of Waqf', 3–23. For a critical approach to sources, see Powers, *Studies in Qu'rān and Ḥadīth*, 123–8, 134, 136, discussing Fāṭima's claim against her father's estate.

two practices: *ḥabs fī sabīl Allāh* and *ʿumrā*. The next significant development in the shaping of the laws of *waqf* was the stipulation of Shaybānī (d. 806) that an endowment for the benefit of a person was valid only if the founder specified a pious function as the endowment's ultimate designation, which would be fulfilled upon the death of the original beneficiary.[54] A further step in the development of the *waqf* doctrine is represented by the work of two leading Ḥanafī jurists, Hilāl al-Ra'y (d. 859) and al-Khaṣṣāf (d. 874), whose extant legal treatises on the subject have been studied by Peter C. Hennigan. Hilāl stated that a legally valid endowment was a perpetual charity (*ṣadaqa mawqūfa*) which, as argued by Shaybānī, would upon the extinction of the original beneficiary serve a charitable purpose. These two jurists drew a legal distinction between the institution of pious endowment and other types of charity that were denoted by terms such as *ṣadaqa* and/or *zakāt*.[55]

Although the sources provide no information on the subject, by the early 730s the spread of *waqfs* in Egypt must have been quite considerable. These early endowments were managed by family members or people designated by the founders. The cadi Tawba ibn Namir reformed the way such foundations were handled and declared that pious endowments are charity (*ṣadaqāt*) for the poor, invoking the Koranic terms *masākīn wa-l-fuqarā'*. He assumed a supervisory role over them and created a special office for this purpose, declaring that he would protect these foundations against corrupt practices and transmission by inheritance. The cadi's struggle for control of economic assets is presented in moral terms, something that gave him the needed leverage to overcome vested interests and change the way this institution functioned.[56]

To what extent Kindī's tenth-century text accurately reflects the realities of Tawba ibn Namir's time (the third decade of the eighth century) is difficult to ascertain, but the cadi's assertion (if accurately quoted) that the poor are the ultimate beneficiaries of a *waqf* pre-dates Shaybānī's stipulation. The spread of the pious endowment institution in Egypt was, apparently, a

[54] Schacht, 'Early Doctrines on Waqf', 444–5, 447; Oberauer, 'Early Doctrines on Waqf Revisited', 1–47. For pious endowments in Ṭarsūs, see Lev, *Charity*, 68–9. Ibn Yūnus, II, 246, quoting a tradition in favour of endowing a horse for the purpose of the holy war.

[55] Hennigan, *The Birth of a Legal Institution*, 52, 61–9; Yanagihashi, 'The Doctrinal Development', 337–8.

[56] Kindī, 346; Tillier, *Histoire des cadis*, 102; Bouderbala, 'Les aḥbās de Fusṭāṭ', 39–40.

unique local development and fiercely defended. In 780, the caliph al-Mahdī appointed Ismāʿīl ibn Alīsaʿ as cadi of Egypt. He is described as the follower of Abū Ḥanifa (d. 767) and an adherent of the legal school of Kūfa, which advocated the nullification of pious endowments. Ismāʿīl ibn Alīsaʿ's legal approach brought him into direct conflict with the Arab-Muslim elite in Fusṭāṭ, which considered the establishment of pious endowments to be a practice authorised by and derived from the deeds of the Prophet, the early caliphs Abū Bakr and ʿUmar I and Ṭalḥa and Zubayr ibn al-ʿAwwām (both were killed at the Battle of the Camel, December 656). A complaint against the cadi was sent to Baghdad. Apparently it did not question his integrity, but his rulings, issued according to a legal doctrine with which the people in Fusṭāṭ were unfamiliar. The caliph dismissed the cadi, implying that a cadi cannot act against evolving local legal tradition, and, one might add, especially not against a tradition which supports an institution with wide socio-economic ramifications.[57] This clash between a foreign cadi and members of the local elite involved the preservation of both local legal identity and local interests.[58] In the broader context of urban socio-legal life this case was not exceptional. The recognition that eighth-century towns had a unique legal identity was widespread.[59]

[57] Ibn ʿAbd al-Ḥakam, *Futūḥ*, 244. Ibn Yūnus, II, 39; Kindī, 371; Maqrīzī, *Kitāb al-Muqaffā*, II, 113–15; Tillier, 'Les 'premiers' cadis de Fusṭāṭ', 228–9. All the people mentioned in the account owned land in the Ḥijāz and certainly elsewhere too, but the status of these lands is not specified. For Ḥijāz, see El-Ali, 'Muslim Estates', 249, 253, 256, 257, 259. Although allusions to endowment of properties for the common good of the early Muslim community in Fusṭāṭ are frequent, the institutional history of the endowment system remains enigmatic. That idea that the most productive lands of Egypt were endowed for the Muslims is rarely stated. See Ibn ʿAbd al-Ḥakam, *Futūḥ*, 89, 92, 98, 100, 101, 104.

[58] Another version of Alīsaʿ's term as cadi puts the whole affair into a completely different context of sexual mores and the apparent indifference of the cadi to somebody being vilified as a sodomite, which is alluded to by the vague term *ma'būn* and the explicit phrase *man yunkaḥu fī duburi-hi*. (For *ma'būn* in the meaning of a male passive sexual partner, see Riḍā, *Muʿjam al-ʿArabiyya al-Klāsīkiyya wa-l-Muʿāṣira*, 1,399.) Perhaps the issue hinted at this account was broader and also involved the question of sexual positions and not just of anal intercourse. Both issues were extensively debated in Islam and, generally speaking, rear-entry vaginal intercourse was permitted, while opinions about anal intercourse were divided. See Kindī, 371–2. For another debate about anal intercourse (*al-waṭ' fī l-dubur*), see Kindī, 379; Tillier, *Histoire des cadis*, 134, 143. Sexual mores were also part of Muslim–Jewish polemics. For a broad discussion of this particular issue, see Maghen, *After Hardship Cometh Ease*, ch. 9.

[59] See Tillier's discussion 'Legal Knowledge and Local Practice', 187–204, esp. 199–200, referring to Ismāʿīl ibn Alīsaʿ's conflict with the local elite in Fusṭāṭ. For the Abbasid preference for Ḥanafī cadis but also attention to local legal identities, see Tsafrir, *The History of an Islamic School of Law*, 27, 95.

The spread of pious endowments in Egypt must have been considerable, and the roots of the phenomena go back to the Umayyad period. One of the earliest references to a pious endowment is the account concerning the governor al-Walīd ibn Rīfāʿa (in office during 727–35), who established a charitable pious endowment without specifying the causes it should serve. The account neatly illustrates the fact that early pious endowments, even those established by people of high standing, could have been set up for unspecified beneficiaries, a situation that Shaybānī tried to curb. There must have been constant debate about the identity of the beneficiaries, and, in the early tenth century, the cadi Ibn Ḥarb decided that the income should go to the foundlings.[60] The longevity of the endowment is rather surprising, and one must assume that it was a very rich and well-managed endowment to yield income for such a long period.

In contrast to al-Walīd ibn Rīfāʿa's endowment, a *waqf* established in 711–12 in Fusṭāṭ highlights the social make-up of the Arab-Muslim population at that time and explicitly names the beneficiaries. Ibn ʿUthmān (his name is also given as Abū ʿUthaym), the protégé of the governor Maslama ibn Mukhallad, endowed a house for his protégés. The account indicates that the process whereby high-ranking Arab-Muslims granted patronage (*walāʾ*) to individuals among the local population began early on. Some of these protégés made a career, gained wealth and granted patronage to others.[61] In this case, in contrast to al-Walīd ibn Rīfāʿa's pious endowment, the original endowment deed specified who were the immediate and the ultimate beneficiaries of the endowment. Actually, there were two hierarchies of charitable stipulations: the immediate beneficiaries were four protégés and their male and female descendants and upon the extinction of their lines the beneficiaries would be the poor and the needy and other named protégés, including

60 The way the cadi reached his conclusion might be called reverse analogical thinking. He was informed that the governor used to publicly vilify ʿAlī and, relying on a *ḥadīth*, stating that a person hostile to ʿAlī is a bastard he inferred that foundlings are the rightful beneficiaries of the endowment. See Ibn Ḥajar, ed. ʿUmarī, 273; Tillier, *Vies des cadis*, 92.

61 For a broader discussion of this issue, see Nawas, 'A Client's Client', 143–58. The process of a protégé having his own clientele had wide social ramifications and is also attested in the context of court slavery. The phenomena of slaves, including eunuchs who belonged to rulers, members of royal families and other high-ranking people of the ruling circles, having their own slaves and eunuchs is well-attested across the whole spectrum of court life in medieval Islam.

volunteers and people on the military payroll who received fewer than 200 *dīnārs* and were not entitled to any inheritance (the technical legal term is *ʿaṣaba*). If no beneficiaries belonging to this category were found in Fusṭāṭ, their share would be added to the share of the poor.

There was constant litigation about who was entitled to the incomes of the endowment and cadis invalidated the judgments of their predecessors. One of these litigations was adjudicated by the cadi al-Ḥārith ibn Miskīn as late as 858. The pious endowment involved a house known as Dār al-Fīl (the House of the Elephant), which generated incomes through being either a commercial building or a residential building in which flats were rented. Again, one may wonder at the longevity of the endowment, its proper management, and the fact that a century and half after its establishment people still asked to be recognised as descendants of the rightful beneficiaries.[62]

Another familial pious endowment, dated by Sobhi Bouderbala to the end of the seventh century, like Ibn ʿUthmān's endowment, specified charitable causes upon the extinction of the family line. In this case a hierarchy of male and female beneficiaries was stated, and upon the extinction of the female line the incomes from the endowment, which included a house, a bathhouse and a kiln, would go for the 'purpose of God' (meaning either the holy war or charitable causes in general), to the poor and to the protégés of the family. However, upon the extinction of the protégés the remaining proceeds of the endowment were designated for the poor in Fusṭāṭ and the *ʿimāra* (benefit/development) of Medina, at the discretion of its ruler.[63]

In the Egyptian context, the administrative changes introduced by Tawba ibn Namir in the way pious endowments were managed were irreversible and recognition of the cadis' supervisory role became firmly established. The cadi ʿAbd Allāh ibn Muḥammad al-Ḥazmī, who was appointed by the caliph al-Hādī and came to Egypt in 786, exceeded the authority of the supervisors of pious endowments, ordered them to repair and maintain endowed properties and punished those who neglected their duties. Al-Ḥazmī's personal

[62] Kindī, 474–5; Tillier, *Histoire des cadis*, 251; Ibn Ḥajar, ed. Guest, 503–5, 506; Tillier, *Vies des cadis*, 47–51, 56. Both Ibn Ḥajar and Maqrīzī (*Kitāb al-Muqaffā*, III, 138–9) provide long and complex accounts of the endowment and its history.

[63] Ibn ʿAbd al-Ḥakam, *Futūḥ*, 135–6; Bouderbala, 'Les aḥbās de Fusṭāṭ', 40–1, with a French translation of the account.

involvement set a pervasive example which was followed by other cadis, although some tried to question the legal obligation to invest in the repair of these properties. The cadi al-ʿUmarī (appointed in 801), for example, was informed that, according to Mālik, this obligation was not necessarily anchored in the endowment deeds specifying the way these properties should be run. The cadi, who is described as a Mālikī jurist who had come from Baghdad, rejected the claim, stating that repairs are necessary to ensure the flow of incomes to the beneficiaries. Al-ʿUmarī's interest in pious endowments went beyond a supervisory role; he is credited with setting up a pious endowment for a dilapidated mosque.

Kindī recounts the history of a mosque built in the Umayyad period and torn down, or allowed to fall into ruin, in the Abbasid period and rebuilt on al-ʿUmarī's initiative after he had heard testimony about its dilapidation. The cadi used 1,000 *dīnārs* from the legacy of a certain person for the setting up a pious endowment, rebuilding of the mosque and construction of shops for its upkeep. Although the terminology *waqf* is not employed by Kindī, he quotes and paraphrases the ruling of the cadi as set down in a document (*qaḍiyya*) issued on that occasion (January–February 804). The document begins by stating that the essence of the cadi's role is to issue judgments. This assertion is followed by a detailed description of the location of the mosque in Fusṭāṭ and refers to the shops which were built to provide income for the mosque's muezzin and staff, while any surplus income was dedicated for charitable causes. The cadi also appointed a certain person to manage the affairs of the mosque and to serve as a trustee for its incomes, its expenditures and the dispensing of charities. The document actually recounts the chain of events that culminated in the cadi's ruling: the testimony concerning the mosque's condition, the cadi's verification of the testimony and his actions in response to the testimony.[64]

Kindī's account of al-ʿUmarī setting up a pious endowment for the mosque ends with an enigmatic remark about a delegation of *qurrā'* who went to Baghdad to complaint to the caliph Harūn al-Rashīd about al-ʿUmarī's handling of the affair. The caliph found that no blame lay with the cadi and retained him in his post. In 810, following the death of the caliph, al-ʿUmarī

[64] Kindī, 406–10; Ibn Ḥajar, ed. Majīd, II, 320–1, 370–1; Tillier, *Histoire des cadis*, 174–7.

was dismissed and the new cadi imprisoned him and some of his associates. The backlash against al-ʿUmarī had a twofold background: it went back to the so-called Ḥaras affair and also involved accusations of misuse or embezzlement of trust money under his supervision and the dismissal of witnesses serving at his court.[65]

The expansion of the cadi's role beyond legal matters came at a cost: it made him vulnerable and entangled him in power struggles for the control of lucrative sources of income. An intriguing question is how al-ʿUmarī could allocate 1,000 *dīnārs* of a legacy to the setting up an endowment. Apparently, this money belonged to the category known as estates with no legal heirs and/or residue of estates to which no heirs were entitled to (*al-mawārīth al-ḥashriyya*), which somehow came under the cadi's control. The extension of the cadis' supervisory role empowered them to freely dispense money untied to any specific purpose.

The dismissal of al-ʿUmarī reflected an ongoing struggle for the control of funds supervised by the cadi, but brought no changes in the way cadis exercised their powers. There was no way back, since the notion that the cadi has supervisory powers became an accepted norm, and the sources throw light on what really was at stake. Cadis, for example, controlled the incomes of pious endowments for the holy war (referred to by Kindī as *aḥbās al-sabīl/amwāl al-sabīl*), which supported the poor soldiers of the regular army (*ahl al-dīwān*) and volunteers. Both types of troops were deployed, or settled, along Egypt's Mediterranean coast from southern Palestine to the town of Barqa in Libya. This system collapsed during the civil war between the brothers al-Amīn and al-Ma'mūn and was restored by the cadi Lahīʿa ibn ʿĪsā al-Ḥaḍramī (812–13). This cadi used the incomes generated by this type of endowment to enlist fresh troops and new volunteers and dispatched them, or settled them, along the coast and paid them salaries. Although Kindī asserts that enlisting troops became a typical activity for a cadi, one may doubt this claim, which should rather be understood in a narrow sense: cadis paid salaries to these coastal garrisons since they controlled the incomes

65 Kindī, 412. The Ḥaras affair involved al-ʿUmarī's ruling in favour of Copts who claimed Arab pedigree. See Lev, 'Coptic Rebellions', 320–3. For more recent discussion of these events and French translation of relevant fragments, see Bouderbala, 'Les māwālī à Fusṭāṭ', 147–51, esp. 149, n. 49; Webb, *Imagining the Arabs*, 188–9, including English translation of poetry fragments.

derived from endowments in their support. In any case, the cadi al-Ḥaḍramī did something that one would expect the governor to do: take care of Egypt's coastal defence.[66]

By the 810s, the cadi Lahīʿa ibn ʿĪsā al-Ḥaḍramī controlled all of Egypt's pious endowments and his judgments were based either on oral testimonies (*bayyina*) or on *iqrār*, that is, acknowledgements made in the court in the presence of a cadi. He declared that making a comprehensive inspection of pious endowments had been his long-standing intention, and he followed the example of his father, who had collected information concerning these foundations from the cadis or the families of the founders.[67] The account indicates that documentation (endowment deeds) concerning *waqfs* was not easily available because of unintentional (or intentional) loss of the original documents. The cadi conscientiously executed his task and made great efforts to maintain the intended designation of the endowments under his supervision, since the original *waqf* stipulations were legally binding and religiously sanctioned.

One must be cautious in making any sweeping generalisation about the cadi's control of all *waqfs*. Ibn Yūnus, for example, recounts the history of a pious endowment which surely was not under the cadi's control. The endowment was set up by Ibn al-ʿAwf al-Zuhrī, a newcomer to Egypt, who was appointed chief of police and died in 825. He owned a garden which he endowed in favour of his son, and the endowment deed was deposited with Ibn Yūnus's father, whose name is mentioned in the document. Ibn Yūnus states that the document is in his possession and that the endowment serves its purpose. Nevertheless, the document included a sentence stating: 'deposit (*wadīʿa*) in favour of the son of Ibn al-ʿAbbās al-Zuhrī, not to be handed to anyone unless demanded by the *sulṭān*.' This was a familial pious endowment administration of which was entrusted to the Ibn Yūnus family, but the superior authority of the government, alluded to by the term *sulṭān*, or the cadi as its representative, was acknowledged.[68] In any case, whatever the extent of

[66] Kindī, 418–19; Tillier, *Histoire des cadis*, 186–7.

[67] Kindī, 383, 394–5, 424; Tillier, *Histoire des cadis*, 148, 161, 193. Kindī's narrative strongly suggests that by the mid-eighth century the cadis also controlled familial pious endowments. See Kindī, 361, 364; Tillier, *Histoire des cadis*, 121, 126.

[68] Ibn Yūnus, II, 138–9.

the cadi's supervisory authority over pious endowments was, disputes about these foundations were brought to his court.

In Fusṭāṭ of the late ninth or early tenth century, a dispute erupted over the question of who was entitled to the profits of a pious endowment set up by a eunuch who served as chief of the Egyptian postal service. He raised a boy, who became a jurist and a beneficiary of endowments set up by his master (or foster-father) in his favour, but others challenged his rights at the cadi's court.[69] Disputes about pious endowments must have been frequent, and numerous literary sources provide further examples of litigation that took place during the Umayyad period.[70]

Familial pious endowments must be understood in the light of Koranic teachings, which have parallels in monotheistic religions, about the care of family and relatives. One can ask what were the chances that the ultimate charitable designations of familial pious endowments would ever be realised. The answer is not necessarily negative. Under medieval and pre-modern conditions the life-span of family lines was relative short, and incomes generated by *ahlī waqfs*, if the *waqf* was extensive and well-managed, could eventually serve the charitable causes specified in the endowment deed.

The Formation of a Procedural-Judicial Tradition

Many of the cadis discussed so far were dynamic and assertive individuals who expanded judicial authority beyond the confines of the court to the financial sphere and management of trust funds. In a parallel but unrelated process, cadis also shaped the procedural aspects of how justice was administrated at their courts. A cadi was assisted by his clerk and witnesses, and a crucial factor in the development of procedural norms was the selection and ratification of the corps of witnesses and definition of the criteria for accepting or rejecting a person as a witness.[71] The question of whose testimony should be accepted was hotly debated in seventh- to eighth-century Muslim society, and Wakīʿs

[69] Maqrīzī, *Kitāb al-Muqaffā*, II, 436–8.

[70] For example, in a reply to a question sent from Egypt about entitlement to incomes of a familial pious endowment, Mālik stated that a third of the income must go for 'the cause of God'. See Ibn Ḥajar, ed. ʿUmarī, 439. For a French translation of the account and discussion, see Tillier, *Histoire des cadis*, 152; Bouderbala, 'Les aḥbās de Fusṭāṭ', 43–5.

[71] For the personnel assisting the cadi, see Tillier, 'Scribes et enquêteurs' 370–404, and the prosopographic data discussed by him.

History of the Cadis highlights many of these deliberations.[72] Shurayḥ ibn al-Ḥārith, cadi of Kūfa in the late 710s, for example, had a firm opinion on the issue. In his view, the testimonies of an owner of a bathhouse, a bathhouse attendant and a slave should be rejected, while he accepted testimonies of young boys and did not reject the testimony of a convicted thief if someone vouched for his probity (*khayr*). Furthermore, he accepted a single testimony sworn on the Koran but severely punished a false witness.[73] The question is how, if at all, the personal views of such opinionated cadis turned into established procedural-judicial tradition. Other cadis who succeeded Shurayḥ ibn al-Ḥārith in Kūfa only accepted a testimony given by two witnesses, as set forth in the Koran, and did not endorse his acceptance of testimony by young boys.[74] The acceptance of a testimony with an oath is known under the technical term *yamīn maʿ al-shāhid*, and the adoption of the practice varied on a regional basis. In Egypt it was introduced and, apparently, consolidated between the 730s and the 780s. The cadi Tawba ibn Namir applied it in cases of lesser significance, and it was also acceptable to the cadi ʿAbd al-Mālik ibn Muḥammad al-Ḥazmī, who followed the legal school of Medina (i.e. the Mālikī school), which accepted this type of testimony.[75]

Going back Wakīʿs text, one gets the impression that in Iraq in the Abbasid period, debate as to whose testimony should be rejected became politicised and cadis, as state officials, were (or found themselves) at the forefront of the battle to uphold Abbasid legitimacy and stem the rising tide of sectarian ideologies. For example, testimony given by a woman described as holding Kharijite views was rejected by the cadi ʿAbd al-Raḥmān ibn ʿAbd Allāh ibn ʿĪsā (also known as ʿUbayd ibn bint Abī Laylā), who served in Kūfa between 765 and 770. What the nature of these views might have been remains unclear. Although Kharijites acquiesced in practice to Abbasid rule, they were considered deviant and as challenging the established socio-political order. This was not an isolated case but rather a matter of policy,

72 For the author and his work, see Masud, 'A Study of Wakīʿ's (d. 306/917) Akhbār al-Quḍāt', 116–28.
73 Wakīʿ, II, 288, 290, 294, 308, 309, 313, 377. For testimony by minors, see Schacht, *The Origins*, 218.
74 Wakīʿ, II, 427–8, III, 85.
75 Kindī, 344–5, 384; Tillier, *Histoire des cadis*, 101, 148. For broader discussion, see Masud, 'Procedural Law', 387–416, esp. 390, 399–401.

and Sharīk ibn ʿAbd Allāh, Abī Laylā's successor in Kūfa (who served as cadi between 770 and 786), barred people belonging to the Murjiites and Rafidis from testifying at court. The use of these appellations in the text is loose, but theology and politics were inseparable in medieval Islam and the fusion of the two had social and institutional ramifications, such as the boycotting of funerals of rival theological groups. The label 'Rafidis', meaning Shiites, though generic, was pejorative, but the drift of the account is that those cadis, by ostracising sectarians, upheld orthodoxy. In some cases the radicalism of the cadis was at odds with the more tolerant society. A cadi of Baṣra, for instance, did not admit the testimony of a person holding Qadarī views (i.e. adhering to the doctrine of free will, used here as a broad abusive nickname), although that person was accepted in local society and renowned for his piety, exemplified by fasting, immersion in prayer, charitable distribution (*maʿrūf*) and the paying of *zakāt* (the obligatory alms tax).[76] The dynamics of exclusion had far-reaching consequences, and people were excluded from giving testimony because they did not perform prayers and pilgrimage.[77] One can understand that in a close-knit, conformist society the performing of prayers was closely watched, but performing pilgrimage was beyond the reach of most since it required considerable financial means. The application of this criterion by the cadi seems an idiosyncrasy.

In broad terms, the issues alluded to by Wakīʿ were also relevant in Fusṭāṭ but are presented in a slightly different form since Kindī is more informative about how the corps of witnesses serving at the cadi's court was selected. In mid-eighth-century Fusṭāṭ, the local custom was to accept the testimony of people known to be righteous, while rejecting the testimony of those who failed to qualify as such. The underlining assumption was that righteousness (*khayr*, *salāma*) implies moral and religious integrity and, concomitantly, reliability. Kindī's narrative alludes to an earlier period before a permanent corps of witnesses was established at the cadi's court. This early practice failed, however, as false testimonies multiplied. The cadi Ghawth ibn Sulaymān, during his second term in office (758–61), initiated a secret screening of

[76] Wakīʿ, II, 427–8; Kindī, 442: Hurvitz, 'Legal Doctrines', 242–4. For funerals as markers of religious controversies, see Zaman, 'Death, Funeral Processions', 27–58.

[77] Wakīʿ, III, 134, 219.

witnesses in order to assess their moral standing. This was not a radical change since no objective criteria for the selection process were introduced. The system of secretly screening witnesses lasted until 790, when it was reformed by Mufaḍḍal ibn Faḍāla. The cadi assigned the task of inquiring about witnesses to his clerk, who became known as the examiner (*ṣāḥib al-masāʾil*), but rumours spread that some people bribed him to declare them fit for testifying (literally, to declare them as imbued with *ʿadāla*, virtue and honour). The cadi subsequently installed ten witnesses at his court, apparently, on a permanent basis. This move was resisted by someone, who restored to poetry and in unequivocal verses called upon God to turn the cadi into an emaciated dog, accusing him of installing criminals as witnesses.[78] This harsh criticism might indicate that serving as a witness was not only a question of social prestige, but also brought some tangible benefits. The impression is gained that the criticism of the cadi was malicious, since he was praised for his scrupulous supervision of orphans' affairs. Another context for the preoccupation of both Ghawth ibn Sulaymān and Mufaḍḍal ibn Faḍāla with the establishment of the witness corps has been suggested by Tillier, who perceives it as part of the procedural judicial innovations that occurred in Egypt.[79]

The cadi Muḥammad ibn Masrūq al-Kindī, appointed in 793, found himself in a situation similar to that of Mufaḍḍal ibn Faḍāla. He is described as a cadi who rigorously dispensed justice, was not afraid to confront tax collectors, and refused invitations by the governor to attend his sessions. His relations with some of the notables of Fusṭāṭ were also strained and he accepted only the testimony of people whom he had selected and registered as witnesses. His deed provoked wide discontent and bitter abusive exchanges took place between the cadi and the dismissed court witnesses.[80] Nonetheless, the notion that a cadi is entitled to appoint and dismiss witnesses took root. In 801, the cadi al-ʿUmarī was unopposed when he chose certain people to serve as witnesses and registered their names while refusing to accept the testimony of others. The issuing of witnesses was high on his agenda, and Kindī

[78] Kindī, 361, 385–6: Tillier, *Histoire des cadis*, 121, 150–1. For the term *ʿadāla* in the context of witnesses, see Lane, *Arabic English Lexicon*, V, 1975a.

[79] See 'Les "premiers" cadis de Fusṭāṭ', 234–7. Ghawth ibn Sulaymān also served as arbitrator in the marital dispute between the caliph al-Manṣūr and his wife Umm Mūsā. See 220–3.

[80] Kindī, 388–9; Tillier, *Histoire des cadis*, 153–4.

offers two conflicting reports as to how it was dealt with. The examiner was entrusted with the task of finding new witnesses, and the instructions given to him were to seek people known for their piety (*sitr* and *faḍl*). The second report claims, however, that a body of 100 witnesses made up of the people of Medina and the *mawālī* of Quraysh and Anṣār was established and that a specific person served as their head (*ra'īs*).[81]

The wording of Kindī's second account is unclear, and it most probably means that people whose origin was Medina and who were descendants of Quraysh and Anṣār and their *mawālī* made up the witness corps.[82] If this interpretation of the text is accepted, it means that inherited social prestige derived from Quraysh and Anṣār forefathers' participation in the events that were associated with the Prophet's life and the formation of Islam was given preference over acquired piety (*sitr* and *faḍl*). One is left to wonder how exactly the protégés of Quraysh and Anṣār became imbued with the prestige of their masters. Clearly, what al-ʿUmarī did was controversial, and, as was the case with Mufaḍḍal ibn Faḍāla, he was criticised in poems which, though less personal and vicious, implied that he impoverished the orphans under his supervision and enriched his associates.[83] It seems that al-ʿUmarī failed to find the right balance between his view of how the witness corps should be selected and public expectations or, to put it differently, between the interests of the various groups that had a stake in this matter. Eventually, he appointed thirty Persians to serve in the witness corps.[84] Turning to a foreign group to serve in such a sensitive capacity could hardly be a popular move and apparently solved nothing, as the problem persisted and other cadis had to address it again.

The cadi Lahīʿa ibn ʿĪsā, during his second appointment (814–20), ordered the examiner to inquire about witnesses every six months and dismiss those tainted with *jurḥa* (suspension). Actually, he was following the example of al-ʿUmarī, who dismissed witnesses sullied by *jurḥa*.[85] Dismissing

[81] Kindī, 394, 395–6; Tillier, *Histoire des cadis*, 161, 162–3.

[82] Ibn Ḥajar's text provides no better reading. It states that around a hundred people of Medina, mostly the *mawālī* of Quraysh and Anṣār, were enlisted as witnesses. See Majīd (ed.), II, 321.

[83] Kindī, 396; see Tillier's translation of the poems *Histoire des cadis*, 163; El-Shamsy, *The Canonization of Islamic Law*, 104–5.

[84] Kindī, 401–2; Tillier, *Histoire des cadis*, 168.

[85] Kindī, 422; Tillier, *Histoire de cadis*, 191. For the judicial context of the term *jurḥa*, see Lane, *Arabic English Lexicon*, II, 405b.

witnesses was one thing but selecting them was another, and the examiner of the cadi ʿĪsā ibn Munkadir (827–30) was criticised for admitting to the witness corps people of no social standing (literally, lacking *qadr* and *bayt*), including vendors, weavers and insincere converts to Islam (*muslimānī*). The whole affair sparked off a fascinating discussion over the very nature of the function (referred to as *ʿadāla/shahāda*) of providing testimony at court. Opponents of the selection process, which admitted market people into the corps of accredited witnesses, claimed that the key criteria for selection should be social respectability (alluded to by the term *mastūr*), while the cadi maintained that it was a religious function (*dīn*).[86] The term *mastūr* is a loose term with a considerable range of meanings and refers to pious virtuous people with roots in local society. Socially-oriented piety typified medieval Muslim urban society, but the sociological terminology of the period is not easy to decipher and the terms *mastūr* and *dīn* seem more overlapping than contradictory. It seems that society was divided over the issue of what really constituted piety and whether social respectability could be combined with having an occupation and earning a livelihood at market.[87]

The question as to what the appropriate social background should be of the people involved in the administration of justice also applied to cadis. The issue comes to the fore through Maqrīzī's biography of the cadi Aṣbagh ibn al-Faraj (*c.* 767–840), who claimed to be a descendant of the *mawālī* of the Umayyad governor of Egypt Aṣbagh ibn ʿAbd al-ʿAzīz ibn Marwān. Other people in Fusṭāṭ disputed the claim, and suggested that he was a scion of *ʿabīd al-masjid*, slaves belonging to a mosque, a group of people installed at mosques by the Umayyads. Aṣbagh ibn al-Faraj was a jurist and an expert on *naẓar* (speculation), who avoided the *miḥna* by going into hiding. His name as a candidate for the post of cadi was mentioned during consultations between the Abbasid general ʿAbd Allāh ibnṬāhir and the civilian elite

86 Kindī, 436; Ibn Yūnus, I, 140–1; Tillier, *Histoire de cadis*, 209. The term *muslimānī* had a range of connotations from obsessive and insulting to neutral, meaning fresh converts to Islam. For the former, see Lev, 'Persecutions and Conversion', 88–9; for the latter, see Tillier and Vanthieghem, 'La rançon du serment', 55, line 2 (text and trans. [néo-musulman]).

87 For the concept of *sitr* and people living by it (*mastūrūn*), see Lev, *Charity*, 10–12; 'The Discourse of Charity', 68–9. Both terms are attested in the Geniza documents. See Cohen, *Poverty and Charity*, 51–3, who shows that in the Jewish context *mastūrūn* meant conjectural poor, or the shame-faced poor.

of Fusṭāṭ as to who should be nominated for the post. Eventually he was nominated, but some participants expressed the view that people referred to as strangers should not be selected for the post of cadi, and the same applied to peasants (*zarrāʿ*), *maqāmisa* and dyers.[88] The rural world ranked low on the social scale of the learned urban elite to which people involved in this conversation belonged, and the same applies to impure occupations such as dying. Although, in this case, merits overcame marginal social background, in medieval society considerations of social hierarchy were always a powerful underlying factor and must be taken into account in any discussion of the administration of justice.

The preoccupation of the sources with the selection process of the witness corps should not obscure the fact that procedures at the cadi's court were dominated by written culture, whose beginnings go back to Sulaym ibn ʿItr's term in office. Whatever place writing occupied in the culture of the pagan Arabs, the world of Late Antiquity was dominated by the written word and the acculturation of the emerging Muslim civilisation into this culture is not surprising. Kindī's double phrasing (*wa-kataba kitāb*^{ān} *bi-qaḍā'ihi* and *sajjala sijill*^{ān} *bi-qaḍā'ihi*, using both Arabic and Arabicised Latin terms) when referring to Sulaym ibn ʿItr's innovation of recording his judgments emphasises the novelty of his deed, which became an established practice and was applied in judicial and non-judicial matters handled by the cadi.[89] Muʿāwiya ibn Ḥudayj, the first cadi to control the money of the orphans, recorded each transaction in which he was involved. The practice of recording depositions and withdrawals of money belonging to orphans in the Treasury was also followed by later cadis.[90]

How endowment deeds were recorded is less clear. Kindī writes that during Tawba ibn Namir's term in office (he was the first cadi to supervise *waqf* foundations) pious endowments became a large *dīwān*, which, in this context, should be understood as referring to the archive holding endowment

88 Kindī, 433–4; Tillier, *Histoire des cadis*, 205–6; Maqrīzī, *Kitāb al-Muqaffā*, II, 213–14, 214–17; El-Shamsy, *The Canonization of Islamic Law*, 100, 101–2. The term *maqāmisa* appears in military context in association with *mawālī*, but remains vague. See the glossary in Guest's edition of Kindī.

89 Kindī, 310; Tillier, *Histoire des cadis*, 59. For the term *sijill* in the Koran, see Jeffery, *The Foreign Vocabulary of the Qu'rān*, 163–4.

90 Kindī, 325, 355.

deeds. Actually, the word *dīwān* came to denote the cadi's archive and is also attested in the context of writing an endowment deed and depositing it at the cadi's *dīwān*.[91] What sort of documents were regularly deposited in the cadi's archive is never explicitly stated, and the statement that the cadi Mufaḍḍal ibn Faḍāla made, during his first term in office (785–6), the deeds (*ṭawwala al-sijillāt/kutub*) of bequests and debt obligations longer remains elusive. Another way of understanding the account is to follow Wael B. Hallaq's interpretation of the term *sijill/sijillāt* as referring to a document that 'consists of a witnessed record of what the *maḥḍar* contained, together with the *qāḍī*'s decision (*ḥukm*) on the case', meaning that the cadi created a new kind of a combined long document.[92] This document-oriented culture that prevailed at the cadi's court is, perhaps, best illustrated by the term *qimṭar*, a briefcase for carrying documents needed by the cadi, an innovation attributed to Muḥammad ibn Masrūq, a Ḥanafī cadi from Kūfa.[93]

When we turn to documentary evidence, a great variety of legal documents emanating from medieval Muslim and non-Muslim courts have survived and even a brief survey of a few well-known corpuses of published Arabic and Judaeo-Arabic documents reveals marriage and divorce documents and deeds of purchase, sale and lease, as well as quittances and various types of acknowledgement documents. Furthermore, the court conducted its business in writing and issued written summons to people to appear before it, while people submitted written requests to judges and the court concerning their

[91] Kindī, 362, 410, describing the establishment of a pious endowment by the cadi al-ʿUmarī for a mosque. For the inclusion of *waqf* deeds in the cadi's archive, see Ziadeh, 'Adab al-Qāḍī', 144; Tillier, 'Le statut et la conservation des archives judiciaires', 273. The history and practice of recording court business by the cadi is extensively discussed by Hallaq. See 'The Qāḍī's Dīwān', 415–36.

[92] Kindī, 379; Ibn ʿAbd al-Ḥakam, *Futūḥ*, 244; Tillier, *Histoire des cadis*, 143; 'The Qāḍī's Justice', 45; Hallaq, 'The Qāḍī's Dīwān', 420, including explanation of the meaning of *maḥḍar* as either a statement made by a witnesses or the minutes of a case examined by the cadi. For a short documentary fragment of minutes of a case that took place before the cadi Mufaḍḍal ibn Faḍāla, see Tillier, 'Deux papyrus judiciaires de Fusṭāṭ', 11–14.

[93] Kindī, 391–2, 437; Maqrīzī, *Kitāb al-Muqaffā*, VII, 234; Hallaq, 'The Qāḍī's Dīwān', 428, 433, who understands *qimṭar* as referring to a 'bookcase in which documents and sheets of papyri were preserved'. For the transfer of the cadi's archive from one cadi to another and the terminology involved in the legal prescriptive literature, see Ziadeh, 'Adab al-Qāḍī', 143–4. For further references, see Tillier, *Vies des cadis*, 44; *Histoire des cadis*, index. For the Semitic roots of the term *qimṭar* and Muḥammad ibn Masrūq's career, see Tillier, 'Les "premiers" cadis de Fusṭāṭ', 17–18.

affairs.[94] Nevertheless, within this document-oriented practice of Muslim courts, oral testimony played a crucial role. When a legal document was drawn it had to be witnessed by at least two people, but when submitted to the court it had no evidential power unless validated by an oral testimony, an oath or formal acknowledgement. To put it differently, in the legal sphere, written culture in itself had no affirmative power and a court could not function without its witness corps. The discourse about who could serve in this corps was motivated by the need to have a reliable body of people to provide oral testimony to empower, so to speak, written documents.

The Cadi and the State

Although cadis were paid state officials, information about their salaries is random and cannot be discussed outside a broader socio-economic context of prices and salaries. We have no idea what could have been the buying power of a *dīnār* in seventh- to ninth-century Egypt and we know nothing about the salaries of other officials at the provincial level. A documentary fragment from 748 indicates a modest monthly salary for a cadi of ten *dīnārs*. This information stands in sharp contrast to literary sources, which indicate much higher levels of remuneration.[95] The cadi ʿAbd al-Raḥmān ibn Ḥujayra (689–702), for example, received a salary of 200 *dīnārs* per annum for executing his judicial duties. In addition, he held the post of preacher/storyteller and wielded responsibility for the Treasury, receiving remuneration of 200 *dīnārs* for each of these assignments. He was also entitled to other benefits which reflected his status as belonging to the Arab-Muslim privileged population, and as a member of the ruling elite he received 200 *dīnārs* as a yearly allocation (*ʿaṭā*ʾ) and an additional 200 *dīnārs* as a special bonus (*jāʾiza*, a gift). The tenor of Kindī's narrative is not negative, and this cadi is not portrayed as greedy but rather as generous towards his extended family, reflecting the spirit of Koranic teachings. Beginning in al-Manṣūr's

[94] See, for example, Khoury, *Chrestomathie de papyrologie arabe*, docs 78, 79, 80 (a denunciation submitted to the court), 81, 82. For summons issued by the cadi Ghawth ibn Sulaymān, see Tillier, 'Deux papyrus judiciaires de Fusṭāṭ', 3–5.

[95] For the documentary evidence, see Al-Qāḍī, 'The Salaries of Judges', 9–10, 12. Kindī, 354; Tillier, *Histoire des cadis*, 114. Any attempt to correlate Ashtor's discussion of prices and salaries with the data presented here is marred by many difficulties. See *Histoire des prix*, ch. 2.

reign cadis' salaries sharply increased to 30 *dīnārs* (and beyond) per month, for reasons which remain obscure.[96]

The case of ʿAbd al-Raḥmān ibn Ḥujayra was exceptional, but equally rare were cases of a salary for the post of cadi being declined. One cadi appointed in the late 710s declined a salary, and the same is recounted about al-Ruʿaynī (761–71), who was a craftsman and continued to practise his trade while serving as cadi and drawing no salary. Actually he was second choice for the post, but the first candidate refused the nomination. Pursuit of learning – earning a living via crafts and commerce and declining the post of cadi – typifies the class of religious scholars of early Islam, and al-Ruʿaynī represents this tradition. In the Egyptian context this is a rare example of such conduct, and one is left to wonder whether Egyptian realities were different.[97]

Although the structure of the provincial government is relatively well-known, there is no data on the salaries of governors and other officials, and any attempt to discuss the position of the cadi within the local administration is marred by many difficulties. The governor was the key figure in the local government and he was assisted by the fiscal administrator, the chief of the postal service, the cadi and, beginning with the rule of Aḥmad ibn Ṭūlūn, the chief of the secret police.[98] The internal hierarchy and the actual disposition of power within the local government are something of an enigma, but the sources paint a picture of parallel lines of responsibility, with the governor having political powers and responsibility over the military while the fiscal administrator was in charge of taxation and expenditure. The chiefs of the postal service and the secret police had no control over real instruments of power such as the military or the administration, and their role can be described as supervisory, with direct access to the local ruler (Aḥmad ibn

[96] Kindī, 317, 377, 421, 435; Tillier, *Histoire des cadis*, 68; Al-Qāḍī, 'The Salaries of Judges', 22, 28. Tillier provides two graphs, spanning the period between al-Manṣūr and al-Ma'mūn, which illustrate this increase. The second turning point in salary increases took place under Hārūn al-Rashīd (786–809). See *Les cadis d'Iraq*, 263–72, esp. 265, 267.

[97] Kindī, 339, 364–5; Ibn Ḥajar, ed. Majīd, I, 46; Tillier, *Histoire des cadis*, 94, 124–5. For broader discussion of accounts of refusal of the appointment to the post of cadi in the earlier centuries of Islam, see Coulson, 'Doctrine and Practice in Islamic Law', 211–26.

[98] Although it is not explicitly stated, Balawī's biography of Aḥmad ibn Ṭūlūn conveys the impression that an internal network of informants was set up, or vastly expanded, by the new ruler of Egypt. References to *aṣḥāb al-akhbār* are abundant in the text. See, for example, 73, 83, 118, 122, 146, 156, 207, 224, 333. For the caliphate, see Silverstein, *Postal Systems*, 114–15.

Ṭūlūn) and a fast line of communication to the caliph in Baghdad.[99] In reality, however, there was no neat division of responsibilities between the different post holders, and spheres of authority overlapped and the demarcation lines between political, fiscal and judicial were ill-defined.

There is no simple answer to the question of what the cadi's position was within the local government. There are no indications that cadis were involved in taxation, but as late as 757, Yazīd ibn ʿAbd Allāh ibn Bilāl, who was appointed to the post of cadi, had previously served as governor of Akhmīm in Upper Egypt. The papyri offer unexpected and rare evidence for his involvement in what seems to be a questionable judicial process while serving as governor. He demanded and received a letter of acquaintance stating that neither any member of his staff nor he personally oppressed the people of the province.[100] A possible insight into the cadi's role within local government is provided by events in which al-Ruʿaynī played a minor by significant part. The case involved financial maltreatment of the Arab population of the village of Atrīb in the Delta (on the lower section of the Nile's arm leading to Damietta) by Ibn ʿUtba, who was in the service of the fiscal administrator of Egypt appointed by the caliph al-Manṣūr.[101] The discontent led to an attempt on Ibn ʿUtba's life, and many of the Arab rioters involved in the incident were arrested. Eventually, a letter was sent to the caliph who, as might be expected, sided with the persecuted population against the oppressor. The letter was sent to the cadi, who insisted on reading it publicly at his court; the caliph's justice was direct and firm but limited in scope: the rioters were set free and the execution of Ibn ʿUtba was authorised. The fiscal administrator drew his own conclusions from the affair and declared that he was seeking a new tax collector for Atrīb who would combine firmness and good judgment.[102]

The cadi's role in this affair was a passive one: he merely served as a channel of communication to convey the caliph's ruling. Quite clearly, the

[99] The first attestation of a postal service in Egypt is from 669. See Sijpesteijn, *Shaping a Muslim State*, 91. For the postal service in early Abbasid Egypt, see Bruning, 'Developments in Egypt's Early Islamic Postal System', 25–40.

[100] Guest 'An Arabic Papyrus', 247–8; Kindī, 359; Tillier, *Histoire des cadis*, 119; 'Du pagarque au cadi', 32.

[101] For the location, see Cornu, *Atlas*, index.

[102] Kindī, 365–7; Tillier, *Histoire des cadis*, 126–8.

cadi was not supposed to serve as an overseer of local government or other state officials. In rare cases, however, certain cadis overstepped their designated role. The most notable case was that of the cadi Muḥammad ibn Masrūq, an authoritative cadi who kept aloof from the governor and brought fiscal administrators/tax collectors (*ʿummāl*) to justice. He also took on the agent of Zubayda (763–831), the wife of Hārūn al-Rashīd and the mother of al-Amīn, who represented Zubayda's interests in the Buḥayra region (the southern part of the Delta), whom he convicted and punished by flogging.[103]

Although cases of cadis taking action on behalf of subjects and confronting state officials were rare, equally rare were charges of corruption and the deliberate perversion of justice.[104] Accusations were levelled against the cadi al-ʿUmarī, but these involved a case submitted to him by the governor rather than a litigation. A quarrel between two Arab tribes erupted about who won a horse race and who was responsible for misdoings during its course. The governor, who was faced with massive disorder, brought the case to the cadi, whose ruling was rejected by the losing side, and he was accused of accepting money to favour the other side. A lively exchange of poetry followed the cadi's decision, which eventually was overturned.[105] In this case the governor was happy to shed responsibility for maintaining public order, and involved the cadi by invoking his impartiality and moral authority.

The real question, however, is how much authority the cadi had in enforcing judgments. In medieval Muslim society coercive powers were widely diffused and exercised by powerful individuals in a variety of contexts, while the history of private prisons goes back to the garrison towns of seventh-century Iraq.[106] In tenth-century Egypt, the power to imprison opponents rested with the rulers and powerful state dignitaries and is illustrated by the misfortunes of Sībawayhi, who was forcibly incarcer-

103 Kindī, 388, 392; Tillier, *Histoire des cadis*, 153, 158. The term 'Buḥayra' lacks geographical precision. It must be taken into account that two internal lakes, with connection to the sea, dotted Egypt's Mediterranean cost: Lake Burullus and Lake Tinnīs. The first was known for fishing, while the second was, in addition to fishing, known for its textile industries on the island of Tinnīs. Most likely Zubayda's agent was more interested in the second region.

104 For Iraqi cadis who confronted caliphs, see Tillier, 'Judicial Authority and Qāḍī's Autonomy', 124–5.

105 Kindī, 402; Tillier, *Histoire des cadis*, 169–70.

106 Anthony, 'The Domestic Origins of Imprisonment', 571–96.

ated at the hospital at the behest of Ṣāliḥ ibn Nāfiʿ, a close associate of Muḥammad ibn Ṭughj al-Ikhshīd. Sībawayhi's second imprisonment was at the Arsenal's tar workshop and took place on the orders of Muḥammad ibn ʿAbd Allāh al-Khāzin, a naval commander apparently in charge of the Arsenal.[107] Important though this aspect of political or private incarceration was, the present discussion focuses on incarceration authorised by cadis and the chiefs of police, who were state officials vested with such powers. Whether the cadi had the power to apply the death penalty is rarely alluded to in the sources. In 785, for example, the cadi Mufaḍḍal ibn Faḍāla wrote to Mālik in Medina asking whether it was permissible to put a Christian who cursed the Prophet to death. Having secured Mālik's approval, he, in co-operation with the governor (or with his tacit consent), put the Christian to death.[108] This was, however, an atypical case. Eighth-century cadis had the power to jail litigants engaged in lawsuits at their courts and their powers also extended, to some degree at least, over other people not involved in lawsuits. The cadi Yaḥyā ibn Maymūn al-Ḥaḍramī, for example, jailed an orphan who complained against him. Other cases that involved cadis who tried to silence their critics were more complex. The cadi Ibn Abī Layth (842–9) faced the criticism of Ibn al-Qaṭṭās, described as a pious man who served as a witness at the court of Ibn Abī Layth's predecessors. Ibn al-Qaṭṭās had a teaching circle at a mosque and accused the cadi of innovations, using the term *bidʿa*, whose wide range of meanings obscures rather than clarifies the nature of the criticism. Following a meeting between the two that ended in rupture and further animosity, someone came to the cadi and claimed that Ibn al-Qaṭṭās was a slave who had never been manumitted. Ibn Abī Layth accepted the testimonies of witnesses who testified to that effect. There are several versions of how the affair subsequently unfolded, but clearly a cadi could muster support when dealing with an opponent and, in this case, he was by far the more powerful side in the dispute. On the other hand, no cadi was above

[107] Ibn Zūlāq, *Kitāb Akhbār Sībawayhi*, 30, 40, 57–8. For the military and naval career of al-Khāzin, see Maqrīzī, *Kitāb al-Muqaffā*, VI, 137–8. Apparently, Ṣāliḥ ibn Nāfiʿ held no official appointments but was closely associated with the Ikhshidid rulers. See Maqrīzī, *Kitāb al-Muqaffā*, II, 315; III, 335; V, 752, VI, 58, and I, 340.

[108] Kindī, 382–3; Tillier, *Histoire des cadis*, 145–6.

suspicion, certainly not Ibn Abī Layth, and the talk in the town was that the testimonies against Ibn al-Qaṭṭās were false.[109]

The cadi ʿĪsā ibn al-Munkadir jailed a litigant who had lost a case in his court and vilified him. He nevertheless provided for the family of the jailed person.[110] As has been shown by Tillier, the conditions in medieval jails were harsh and basic needs such as nutrition and hygiene were not guaranteed. One can only wonder how Yūnus ibn ʿAbd al-Aʿlā, who was jailed for seven years, survived the ordeal. He, along with other people, served as executor of a will and was accused of fraudulent handling of money. He was jailed by the cadi Ibn Abī Layth and set free only upon the arrival of Qawṣara, al-Mutawakkil's special envoy to Egypt. When he regained his freedom, Yūnus ibn ʿAbd al-Aʿlā did not accuse the cadi, but the witnesses whose false testimony had led the cadi astray.[111] Ulrich Rebstock has pointed out that there were no institutional instances that could rectify judicial mistakes committed by cadis, and the same applies to cases of cadis misusing of power.[112] Actually it was a broader problem, since neither the state administration nor the administration of justice system contained checks-and-balance apparatuses and the ultimate power to redress misdeeds lay with the ruler (the *maẓālim* institution).

The clearest evidence for the existence of a jail run by a cadi comes from Aḥmad ibn Ṭūlūn's reign. In a response to a petition, the emir ordered his confidant to provide a list of the prisoners, their conditions and the reasons for their imprisonment. It turned out that the total debt of the people jailed at the cadi's prison was 20,000 *dīnārs*, and Aḥmad ibn Ṭūlūn paid the money. Needless to say he won the prisoners' gratitude and intercessory prayers and, on a higher level of the Koranic ethics of almsgiving, he followed Koran 9:60 which enjoins distribution of charity to prisoners and debtors. Imprisonment of debtors by cadis was a medieval reality and many rulers did

109 Kindī, 341, 456–7; Tillier, *Histoire de cadis*, 233–4.

110 Ibn Ḥajar, ed. Majīd, I, 25; Kindī, 439; Tillier, *Histoire de cadis*, 213.

111 Kindī, 454–5; Tillier, *Histoire de cadis*, 230–1. According to one account, Ibn Abī Layth was aware of his grave mistake and acknowledged Yūnus ibn ʿAbd al-Aʿlā's magnanimity towards him. See Ibn Ḥajar, ed. Majīd I, 142. For the harsh realities of medieval jails, see Tillier, 'Vivre en prison', 643–55; 'Les prisonniers dans la société musulmane', 191–212, including a discussion of the difference between political and judicial imprisonment.

112 See 'A Qāḍī's Errors', 33.

what Aḥmad ibn Ṭūlūn had done.[113] Common though the jailing of debtors was, it does not necessarily undermine Irene Schneider's observation that punitive detention played a relatively minor role in the legal literature and the administration of justice, while flogging and shaming were the main means of punishment.[114]

So far, the cadi's dependence on the state has been stressed, but it went even deeper: the cadi was also dependent on the public and cadis bent to public opinion. Although the sources provide little information concerning this issue, two events are highly suggestive and shed light on the problem. The first event to be discussed concerns the highly respected and appreciated cadi Abū Ṭāhir al-Dhuhlī, who served in the 960s. He declared that a young child does not become Muslim upon the conversion of his Christian mother (her husband did not convert). His decision was met by uproar. People claimed that it contradicted both Shīʿī (*ahl al-bayt*) and Shāfiʿī law, and the cadi yielded to the public and changed his legally sound decision.[115] The second event took place earlier during the Ikhshidid period and involved Copts who approached the ruler and asked to restore a collapsed church. The cadi Ibn al-Ḥaddād and another Mālikī jurist issued legal opinions denying their request, but another jurist allowed the restoration. Angry people surrounded his home and were about to set it on fire. The ruler, threatened with public disorder and relying on the opinion of the majority of the jurists, yielded to the popular demand.[116] It can be said that the two jurists whose rulings were

[113] Balawī, 184–5. The text implies that the money paid for the release of those prisoners covered their debts, but debt (*dayn*) is not mentioned in the account. For a prisoner abandoned to his fate, see Balawī, 234–7. For home arrest imposed on a dignitary and those who interceded on his behalf, see Balawī, 237–9. Tillier and Vanthieghem assume that the prison log they have published ('Un registre carcéral'), which specifies how debtors were set free from a prison, belonged to a prison run by the chief of the police. Their assumption hinges on the identification of Faḍāla ibn al-Mufaḍḍal (the son of the cadi al-Mufaḍḍal ibn Faḍāla) as chief of police in January 806(?). In Balawī's account dealing with the release of the prisoners from the cadi's jail, Ibn Faḍāla is referred to as Aḥmad ibn Ṭūlūn's agent (*wakīl*) and plays a key role in these events. For the release of debtors, see Tillier, 'Prisons et autorités urbaines', 396; Lev, *Charity*, 25, 44–5.

[114] See, 'Imprisonment', 170. For a wider treatment of the subject, see Lange, *Justice, Punishment*, 44–8.

[115] Ibn Ḥajar, ed. Guest, 586. Although not alluded to, the Muslim concept of *fiṭra* argues that a child is born a *tabula rasa* and his religion is determined by his parents.

[116] Ibn Ḥajar, ed. Guest, 554–5, quoting Ibn Zūlāq. Although no details are given, the issue at stake was complex and the main question was whether the church in question could be regarded as ancient, i.e. pre-dating the Muslim conquest of Egypt. In such cases, under certain conditions,

opposed by the public displayed professionalism and a legal frame of mind, paying no attention to the possible social repercussions of their decisions. However, when faced with popular anger al-Dhuhlī retreated to placate the public.

Conclusions

It is possible to reconstruct the evolution of the post of cadi, relying on both literary and documentary sources. Tenth-century writings and Mamlūk historiography depict the cadi as a paid state official whose judicial responsibilities were compounded with other assignments. From the state perspective, during the eighth century the cadi institution become associated with the administration of justice, and the combining of posts such as cadi and chief of police or cadi and preacher/storyteller ceased. The nature of the post was, however, largely shaped by processes that took place from below from the ranks of the people who occupied the post. This bottom-up process began during Sulaym ibn ʿItr's term in office. He is described as issuing written rulings in inheritance cases and his dealings with other state officials are described as an exchange of missives. The process gained momentum during the second half of the seventh century, and between 705 and 810 cadis acquired responsibility for supervision/administration of various trust funds, not money obtained through the tax collection system.

The stages of the process can be summarised as follows: in 705, for the first time, orphans' monies came under the supervisory authority of the cadi and remained in the hands of cadis throughout the middle ages. The involvement of cadis with the management/supervision of *waqfs* began during the 730s, but cadis never achieved full control over the *waqf* institution. By the first decade of the ninth century, the cadi also supervised the monies of absent people and legacies with no legal heirs. This accumulation of extra-judicial authority made the cadi a powerful figure at the centre of an urban business network unconnected with state administration, and he, like members of ruling families, courtiers, emirs and private businessmen, moved freely across a multiple divide of roles. The extension of the cadi's authority is a reflection

the restoration was allowed. Frequently, in such cases the jurists differed and the decisions taken by the rulers were more politically inspired than legally informed. See Lev, 'The Fatimid Caliphs', 396–7.

of medieval realities in which the amalgamation of responsibilities was a norm and no clear-cut distinction between ex-officio activities and semi-private and private commercial-financial dealings existed.

The extension of the cadi's responsibilities was driven by a quest for power, influence and financial rewards. In a parallel but unrelated process, cadis also shaped proceedings at their courts. Cadis chose their clerks and controlled the appointment and dismissal of witnesses. The first references to the debate as to how the selection of witnesses should be conducted are from 758–61, and no acceptable solution was reached during the second half of the eighth or the ninth century. No clear criteria were put forward, and the main debate concerned whether the selection process should be socially inclusive or selective. The outcome was quite clear: people belonging to sectarian religious and theological groups were left out, and social prestige was the driving force behind the selection process. A certain degree of congruence between belonging to the witness corps and acting as a financial trustee with responsibility for various funds on behalf of the cadi is discernible, but how widespread this congruence was remains unknown.

That caliphs were involved in legal matters, and in the way the cadi administrated justice, is a truism, and the question that should be asked is when this ceased. Tillier has devoted extensive discussion of the topic, which relies on a wide range of sources and spans the period from al-Manṣūr's reign to the post-*miḥna* period.[117] The sources for the study of the cadi institution in Egypt are far more restricted and offer no clear answer; the impression is that it simply faded away, but never entirely ceased. The reappointment of Ḥārith ibn Miskīn illustrates this point. The caliph was aware of the cadi's independence and integrity when investing him with judicial authority for the second time, but dismissed him again when he threatened the economic interests of the ruling family. However, the question of a cadi confronting the regime on social issues should be separated from the issue of constant caliphal involvement in legal matters and court cases adjudicated by the cadi. The impression is that this kind of involvement ceased following the end of the *miḥna* and the appearance of *madhhab*-oriented cadis.[118]

[117] See *Les cadis d'Iraq*, Chapter 9, entitled 'La lutte pour l'autorité judiciaire', 577–684.

[118] Cf. Tillier's concluding remarks of his long discussion of the topic. See *Les cadis d'Iraq*, 683–4.

It can be argued that during the tenth century, if not earlier, the notion of the cadi's judicial sovereignty became solidified. How this trend related to the social standing of the cadi in his society is, however, a different question. The way in which the cadi institution had evolved made the recipient vulnerable and susceptible. Firstly, the cadi acted as a single judge with no clearly structured mechanism of appeal on his rulings. Secondly, the cadi's involvement with the supervision and management of various trust funds could tarnish his reputation and call his integrity into question. Although the post was of paramount importance, it was beset by structural flaws.[119]

[119] Tillier, 'Qadis and Their Social Networks', 123–41, esp. 134–41, which discusses the attempts of Shāfiʿī and Ḥanafī jurists to define the distinction between the cadi's professional and private life.

2

Sunnī Rulers and their Cadis

Cadis at the Forefront of Political Life

The history of Egypt between 868 and 969 was marked by the rule of two short-lived semi-independent local dynasties, the Tulunids (868–905) and the Ikhshidids (935–69), and an intermit period of direct Abbasid control (905–35). During that period the cadi institution saw few long-serving cadis, as well as a rapid turnover in the post, increasing politicisation of the post, and growing dependence of the cadis on their political masters. When Aḥmad ibn Ṭūlūn arrived in Egypt the cadi was Bakkār ibn Qutayba, a Ḥanafī jurist from Baṣra, where he studied the *shurūṭ* literature (formularies). In 860, he was appointed by the caliph al-Mutawakkil and received the exorbitant monthly salary of 168 *dīnārs*.[1] He is described as a pious unmarried person and as a conscientious cadi, who made every effort to ensure the credibility of testimonies submitted at his court and kept a watchful eye on the trustees who handled various funds supervised by the cadi. He was also involved in the local world of learning and the transmission of prophetic traditions.[2] It may be said that Bakkār ibn Qutayba was a professional cadi in a long tradition of scrupulous cadis who executed their duties properly, but his career was overshadowed by his complex relations with Aḥmad ibn Ṭūlūn.

Aḥmad ibn Ṭūlūn respected Bakkār ibn Qutayba, who was not a yes-man, but a stern cadi who applied the law appropriately. In one case, a tax farmer (or tax contractor, literally 'one of the *mutaqabbilūn*') who owed money to

[1] In comparison to Bakkār ibn Qutayba's salary, the keeper of the Nilometer, built in Fusṭāṭ on the orders of Mutawakkil, received a salary of 6 *dīnārs* per month, which must be have been regarded as adequate. See Ibn Ḥajar, ed. Majid I, 144.

[2] Kindī, 477 (Ibn Burd); Ibn Ḥajar, ed. Guest, 505–6; Tillier, *Vies des cadis*, 53–5.

Aḥmad ibn Ṭūlūn died and the chief tax-collector asked the emir to order the cadi to sell the debtor's house. Tax contracts were complex legal and financial transactions, and in this case the tax farmer/contractor himself guaranteed the deal and did not transfer the guarantee to a third party.[3] In any case, Bakkār ibn Qutayba proceeded in an orderly way. He verified the existence of the debt, then the debtor's ownership of the house, and, finally, requested Aḥmad ibn Ṭūlūn to swear that he was the creditor. The gist of the account seems to be the remark that the debtor left small children and that the sale of the house had grave consequences for them. The cadi, however, sought no social justice or mitigating circumstances: he applied the law. In another case, the cadi nonetheless took a broader approach to the law and its application. The circumstances of the second case were also rooted in the tax farming/contracting system and bore resemblance to the first case, with one significant difference: the debtor fled, and his house was endowed. Balawī, Aḥmad ibn Ṭūlūn's biographer, provides a supposed transcript of the conversation in which Aḥmad ibn Ṭūlūn addressed Bakkār ibn Qutayba saying: 'Your mentor teaches that dissolving of pious endowments is religiously/legally (*dīn*) permitted. Thus annul the pious endowment of this fugitive so that we can take the money belonging to the government [*sulṭān*] from him.' Bakkār ibn Qutayba preferred to avoid the legal aspect of the issue (i.e. Abū Ḥanīfa's views about the permissibility of dissolving pious endowments) and came up with a non-legal argument, saying: 'Don't do that. Don't set a custom (*sunna*) that others will use against you. The reason is that you have established charitable pious endowments and if you annul (those) of others (yours) will be dissolved too.' Supposedly, the emir was grateful for the advice.[4]

There are no indications that the cadi had any involvement in the tax-collecting system, and in these two cases his involvement was limited to the legal fall-out from the way the system worked. The sources provide no

[3] For the ninth-century meaning of the terms *qabāla* as tenancy and of *qabbāl* as tax collector, see Frantz-Murphy, *The Agrarian Administration*, 94–5. For the practice of guarantee in the tax collection system, see Sijpesteijn, 'Profit Following Responsibility', 98–130.

[4] Balawī 179. Echoed and elaborated by Ibn Ḥajar, ed. Guest, 508–9; Tillier, *Vies des cadis*, 59–60. Maqrīzī's account is closer to Balawī's text. See *Kitāb al-Muqaffā*, II, 452. The endowment of houses in favour of family members must have been quite common. For an example of such a *waqf* created by the Banū ʿAbd al-Mu'min family of the Fayyūm between 864 and 872, see Rāġib, *Merchands d'étoffes du Fayyoum*, doc. 12.

hint that economic aspects had any significance in the relations between Aḥmad ibn Ṭūlūn and Bakkār ibn Qutayba, who rendered the emir important services and maintained financial independence from him. The cadi, for example, invalidated the letters of safety given to the rebels who supported the attempted putsch by al-ʿAbbās, Aḥmad ibn Ṭūlūn's son, in 879. Although one may wonder whether Baghdad really regularly paid Bakkār ibn Qutayba's salary during the twenty years he served as cadi in Egypt, we know nothing about his financial situation. He must have been either well-off or living modestly, and made no use of the 1,000 *dīnārs* bonus that Aḥmad ibn Ṭūlūn used to send him every year.[5]

Although the cadi challenged neither the authority nor the legitimacy of the emir, relations between the two become strained because of politics. Nothing in the relations between them can explain Bakkār ibn Qutayba's lack of total support for Aḥmad ibn Ṭūlūn's blatant intervention in Abbasid dynastic politics in favour of the caliph al-Muʿtamid against his brother and heir apparent al-Muwaffaq, as exemplified by the document proclaimed in Damascus in 883 on the emir's instigation. Aḥmad ibn Ṭūlūn secured the support of the leading cadis of Syria, jurists and notables for the proclamation which condemned al-Muwaffaq for his mistreatment of the caliph and demanded his removal from the position of heir apparent, declaring the fight against him *jihād* and obligatory. Bakkār ibn Qutayba and two other Egyptians jurists were the only dissidents who refused to sign the document as witnesses.[6] The sources do not offer coherent information about what seems to be Bakkār ibn Qutayba's complex approach to the problem: he partially supported the proclamation, but had his reservations too. Aḥmad ibn Ṭūlūn was infuriated and jailed the cadi, but Bakkār ibn Qutayba's imprisonment was not harsh and he outlived Aḥmad ibn Ṭūlūn for forty days (both died in 884). Bakkār ibn Qutayba's biographers lament that the funeral of such a virtuous and pious person was not attended by state dignitaries. The meritorious qualities of the deceased were, nonetheless, grafted onto his grave and supplicatory prayers at his burial place were answered.[7]

[5] Ibn Ḥajar, ed. Guest, 512; Tillier, *Vies des cadis*, 66–7; Maqrīzī, *Kitāb al-Muqaffā*, V, 707. For the complex relations between the emir and cadi, see Tillier, 'The Qāḍīs of Fusṭāṭ Miṣr', 208–10.

[6] For the 883 events in Damascus, see Bonner, 'Ibn Ṭūlūn's Jihād', 573–605.

[7] Ibn Ḥajar, ed. Guest, 514; Tillier, *Vies des cadis*, 70–1.

According to Ibn Zūlāq, following Bakkār ibn Qutayba's death no cadi was appointed for seven years and during those years justice was dispensed by the *maẓālim* court. Ibn Zūlāq's statement is enigmatic and should not be taken too literally; he possibly meant that no cadi was officially nominated for a long period, not that the post was abolished or left vacant. According to Ibn Zūlāq, Khumārawayh, Aḥmad ibn Ṭūlūn's son and successor, appointed Muḥammad ibn ʿAbda ibn Ḥarb (833–925) to the *maẓālim* court and only in 891 was he also appointed cadi. It was a joint appointment made by the emir and the Abbasid caliph.[8] In any case, Ibn Zūlāq's account draws attention to the tension between the cadi's jurisdiction and the *maẓālim* institution. Ibn Ḥajar, for example, states that Aḥmad ibn Ṭūlūn persisted in holding *maẓālim* sessions, and people turned to his court and avoided the justice dispensed by the chief of the police in criminal cases, and Bakkār ibn Qutayba found himself idle. Ibn Ḥajar's statement is a general observation devoid of any time frame and context, and one is left puzzled as to its meaning. By patronising the *maẓālim* court Aḥmad ibn Ṭūlūn manifested political authority, and this might also have been an attempt to belittle, not to say marginalise, Bakkār ibn Qutayba, who refused to accept oaths taken in the name of the emir and insisted on taking oaths only in the name of God.[9] In any case, it was a powerful demonstration of political dominance over the judiciary.

Ibn Ḥarb's nomination as cadi in 833 solidified his integration into the regime. Ibn Zūlāq paints a complex portrait of Ibn Ḥarb's personality, describing him as an oppressive person who seized properties and, at the same time, as an open-handed person and an authority on prophetic traditions. The first thing that strikes the reader is the wealth that Khumārawayh lavished on Ibn Ḥarb, who received a monthly salary of 3,000 *dīnārs*. In addition to occupying the post of cadi and having responsibility for the *maẓālim* court, Ibn Ḥarb also presided over cases of inheritances, and supervised pious

[8] Ibn Zūlāq's account is quoted by both Ibn Ḥajar (ed. Guest), 501 and Maqrīzī (*Kitāb al-Muqaffā*, VI, 9); Tillier, *Vies des cadis*, 71. For the tension between the *maẓalim* court and cadi's jurisdiction, see Tillier, 'The Qāḍīs of Fusṭāṭ-Miṣr', 209–10; 'Qāḍīs and the Political Use of Maẓalim', 49–50.

[9] Ibn Ḥajar, ed. Guest, 511, 512; Tillier, *Vies des cadis*, 65, 67. In Damascus, during the *miḥna*, the *maẓalim* court replaced the cadi (dismissed because of his views) for several years. See Tillier, 'Qāḍīs and the Political Use of Maẓalim', 48.

endowments and the markets. If one takes a long-term view of the evolution of the post of cadi, it can be argued that the delegation of these responsibilities exemplifies a twofold process. The state ratified the long process typified by cadis who extended their responsibilities to include supervision of trust funds, and, in this case, the ruler vested the cadi with new authority over the markets and made the *muḥtasib* answerable to him. Although Ibn Ḥarb entrusted the management of pious endowments to al-Ṭaḥāwī, his confidant, he invested money deposited with him by other people. His financial affairs diversified: he became a financier-banker.

Ibn Ḥarb, for example, received a deposit from the administrator ʿAlī ibn Aḥmad al-Mādharāʾī, who also deposited money with Ibrāhīm ibn Hārūn al-ʿAbbāsī. When ʿAlī's son Abū Bakr enquired about these deposits the two trustees gave completely different answers regarding how they had handled the deposited money. Ibn Ḥarb claimed that he had followed instructions and bought a rural property in Baṣra, while al-ʿAbbāsī handed Abū Bakr a vast sum of money. A grateful Abū Bakr bought a house worth 5,000 *dīnārs* for al-ʿAbbāsī.[10] The account leaves the question open as to whether al-ʿAbbāsī returned only the capital or the capital with a profit, and the general drift of the account is equally enigmatic: is Ibn Ḥarb implicitly being criticised for investing in a far-away, not easily accessible rural property? Ibn Ḥarb's extensive financial dealings typify the lack of a clearly defined demarcation line between the private financial dealings of a cadi and his public duties.

In terms of wealth, Ibn Ḥarb belonged to a small group of the super-rich. He displayed his wealth, and used it to solidify his position as a state dignitary who also played a leading role in the local world of learning. Two of Ibn Ḥarb's most important status symbols were the opulent house in which he lived, which cost 100,000 *dīnārs*, and his retinue of a hundred slaves, including eunuchs. He also bestowed patronage on people, lavished money on those who approached him, and cultivated jurists and transmitters of prophetic traditions. Ibn Ḥarb's grandiose lifestyle involved throwing receptions on the occasion of the great religious festivals, which were attended by the civilian and military elite of the state.[11]

[10] Ibn Ḥajar, ed. Guest, 516, 518; Tillier, *Vies des cadis*, 74, 76–7.

[11] Ibn Ḥajar, ed. Guest, 515, 516, 517; Maqrīzī, *Kitāb al-Muqaffā*, VI, 11.

From Khumārawayh's point of view, the investment in Ibn Ḥarb was fully justified. The cadi is described as a bold, assertive person who successfully mediated between Khumārawayh and the emirs during the strife between them. Ibn Ḥarb's position was, however, entirely dependent on Khumārawayh's sway over power. The cadi's attempt to create an independent power base buttressed by slaves, wealth and patronage was not enough to secure his position following the killing of Khumārawayh in Damascus in 896. Actually, he had failed to win the support of the *ʿulamāʾ* class and was accused of dishonesty in the transmission of prophetic traditions. Ibn Zūlāq disputes the accusation, which, most likely, was politically motivated.[12] For a few months during 896, the reins of power were held by Khumārawayh's son Jaysh, and later by another son of his, Hārūn (896–904). During the short and stormy reign of Jaysh, Ibn Ḥarb went into hiding, where his resources were large enough to keep him alive and safe for several years. Al-Ṭaḥāwī fared worst: he was obliged to submit a detailed account of the way he had handled *waqf* properties during Ibn Ḥarb's tenure as cadi.[13]

In 897, Hārūn appointed Abū Zurʿa as cadi, and the way the nomination document was formulated reflected Tulunid political vision: it was stated that he had been nominated cadi of Egypt and the Syrian provinces held by the Tulunids. Although the term 'supreme cadi' (*qāḍī al-quḍāt*) is not mentioned, the appointment resembled the Abbasid post of supreme cadi. Abū Zurʿa's nomination was a political statement and a reward for a staunch Tulunid supporter. In 833, Abū Zurʿa was personally involved in cursing al-Muwaffaq on Aḥmad ibn Ṭūlūn's instigation, and he barely escaped retribution when al-Muwaffaq temporarily seized Damascus during 884–6.[14]

Abū Zurʿa was a native of Damascus, a scion of a Jewish family which had converted to Islam and a rich landowner. His adherence to the Shāfiʿī school of law is much emphasised and reflects the claim that the Shāfiʿī *madhhab* replaced adherence to al-Awzāʿī's legal teaching in Damascus and Syria

[12] Tillier, 'The Qāḍīs of Fusṭāṭ-Miṣr', 212–13.

[13] Kindī, 479–80 (Ibn Burd); Ibn Ḥajar, ed. Guest 518; Tillier, *Vies des cadis*, 76–7.

[14] Kindī, 489 (Ibn Burd); Ibn Ḥajar, ed. Guest; Maqrīzī, *Kitāb al-Muqaffā*, VI, 190–1; Tillier, *Vies des cadis*, 77–81.

during the ninth century.[15] Abū Zurʿa married into the Madharāʾī family, and in terms of wealth and status he was part of the civilian administrative elite of the Tulunid state. Although he had enemies in Damascus, he forged ties beyond his social circle with the poor and pious, and as cadi he showed spectacular magnanimity towards an impoverished debtor. He survived the overthrow of the Tulunid regime and returned to Damascus to take the post of cadi on behalf of the Abbasids.[16]

Aḥmad ibn Ṭūlūn's successors firmly integrated their cadis into the state structure, while state patronage was instrumental in turning them into influential personalities in the Fusṭāṭ milieu of scholars and notables. Both Ibn Ḥarb and Abū Zurʿa earned a name as charitable people, and whether this was a move dictated or inspired by the Tulunid rulers, as assumed by Tillier, or a personal inclination remains unknown. In the case of Abū Zurʿa, his association with the rulers had no adverse effect on the way he executed his judicial duties.[17]

During the intermit period of Abbasid direct rule, Egypt's most renowned cadi was ʿAlī ibn al-Ḥusayn ibn Ḥarb, who came from Baghdad and served between 906 and 923. He was a Shāfiʿī jurist, and within the Shāfiʿī school the disciple of Abū Thawr. He impressed his contemporary tenth-century biographers by his learning, especially in prophetic traditions, piety and asceticism, and is described as the last cadi to whom the emirs of Egypt showed reverence.[18] He was a meritorious, experienced and learned cadi who, prior to his appointment in Egypt, had served as cadi in the town of Wāsiṭ in Iraq.[19] Following Ibn Ḥarb's dismissal (he died in Baghdad in 931), the appointment of cadis in Egypt became chaotic and were made by the caliph, or the supreme cadi of the caliphate, or the emir of Egypt.[20] Some of those

15 Ibn Ḥajar, ed. Guest, 518–20; Tillier, *Vies des cadis*, 77–8.

16 Ibn Ḥajar, ed. Guest, 521–3; Tillier, *Vies des cadis*, 82–3.

17 Tillier, 'The Qāḍīs of Fusṭāṭ-Miṣr', 212. Abū Zurʿa's biographers praise him as a conscientious cadi. See, for example, Maqrīzī, *Kitāb al-Muqaffā*, VI, 190, 194.

18 This point is much emphasised by Tillier, see 'The Qāḍīs of Fusṭāṭ-Miṣr', 213–14.

19 Kindī, 481 (Ibn Burd); Ibn Ḥajar, ed. Guest, 523–5; Tillier, *Vies des cadis*, 85–9, 93–4. The field of *ḥadīth* studies in ninth- to tenth-century Egypt was dominated by the towering figure of al-Nasāʾī (d. 915), of whom Ibn Ḥarb was a student. See Ibn Ḥajar, ed. Guest, 524; Melchert, 'The Life and Work of al-Nasāʾī', 377–407.

20 For appointments made by the caliph in 926–7 and 929, see Kindī, 484 (Ibn Burd); Ibn Ḥajar, ed. Guest, 537, 539. For appointments made by the chief cadi in 933, 935–6, 938–9 and 940–1,

nominated cadis of Egypt preferred to stay in Baghdad, and sent nominees on their behalf to Fusṭāṭ or appointed local people to the post.[21] Furthermore, some of the appointees served for very short periods of time while others were repeatedly appointed to the post.[22] Very few cadis during this period were meritorious people who executed their duties properly.

Some of the problems that typified the period of renewed Abbasid direct rule over Egypt also continued in the Ikhshidid period, and clear-cut separation between the two periods is difficult. Quḍāʿī's accounts shed some light on how cadis were appointed in Egypt during the Ikhshidid period. He suggests that two cadis (Muḥammad ibn Badr and ʿAbd Allāh ibn Aḥmad ibn Zabr) were appointed directly by the caliph al-Rāḍī (934–40). Other appointments were made directly by Muḥammad ibn Ṭughj (935–46), who installed the cadi al-Ḥusayn ibn Aḥmad ibn Abī Zurʿa and his deputy Abū Bakr Muḥammad ibn Aḥmad ibn al-Ḥaddād. The nomination of Ibn Abī Zurʿa was also approved by the Abbasid supreme cadi (Muḥammad ibn al-Ḥusayn ibn Abī al-Shawārib), who issued for him an official letter of appointment (*ʿahd*). Other appointments made by Muḥammad ibn Ṭughj were reconfirmed by Muḥammad ibn al-Ḥusayn ibn Abī, al-Shawārib's successor in the post of supreme cadi. The drift of Quḍāʿī's accounts is that reconfirmation of appointments by the Abbasids was a matter of policy.[23]

The appointment of Ḥusayn ibn Abī Zurʿa (898–939) illustrates another significant point: the *madhhab* affiliations of the appointee. Ibn Abī Zurʿa, the son of the cadi Abū Zurʿa, was born in Egypt and educated as a Shāfiʿī jurist. He became cadi of Damascus in 924, being appointed by the supreme Abbasid cadi. In 937, Ibn Abī Zurʿa came to Fusṭāṭ to assume the post of cadi of Egypt, while keeping authority over the cadi institution in Palestine

see Kindī, 485, 488, 489 (Ibn Burd). For a cadi appointed by the emir Ibn Ṭughj in 935–6, see Ibn Ḥajar, ed. Guest, 552.

21 Ibn Ḥajar, ed. Guest, 531; Tillier, 'The Qāḍīs of Fusṭāṭ-Miṣr', 215.

22 In 925–6, three cadis served in Fusṭāṭ for short periods of time, while Aḥmad ibn Ibrāhīm ibn Ḥammād served in Egypt three times (in 926–8, 929–32 and 933–4). See Kindī, 482–3, 484, 486 (Ibn Burd). It was not an isolated case: ʿAbd Allāh ibn Aḥmad ibn Zabr served four times as cadi. The first nomination took place in 926 and lasted for six months, while other nominations took place in 932–3, 935–6 and 940–1. See Kindī, 483–4, 487, 489 (Ibn Burd). For a full list of Egypt's rulers, Abbasid governors and cadis during 868–969, see Tillier, 'The Qāḍīs of Fusṭāṭ-Miṣr', 221–2.

23 See *Kitāb al-Inbā'*, 331–2; *Ta'rīkh al-Quḍāʿī*, 520–1.

(Ramla and Tiberias) and Syria (Damascus and Homs) too. His powers in Egypt were equally sweeping and included Alexandria, and supervision over cases of inheritance, the mint and pious endowments. Having such vast and diversified responsibilities he became a central figure in a network of patronage by appointing deputies.[24] Supervision of pious endowments must have been an especially coveted nomination and there was turnover in deputies appointed for the post. Ibn Abī Zurʿa deputed Aḥmad ibn al-Ḥaddād (also a Shāfiʿī jurist) to serve as cadi, but dismissed him and later reappointed him following persuasive mediation by a prestigious Shīʿī notable. Unusual though the scope of Ibn Abī Zurʿa's responsibilities was, he was a professional jurist praised for his judicial skills, and was described as a *bon vivant.*[25]

Ibn Abī Zurʿa's deputy Aḥmad ibn al-Ḥaddād (878–955) was a mild ascetic, a learned Shāfiʿī jurist and a prolific author, including on the subject of *furūʿ* (literally, branches, i.e. derivative principles of law or, in this case, derivative principles of the Shāfiʿī school).[26] Aḥmad ibn al-Ḥaddād's qualifications were exceptional, since other cadis are described as lacking knowledge of the law and as having no judicial skills,[27] being hampered by old age,[28] or corrupt.[29] To what extent, in the overall assessment of the period, one can speak of the judicial autonomy of the cadis in Egypt is a matter of opinion.[30] Various aspects of this question have been discussed by Tillier and Steven Judd, and my departure point is Judd's observation that, during the Umayyad period, the typical area of the cadi's jurisdiction was family law, involving cases such as marital strife, divorces and inheritance disputes. On the other hand, cadis were not involved in criminal justice (murder) cases, nor in heresy trials or the division of spoils.[31] Significant though these observations are, the

[24] Clearly alluded to by Maqrīzī. See *Kitāb al-Muqaffā*, III, 642–5, esp. 645.

[25] Maqrīzī, *Kitāb al-Muqaffā*, III, 642–5; Ibn Ḥajar, ed. Guest, 562–4; Tillier, *Vies des cadis*, 143–5.

[26] Kindī, 487, 491–2 (Ibn Burd); Ibn Ḥajar, ed. Guest, 551–7; Tillier, *Vies des cadis*, 126–36 (including translation of poetry fragments); Maqrīzī, *Kitāb al-Muqaffā*, V, 253–9, quoting, in addition to in Ibn Zūlāq, Quḍāʿī's *Kitāb al-Khiṭaṭ*.

[27] This was the cause of Ibrāhīm ibn Muḥammad al-Kurayzī, who served as cadi during 924–5. Kindī, 482 (Ibn Burd); Ibn Ḥajar, ed. Guest 534–5; Maqrīzī, *Kitāb al-Muqaffā*, I, 303–4.

[28] Ibn Ḥajar, ed. Guest, 538.

[29] Although ʿAbd Allāh ibn Aḥmad ibn Zabr served four times as cadi, he is described as corrupt. Ibn Ḥajar, ed. Guest, 540, 541.

[30] Tillier, 'The Qāḍīs of Fusṭāṭ-Miṣr', 214–15.

[31] Judd, 'The Jurisdictional Limits of Qāḍī Courts', 45–56, esp. 48–9, 52–4.

Umayyad period was marked by the constant involvement, or intervention, of rulers both in shaping the law and in court cases. Furthermore, the literary sources from which we have derived most of the information about these matters have their limitations. While *waqf* disputes are frequently referred to, no other commercial cases with legal ramifications are reported. Thus our ability to define what the areas of a cadi's jurisdiction really were is limited. Tillier's work offers a broader perspective on the question and illustrates many cases of direct confrontation between cadis and caliphs on economic issues that were outside what one would think of as the typical sphere of cadi's jurisdiction. ʿUbayd Allāh ibn al-Ḥasan al-ʿAnbarī, the cadi of Baṣra (773–83, d. 784), for example, clashed with the caliph on questions such as the taxation of lands around Baṣra and the legitimacy of land grants bestowed by the caliph on favourites.[32] Al-ʿAnbarī not only clashed with al-Mahdi (775–85), but also addressed a letter to the caliph which dealt with administrative issues and the cadi institution. Al-ʿAnbarī maintained that legal decisions should be derived from the Koran, the *sunna*, the consensus of the jurists and the individual reasoning of the cadi. He did not deny the caliph's superior position, but argued for the cadi's judicial independence.[33] I would argue that in traditional pre-modern society the value of prescriptive literature in setting institutional norms was limited and it was up to the individual to set ethical boundaries for himself while occupying a post. Furthermore, the structural flaws of the cadi institution were counter-conducive to the firm establishment of judicial autonomy. There was no appeal on the cadi's rulings, and so other state officials and institutions (*maẓālim*) were frequently approached. The cadis' involvement with trust funds had the potential to compromise their integrity, making the distinction between judicial and non-judicial spheres of activity altogether blurred. In these circumstances, the struggle to maintain 'judicial autonomy' was an uphill battle.[34]

Many reports referring to cadis who served between 868 and 969 alluded to the extra-judicial functions of cadis as supervisors of various funds, and

[32] See 'Un traité politique du IIe/VIIIe siècle', 142–4; 'Judicial Authority and Qāḍī's Autonomy', 124–5.

[33] For a French translation of al-ʿAnbarī's letter, see Tillier, 'Un traité politique du IIe/VIIIe siècle', paras 2–4, discussion, 151–3, and Zaman, *Religion and Politics*, 85–91, esp. 89–91.

[34] See the discussion in Chapter 1 and notes 134–5, referring to Tillier's publications.

there are no indications that any ethical code covering how these duties should be discharged had evolved. For example, the cadi Abū al-Dhikr Muḥammad ibn Yaḥyā, who held the post for three months in 924–5, is described as a stern cadi who rigorously supervised the accounts of court trustees. He was a native of Egypt, a sick old ascetic, chosen for the post by the local agreement of people of his class (*nās*) in Fusṭāṭ. In total contrast to Abū al-Dhikr, Ibrāhīm Muḥammad al-Kurayzī, who served in 924–5, came from Baghdad and was scorned for his lack of legal skills. Upon arrival at Fusṭāṭ he immediately seized the court trustees' deposit box (*mawda'*) which contained 50,000 *dīnārs*. He also seized the incomes of pious endowments.[35] Other cadis, although they were foreigners who served for short periods, behaved differently. Muḥammad ibn Mūsā al-Sarakhsī, for example, who came from Baghdad and served as cadi in 934 for few months, was an authoritative cadi careful in accepting testimonies and stern in releasing orphans' monies and incomes from pious endowments to the rightful recipients. He was also high-handed with the supervisors of pious endowments and reduced the remuneration of 500 *dīnārs* that one of them claimed for himself to 10 *dīnārs* per day's work, paying him 30 *dīnārs* in toto. Nonetheless, by the standards of the period this was very high, not to say exorbitant, pay.[36] The inescapable conclusion is that the way cadis exercised their extra-judicial duties was highly personal, and oscillated between the demonstration of high professional ethics and the perception of the post, by some, as an instrument for personal gains and aggrandisement.

There was constant struggle for the control of the lucrative extra-judicial responsibilities held by cadis, and one of the solutions was to split the judicial and supervisory responsibilities. In 925–6, on the intervention of the powerful administrator Ibn al-Furāt, the judicial and extra-judicial spheres of

[35] Ibn Ḥajar, ed. Guest, 535, 554; Maqrīzī, *Kitāb al-Muqaffā*, I, 303–4. In 926–7, the *mawda'* contained 80,000 *dīnārs*. See Ibn Ḥajar, ed. Guest, 536. For both cadis, see Tillier, *Vies des cadis*, 99–101, 101–2.

[36] The 500 *dīnārs* claimed by the supervisor represented a deal involving 5,000 *dīnārs* paid for buying a profitable property for the endowment. The cadi suspected that the supervisor was involved as a partner in the deal, but the supervisor claimed that he had worked on the accounts concerning the deal for three days. Ibn Ḥajar, ed. Guest, 549. In 926, the cadi Aḥmad ibn Zabr, infamous for his corruption, allocated a salary of 30 *dīnārs* to the supervisor of the pious endowments of the (Tulunid?) hospital in Fusṭāṭ. Ibn Ḥajar, ed. Guest, 540; Tillier, *Vies des cadis*, 134.

responsibility were separated, but it must have a temporary arrangement. In 941–2, in similar circumstances, the same separation took place again. The cadi al-Jawharī, appointed by the emir Ibn Ṭughj al-Ikhshīd, quarrelled with Bakrān al-Ṣabbāgh, who solicited the emir to dismiss the cadi and to split the responsibility for jurisdiction and for pious endowments.[37] The request was granted and Bakrān was appointed cadi responsible for Egypt's provinces.[38]

The period of quick turnovers in the post of cadi and the appointment of unqualified persons came to an end in 959 with the nomination of Abū al-Ṭāhir al-Dhuhlī (892–978). He was a Mālikī jurist, scion of an Iraqi family of cadis who had received the standard education of the period, which involved the Koran and the prophetic traditions, and his judicial career included a short appointment as cadi of the Round City of Baghdad (Madinat al-Manṣūr), the caliphal town or complex, and appointments as cadi in Wāsiṭ and Baṣra, his home town. During his service in Wāsiṭ he acquired first-hand experience of the political embroilments surrounding judicial assignments and posts. It is claimed that he was expelled from the town by Bakjam the Turk. Later on he was appointed cadi of Damascus, but lost his position, being chased away from the town by popular protest supported, or manipulated, by Kāfūr. In spite of the alleged involvement of Kāfūr in al-Dhuhlī's downfall in Damascus, he arrived in Fusṭāṭ and became popular with the key people in the town. When the issue of appointing a new cadi came to the fore they took action to secure the nomination for him, and 3,000 *dīnārs* were offered to Kāfūr to allow the appointment. Nonetheless, only the intercession of the eunuch Naḥrīr with Kāfūr had the desired effect. The circumstances behind al-Dhuhlī's nomination say little about his personality and integrity as cadi. He enjoyed the support of notables and court witnesses in Fusṭāṭ, while nomination of a cadi was always a political decision and intercession, the enlisting of support and bribes were part of the nomination process. Al-Dhuhlī had a reputation as a transmitter of prophetic traditions and as an easygoing person. He was criticised by Kāfūr, who claimed that his too-

[37] By the tenth century the norm was that the cadi held responsibility for pious endowments. See Ibn Ḥajar's *en passant* remark about the cadi Aḥmad ibn Ibrāhīm ibn Ḥammād, referring to his first term in office (926–9). Implicitly, the combination of these two responsibilities was state policy. See Ibn Ḥajar, ed. Guest, 537; Tillier, *Vies des cadis*, 105–7, esp. 105.

[38] Kindī, 490–1 (Ibn Burd); Ibn Ḥajar, ed. Guest, 536–7, 571; Tillier, *Vies des cadis*, 157–8, 159.

friendly relations with his companions impaired his authority (*hayba*) as cadi. Al-Dhuhlī disagreed and did not change his ways, but he internalised the experience he had in Damascus and changed his practices as judge, becoming less stern and more lenient in carrying out his duties.[39] Whatever al-Dhuhlī's relations with Kāfūr were, he commanded respect and was a towering figure among the civilian elite of Fusṭāṭ, and, like many other people of this milieu, he made a smooth transition from the Ikhshidid to the Fatimid period.

Cadis and the Provincial Towns

By the second half of the tenth century the cadi institution had spread to provincial towns, and the end result of this process is shown in Ibn Ḥawqal's description of the Delta, which depicts a world of humble hamlets, semi-urban villages and provincial towns. The account begins with the western branch of the Nile and the Mediterranean coast between Alexandria and Burullus. The data derived from Ibn Ḥawqal are used in conjunction with Georgette Cornu's map of ninth- to eleventh-century Egypt. One must bear in mind, however, the complexities of Ibn Ḥawqal's description. In the tenth century there were areas with a mixed Coptic-Muslim population as well as areas with a homogeneous Coptic population unaffected by Islamisation. The presence of government agencies in the form of governors, tax collectors, the military and cadis was widespread, testimony to the degree to which Islam had penetrated the diversified rural world of the Delta. In places like the town of Sanhūr in the northern part of the Delta, and the town of Shābūr on the Nile branch leading to Rashīd, the presence of troops and tax collectors offers no clue as to the composition of the local population.[40] Meanwhile in places such as Juraysiyyāt and Subk al-ʿAbīd, north of Shaṭnūf, the presence of a Muslim population is alluded to by references to mosques or *minbars* but no cadis are mentioned in these places.[41]

Judicial institutions are not at the focus of Ibn Ḥawqal's descriptions. He employs two terms, *qāḍī* and *ḥākim*, which, I would argue, are

[39] Ibn Ḥajar, ed. Guest, 581–3; Maqrīzī, *Kitāb al-Muqaffā*, V, 189–92; Tillier, *Vies des cadis*, 173–8.

[40] Ibn Ḥawqal, 138, 140. For a French translation, see Wiet, *Configuration de la terre*, 138–41, and detailed discussion in Lev, 'Coptic Rebellions', 331–5.

[41] Ibn Ḥawqal, 138, 139.

interchangeable. Shubru Alaw, for example, situated at the heart of the Delta (Baṭn al-Rīf) between Tarnūṭ and Manūf, is described as having a congregational mosque, a *qāḍī* and a tax collector. Tarnūṭ had a mixed Muslim and Coptic population with a strong presence of government agencies in the form of troops and a tax collector. Manūf was a big town in the midst of a grain and flax-growing region, with a *ḥākim*, a tax collector, a congregational mosque and amenities (bathhouses), and markets. North of Manūf there was al-Bundāriyya and the town of Maḥallat al-Maḥrūm, which seem to have had sizeable, if not exclusive, Muslim populations. Both places were seats of a *sulṭān*, a *qāḍī* and a base of military contingents.[42]

Ibn Ḥawqal goes on to describe eleven other places in which *ḥākim* and state officials, referred to as *ʿāmil* (tax collector), *sulṭān* and *ṣāḥib al-maʿūna*, resided. The meaning of *sulṭān*, in this context, is vague, while *ṣāḥib al-maʿūna* is usually understood as 'chief of police' but can also be understood as meaning a commander of local contingents (*ʿaskar*, troops). Some of the places, such al-Ṣāfiyya, a big village (*ḍiyāʿ*), and the town of Farnwa, on the desert edge, had a mixed Muslim and Coptic population, congregational mosques and churches. The population make-up of the tenth-century Delta was complex and the presence of a cadi in conjunction with government agencies indicates a sizeable but not exclusive presence of Muslim populations.[43]

The question is how the cadi institution spread from Fusṭāṭ to the provincial towns, and, as stated earlier, we are hampered in answering it by our inadequate knowledge of the Islamisation process and its history. Nonetheless, by following the terminology of both literary and documentary sources we can partially discern the spread of the institution. Tillier has compiled a partial list of cadis of Alexandria which begins with an appointment made in 708 and runs, with many gaps, to the early tenth century. Further details about early cadis of Alexandria are provided by Bruning, while the first cadi of Rashīd, on the Mediterranean coast, is known only from the early tenth century.[44] The relative abundance of information about cadis in Alexandria

42 Ibn Ḥawqal, 141.

43 Ibn Ḥawqal, 141–3.

44 See Tillier's Introduction to *Histoire des cadis*, 23–4; Bruning, *The Rise of a Capital*, 140–5. Various aspects of Arab presence in Alexandria are extensively discussed by Bruning. See Chapters 1–2.

reflects the Arab presence in the town and perhaps also indicates a process of Islamisation. It can be argued that the same applies to the town of Ikhmīm, in Upper Egypt, which had a cadi during the 750s.[45] By the ninth century powerful cadis such as Ḥārīth ibn Miskīn appointed cadis in provincial towns on their behalf, but references to such individuals are rare in the literary sources. Abū Yaʿqūb al-Shāshī, for example, was a Ḥanafī jurist from Khurāsān who immigrated to Egypt, where he died in 937. His was no spectacular career, but he served as a provincial cadi in Egypt.[46]

The cadi institution in Egypt's provincial towns is also attested in documentary sources. For example, a partially preserved text on a papyrus begins with *basmala* and continues: 'This document is written by Ḥasan ibn Yaʿqūb, the deputy (*khalīfa*) of Yaḥyā ibn Saʿīd, the deputy of the cadi ʿIsā ibn Munkadir in the Fayyūm.' [47] ʿIsā ibn Munkadir served as cadi in Fusṭāṭ between 827 and 929, and the chain of deputation of judicial responsibilities can be explained as follows. ʿIsā ibn Munkadir chose Yaḥyā ibn Saʿīd to serve as deputy in the Fayyūm (most likely meaning Madīnat al-Fayyūm), while he deputed Ḥasan ibn Yaʿqūb to serve as cadi in one of the villages of the Fayyūm. If this was indeed the chain of deputation, it means that the fragment was written at village level in the Fayyūm.

The existence of courts in the major towns of Upper Egypt in the eighth to ninth centuries is well-attested in the documentary record. Although the appearance of the term *qāḍī* in documents is rare, the phraseology in the papyri is identical to that of Ibn Ḥawqal.[48] In ninth- to tenth-century Ashmūnayn, the court is referred to as *majlis al-ḥukm* and *majlis al-taḥakkum al-ʿazīz* and the judge as *qāḍī*. In other documents whose provenance is unknown, the terms used are *majlis al-ḥukm* and *ḥākim*.[49]

The above-mentioned references to literary and documentary sources

[45] Ibn Yūnus, I, 205, 392–3; see Tillier's Introduction to *Histoire des cadis*, 24; Bruning, *The Rise of a Capital*, 144–5.

[46] Maqrīzī, *Kitāb al-Muqaffā*, II, 52, VI, 464, referring to the cadi of Rashīd on behalf of Ḥārīth ibn Miskīn. Ibn Ḥawqal's description of Rashīd offers no clue as to the long-established Muslim population in the town.

[47] Sijpesteijn, 'Delegation of Judicial Power', 61–84, esp. 65 (text and trans.).

[48] See, for example, a document from 811 (provenance unknown), referring to the decision of the cadi ʿAmr ibn Abī Bakr in an inheritance case. Grohmann, *Arabic Papyri*, I, doc. 51.

[49] Khoury, *Chrestomathie*, docs 78, 79, 81, 82, 83; *Papyrologische Studien*, docs 31, 32, 33.

reflect long evolutionary process, mostly hidden from our eyes, which took place at the provincial level. Mikhail, for example, has noted that increasing Islamisation rendered the *lashane* (village level official), local bishops and holy men ineffective in the administration of justice, while Copts increasingly turned to the cadi and Islamic law. This process gained momentum after the eighth century.[50] As mentioned in the Introduction, Reinfandt argues that in the early Islamic period, at the provincial level, the administration of justice was in the hands of low- and mid-level administrators, while complaints were addressed to provincial governors (the *pagarchs*/*ṣāḥib al-kūra*) and, more rarely, to the governor of Egypt.[51] Tillier has argued that during the Byzantine period the *pagarchs* exercised judicial authority, and the combination of political and judicial authority is also exemplified by the letters of Qurra ibn Sharīk. The diffusion of the cadi institution into provincial towns took place during the early Abbasid period, and Tillier perceives a strong link between Islamisation and the spread of the institution.[52]

The beginning of the eighth century is also seen by Sijpesteijn as a turning point marked by the more extensive presence of Muslims in the Egyptian countryside and the replacement of Coptic *pagarchs* by Muslims, with inevitable consequences for the administration of justice and the maintainance of law and order.[53] As Frantz-Murphy stresses, the eighth century also saw the Coptic Church losing its intermediary position between the Coptic rural taxpayer and Muslim government.[54] The most recent contribution to this discussion has been made by Bruning, who emphasises the interconnection between the settlement of Arabs in provincial towns, the process of Islamisation and the spread of the cadi institution.[55]

The Cadis and the Application of the Law

By the time of the Fatimid conquest of Egypt, Islamic law had a fully developed legal framework. In the words of Robert Gleave: 'In the ninth century

[50] See *From Byzantine to Islamic Egypt*, 156–7.
[51] See 'Local Judicial Authorities', 129, 135.
[52] See 'Du pagarque au cadi', 21, 22, 25, 31, 32, including documents pertaining to tenth-century Ashmūnayn.
[53] See *Shaping a Muslim State*, 103, 147.
[54] See 'The Economics of State Formation', 101–6.
[55] *The Rise of a Capital*, 148–53.

Muslim jurists began to conceive of the law as a coherent body of legal norms rather than as a collection of disconnected rules.'[56] During the ninth century the first works of legal theory (*uṣūl al-fiqh*) were composed, and the genre gained popularity during the tenth century. Fragments of early treatises on the subject can be reconstructed from the *Ikhtilāf Uṣūl al-Madhhāhib* (*Differences about the Principles of Jurisprudence among the Schools of Law*), by the foremost Fatimid jurist, Qāḍī al-Nuʿmān (see Chapter 3). For the current discussion, the most relevant passage is that quoted by Devin Stewart from the work of the cadi Abū ʿUbayd al-Qāsim ibn Sallām (d. 839), which in Stewart's translation goes as follows:

> The sources of legal rulings (*uṣūl al-aḥkām*) which the judge cannot transgress to adopt [*sic*] are: the Book, the Sunnah, and what the leading jurists and righteous ancestors have ruled on the basis of consensus and *ijtihād*. There is no fourth category.[57]

The change from a situation in which the administration of justice preceded the formation of the law (seventh–eighth centuries) to the perception 'of the law as a coherent body of legal norms', from which judicial rulings should be derived (as exemplified in the above quotation), can be described as a shift from *ra'y* to *madhhab*. The range of meanings attributed to the term *ra'y* (personal view) varies from discretion (*istiḥsān*) and sound opinion to legal reasoning. Schacht has argued that issuing judgments relying on *ra'y/istiḥsān* could have been informed by customary practice, administrative regulations, Koranic regulations and recognised Islamic religious norms.[58] Yasin Dutton maintains that *ra'y* involved various methods of legal reasoning, including consideration of public good, which by its very nature is more discretionary than legal reasoning. [59]

[56] See 'Deriving Rules of Law', 57.

[57] See 'Muḥammad B. Dā'ūd al-Ẓāhir Manual of Jurisprudence', 99–158, esp. 104–5. There is a large literature on the subject. See, for example, Stewart, 'Muḥammad B. Jarīr al-Ṭabarī's al-Bayān ʿan Uṣūl al-Aḥkām', 321–48, esp. 348, where he states that by the late ninth century 'nearly all of the established *madhhabs* had one or more manuals of *uṣūl al-fiqh*'. See also Hallaq, 'Uṣūl al-Fiqh: Beyond Tradition', 172–202, who argues for the congruence in Islam between law and social life (181–2).

[58] See *An Introduction*, 25–6, 37. The literal meaning of the term *istiḥsān*, deeming something good, is very close to *istiṣlāḥ*, meaning something in the public interest. Both terms refer to a legal method of deriving rulings in the absence of any applicable text.

[59] See *The Origins*, 34–5.

The possibility that the Koran could provide a unifying frame of reference for deriving rules of law has been discussed by Noel J. Coulson. He shows how two Egyptian cadis, Ibn Ḥujayra (688–702) and Tawba ibn Namir (733–7), understood differently the Koranic injunctions about the rights of a finally-repudiated wife during her ʿ*idda* (waiting period). The topic was controversial, and in 703–4 it had been examined in the presence of the governor, who, at the request of the caliph, assembled the learned people in Fusṭāṭ (*ashyākh*) for a discussion. The caliph was interested to learn what the people of Fusṭāṭ (*ahl Miṣr*) thought about the issue since the opinions of the people of Syria (*ahl Shām*, possibly meaning Damascus) were divided. Kindī does not elaborate about the opinions expressed at the meeting, but one of the participants, Yūnus ibn ʿAṭiyya, impressed the governor, who appointed him cadi and also vested him with responsibility for the police.[60]

Kindī's accounts reflect a lively and continuous dialogue between cadis and caliphs and add weight to Schacht's statement that, during the second half of the seventh and the first half of the eighth century, 'the administrative and legislative activities of the Islamic government cannot be separated'.[61] Recent scholarship on the Umayyad period vindicates Schacht's statement and provides a more nuanced picture of caliphal involvement in the legal arena. Patricia Crone and Martin Hinds have pointed out that the involvement of the Umayyad caliphs in the legal arena had a corollary in the perception of them as deputies of God on earth and in their role as political and spiritual guides implementing God's ordinances.[62] The degree of the caliphal entanglement in legal matters is revealed by ʿAbd al-Razzāq al-Ṣanʿānī's Muṣannaf, which is considered 'one of the earliest preserved compilations of mainly legal traditions, dating from the second/eighth century'. Tillier's study of the work has shown that Umayyad caliphs responded to legal queries sent to them by both provincial officials and cadis. Particularly interesting is

60 Coulson, *A History of Islamic Law*, 31–2, 34–5; Kindī, 317, 323–3, 344; Tillier, *Histoire des cadis*, 68, 74, 100. Although Schacht's notion that schools of law evolved from regional to personal is questioned in recent scholarship, Kindī's tenth-century text, alluding to events in the first decade of the eighth century, is implicitly more in line with Schacht's perception of the process. For Hallaq's criticism of Schacht, see 'From Regional to Personal', 20–1.

61 See *An Introduction*, 15. This topic is extensively treated by Schacht in *The Origins*, Part Three.

62 See *God's Caliph*, ch. 4, esp. 43–8.

the case of ʿUmar II, who usually issued rescripts to governors but, in the case of Egypt, corresponded directly with cadis.[63]

The cadi's dependence, voluntary or not, on the caliph as the supreme authority over judicial matters is illustrated by a conversation that took place between the cadi ʿĀbis ibn Saʿīd and the Umayyad caliph Marwān ibn al-Ḥakam in Egypt in 684, during the rebellion of ʿAbd Allāh ibn al-Zubayr. The cadi, who was also responsible for the police, unequivocally stated that he always relied on his own knowledge when passing judgments and consulted with others when necessary. His statement came in response to a direct question posed by the caliph, and the cadi explained that neither the Koran nor the Koranic law of inheritance guided him in his judgments. The caliph was, apparently, pleased with the answer and confirmed him as cadi. According to another report, in some inexplicable way typical of a true believer the cadi was, nonetheless, familiar with the Koran and its teachings on the laws of inheritance. The first report might be seen as reflecting the age of discretionary *ra'y* prior to the formation and solidification of Islamic law. Kindī, however, wrote when schools of law reigned supreme, and the second report was intended for his contemporary readers: inadvertently, the cadi knew the Koran and its legal teachings. Kindī's narrative also hints that the caliph might have been politically motivated in endorsing the cadi, since he was one of his staunch supporters and control of Egypt was a matter of great importance when dealing with Ibn Zubayr's rebellion.[64]

One may ask what the legal education, if any, was of those nominated as cadis in the period when discretionary *ra'y* reigned supreme. The evidence is contradictory. The cadi Ghawth ibn Sulymān (appointed in 753), for example, is described as an agreeable person but not much of a jurist. He nevertheless had a broad, though unspecified, knowledge of judicial matters and how they should be handled.[65] It can be argued that this characterisation is unsurprising and rather typical of the discretionary *ra'y*-oriented cadis,

[63] See 'Califes, émirs et cadis', 147–90, esp. 168–170, 172–5, 177. For ʿAbd al-Razzāq's Muṣannaf, see Motzki, 'The Author and His Work', 171–201, esp. 176; 'The Muṣannaf of ʿAbd al-Razzāq al-Ṣanʿānī', 1–21.

[64] Kindī, 311–12; Tillier, *Histoire de cadis*, 61–4; Juynboll, *Muslim Tradition*, 83.

[65] Kindī, 357; Tillier, *Histoire des cadis*, 117. For another example of an excellent cadi with inadequate legal training, see Simonsohn, *A Common Justice*, 80.

who brought to the post valuable extra-legal skills. If the Kadijustiz paradigm has any relevance for the present inquiry, it can be argued that the period of discretionary justice represents a stage when cadis actively participated in the shaping of the law and the justice they dispensed was, if not arbitrary, highly personal, while their frequent consultations with the caliph aimed at providing higher authority for their rulings.

Many of Kindī's accounts refer to ʿUmar II's instructions sent to his cadis, but occasionally the caliph withheld his opinion from a cadi. For example, ʿUmar II refused to advise the cadi ʿIyāḍ ibn ʿUbayd Allāh on what should be done with a boy who had violated a girl with a finger. ʿUmar II maintained that the cadi should use his discretion in resolving the matter. Eventually a compensation of fifty *dīnārs* was awarded to the girl.[66] One may wonder whether the cadi would have undermined his authority and bothered the caliph with such a question, waiting for weeks, if not months, for an answer while leaving the case unresolved. In other cases with wider socio-legal ramifications the quest for caliphal intervention seems more probable, and caliphs had no inhibitions about instructing the cadi on what needed to be done. Caliphal involvement is highlighted by a case concerning *shufʿa*, that is, the question of who has a pre-emptive right to purchase co-owned property – the co-owners or a neighbour. The caliph ordered that the co-owners should be granted priority in contrast to the practice of according the property to a neighbour. In fact, the caliph offered the cadi a detailed exposition of his view on the matter.[67] Whether due to political considerations or personal relations, the consultations between ʿIyāḍ ibn ʿUbayd Allāh and ʿUmar II on judicial matters were frequent and involved diverse aspects of the administration of justice. Kindī, for example, quotes ʿUmar II's official letter from 718 in which the caliph states that he is responding to an inquiry submitted by the cadi which involved the case of a debtor who upon his death had many debts but no means to repay them. He also had nine young slave girls (*walāʾid*) either born to him or bought by him, and the caliph provided detailed instructions as to how the case should be handled.[68]

[66] Kindī, 334; Tillier, *Histoire de cadis*, 89.

[67] Kindī, 334–5; Tillier, *Histoire des cadis*, 89–90; Yanagihashi, *A History of the Early Islamic Law of Property*, 9, 141.

[68] Kindī, 336–7, 338–9; Tillier, *Histoire des cadis*, 91–2.

One can always argue that the reports about cadis consulting the caliph are in line with ancient and medieval Middle Eastern norms and depictions of the ruler as lawgiver and dispenser of justice, and are part of a more comprehensive process of transformation from Late Antiquity to early Islam. Furthermore, early caliphs claimed religious legitimisation and authority and involvement in legal matters came naturally to them. Another perspective on consultations between cadis and ʿUmar II is offered by Abū Zurʿa, who credits the caliph with a comprehensive vision on legal matters and states that he wished to create what seems to be a unified system of *aḥkām* for the people (*nās*) and army (*ajnād*). The term *aḥkām* must be understood as referring to judicial rulings (or more broadly to law), but the intended unification of the legal system remains ambiguous since there are no indications that civilians and the military were legally treated differently. Abū Zurʿa continues by stating that the caliph wished to appoint, in cities (*amṣār*) and provinces (*ajnād*), descendants of the Companions of the Prophet as cadis to effect reconciliation (*ṣulḥ*) between the people. The ambiguity of the account persists because of the double meaning of the term *jund* (pl. *ajnād*), which usually refers to the army/military, but in the context of the administrative geography of Syria-Palestine to a province.[69]

In contrast to the (still) enigmatic legal policies of ʿUmar II, the relationships between cadis and caliphs in the Abbasid period involved two parallel processes: firmer control of the process of appointment, and consolidation of the notion that cadis are independent in their judgments. Direct appointment of cadis by the caliph became the norm under al-Manṣūr (754–75), and Hārūn al-Rashīd (786–809) created the post of chief cadi (*qāḍī al-quḍāt*). Jany has persuasively argued that this was an internal development unrelated to the Sasanian *mōbedan mōbed*, which was the title of the Zoroastrian high priest and supreme judge. Tillier has questioned the prevailing wisdom that the new post created a centralised hierarchical judicial system, and has pointed out that the system was marked by ill-defined lines of responsibility and that its impact on Egypt up until the Tulunid period was meagre.

[69] Abū Zurʿa, 202. For the meaning of *ajnād* in the context of the administrative geography of Muslim Syria and its Byzantine precedents, see Haldon, 'Greater Syria in the Seventh Century', 2–3, 6–7.

Furthermore, in the second half of the ninth century, after al-Mutawakkil's reign (847–61) the post of chief cadi was in decline.[70] One can argue that, whatever Umayyad and Abbasid legal policies were, the long-term trend was away from discretionary *ra'y* towards a judicial system based on codified law as embodied by the emerging schools of law and towards the authority of the *madhhab* and *madhhab*-oriented cadis who derived law differently from the *ra'y*-oriented cadis.

Rich though Kindī's history of the Egyptian cadis is, the text does not reflect the late eighth- to ninth-century debate between *aṣḥāb/ahl al-ra'y* and *aṣḥāb/ahl al-ḥadīth* as to how law should be derived. The traditionalists (*aṣḥāb/ahl al-ḥadīth*) maintained that, alongside with the Koran, law should be derived from *ḥadīth*. These two opposing views were eventually combined in the legal system typified by the schools of law. These developments took place from below and were only loosely related to the state. Another development that took place from below involved the notion that cadis are independent in their judgments and derive their judicial authority from God and that their foremost obligation is towards the Muslim community.[71]

Although much used, the term *madhhab* escapes neat definition, and the limitations of the English translation 'school of law' have been pointed out by Bernard Weiss. In legal usage, the term signifies a body of doctrines associated with a jurist.[72] While keeping in mind the amorphous nature of the terms *ra'y* and *madhhab*, one can examine Tillier's list of the cadis of Fusṭāṭ between 644 and 680, which also includes a heading referring to *madhhab* affiliation. The first cadi mentioned as having a *madhhab* identity is ʿIsmāʿīl ibn Alīsaʿ (780–3), who, relying on Abū Ḥanifa, insisted on the nullification of pious endowments in Egypt. It is the first case in which the cadi's judgment was informed by a legal doctrine, or positive law, and one can argue that it is firmly in line with Hallaq's emphasis on personal adherence to the teaching of a leading jurist. ʿIsmāʿīl ibn Alīsaʿ's adherence to the doctrine of Abū Ḥanifa pre-dates the emergence of fully-fledged Ḥanafī *madhhab*. Actually, cadis having a clear *madhhab* identity are rare during the

70 Jany, 'Persian Influence', 149–68; Tillier, *Les cadis d'Iraq*, 131–5.

71 Tillier, 'Judicial Authority and Qāḍī's Autonomy', 119–31, with cross-references to his other publications, and to sources and literature.

72 See 'The Madhhab', 1.

eighth century and more frequent during the ninth. Tillier's list of cadis who served in Fusṭāṭ between 800 and 860 includes eighteen names, of which five are referred to as Mālikis and four as Ḥanafīs, leaving eleven cadis with no alluded-to *madhhab* identity.[73] Illuminating though the list of cadis with or without indications of *madhhab* affiliations is, the scope of the investigation must be expanded to also include legal texts composed in Egypt. Jonathan E. Brockopp, for example, perceives Egypt as being the birthplace of the Mālikī and Shāfiʿī schools of law and the place where the first legal compendiums were written.[74]

Coulson's critical acumen when reading Kindī sheds light on the question of to what extent doctrinal differences between the schools of law influenced the judicial process. A case in point is the dispute as to who the rightful beneficiaries were of the *waqf* known as The House of the Elephant (see Chapter 1). As Coulson has pointed out, the case hinged on the interpretation of who the 'descendants' were in the *waqf*'s original stipulations.[75] Kindī's long account of the affair begins with the ruling of the cadi Hārūn ibn ʿAbd Allāh (832–40), who is identified by Ibn Ḥajar as a Mālikī jurist.[76] He ruled that sons of daughters (*ʿaqib*) should be excluded from the list of beneficiaries. The cadi Muḥammad ibn Abī l-Layth (841–51), who is described as a follower of the Kūfa school of law (meaning he was a Ḥanafī jurist), annulled Hārūn ibn ʿAbd Allāh's ruling and allotted a share of the *waqf*'s revenues to the offspring of Banū l-Sāʾiḥ. The third ruling in this case was issued by the cadi Ḥārith ibn Miskīn (851–9), a Mālikī jurist (a follower of the legal school of Medina), who nullified the ruling of his immediate predecessor in the post and denied the offspring of Banū l-Sāʾiḥ a share in the *waqf* revenues. Isḥāq ibn Ibrāhīm of the Banū al-Sāʾiḥ family resorted to the *maẓālim* institution and brought his grievance to the caliph, or, to put it differently, he appealed against the ruling of the cadi (see Chapter 6). Kindī is very clear that the

[73] See Tillier's Introduction to *Histoire des cadis*, 24–30. For Egypt's strong Mālikī identity and the emigration of Ḥanafī jurists to Egypt, see Tsafrir, *The History of an Islamic School of Law*, 95–9. For the nomination of Isḥāq ibn Furāt, a prominent member of Mālik's circle in Egypt, for the post of cadi (he served between 800 and 801), on the recommendation of Shāfiʿī', see, Kindī, 393; Tillier, *Histoire des cadis*, 159–60.

[74] See 'The Formation of Islamic Law', 123–40, esp. 124, 136.

[75] A *History of Islamic Law*, 87–8.

[76] Kindī, 443; Ibn Yūnus II, 246; Tillier, *Histoire des cadis*, 218, n. 925.

issue at stake was the interpretation of law according to *madhhab* guidelines. The jurists in Baghdad who were charged with re-examining the case were Ḥanafīs, and they quashed Ḥārith ibn Miskīn's ruling. Ḥārith ibn Miskīn asked the caliph to be relieved of his duties as cadi and his request was granted (see Chapter 1).

It seems that Ḥārith ibn Miskīn's resignation had some impact in Baghdad, and the decision of the Ḥanafī jurists in the capital was suspended, so to speak, and the case entrusted to the cadi Bakkār ibn Qutayba, who was instructed to grant Isḥāq ibn Ibrāhīm ibn al-Sā'iḥ what Ḥārith ibn Miskīn had denied him. Although Kindī's text explicitly says that Bakkār ibn Qutayba was ordered to uphold the decision of the Ḥanafī jurists in the capital, his decision was not a foregone conclusion. Bakkār ibn Qutayba disliked the quashing of Ḥārith ibn Miskīn's ruling and had to be persuaded to reaffirm Isḥāq ibn Ibrāhīm ibn al-Sā'iḥ's right to enjoy income from the disputed *waqf*.[77]

The way law was derived greatly changed during the ninth century, and the *madhhab* system, in the words of Paul R. Powers, 'had taken shape as a distinctive feature of Islamic civilization' and permeated many spheres of intellectual activity and public life. The *miḥna* policy imposed between 833 and 848 attempted to enforce the doctrine about the 'createdness' of the Koran. The cadis, court witnesses and *ahl al-ḥadīth* were forced to declare their adherence to the state's proclaimed doctrine. The caliph's letter sent to Fusṭāṭ announcing the *miḥna* also included the request to reject *tashbīh* (anthropomorphism), which was the term chosen for the opposing view that the Koran is co-eternal with God. The policy was implemented, but some jurists went into hiding and the role of the Mālikī cadi Hārūn ibn ʿAbd Allāh in these events is ambiguous. He certainly had to comply with the policy, but refused the demand by the caliph al-Muʿtaṣim (833–42) to impose it on the jurists.[78] He was dismissed, while the newly appointed Ḥanafī cadi Muḥammad ibn Abī l-Layth had, prior to his appointment, agreed to carry out the policy.

77 Kindī, 474–5; Tillier, *Histoire des cadis*, 249–50.

78 The exact dating of the letter is vague. For these events, see Kindī, 445–8; Tillier, *Histoire des cadis*, 221–3.

Kindī states that *miḥna* was lightly applied during al-Muʿtaṣim's reign, but stringently and widely enforced under al-Wāthiq (842–7). Wider segments of the learned class were subjected to the *miḥna*, including muezzins and teachers at the Koranic schools for boys. The public was exposed to the tenets of the doctrine, upheld by the state in the form of writings on mosques: There is no God but God, Lord (of the created) Koran. The world of learning was also affected by the policy since Mālikī and Shāfiʿī jurists were banned from mosques, meaning they were not allowed to use the mosques as venues for teaching law. To avoid the *miḥna* administrated by Muḥammad ibn al-Layth many fled Egypt.[79]

Muḥammad ibn al-Layth was a high-handed cadi, and his arrest in 850 revealed how unpopular he was. The arrest ordered by the caliph al-Mutawakkil was motivated by a financial investigation launched from Baghdad, and the cadi and family members suffered many tribulations. The backlash against social groups associated with the *miḥna* took place under the cadi Ḥārith ibn Miskīn, himself a victim of the *miḥna*, who expelled Ḥanafīs and Shāfiʿīs from the mosque, meaning the Ancient Mosque in Fusṭāṭ, and dismissed a group of muezzins.[80]

If al-Ma'mūn's motivation for imposing the *miḥna* was to crush potential political adversaries and those who opposed his self-view as *imām al-hudā* (rightly-guided ruler chosen by God whom subjects have to obey), one may ask what the relevance was of the *miḥna* in the Egyptian context.[81] No real threat to Abbasid rule could emanate from Egypt, but the *miḥna* was a powerful reminder of the coercive powers of the state directed first of all against its employees (cadis) and those indirectly dependent on it.

The termination of the *miḥna* policy did not change the disparity between the authoritative state and society dependent on it, and the co-operation between rulers and the learned class continued and took many forms. Furthermore, the termination of the *miḥna* was instrumental in the

[79] Kindī, 451, 453; Tillier, *Histoire des cadis*, 226–7; Maqrīzī, *Kitāb al-Muqaffā*, V, 88. For the Abbasid regime's intention of inculcating the doctrine about the 'createdness' of the Koran via teachers of Koranic schools for boys, see Cook, *Commanding Right*, 105, n. 176.

[80] Kindī, 469. There is an extensive literature on the *miḥna*. See for example Cooperson, *Classical Arabic Biography*, 33–40, with ample references to sources and literature.

[81] For al-Ma'mūn's pretensions for juridical powers, see El-Hibri, *Reinterpreting Islamic Historiography*, 97, 102–3, 139.

coming to fruition of the growing *madhhab* identity, a process that took place from below. The ninth century was a formative period in the long evolution of the *madhhab* as both legal school and social organism. The association between rulers and legal schools also became the norm. Although late, the account of Ibn Zayyāt (d. 1411) sheds some light on the issue. According to him, in the Fusṭāṭ of the 960s money was distributed among the adherents of the Mālikī school of law by the Umayyad rulers of Spain. On the solicitation of the jurist and cadi Abū Bakr al-Ḥaddād, Kāfūr extended even greater support for the Shāfiʿī jurists.[82] *Madhhab* identities hardened in the later Middle Ages, encapsulated in the term *taʿssub*, meaning zealous adherence to a certain *madhhab* typified by bitter rivalry with other schools.

Ibn Ḥajar's and Maqrīzī's remarks about the legal education of the cadi Bakkār ibn Qutayba in Baṣra reveal another aspect of the formative process of ninth-century law. Both assert that the future cadi studied *ḥadīth*, jurisprudence and works of *shurūṭ* (formularies) with Hilāl ibn Yaḥyā (known as Hilāl al-Ra'y), a famous Ḥanafī jurist from Iraq. Bakkār ibn Qutayba can be described as a *faqīh-cum-shurūṭī* type of jurist, to use a term coined by Hallaq. In Egypt, Bakkār ibn Qutayba became a central figure in the local world of learning and one of his most famous students of *ḥadīth* was Aḥmad ibn Muḥammad al-Ṭaḥāwī, the author of several books on *shurūṭ*. Both Jeanette A. Wakin and Hallaq have emphasised the tendency of Ḥanafī jurists to compile works on *shurūṭ* and, more significantly, the key role of these works in the formation of Islamic law.[83] The list of Bakkār ibn Qutayba's treatises relevant for the work of the cadi's court includes three titles: *Kitāb al-Shurūṭ*, *Kitāb al-Maḥāḍir wa-l-Sijillat* and *Kitāb al-ʿUhūd wa-l-Wathāʾiq*. The *Kitāb al-Maḥāḍir wa-l-Sijillat* was a work that specified how the minutes of the court and the cadi's judgment should be written. Although the terms *wathāʾiq* and *shurūṭ* are considered synonymous, the title *Kitāb al-ʿUhūd wa-l-Wathāʾiq* indicates that this was a manual specifying how documents presented to the court should be written. Another work (title not given)

[82] See 190–1. Abū Bakr al-Ḥaddād served as cadi twice for a few months during 936 and 944. See Kindī (Ibn Burd), 487, 491.

[83] Kindī (Ibn Burd), 477; Ibn Ḥajar, ed. Guest, 505; Tillier, *Vies des cadis*, 53–4; Maqrīzī, *Kitāb al-Muqaffā*, II, 442; Hallaq, 'Model Shurūṭ Works', 122–3, 115, 128; Wakin, *The Function of Documents*, 12–13, 18–22.

was an extensive polemical tract which defended Abū Ḥanifa while refuting Shāfiʿī.[84]

Al-Ṭaḥāwī's literary output was large and diverse. It includes works such as *Kitāb al-Shurūṭ al-Kabīr*, *Kitāb al-Shurūṭ al-Ṣaghīr* and *Kitāb al-Maḥāḍir wa-l-Sijillat*. Other works were devoted to *fiqh*, *ḥadīth* and the Koran. Al-Ṭaḥāwī also wrote legal monographs on issues such as inheritance and testaments. One title stands out, *Ikhtilāf al-Fuqahā'*, which can be described as reflecting the slow crystallisation of the schools of law and disagreements as to how law should be shaped and rulings derived. This title also can be seen as reflecting a personal change in al-Ṭaḥāwī's life, from his being considered a follower of Shāfiʿī to being the most prominent personality among the followers of Abū Ḥanifa in Egypt.[85]

Although, in medieval Muslim courts, documents were subordinated to oral testimony, formularies served a purpose. These documents were not contracts in the legal sense of the term, but they established the validity of transactions and facilitated the working of the court. Bakkār ibn Qutayba, al-Ṭaḥāwī and the earlier-mentioned Qāsim ibn Sallām were legal scholars and practitioners of law. Bakkār ibn Qutayba and Qāsim ibn Sallām served as cadis while al-Ṭaḥāwī held the position of a supervisor of pious endowments. Their lives illustrate the emerging congruity between legal doctrine and how cadis derived their rulings. The contribution of Arabic papyrology to the question of congruity between law and judicial practice focuses on the *shurūṭ* literature. Khan, for example, has noted that deeds of purchase recording the purchase of land properties in Fatimid Fusṭāṭ follow al-Ṭaḥāwī's formularies specified in the section on sales in his *Kitāb al-Shurūṭ al-Kabīr*.[86]

When we take a broad view of the ninth century, we see that it was a period which saw a shift from administration of justice informed by *ra'y* to *madhhab*-oriented cadis. Two other characteristics of the *sharīʿa* were

[84] Maqrīzī, *Kitāb al-Muqaffā*, II, 453. How documents that recorded private transactions were written in order to serve as acceptable evidence (*ḥujja*) in court is discussed by Sijpesteijn, 'Making the Private Public', 83–5. I owe this reference to the kindness of one of the anonymous readers on behalf of EUP.

[85] Maqrīzī, *Kitāb al-Muqaffā*, I, 720–4; Wakin, *The Function of Documents*, 23, n. 6.

[86] See *Bills*, 175.

also forged during that time: the identification of certain schools of law with geographical regions (the Muslim West with Malikism, Baghdad with Hanbalism and the Turkish world with Hanafism) and *ikhtilāf*. The term stands for both legal differences between the schools and a divergence of opinions within a school, which ensured legal dynamism and change.

3

Ismāʿīlī Rulers and the Judicial System

Militancy and Pragmatism

Fatimid history in its North African and Egyptian–Syrian phases is relatively well-known, and references to cadis are quite frequent in the works of Heinz Halm, Ayman Fu'ād Sayyid and Michael Brett. As regards its two main components, the justice dispensed by the cadi and by other state officials such as the market supervisor, the system of administration of justice during the North African period, has been discussed by Farhat Dachraoui, who focused on the Mālikī legal background of North Africa and the complex relations of the Mālikī jurists with the Aghlabids and the Fatimids. Dachraoui has also discussed the Aghlabid administrative precedents, such as combining responsibilities for the markets with *maẓālim*.[1]

The various institutions that made up the system of administration of justices are discussed by Sayyid in his book about the Fatimid state in Egypt. The cadi institution, however, is discussed separately from legal issues such as inheritances where there are no legal heirs and pious endowments, and the way the cadi dealt or failed to deal with them.[2] The cadis of the Nuʿmān family played a crucial role in the development of the cadi institution in Fatimid Egypt, and Richard J. H. Gottheil, who wrote at the beginning of the twentieth century, was the first to translate and publish fragments

[1] See *Le califat fatimide*, 397–422, esp. 399, 419–20.

[2] See *Al-Dawla al-Fāṭimiyya fī Miṣr*, 361–9, 539–43, 543–7. For other brief discussions of certain components of the Fatimid system of the administration of justice, see Haji, 'Institutions of Justice in Fatimid Egypt', 198–214; Magued, 'De quelques juridictions fatimides en Égypte', 48–60; 'La fonction de juge suprême dans l'État fatimide en Égypte', 45–56.

concerning members of the family from Ibn Ḥajar's history of the Egyptian cadis.[3]

This chapter treats the Fatimid period as a whole, and relies on extensive fragments of Fatimid documents preserved in the literary sources pertaining to the appointment of supreme cadis during the late tenth and early eleventh centuries. It also tries to present an integrative discussion of legal issues and their administrative ramifications. While relying on the existing literature and the larger range of sources currently available, my approach is primarily informed and influenced by the broader perspectives that study of law and medieval Islamic history have to offer to a student of Fatimid history. The first issue that must be addressed is the paradox that the administration of justice under the Fatimids in North Africa preceded, and in Egypt paralleled, the formation of Fatimid law. This evokes the realities of the seventh to eighth centuries, when administration of justice in early Islam preceded the formation of the law. However, contrary to their Umayyad and Abbasid predecessors, the Fatimids could draw on the political experience of Muslim states in terms of how administration of justice was carried out.

For the establishment of Fatimid rule in North Africa, we have the authoritative account of Qāḍī al-Nuʿmān (d. 974), who was both the creator of Fatimid law and the historian of the Fatimid mission (*daʿwa*) and state (*dawla*) during their Ifrīqiya (Tunisia) stage. Authoritative though Qāḍī al-Nuʿmān's account is, some points are left perhaps deliberately vague. Qāḍī al-Nuʿmān, for example, describes the Berbers of the Kutāma who sheltered the Fatimid propagandist Abū ʿAbd Allāh and became staunch Fatimid supporters as a free tribal society divided into clans, with religious and judicial authority exercised by people who possessed *ʿilm*, knowledge. Whether this was knowledge of Islamic law or tribal legal tradition remains unexplained. Undoubtedly, the Kutāma were a Muslim society and Abū ʿAbd Allāh befriended them in Mecca when they performed the pilgrimage, but this does not necessarily mean that they lived according to every iota of Islamic law. Qāḍī al-Nuʿmān is equally vague when he describes the tenets of Abū ʿAbd Allāh's preaching, which was about religion, piety and the rights of ʿAlī and the *imāms* of his line. Those who responded to the preaching are

[3] See 'A Distinguish Family of Fatimid Cadis', 217–96.

described as yearning for God, seeking an approach to Him and expecting spiritual rewards for good deeds.[4] Writing centuries later, Idrīs ʿImād al-Dīn (d. 1468), the chief propagandist of the Ṭayyibī Ismāʿīlīs in Yemen, offers no better perspective on Abū ʿAbd Allāh's preaching and activity among the Kutāma, which he presents in idealised form as imbued with uncompromising Islamic legal values of justice and the wiping out of oppression. Abū ʿAbd Allāh's justice was harsh, and when the need arose to execute a guilty person he delegated the task to the family of the accused.[5]

During the period that followed the collapse of the Aghlabid regime (25 March 909) and before the coronation of ʿUbayd Allāh al-Mahdī (5 January 910), as the first reigning Fatimid ruler Abū ʿAbd Allāh had to deal with the situation in Kairouan, the biggest and most important town of Ifrīqiya.[6] His first priority was to establish law and order and to show that his rule was different from that of the Aghlabids. He prohibited alcohol and installed a Shīʿī person, Muḥammad ibn ʿUmar al-Marwarrudhī, as cadi in Kairouan, who, in letters and documents he issued, used the title 'Supreme Cadi' while the justice he administrated was based on the utterances of the *imāms*.[7] For this period (March 909–January 910) we also have a new, recently published text from inside Ismāʿīlī ranks which speaks in disparaging terms about the Sunnī, mostly Mālikī, population of Ifrīqiya and the role of the cadi. The population is referred to as a garbage heap and the cadi as a sweeper. The needs of the population for a cadi are also belittled, and described as limited to the supervision of the markets and weights, implying that in their view a cadi for the Sunnī population was no more than a market supervisor.[8]

Al-Marwarrudhī is described as belonging to Ahl Khurāsān, meaning the descendants of the Khurāsānī troops dispatched to Ifrīqiya during the reign of the Abbasid caliph al-Manṣūr. Between 909 and 916 he served as cadi and was deeply involved in the local Kairouan scene and the life of the state.

[4] Qāḍī al-Nuʿmān, *Iftitāḥ*, 64–6, 73, 76.
[5] See *ʿUyūn al-Akhbār*, 106.
[6] For an extensive discussion of this period, see Halm, *The Empire of the Mahdi*, 118–47; Brett, *The Rise of the Fatimids*, 72–108; Dachraoui, *Le califat fatimide*, 109–25.
[7] Qāḍī al-Nuʿmān, *Iftitāḥ*, 215; Ibn ʿIdhārī, I, 150–1, 152. For al-Marwarrudhī's appointment, see Madelung, 'The Religious Policy of the Fatimids', 98–9.
[8] For Ibn al-Haytham's *Kitāb al-Munāẓarāt*, see Madelung and Walker, *The Advent of the Fatimids*, 45–55, and 64–5 (Arabic text); 116–17 (English trans.).

Being a scion of a long-established social group in the region and enjoying the advantages of his post, he became involved in extensive commercial and financial dealings with the notables and merchants of Kairouan. This kind of involvement in urban commercial life was rather typical of cadis and their standing in a local society; less typical were the accusations that, driven by greed, he was responsible for the death of a merchant whom he persecuted. He died in 916 under torture in murky circumstances, at the hands of the ruler whom he had served.[9]

Al-Marwarrudhī also implemented the Ismailisation of the religious life in Kairouan by abolishing the supererogatory *tarāwīḥ* prayers in Ramaḍān and introducing the Shīʿī formula of the call to prayer. The Fatimid propagandists and their local supporters who gained political power by violence had no hesitation in unleashing violence and imposing their world view on the population. Abā ʿAbd Allāh instructed the leaders of the Kutāma to call the people to adopt their brand of Islam (*madhhab*), and he had some success. Messianic expectations focused on ʿUbayd Allāh al-Mahdī resonated in the local society, and certain people in Kairouan eagerly anticipated the rule of the *imām*. Prior to the coronation of ʿUbayd Allāh al-Mahdī, two jurists were put to death in Kairouan, having been accused of opposing the new regime by belittling ʿAlī and comparing him to the other caliphs of Medina. The executions were authorised by Abū l-ʿAbbās, Abū ʿAbd Allāh's brother, who is described as having been outraged at the fomenting of unnecessary hostility towards the regime.[10]

With the coronation of al-Mahdī, the Ismailisation of religious life in the public sphere took the form of state-sponsored policy and involved the cursing of the companions of the Prophet (with three exceptions) and his wife, while al-Marwarrudhī compelled the Sunnī jurist of Kairouan to issue legal opinions according to the legal system of Jaʿfar al-Ṣādiq. The level of al-Marwarrudhī's legal expertise in Shīʿī jurisprudence is difficult to gauge, but this proved to be no obstacle since legal guidance and instruction came

[9] Ibn ʿIdhārī, I, 151, 169, 173.

[10] Abū l-ʿAbbās is depicted as a mindless militant who suggested expelling Mālikī jurists from Kairouan, a move blocked by his brother. Ibn ʿIdhārī, I, 150, 152–3, 155. For a broader discussion of violence in Fatimid history, see Lev, 'From Revolutionary Violence to State Violence', 67–86.

from the fountain-head of al-Mahdī, who disapproved of irrevocable divorce (*ṭalāq batta*) pronounced by a single formula and the exclusion of uterine heirs, but allowed the granting of a whole inheritance to a daughter, in the absence of male heirs, to the exclusion of agnates.[11]

Wilferd Madelung has pointed out that in pre-Fatimid North Africa Mālikī jurists adopted a vehement anti-Shīʿī policy and that Mālikī bibliographical dictionaries are a biased source for the Fatimid period.[12] These are important observations, but the whole North African phase of Fatimid history was markedly violent and violence was a political tool of the Fatimid regime.[13] Although the killing of the jurists in 909 in Kairouan is presented as sparking a row between the two brothers who brought the Fatimids to power, other sporadic violent acts committed, or authorised, by the Fatimid rulers followed. In 919, a muezzin was put to death for omitting the Shīʿī formula of the call to prayer, and in 921 two other people met the same fate, being accused of preferring some companions of the Prophet over ʿAlī. In 923, a jurist was put to death for issuing legal opinions based on Mālikī law. These events took place in Kairouan, and it appears that the regime created an atmosphere of fear by encouraging incriminations and was attentive to denunciations. These cases of state oppression pale in comparison to the massive violence that was applied against internal heretics within the Fatimid movement. In Kairouan and other places, there were Fatimid supporters who completely deviated from Islam by permitting alcohol and pork and violating Ramaḍān, while some of them worshipped al-Mahdī. Hundreds were arrested, and many died in prisons.[14]

When Qāḍī al-Nuʿmān's writings, as well as late Sunnī North African and Egyptian historiography, are examined, two points are clearly borne out:

[11] For al-Mahdī's legal injunctions, see Ibn ʿIdhārī, I, 155, 159–60; Poonawala, 'Al-Qāḍī al-Nuʿmān and Ismāʿīlī Jurisprudence', 117–45. For critical re-examination of the Fatimid inheritance laws, with ample references to sources and literature, see Cilardo, *The Early History of Ismāʿīlī Jurisprudence*, 10–15. Irrevocable divorce pronounced by a single formula is considered by the Ismāʿīlīs as *ṭalāq al-bidʿa*, see Ibn al-Haytham's *Kitāb al-Munāẓarāt*, 73 (text), 127 (trans.). I am grateful to Tillier for his comment on the issue.

[12] See 'The Religious Policy of the Fatimids', 99–102.

[13] For Qāḍī al-Nuʿmān's perception of God's manifestation through war and carnage, helping (the Fatimids) to overcome the stubborn enemies of His cause, see Lev, 'From Revolutionary Violence to State Violence', 71.

[14] Ibn ʿIdhārī, I, 172–3, 186, 187, 188.

from the beginning, Fatimid rulers did appoint cadis, and they also imposed religious rites typically associated with the brand of Islam they professed.[15] The cadi Aflaḥ ibn Hārūn al-Malūsī, for example, was appointed by al-Mahdī cadi of Rakkāda and Mahdiyya and had previously served as *dāʿī*, famous for introducing sessions of Ismāʿīlī teaching to women. Whether he simultaneously kept his position as *dāʿī* remains unknown, but Idrīs ʿImād al-Dīn vaguely alludes to his legal training.[16] Qāḍī al-Nuʿmān's career is better documented. In June 951, he was actually appointed de facto supreme cadi of the Fatimid realm in North Africa.[17] At that time he served as cadi of Tripoli and, according to his own testimony, he was summoned by Manṣūr (946–53) to Manṣūriyya (or Ṣabra, a palace city south of Kairouan). He arrived there on a Friday morning and was immediately appointed and ordered to proceed to the Friday mosque of Kairouan to perform the prayers and deliver a sermon. He was accompanied by an armed escort and the highest-ranking members of the court, and his letter of appointment stated that he was nominated cadi of Manṣūriyya, Mahdiyya, Kairouan and other towns of Ifrīqiya. He was instructed to uphold justice among the people and to show no preference for the noble and mighty over the commoner and the humble.[18]

The dilemma that Fatimid rulers faced during the mid-tenth century is highlighted by the account that the cadi of Barqa refused to implement the Shīʿī law (*madhāhib ahl al-bayt*) in his judgments, and suffered bestial public execution in Kairouan. Although the report about his execution can be doubted since al-Manṣūr's policies towards political opponents were reconciliatory, the difficulties in implementing Shīʿī law were real. One must ask what Fatimid legal texts were available at that time and what the pool, if any, was of jurists trained in *madhāhib ahl al-bayt*.[19] It seems that al-Manṣūr (946–53) made an effort to reach out to the Sunnī majority of Ifrīqiya and to

[15] During Fatimid rule in North Africa cadis were appointed in the towns of Barqa, Raqqāda and Tripoli. In 925, in Kairouan, a person was nominated for the *maẓālim* court. Ibn ʿIdhārī, I, 153, 159, 188, 189, 190. For a systematic listing of cadis appointed by the Fatimid rulers in North Africa, see Ibn Ẓāfir, ed. ʿAlī ʿUmar, 96, 98, 101, 106.

[16] See *ʿUyūn al-Akhbār*, 211–12; Halm, *The Empire of the Mahdi*, 153, 375; Brett, *The Rise of the Fatimids*, 138, 154.

[17] Maqrīzī's, *Kitāb al-Muqaffā*, II, 173–4.

[18] For Qāḍī al-Nuʿmān's recollections, see his *Kitāb al-Majālis*, 51, 53, 75, 348.

[19] For al-Manṣūr's policies, see Al-Anṭākī, 109; Maqrīzī, *Kitāb al-Muqaffā*, II, 130, 173–4, 175–6; Idrīs ʿImād al-Dīn, 350, 379.

co-opt the Sunnī religious class to support the regime. In 952, for example, when the Byzantines made a request for a truce and offered a payment the proposal was brought before assembly of Shīʿī and Sunnī jurists, who represented the three Sunnī legal schools present in North Africa, for a debate. Qāḍī al-Nuʿmān was instrumental in conveying the jurists at the palace and they ruled, as one would expect, that only the opinion of the ruler matters (al-Manṣūr was in favour of accepting the truce). On their way out they met al-Manṣūr's heir apparent, to whom they paid respect and whom they informed about the meeting.[20]

Al-Manṣūr's invitation of Sunnī jurists to serve as a rubber stamp for political decisions was an empty gesture, but it illustrates Qāḍī al-Nuʿmān's pivotal role in the judicial arena as the creator of the Fatimid law, as cadi and as member of al-Manṣūr's inner circle. Qāḍī al-Nuʿmān entered into the service of the Fatimid rulers in 925 and was close to many of them. He was a prolific author who wrote on a wide range of topics, including law, theology and history, and his *Daʿā'im al-Islām* (*Pillars of Islam*) became the most important Fatimid legal text.[21] The book was composed on the behest of al-Muʿizz (in Ifrīqiya 953–73, in Egypt 973–5), who served as editor-in-chief, and Qāḍī al-Nuʿmān claims that the text was popular, while al-Muʿizz made efforts to promote the book and approved its use as a legal text.[22] In another case, the initiative of writing a book came from Qāḍī al-Nuʿmān, who asserts that he responded to a demand from cadis and learned people for a concise book consisting of the sayings of the people of Ahl al-Bayt that could be understood and easily remembered. Qāḍī al-Nuʿmān indeed composed such a text, and he called it *Kitāb al-Dīnār* since he stipulated that anyone copying the book should pay a *dīnār*. Al-Muʿizz was pleased with the book, but gave it the more dignified title *Kitāb al-Ikhtiṣār li-Ṣaḥīḥ al-Āthār ʿan al-A'imma al-Aṭhār* (*The Abridged Book of Sayings of the Pure Imāms*), insisting that the new title better reflected the book's content. Idrīs

20 Maqrīzī, *Kitāb al-Muqaffā*, II, 175.

21 For Qāḍī al-Nuʿmān's literary output, see Fyzee, 'Qāḍī an-Nuʿmān', 1–32; Poonawala, 'Al-Qāḍī al-Nuʿmān's Work', 109–15. For the family's legal leanings, see Poonawala, 'A Reconsideration of Qāḍī al-Nuʿmān's Madhhab', 572–80. For Qāḍī al-Nuʿmān's book on the Fatimid *daʿwa* and state in North Africa, see Poonawala, 'The Beginning of the Ismāʿīlī Daʿwa', 338–63.

22 See *Kitāb al-Majālis*, 306.

ʿImād al-Dīn explains that the book was actually an abridgement of *Daʿāʾim al-Islām* and that its other title was *Ikhtiṣār al-Āthār fī mā Ruwiya ʿan al-Aʾimma al-Aṭhār*.[23] Qāḍī al-Nuʿmān's close relations with al-Muʿizz brought him the post of authorised teacher of Ismailism. Teaching sessions took place at the palace on Fridays and became known as *majālis*. In unspecified circumstances, al-Muʿizz also entrusted Qāḍī al-Nuʿmān with the teaching of Ismāʿīlī esoteric lore (*ʿilm bāṭin*).[24]

During al-Muʿizz's reign in North Africa, Qāḍī al-Nuʿmān laid the foundation of Fatimid law, while the *imām* promoted further Ismailisation of the religious life. In 960, al-Muʿizz proclaimed new ordinances about the performance of religious rites in the public domain. The most significant directive seems to be the one which ordered the exclusive use of the Shīʿī formula for the call to prayer. Other directives regulated the performance of prayers and restricted the blind reciters of the Koran to practising their trade exclusively during funerals and not during other mourning or commemorative rituals performed at the cemeteries.[25]

A knowledge of Fatimid religious policies in North Africa is essential for understanding the policies in Egypt, which were a continuation of deep undercurrents that governed the conduct of the Fatimid state (e.g. animosity towards the Mālikī school of law).[26] However, in comparison to North Africa, the Egyptian phase was characterised by more restrained use of violence as a tool for imposing religious policies. Experience made the Fatimids aware that the vast majority of their subjects were Sunnīs who adhered, sometimes vehemently, to their legal schools and perceived the Fatimids as heretics against whom holy war should be waged.[27] Unable to win the hearts and minds of the Sunnī majority either in North Africa or in Egypt, the Fatimids adopted

23 Qāḍī al-Nuʿmān, *Kitāb al-Majālis*, 359–60; Idrīs ʿImād al-Dīn, 562–3; Cilardo, *The Early History of Ismāʿīlī Jurisprudence*, 34–6. For other books composed by Qāḍī al-Nuʿmān under al-Muʿizz's supervision and approval, see *Kitāb al-Majālis*, 117–18, 396–7, 401, 430, 545.

24 See *Kitāb al-Majālis*, 386–7, 545–6.

25 Ibn ʿIdhārī, I, 223; Brunschvig, 'Fiqh fatimide', 13–20, who relies on a wide range of sources, including a careful study of *Daʿāʾim al-Islām*.

26 In 1025, for example, the remaining Mālikī jurists were expelled from Fusṭāṭ. See Maqrīzī, *Ittiʿāẓ*, II, 175.

27 For the declaration of *jihād* against the Fatimids by the Mālikī jurists of Kairouan and the pious (*ʿubbād*) during the rebellion of Abū Yazīd, see Ibn ʿIdhārī, I, 217 (quoting Ibn Raqīq's *Taʾrīkh al-Ifrīqiyya*); Young, 'Abū l-ʿArab al-Qayrawānī', 59.

a pragmatic approach that sought to reassure and placate the Sunnī population while partially implementing the Ismāʿīlī law and imposing their rituals in the public sphere. In the long run, the failure to propagate Ismailism and pragmatism ensured the survival of extensive Sunnī learning in Fatimid Egypt and, in Alexandria, a strong presence also of Mālikī jurists.[28]

Jawhar's letter of safety (*amān*), issued upon the conquest of Egypt, manifests Fatimid policies on both the declarative and practical levels. It states that the Fatimids would 'promote justice, spread righteousness (*al-ḥaqq*) and terminate oppression'. This general proclamation was followed by a more concrete reference to the inheritance law, which would be conducted 'according the Book of God and the tradition of the Prophet', and the seizure of inheritances with no legal heirs by the treasury would cease. The references to the Koran and the practice of the Prophet are followed by what might be described as a proclamation of overall Muslim unity: 'Islam is one and applied law.' This ecumenical spirit is also reflected by other statements that refer to the 'righteous ancestors of the Muslim community among the companions of the Prophet and their followers' and the 'jurists of the towns who apply law and issue legal opinions according to their legal schools'. These conciliatory but general, not to say amorphous, references are followed by a more concrete proclamation which states that the call to prayer, the prayers, the rites of Ramaḍān and the breaking of the fast, the alms tax, the pilgrimage and the holy war will be conducted according to what God has commanded, His book, and what has been laid down by the Prophet's practice.[29]

In practical terms, the invocation of God's command, His book and the Prophet's practice were empty declarations, and contemporary people must have been aware of this. By the second half of the tenth century, Islamic political tradition had shown that the interpretation of religion and the application of law and rites was a government monopoly. This reality is illuminated by an encounter (discussed later in this chapter) that took place in 1122, when al-Ṭurṭūshī, the leading Mālikī jurist in Alexandria, came to the court of al-Ma'mūn al-Baṭā'iḥī, the non-Ismāʿīlī vizier of the Fatimid state, and made

[28] Cortese, 'Voices of the Silent Majority', 345–66.

[29] Maqrīzī, *Ittiʿāẓ*, I, 105. For extensive discussion of the document, see Bianquis, 'La prise du pouvoir', 68–71, 73–4; Halm, *The Empire of the Mahdi*, 412–13; Brett, *The Rise of the Fatimids*, 301–3.

several demands. The jurist was reminded, if he needed reminding, that the way law was applied was a disputed issue and, eventually, a political decision.

Even on the declarative level, Jawhar's letter of safety did not promise freedom of religion to the Sunnīs, and in any case, religious freedom was not a principle especially cherished during the Middle Ages. Ismailism can be described as the 'state religion' of the Fatimid state, and one can adopt Samuel M. Stern's observation that it 'enjoyed a privileged position insofar as its legal doctrines were applied by the judiciary and its particular ritual was, at least in the main centres, enforced on public occasions'.[30] The scope and limits of the Fatimids' drive to implement their law in the legal domain are manifested through the elevation of the Nuʿmān family to the position of the highest judicial authority in the state.

The Cadis of the Nuʿmān Family

At the time of the Fatimid conquest of Egypt, the cadi in Fusṭāṭ was al-Dhuhlī, an experienced and politically savvy cadi who knew how to adapt to changing political circumstances. Eager to preserve his position, he made the necessary adjustments to satisfy the new political masters. Al-Dhuhlī's first experience with the Fatimids went very well. As a member of the Fusṭāṭ elite he participated in the delegation that went to meet and negotiate with Jawhar and signed Jawhar's letter of safety as witness. Later on, when the military factions in Fusṭāṭ decided to fight Jawhar, he sanctioned waging war against them. This was an oral approval given during a conversation with Jawhar and came as a reply to the question of whether fighting those who obstruct one's path to the holy war is allowed. When the cadi assured Jawhar that fighting in such circumstances was allowed, he asked whether killing in such circumstances was also allowed, and was again given a positive reply.[31] Jawhar's reference to holy war was not incidental, since the Fatimid conquest of Egypt was explained as motivated by the wish to wage holy war on Byzantium.

In 973, al-Dhuhlī's meeting with al-Muʿizz went even better. When asked by al-Muʿizz how many caliphs he had seen, the cadi answered that except for him he had seen none. Al-Muʿizz was very pleased, since, as the

[30] See *Studies in Early Ismailism*, 236.

[31] Maqrīzī, *Ittiʿāẓ*, I, 103, 107, 108.

historian Ibn Zūlāq explains to his readers, al-Dhuhlī had lived through the reign of eight Abbasid caliphs.[32] According to Ibn Ḥajar, the price al-Dhuhlī had to pay for maintaining his position was to judge inheritance and divorce cases according to *ahl al-bayt*, meaning the Shīʿī or Ismāʿīlī law, and to declare the beginning of the holy months of Rajab, Shaʿbān and Ramaḍān by calculations and not by the appearance of the new moon.[33]

The services al-Dhuhlī rendered to the Fatimids helped him to maintain his position as cadi, but from the Fatimid point of view he was an obstacle. The first step taken against him was taken by Jawhar, who divested him of responsibility for pious endowments and entrusted it to somebody else.[34] Such splitting of responsibilities had its precedents, and Jawhar's underlying motive was financial. A more threatening development took place under al-Muʿizz, with the appointment of Ibn Abī Thawbān as cadi for the Fatimid Berber troops, with responsibility of hearing their grievances. This followed the death of the previous cadi who had held this position, and the appointment can be seen as a Fatimid internal affair unrelated to the wider context of the Fatimids' relations with the Sunnī elite in Fusṭāṭ and the population at large.[35] The events that unfolded proved to be strange and confusing, indicating that from the very beginning Ismāʿīlī rulers and the Sunnī majority became entangled in a complex web of interrelations.

According to Maqrīzī's version of events, Ibn Abī Thawbān, on his own initiative, extended the sphere of his responsibilities, encroached on al-Dhuhlī's judicial domain and began to act as cadi for the Sunnī population of Fusṭāṭ. He accepted the testimony of court witnesses and issued written judicial decisions, compelling witnesses to style him 'Cadi of Fusṭāṭ and Alexandria'. He even deputed a cadi to serve on his behalf.[36] This was a perfectly acceptable practice, since so many cadis before him had done the same: actively extended their sphere of authority, set precedents and assumed responsibilities that were never officially given to them. The

[32] Maqrīzī, *Ittiʿāẓ*, I, 137; Ibn Ḥajar, ed. Guest, 584; Tillier, *Vies des cadis*, 179.

[33] Ibn Ḥajar, ed. Guest, 584; Tillier, *Vies des cadis*, 178–9. For the fundamental differences between the Imāmī–Ismāʿīlī laws of inheritance and the Sunnī schools, see Cilardo, 'Some Peculiarities of the Law of Inheritance', 127–37.

[34] Maqrīzī, *Ittiʿāẓ*, I, 121.

[35] Maqrīzī, *Ittiʿāẓ*, I, 143.

[36] Maqrīzī, *Ittiʿāẓ*, I, 138.

competition between al-Dhuhlī and Ibn Abī Thawbān can be described as rivalry between an Ismāʿīlī cadi and a Sunnī cadi who made some necessary adjustments in the legal sphere. Some Sunnīs, in their 'legal shopping' (so to speak), preferred the Ismāʿīlī cadi, who enjoyed the support of the regime, but Ibn Abī Thawbān's estrangement from the local legal scene proved disastrous for him.

In an undated report, Ibn Ḥajar states that al-Muʿizz ordered cadis to apply the legal principle that a daughter inherits the whole estate in the absence of a brother or sister. Idrīs ʿImād al-Dīn claims that such an order had been issued already by Jawhar.[37] A female plaintiff, undoubtedly aware of these edicts, thought that her inheritance case would be better served at Ibn Abī Thawbān's court and approached al-Muʿizz, who ordered that her case should be dealt with by the Ismāʿīlī cadi. Apparently totally unaware of the behind-the-scenes machinations, Ibn Abī Thawbān ruled in her favour concerning a disputed property. The implied gist of the account is that he applied al-Muʿizz's directive and the Fatimid law. Ibn Abī Thawbān must have been totally unaware of al-Dhuhlī's early ruling, supported by the testimony of witnesses, that the property in question was a pious endowment. When Abī Ibn Thawbān's decision was read, the witnesses protested and various accusations were made about who had falsified the testimonies, while Abī Ibn Thawbān had to defend himself against the accusation of unauthorised use of the title 'Cadi of Fusṭāṭ and Alexandria'. The uproar reached Yaʿqūb Ibn Killis, a powerful administrator and member of al-Muʿizz's inner circle, who informed his master about the scandal. Al-Muʿizz was caught in an impossible dilemma: on the one hand he had ordered application of the Ismāʿīlī law of inheritance; on the other, he had been led astray by his incompetent cadi. What he did can be described as an attempt at damage limitation: he quashed Abī Ibn Thawbān's judgment. This was too much for Abī Ibn Thawbān, who fell ill and died. He must have felt betrayed, since he was the first Ismāʿīlī cadi to have applied Ismāʿīlī law at the behest of his political master, but was abandoned by his *imām*.[38] On another level, the case demonstrated how easily the

[37] Ibn Ḥajar, ed. Guest, 587; Idrīs ʿImād al-Dīn, 695.

[38] Ibn Ḥajar, ed. Guest, 584, 586, 587–8; Bianquis, 'Prise du pouvoir', 94–6; Tillier, *Vies des cadis*, 179–80.

embryonic Fatimid system of the administration of justice was manipulated, and how powerful were the Sunnī jurists and court witnesses in Fusṭāṭ.

Having survived Ibn Abī Thawbān's threat to his position, al-Dhuhlī faced far more formidable opponents, the Nuʿmān family. Following the death of Qāḍī al-Nuʿmān in 974, his son ʿAlī (born 949) was appointed cadi, but the nature of this appointment remains somewhat elusive. He used to hold court at his home (the family house was in Fusṭāṭ) and at the Ancient Mosque; however, al-Dhuhlī continued to exercise his judicial duties as cadi in Fusṭāṭ. ʿAlī also managed to secure the family's traditional hold on the teaching of Ismailism. He began to lecture on Fatimid law at the Azhar mosque in Cairo, and the text he chose was his father's abridgement of *Daʿāʾim al-Islām*, known as *al-Iqtiṣār*.[39]

In spite of the dominant position of the Nuʿmān family as Ismāʿīlī cadis and members of al-Muʿizz's inner circle, ʿAlī's appointment did not undermine al-Dhuhlī's position. This was further testimony to Fatimid pragmatism and the power of Sunnī judicial circles in Fusṭāṭ. Furthermore, during al-Muʿizz's rule in Egypt (973–5), the regime was still experimenting with how to govern the country properly. In 973, for example, vast administrative responsibilities were entrusted to two administrators, Yaʿqūb ibn Killis and ʿAslūj, which involved supervision of the markets, the police, the grain ports in the capital, endowments and inheritances. They were also given responsibility for the *maẓālim*, but, in this particular case, *maẓālim* meant the hearing of grievances pertaining to tax collection and fiscal matters. The most daring Fatimid administrative innovation involved the way pious endowments were administrated. The regime coveted these incomes and, in the first stage of the reform, payments were released to the rightful recipients only upon presentation of proofs of entitlement. Eventually, the Fatimids accepted a bid of 1.5 million *dirhams* for farming out these revenues, on a yearly basis. The bidder was supposed to pay the recipients and transfer any surplus income to the state.[40] The appointment of Yaʿqūb ibn Killis and ʿAslūj reveals a world view

[39] Maqrīzī, *Ittiʿāẓ*, I, 149, 208–9, 215, 217, 223, 227; Ibn Ḥajar, ed. Guest, 585, 587. For the difference between teaching Fatimid law and Ismailism, see Halm, *The Fatimids and Their Traditions of Learning*, 45–50. For Qāḍī al-Nuʿmān's early career as cadi, see Walker, 'The Relations between the Chief Qāḍī and Chief Dāʿī', 75–80.

[40] Maqrīzī, *Ittiʿāẓ*, I, 148, 208.

that perceived no clear distinction between judicial and administrative functions either at the institutional or on personal levels. Al-Muʿizz, for example, made an attempt to use al-Dhuhlī and his witnesses as source of information for what went on in Fusṭāṭ, and a liaison official was suggested for passing information from the cadi to the caliph, but al-Dhuhlī refused to co-operate.[41]

The appointment (or re-appointment) of ʿAlī ibn al-Nuʿmān (in 976) as cadi again demonstrates the thinking that judicial and certain administrative functions were congruous. It was a pompous state event with the ceremony taking place at the Azhar, and conveyed the unique Fatimid perception of the cadi's role in the state: he was part of the ruling establishment, with executive powers symbolised by the sword he carried. Without the title 'Supreme Cadi' being evoked, he was appointed cadi of Egypt and Syria and of territories over which the Fatimids pretended to claim political authority, such as the holy cities of Arabia and the Maghreb. He was also entrusted with responsibility for the performance of religious rituals at the mosques such as preaching and leading prayers. His other responsibilities included application of the inheritance laws, supervision of the mint, and supervision of the purity of gold and silver coinage and the production of weights and measures (a function known as *ʿiyār*, the place of production being known as *dār al-ʿiyār*).[42] Although there are similarities between ʿAlī ibn al-Nuʿmān's appointment and a few pre-Fatimid precedents such as cadis being entrusted with responsibility for the mint, they should not be exaggerated since those were isolated incidental cases, while under the Fatimids the conferment of such responsibilities became state policy. Fatimid policy in Syria heralded the type of responsibilities that eventually were conferred on the supreme cadi. In 973, a person of Husaynid lineage from Kūfa was appointed cadi of Syria, with responsibility for the mint and markets, and rewarded with 6,000 *dirhams*. This was not an isolated case: a year later, a Shīʿī person from Ramla was appointed cadi of the town, with responsibility for conducting prayers, and supervision of the markets, the mint and pious endowments.[43]

In his official capacity ʿAlī ibn al-Nuʿmān was cadi and state administra-

[41] Maqrīzī, *Ittiʿāẓ*, I, 144–5, 146, 217, 224.
[42] Ibn Khallikān, V, 417; Ibn Ḥajar, ed. Guest, 589.
[43] Maqrīzī, *Ittiʿāẓ*, I, 217; *Kitāb al-Muqaffā*, V, 212.

tor, but he was also the head of a family. In his familial role he deputed his brother Muḥammad to serve as cadi, and he immediately went to the Mediterranean towns of Tinnīs, Damietta and Farāma, and there appointed cadis on his own behalf. This was not an incidental move, since Tinnīs and Damietta were the most important centres of textile production and *ṭirāz* workshops. Textiles, and especially inscribed fabrics (*ṭirāz*), came to occupy a unique place in Fatimid political culture and international relations and were sent as gifts to Mecca and to foreign rulers. The cadis of the Nuʿmān family came to control the *ṭirāz* workshops which produced these textiles and their delivery to the court. By the power of state appointment and through typical personal drive to extend authority, the newly installed Ismāʿīlī cadi seized unprecedented responsibility over a crucial sphere of the state's political and economic life. One can only appreciate Nuʿmān's family's acute understanding of what constituted Egypt's non-agricultural wealth.[44]

ʿAlī ibn al-Nuʿmān's letter of appointment paved the way for the assumption of full and exclusive judicial powers, at the expense of al-Dhuhlī. Although al-Dhuhlī became old and infirm, he had hopes of handing down his position to a son. He made this request during what is described as incidental encounter with al-ʿAzīz, who refused but kept him in his post.[45] It was stated in ʿAlī's letter of appointment that if one of the litigants chose to bring the case before him and not before al-Dhuhlī, the other must comply with the request. Three days after the official inauguration of ʿAlī, his brother Muḥammad went to the Ancient Mosque in Fusṭāṭ and read ʿAlī's letter of appointment, while al-Dhuhlī and his supporters knew what the new appointment entailed for them. ʿAlī's appearance in the Ancient Mosque was a carefully staged state event intended to project the significance and magnificence of the occasion and to demonstrate the social support that the new regime enjoyed. Whether it was coerced, opportunist or genuine, the regime and its Ismāʿīlī cadi did enjoy social acceptance. A large entourage made up of court witnesses and court trustees, merchants and notables accompanied

[44] Ibn Ḥajar, ed. Guest, 590. For the role of members of the Nuʿmān family in delivering textiles from Egypt's Mediterranean towns to the court, see Maqrīzī, *Ittiʿāẓ*, I, 283. There is an interesting precedent from Kāfūr's rule: it is said that the cadi of Asyūṭ gave him every year a present of textiles worth of 50,000 *dīnārs*. See Ibn Ẓāfir, ed. ʿAlī ʿUmar, 80.

[45] Ibn Ḥajar, ed. Guest 585; Tillier, *Vies des cadis*, 180.

ʿAlī ibn al-Nuʿmān from Azhar to his home, and three days later to the Ancient Mosque in Fusṭāṭ. ʿAlī ordered al-Dhuhlī to move his court from the mosque to his home, and he understood that his career was over and resigned. His supporters remained loyal to him to the very end, some of the more vocal ones being arrested by the chief of police and later on released on ʿAlī's intervention. ʿAli was so cautious in his approach to al-Dhuhlī that he even refrained from inquiring about the court archive (*dīwān al-ḥukm*).[46]

The regime's tolerance of al-Dhuhlī as a parallel cadi for nine years is indicative of its pragmatism, which should not obscure the fact that the long-term goal was to grant Ismāʿīlī law a dominant position in the state, ʿAlī ibn al-Nuʿmān being the one to implement the policy. The way he carried out the task assigned to him is illuminating: in addition to appointing his brother as deputy he also set a precedent of deputing Sunnī jurists on condition they would apply the Fatimid law. His choice of deputy was a Shāfiʿī jurist, al-Ḥasan ibn Khalīl.[47] The Fatimid paradox – the need to administer justice in Egypt while Ismāʿīlī law had been just created – is here fully illustrated. Apparently there were as yet no trained Ismāʿīlī jurists, and any willing and competent jurist could master the unique features of the Fatimid law and serve as an Ismāʿīlī cadi. Another way of understanding the appointment is to argue that the appointed jurist applied the Fatimd law only in cases in which it diverged from the Shāfiʿī school of law.[48]

The drive to grant the Fatimid law a predominant position in the state was, however, complicated by the rivalry between the Nuʿmān family and the vizier Ibn Killis, whose intervention in the administration of justice went back to al-Muʿizz's reign and the Abī Ibn Thawbān affair in which Ibn Killis played the role of advisor behind the scenes, keen to distance his master from the deeds of others. His struggle against the Nuʿmāns was different: personal and uncompromising. In 980, Ibn Killis appointed ʿAlī ibn Saʿīd al-Juljūlī chief of the Lower Police in Fusṭāṭ and he began to act as cadi too. Usually,

[46] Ibn Khallikān, V, 417; Maqrīzī, *Kitāb al-Muqaffā*, V, 198.

[47] Ibn Ḥajar, ed. Guest, 589–90.

[48] For the differences between Fatimid law and Sunnī schools of law, including marriage, see Fyzee, 'The Fatimid Law of Inheritance', 61–70. Some of Qāḍī al-Nuʿmān's legal writings are characterised by a compromise between Imāmī and Zaydī law. See Madelung, 'The Sources of Ismāʿīlī Law', 29–40. For broader discussion see Cilardo, *The Early History of I Ismāʿīlī Jurisprudence*, 9–21.

the separation between the judicial authority of the cadi and criminal justice administered by the chief of police was clearly maintained, but with some initiative on al-Julјūlī's part the line was easily crossed. This development destabilised the system and friction was inevitable. A litigant whose case was adjudicated by al-Juljūlī complained to the vizier that ʿAlī ibn al-Nuʿmān disapproved of the judgment issued in his case. The vizier pronounced that each cadi is independent in his decisions and that no one was allowed to appeal to the other judge.[49] This dictate was a rule-breaking pronouncement: Ibn Killis created ex-nihilo, so to speak, a position of cadi without formal authorisation and with no letter of appointment.

Ibn Killis's intervention in the administration of justice was opportunistic and, from the Fatimid point of view, detrimental. Furthermore, the overall policies of the regime are difficult to gauge. In 978, for example, Ibn Killis invited to Egypt Aḥmad ibn al-Minhāl, described as an Ismāʿīlī cadi who replaced Qāḍī al-Nuʿmān as cadi of Tunis, Manṣūriyya and Kairouan. Upon his arrival he was officially entrusted with responsibility for the *maẓālim* court in Fusṭāṭ and the whole of Egypt. In another version of events, the cadi sought refuge with the Fatimids. In any case, his arrival enjoyed al-ʿAzīz's support and an official letter of appointment was issued to him. This move can be interpreted as signifying a further Ismailisation of the judicial system since people were granted the opportunity to appeal to a Fatimid cadi when dissatisfied with judgments passed by other cadis in the service of the regime, whose method of deriving rulings remains unknown. Ibn al-Minhāl, however, was also allowed to serve as cadi, and most of the litigants in Fusṭāṭ preferred him over ʿAlī ibn al-Nuʿmān. Ibn Ḥajar, who wrote for his contemporary fifteenth-century readers, explains that Ibn al-Minhāl was not deputed by ʿAlī ibn al-Nuʿmān and that the Fatimids allowed two official cadis to serve in a town. Notwithstanding Ibn Ḥajar's need to explain what seemed to him as an anomaly, it appears that the explanation for Minhāl's appointment must be sought in the realm of Ibn Killi's rivalry with ʿAlī ibn al-Nuʿmān. Ibn Killis also challenged the authority of the Nuʿmān family in the legal sphere. He composed a book of law, which must have enjoyed popularity and which, after his death in 1025, was taught by the Fatimid propagandists. Ibn Killis's

[49] Ibn Ḥajar, ed. Guest, 591.

encroachment on the judicial domain of the Nuʿmāns can be explained by his close personal relations with al-ʿAzīz and his extraordinary position at the court. It can also be said that any autocrat encourages competition among his subordinates to enhance their dependence on him. In this case the competition, which continued until Ibn Killis's death in 990, brought havoc in the way justice was administered and was counter-productive in terms of the Ismailisation of the judicial system.[50]

ʿAli died on 6 Rajab 374/3 December 984, and the prayers at the funeral were conducted by al-ʿAzīz himself. On 23 Rajab/20 December his brother Muḥammad (born 951) was appointed cadi, but the ceremony was marked by his sickness and inability to attend the full event. He was given the insignia of the cadi, a cloak and sword, and entrusted with the supreme judicial authority in Egypt (the capital Cairo-Fusṭāṭ and Alexandria are specifically mentioned), the holy cities of Arabia and Syria. Whether the Fatimids exerted any influence over the nomination of cadis in Mecca and Medina is doubtful. More meaningful were other responsibilities conferred on him, which included the supervision of prayers, inheritances and the *ʿiyār* function.

In the beginning, Muḥammad's nomination did not disrupt inter-family relations and the newly-appointed cadi authorised his nephew Ḥusayn ibn ʿAlī to serve as a cadi. In Alexandria, Muḥammad deputed his son Abū l-Qāsim ʿAbd al-ʿAzīz to serve as cadi and this move enjoyed the support and authorisation of al-ʿAzīz. This nomination was in line with the drive of the Nuʿmān family for presence and influence in Egypt's Mediterranean port towns and, in this case, family and state interests tallied. The situation in Damascus was more complex since at the time of Muḥammad's appointment the cadi who served there was ʿAbd Allāh ibn Muḥammad ibn Rajāʾ, whose position was unaffected by Muḥammad's appointment. Only upon his death was the declaration that Muḥammad wields judicial authority over Syria implemented. Muḥammad's son Abū l-Qāsim ʿAbd al-ʿAzīz was deputed by his father to serve as cadi of Damascus and replaced in Alexandria by Muḥammad's nephew Jaʿfar ibn Aḥmad ibn al-Nuʿmān.[51]

In 985, Muḥammad's branch of the Nuʿmān family entered what might

[50] Ibn Ḥajar, ed. Guest, 591–2; Maqrīzī, *Ittiʿāẓ*, II, 175; *Kitāb al-Muqaffā*, I, 655–6.

[51] Maqrīzī, *Kitāb al-Muqaffā*, VII, 347–8, 349.

be described as strategic marriage alliances with the Jawhar family when Muḥammad's son married Jawhar's daughter. As might be expected at that high level of the ruling establishment, the marriage was sanctioned by al-ʿAzīz and turned into a court event. When intra-Nuʿmān family relations are considered, it may be said that collaboration and the sharing of judicial appointments between the two branches of the family were short-lived. Muḥmmad's drive to raise his family branch to a prominent position brought about the dismissal of Ḥusayn ibn ʿAlī in 987.[52] In 993, perhaps because of illness and a wish to enhance his son's position, Muḥammad conferred judicial duties in Cairo and Fusṭāṭ on his son Abū l-Qāsim ʿAbd al-ʿAzīz. The appointment came after an earlier move in 992 when Muḥammad deputed Mālik ibn Saʿīd al-Fāriqī to be cadi of Cairo.[53]

Although Muḥammad's position as cadi enjoyed firm state support, the usual considerations and constraints that governed cadi conduct also applied to him. He sought public support for his judgments and, like many of his predecessors, began his term in office by appointing about thirty new witnesses, while in early 991 his son appointed new witnesses among the *ashrāf*. Arabic medieval terminology pertaining to social classes is imprecise, and in this context the term refers either to Shīʿī families of the Hasanid and Husaynid lines or to urban notables in general. This move illustrates the cadi's need, no matter how powerful he was, to seek social support for his position and judgments and, irrespective of our understanding of the term *ashrāf*, this support was sought among the upper urban echelon.[54]

Whatever social support Muḥammad could have derived from the nomination of new witnesses, the struggle with Ibn Killis went on unabated and the vizier's intervention in judicial affairs continued. In 985, for example, Muḥammad was criticised for granting permission to marry to a girl who was not legally of mature age and the vizier brought the affair to the attention of al-ʿAzīz, who nullified the marriage. The vizier also asserted his dominance over the cadi by summoning him and his court witnesses and rebuking them for their carelessness. Only following the death of Ibn Killis did the

[52] Ibn Khallikān, V, 419–20; Maqrīzī, *Kitāb al-Muqaffā*, III, 620.
[53] Ibn Khallikān, V, 421; Maqrīzī, *Ittiʿāẓ*, I, 275.
[54] Ibn Ḥajar, ed. Guest, 593, 594.

Nuʿmāns consolidate their position as the leading family of jurists with deep involvement in the state's affairs. In 993, Muḥammad became involved in the management of state finances while another member of the family (Yaḥyā ibn al-Nuʿmān) supervised the delivery of textiles produced in Tinnīs and Damietta to the court. In 993, Muḥammad ibn al-Nuʿmān was also assigned to lecture on the lore of the Prophet's family (*ʿulūm āl al-bayt*) at the palace, attracting great crowds. These appointments solidified Muḥammad's position and quite naturally he performed the last rites for al-ʿAzīz at his burial. He also paid him the last tribute at the festival of The Breaking of Ramaḍān when, ascending the *minbar*, he kissed the place where al-ʿAzīz used to sit.[55]

Quite naturally, the cadis of the Nuʿmān family were committed to enforcing the application of the Fatimid law, the creation of their father, and Abū l-Qāsim ʿAbd al-ʿAzīz appointed a Shīʿī person (Jaʿfarī) to issue legal opinion according to *madhhab ahl al-bayt*, meaning Fatimid law. He must have done so in his capacity as cadi of Cairo-Fusṭāṭ, but the nomination was opposed by jurists in the Ancient Mosque in Fusṭāṭ. Some protesters were punished by a public parade in the town, a widely practised type of punishment known as *tashhīr* (shaming).[56] Apparently, the logic behind the appointment was to create a body of legal opinion based on Fatimid law and to encourage cadis to mould their judgments on them or to allow litigants to challenge judgments issued by Sunnī cadis by relying on those legal opinions. To what extent this rather bold and original attempt at gradual Ismailisation of the judicial system succeeded remains unknown. The originality of the move lies in its attempt to Ismailise the law from above by providing a Fatimid legal framework that could be referred to without changing the judicial personnel. Any Sunnī cadi knowing that his judgment could be challenged through reliance on legal opinions inspired by Fatimid law would think twice before issuing a judgment.

Muḥammad is praised by both Ibn Zūlāq and Musabbiḥī for his personal qualities, his manners, his open-handness and the way he executed his judicial duties, and these praises are difficult to harmonise with the accusations concerning embezzlement of the orphan's fund. Furthermore, the impression

[55] Maqrīzī, *Ittiʿāẓ*, I, 277, 283, 285, 292.
[56] Ibn Ḥajar, ed. Guest, 594.

is that this went on for a long time and was widely known about, and that the regime turned a blind eye. Changes came only following Muḥammad's death on 4 Ṣafar 389/25 January 999.[57] The post of cadi remained vacant for nineteen days and, eventually, in spite of his physical weakness and contrary to expectations, Ḥusayn ibn ʿAlī ibn al-Nuʿmān was nominated as cadi. He was summoned to the palace and cautioned not to take money from people, and al-Ḥākim shared with him his view as to why the embezzlement of the orphan's fund had taken place: cadi remuneration was not high enough. Ḥusayn's overall pay was increased, and included gifts and incomes from grants of land (*iqṭāʿ*), and al-Ḥākim told him: 'I have enriched you and you have no need to take money belonging to Muslims.'[58] Maqrīzī, relying on Musabbiḥī, provides a rare insight into al-Ḥākim's mindset: people were driven by greed, while he, knowing their weakness, lavished on them money and gifts. If al-Ḥākim's mindset as revealed by this conversation is correctly interpreted, it offers a clue to understanding his generosity towards low-ranking employees of the state and commoners. It also explains his insistence that his killings were not motivated by greed.

At that time of Muḥammad's death, he owed 20,000 *dīnārs* to the orphans' fund and the trustees who handled the money were required to submit their accounts. Muḥammad's son and his clerk were asked to provide explanations, and they claimed that the money from the orphans' fund was given to various people in the form of loans. The recovery effort was vigorously supervised by Fahd ibn Ibrāhīm, the Christian scribe of the eunuch Barjawān who was the strongman behind the scenes and instrumental in Ḥusayn's nomination. Eventually, Ḥusayn ordered the sale of his uncle's estate, which yielded 7,039 *dīnārs*, and 4,000 *dīnārs* were recovered from trustees and witnesses, but 9,000 *dīnārs* were still missing. The cadi also ordered a reorganisation of the way the fund was handled and the money held by trustees and witnesses was transferred to a new depository established at Zuqāq al-Qanādīl Street in Fusṭāṭ. Any withdrawal of money from the depository required the testimony of four witnesses.[59]

[57] The prayers at his funeral were performed by al-Ḥākim. Ibn Khallikān, V, 420, 421; Ibn Ḥajar, ed. Guest, 592.

[58] Maqrīzī, *Ittiʿāẓ*, II, 22–3; *Kitāb al-Muqaffā*, III, 621.

[59] Maqrīzī, *Kitāb al-Muqaffā*, III, 622. For other sets of figures and the claim that the

Ḥusayn's investiture ceremony and letter of appointment were in line with the Fatimid tradition established in Egypt: he was given a sword and vested with judicial authority over Cairo, Fusṭāṭ and Alexandria, and the usual phraseology also asserted that his authority extended over Syria, Arabia and the Maghreb. In addition, he was entrusted with overall responsibility for the performance of prayers and preaching at the mosques and given the authority to supervise the mint, the *ʿiyār* and the *ḥisba*. In line with the family drive to control important spheres of economic activity, Ḥusayn appointed his brother cadi of Alexandria and conferred on him responsibility for the *ʿiyār*. Other judicial appointments were given to people outside the family: Ḥusayn ibn Muḥammad ibn Ṭāhir was deputed to serve as cadi of Fusṭāṭ and Mālik ibn Saʿīd al-Fāriqī to serve as cadi of Cairo. Inheritance cases (*furūḍ*) were delegated to Aḥmad ibn Muḥammad ibn Abī l-ʿAwwām, who was also given responsibility for the orphan's fund. Ḥusayn was also entrusted with responsibility for the Fatimid propaganda (*daʿwa*) and the teaching of Ismailism at the palace (*majālis al-ḥikma*).[60]

Ḥusayn did not enjoy undisputed judicial predominance for long, and his authority was challenged by another member of the extended Nuʿmān family. The difficulties began with the nomination of Muḥammad's son Abū l-Qāsim ʿAbd al-ʿAzīz to the *maẓālim* court (3 Rajab 390/9 June 1000), and he was also authorised to accept oral evidence supplied by witnesses (*bayyina*). His letter of appointment was read at the Ancient Mosque in Fusṭāṭ and, within a few months, the judicial system was wrecked by disputes and quarrels since people wondered who was in charge of the jurisdiction, especially as some witnesses refused to co-operate with Abū l-Qāsim ʿAbd al-ʿAzīz. The accounts convey the impression that in this case the *maẓālim* court actually served as an appeal instantia.

Relations between the Nuʿmān family and the Fatimid rulers were complex, and why al-ʿAzīz or al-Ḥākim preferred one branch of the family to the other remains beyond our grasp. It seems that in this case the disruption of the system that followed Abū l-Qāsim ʿAbd al-ʿAzīz's nomination was

debt was as high as 36,000 *dīnārs*, see Ibn Ḥajar, ed. Guest, 595; Maqrīzī, *Ittiʿāẓ*, II, 21–2.

[60] Ibn Ḥajar, ed. Guest, 596–7 (quoting Musabbiḥī); Maqrīzī, *Ittiʿāẓ*, II, 24; *Kitāb al-Muqaffā*, III, 623.

a completely unforeseen result, and the regime was quick to minimise the damage by issuing a letter to Ḥusayn which stated that he was trusted as cadi and propagandist and was in charge of the jurisdiction. The formula that ended al-Dhuhlī's career, which stated that if one of the litigants prefers a cadi the other must comply, was reused to settle a completely different type of dispute. In this case the two competing cadis were Ismāʿīlīs, but if one litigant preferred one of them the other had to comply. In order to leave no doubt as to the regime's preferences Ḥusayn was given the title of supreme cadi and instructed to use it, while people were ordered to address him in that way. Al-Ḥākim's address to Ḥusayn ends with the proclamation 'Exercise your judgments with God's help and ours'.[61] Al-Ḥākim's self-allusion as the supreme judicial authority reveals the gap between Sunnī and Ismāʿīlī legal thinking: by the year 1000 the *madhhab* paradigm constituted the framework of the Sunnī legal system, while in Ismāʿīlī Islam, as during the seventh to eighth centuries, the opinion of the ruler mattered. Although by that time Ismāʿīlī law had already been formulated, it was subjected to the higher authority of the *imām*, reflecting his pivotal role in the Ismāʿīlī universe.

Ḥusayn, like many others, did not survive al-Ḥākim's reign: he was dismissed from his post and later executed, in 1005. Earlier, in 1001, he had survived an assassination attempt and a large bodyguard unit had accompanied him since then, but no one could save him from the wrath of the monarch. Musabbiḥī, quoted by Maqrīzī, offers an explanation for Ḥusayn's execution, claiming that someone complained to al-Ḥākim that the cadi had withheld an inheritance worth 20,000 *dīnārs* which had been deposited with him. The accusation was verified and Ḥusayn repented and begged forgiveness. The explanation inspires little confidence and seems apologetic, aiming to explain why the *imām* turned against a staunch Ismāʿīlī supporter.[62]

On 16 Ramaḍān 394/7 July 1004, Abū l-Qāsim ʿAbd al-ʿAzīz ibn Muḥammad al-Nuʿmān was nominated as cadi of the realm, and titled as follows:

[61] Maqrīzī, *Ittiʿāẓ*, II, 40–1; *Kitāb al-Muqaffā*, III, 624, 626–7.

[62] Maqrīzī, *Ittiʿāẓ*, II, 59; *Kitāb al-Muqaffā*, III, 630 (quoting Musabbiḥī); Ibn Ḥajar, ed. Guest, 596–7, 598–9, offers the same explanation, quoting Ibn Raqīq's *Ta'rīkh al-Ifrīqiyya*. It seems that this account is also derived from Musabbiḥī and cannot be considered independent verification.

> The supreme cadi ʿAbd al-ʿAzīz, the cadi of the servant of God and His friend Manṣūr Abī ʿAlī Imām al-Ḥākim, Commander of the Faithful, God's prayers for him and his pure ancestors, [is appointed to] Cairo al-Muʿizziya, Fusṭāṭ, Alexandria, the two holy cities of Arabia, the Syrian provinces, Raḥba, Raqqa, the provinces of the Maghreb and what God had conquered and will conquer for the Commander of the Faithful from the lands of the east and west.[63]

This formula neatly summarises the *imām*'s view of himself as ruler by God's grace and the supreme cadi's dependence on him. Ibn Ḥajar's citation of the letter of appointment is, however, partial since the range of Abū l-Qāsim ʿAbd al-ʿAzīz's responsibilities was more extensive. During his term in office he held responsibility for the *maẓālim* court and the pious endowments of mosques. He was also appointed supreme propagandist of the Fatimid state with responsibility for a range of activities, including teaching Ismāʿīlī law, and his book of choice was his grandfather's *Ikhtilāf Uṣūl al-Madhāhib* (see Chapter 2). His other tasks involved the supervision of the Dār al-ʿIlm, the learning institution established by al-Ḥākim, and the collection of taxes (*najwa* and *fiṭra*) paid by Ismāʿīlī believers.

Abū l-Qāsim ʿAbd al-ʿAzīz also introduced many personal changes within the judicial system. He deputed Abū l-Ḥasan Mālik ibn Mālik ibn Saʿīd al-Fāriqī to serve as cadi in Fusṭāṭ and dismissed many of the provincial cadis appointed by Ḥusayn, replacing them with his own appointees.[64] On 16 Rajab 398/27 March 1008, however, Abū l-Qāsim ʿAbd al-ʿAzīz was dismissed and replaced by Mālik ibn Saʿīd al-Fāriqī. This change in fortunes took Abū l-Qāsim ʿAbd al-ʿAzīz by total surprise, but the dismissal did not mark the end of his career. For a short period of time during late 1009 and 1010 he was in charge of the *maẓālim* court. He was executed in 1011.[65]

One can view the nomination of al-Fāriqī as supreme cadi as marking

[63] Ibn Ḥajar, ed. Guest, 599–600.

[64] Maqrīzī, *Ittiʿāẓ*, II, 50; Ibn Ḥajar, ed. Guest, 601. For the establishment of the Dār al-ʿIlm, see al-Anṭākī, 188; Halm, *The Fatimids and Their Traditions of Learning*, 71–8. For the fortunes and misfortunes of al-Fāriqī family, see Walker, 'Another Family of Fatimid Chief Qāḍīs', 49–69.

[65] Maqrīzī, *Ittiʿāẓ*, II, 71, 73, 74, 77, 78, 82, 85, 86–7, for Abū l-Qāsim ʿAbd al-ʿAzīz's fall from favour and demise; Ibn Ḥajar, ed. Guest, 602–3.

an important shift from Ismāʿīlī cadis to outsiders, but nothing changed in the state's perception of the cadi's role. The appointment ceremony followed the usual Fatimid protocol for such occasions: the letter of appointment was read first in the palace (more specifically at the Treasury). Later, the newly appointed cadi, equipped with sword and dressed in gold-embroidered attire, accompanied by a huge procession paraded to the Ancient Mosque in Fusṭāṭ. From the beginning of his term in office al-Fārikī was entrusted with responsibility for the *daʿwa* (i.e. Fatimid propaganda and/or the teaching of Ismailism). Al-Fāriqī had to depute a cadi to take over his position as cadi of Cairo, and he selected Ḥamza ibn ʿAlī ibn Yaʿqūb al-Ghalbūnī, but this appointment proved problematic. Al-Fāriqī had to dismiss him following a complaint and Ḥamza went into hiding, but was captured and executed.[66] The whole mishap bore no negative consequences for al-Fāriqī, who skilfully proved how to survive al-Ḥākim's reign of terror, for some time. He won for himself a name as a generous person. It might have been a genuine generosity or an instrumental survival technique, a mimicking of the deeds of al-Ḥākim, whose gift-giving became notorious rather than famous since it was perceived as a squandering of state resources. Al-Fāriqī was instrumental in bestowing largesse on the Shīʿī notables of Mecca and Medina on behalf of al-Ḥākim, and conferred gifts and *iqṭāʿ* grants on others.[67] Al-Fāriqī's generosity also took place in the judicial arena. He is depicted as a kind of 'social-worker' cadi who helped the poor who appeared at his court. One case is particularly illuminating: a man who had stolen a silver lamp from the Ancient Mosque was brought for trial before al-Fāriqī and admitted the stealing of 'my God's money', but defiantly argued that he was a poor person who had to take care of the marriage of his daughters, declaring that 'spending on them is better than this thing hung at the mosque'. The scene turned emotional, with the poor man weeping and the cadi soothing him and eventually providing 3,000 *dīnārs* for the daughters' marriage.[68] The whole account moves between the harsh realities of everyday life, in which securing a proper marriage for girls depended on the ability to provide a dowry, and the ancient monotheistic

[66] Ibn Ḥajar, ed. Guest, 604, 608–9; Maqrīzī, *Ittiʿāẓ*, II, 72.
[67] Ibn Ḥajar, ed. Guest, 605–6.
[68] Ibn Ḥajar, ed. Guest, 607.

dilemma, whether funds dedicated to God should serve religious institutions (or, in another context, the Church) or the poor.

Al-Fāriqī was executed on 25 Rabīʿ II 405/23 October 1014. He had enjoyed a long judicial career of two decades and for six years had served as supreme cadi, a period which was marked by a complete blurring of judicial and administrative duties and a constant preoccupation with state affairs at the expense of judicial obligations. Al-Fāriqī's judicial/administrative duties involved the supervision of the *maẓālim* court (from 1011), pious endowments, the mint, the *dār al-ʿiyār* and *daʿwa*. His other administrative responsibilities can be described as clerical, and included reading the correspondence of both provincial governors and Fatimid propagandists addressed to al-Ḥākim, and paying them.[69] Under al-Ḥākim the supreme cadis were increasingly drawn into the state orbit and had to deal with state affairs. They had little choice, as they lived under awe-inspiring monarchs who ruled through a reign of terror. As long as al-Ḥākim favoured al-Fāriqī it was a most rewarding association both personally and materially. Al-Fāriqī lived in Cairo, dined at al-Ḥākim's table and was handsomely rewarded by generous payments and grants of property.[70]

Following the killing of al-Fāriqī no cadi was appointed for a period of around three months, and the nomination process is described as a series of consultations between al-Ḥākim and members of the Dār al-ʿIlm, who recommended the Ḥanafī jurist Aḥmad ibn Muḥammad ibn Abī l-ʿAwwām, scion of a well-established learned family. The recommendation was accompanied by the revealing explanation that the candidate was a trustworthy person, a Miṣrī (i.e. a person from Fusṭāṭ) who knew the people of the town and was knowledgeable in judicial matters (*qaḍāʾ*). They were, of course, aware of the legal differences between the ruler and the jurist, but insisted that Ibn Abī l-ʿAwwām's advantages outweighed this hindrance, and al-Ḥākim agreed with them.[71] One is surprised that people who belonged to an institution set up by al-Ḥākim were asked for their opinion at all, and at their boldness in emphasising the local and Sunnī characteristics of their candidate, implying

[69] Ibn Ḥajar, ed. Guest, 608; Maqrīzī, *Ittiʿāẓ*, II, 85, 106–7.

[70] Ibn Ḥajar, ed. Guest, 605, 606.

[71] Ibn Ḥajar, ed. Guest, 610.

the foreign character of the dynasty that remained unaltered even after four decades of Fatimid rule.

When seen within the wider context of the judicial situation in the Fatimid capital the recommendation seems less surprising, since Ibn Abī l-ʿAwwām was part of the Fatimid system of administration of justice. In 994, Muḥammad ibn al-Nuʿmān appointed him as a court witness and, in 999, Ḥusayn ibn ʿAlī appointed him to judge inheritance cases as deputy of the cadi of Fusṭāṭ. In this capacity he surely had to apply the Fatimid law; therefore, the Ḥanafī background of Ibn Abī l-ʿAwwām posed no difficulties.[72]

On 21 Shaʿbān 405/14 February 1015, he was inaugurated as supreme cadi. The customary dual ceremony, taking place at the palace and Ancient Mosque, was performed and he was invested with judicial authority over the Fatimid realm: Fusṭāṭ, Cairo, Alexandria, Egypt's provinces, Syria, the holy cities of Arabia, Barqa, the Maghreb and Sicily. In Palestine judicial authority was, however, in the hands of another cadi. Ibn Abī l-ʿAwwām was also invested with the usual sweeping responsibilities for the performing of prayers and sermons in the mosques, the pious endowments of mosques, the mints in the Fatimid territories, and paying salaries and rendering charitable payments. He also wielded responsibility for inheritance cases, and four jurists were placed at his court to ensure that his judgments were in accordance with the legal precepts of the dynasty.

Ibn Abī l-ʿAwwām had a busy weekly schedule and divided his time between the Ancient Mosque in Fusṭāṭ (Mondays and Thursdays) and the Azhar Mosque in Cairo (Tuesdays), while Sundays he spent at the palace, informing al-Ḥākim about judicial affairs and cases. On Fridays he accompanied al-Ḥākim for prayers, but Wednesday he kept as a day of seclusion and worship at a house he bought in the cemetery.

Two of Ibn Abī l-ʿAwwām's deeds as cadi are singled out by his biographers, although their context and implications remain vague. He moved the cadis' archives from the cadis' houses to the Treasury kept at the Ancient Mosque in Fusṭāṭ and dismissed 400 witnesses out of 1,500. Ibn Abī l-ʿAwwām's greatest luck, or achievement, was to survive the events associated with the preaching of Ḥamza ibn ʿAlī, who propagated the cult

[72] Maqrīzī, *Kitāb al-Muqaffā*, I, 604.

of al-Ḥākim. Ḥamza's associates came to the Ancient Mosque, announcing God's incarnation in al-Ḥākim, and three of them demanded Ibn Abī l-ʿAwwām read a letter to that effect. He refused, saying that he must first confer with al-Ḥākim. Eventually, Ḥamza and his associates were killed in violence that erupted in the wake of their preaching, but the cadi escaped these events unscathed, as well as al-Ḥākim's wrath for the killing of Ḥamza and his men. Ibn Abī l-ʿAwwām not only survived these violent events, he also survived al-Ḥākim's demise and retained his position during the transition from al-Ḥākim to al-Ẓāhir. He died on 20 Rabiʿ I 416/21 May 1025.[73]

Behind the Scenes of the Fatimid Judicial System: The Social World of the Supreme Cadi

Ibn Abī l-ʿAwwām's remarkable career is a convenient point to shift the discussion from legal issues to the social context in which Fatimid supreme cadis of the tenth and eleventh centuries operated. The sources are rich enough to allow such discussion, especially the surviving sections of Musabbiḥī's chronicle, which offer glimpses behind the scenes of the Fatimid judicial system beyond what Ibn Ḥajar and Maqrīzī have to offer.

Qāḍī al-Nuʿmān, the father of the Nuʿmān dynasty, lived in Fusṭāṭ and commuted daily to Cairo. At first glance his choice of residence seems strange, since one would expect him to prefer Cairo over Fusṭāṭ. However, many Maghribians who came to Egypt with Jawhar and al-Muʿizz (in 969 and 973) settled in Fusṭāṭ and lived there during the reigns of al-ʿAzīz and al-Ḥākim (975–1021). What happened to the Nuʿmān family residence following the death of Qāḍī al-Nuʿmān remains unclear. His son Muḥammad lived in, or had a house in, Cairo while Ḥusayn ibn ʿAlī lived in the Ḥamrā' district of Fusṭāṭ along the canal, and the house was a gift from al-Ḥākim. The connection of the Ismāʿīlī cadis of the Nuʿmān family with Fusṭāṭ went beyond the question of their place of domicile as they held court sessions in the Ancient Mosque on Mondays and Thursdays, and the same was true for

[73] Ibn Ḥajar, ed. Guest, 610–11, 612; Maqrīzī, *Kitāb al-Muqaffā*, I, 603–6; *Ittiʿāẓ*, II, 108–9, 110, alluding to the cadi's involvement with the Ismāʿīlī *daʿwa*. For these events and the teachings associated with al-Darazī and Ḥamza, see Hodgson, 'Al-Darazī and Ḥamza in the Origin of the Druze Religion', 5–20, including a chronology of events; Bryer, 'The Origins of the Druze Religion', 5–27.

Mālik ibn Saʿīd al-Fāriqī.[74] One can perceive the Ismāʿīlī supreme cadis of the Nuʿmān family as a link between (perhaps even a kind of go-between) the ruler and the Sunnī population of the capital city, a factor much emphasised in support of Ibn Abī l-ʿAwwām's nomination.

Musabbiḥī's reports allow us to re-examine the sweeping assertions about the supreme cadis' responsibilities as stated in their letters of appointment. Undoubtedly, these letters were empowering documents and explicit references to that effect can be found in the sources. An eleventh-century cadi in Damascus owed his appointment to the supreme cadi in Cairo, but in many other cases the realities were far more complex. The possibility of appointing a supreme cadi without a letter of appointment (*bi-ghayr taqlīd*) is alluded to once during the eleventh century.[75] Musabbiḥī's narrative indicates that the appointment of cadis to key towns such as Tinnīs and Ramla (the most important town in Palestine) was done directly by the regime and not through the supreme cadi. This is clearly borne out by the appointment ceremony of Abī l-Faraj ibn Mālik ibn Saʿīd al-Fāriqī as cadi of Tinnīs (1st Jumada II 414/23 June 1023). He was draped in golden dress that included a head-cap and mantle which resembled the golden clothing in which the supreme cadis of al-Ḥākim's period were dressed on appointment ceremonies.[76] These woven gold items were considered state insignia and bestowed on appointees at the investiture ceremonies of state officials. It is quite possible that the supreme cadi had the power to depute cadis to serve in less significant provincial towns, but appointments to key provincial towns remained the privilege of the ruler.

Other disparities between responsibilities vested through letters of appointment and day-to-day realities are also revealed. Fatimid supreme cadis were granted authority to oversee the performance of prayers and sermons at the mosques, but this does not mean that they were not challenged by others. In 1024, the preacher at the Rāshida congregational mosque in Cairo went to Tyre in the company of the newly appointed governor. The supreme cadi Ibn Abī l-ʿAwwām exercised his authority and appointed Abū

[74] Ibn Ḥajar, ed. Guest, 587, 594, 599, 604.
[75] Maqrīzī, *Kitāb al-Muqaffā*, I, 209, II, 90.
[76] Musabbiḥī, 3; Ibn Ḥajar, ed. Guest, 604, 610–11.

Ṭālib ʿAlī ibn ʿAbd al-Samīʿ al-ʿAbbāsī as preacher at the mosque. One of the palace eunuchs, however, appointed another preacher (Ibn ʿUṣfūra) and a compromise between the two had to be worked out. Eventually, the appointee of the unnamed palace eunuch came to serve as replacement for ʿAbd al-Samīʿ al-ʿAbbāsī, but, significantly, the superior authority of a long-serving, well-established supreme cadi over a eunuch of the court was not a foregone conclusion.[77]

It seems that other activities that took place at mosques were not affected at all by letters of appointment issued to Fatimid supreme cadis. In 1087, Ibn al-Jawharī, who had been the *wāʿiẓ* (preacher, admonisher) in the Ancient Mosque in Fusṭāṭ, died. He is described as belonging to a family with a long tradition of *waʿẓ* and learning. Fatimid rule and Ismailisation of the law and religious life had no effect on the family involved in this occupation and the tradition of *waʿẓ* continued well into the twelfth century.[78]

Supreme cadis were also involved in matters that went beyond the functions and responsibilities mentioned in their letters of appointment. This involvement was a reflection of the fact that letters of appointment elevated the supreme cadi to the rank of the ruling establishment, which applied to all of them, not only to members of the Nuʿmān family. Ibn Abī l-ʿAwwām, for example, was asked to supervise works done on the Nilometer, and his involvement was required because of enmity between two state dignitaries: the Nilometer's supervisor and the person in charge of the arsenal.[79]

Perhaps the greatest merit of Musabbiḥī's chronicle is that it sheds light on matters beyond the functional aspects of the Fatimid judicial system: it highlights the diversified social circles in which the supreme cadi moved, which included his immediate professional milieu, the wider learned class and the people of the court. In April 1024, the supreme cadi attended and performed prayers at two funerals in Fusṭāṭ. The first was of a court witness Ibn Ḥājj Yaḥyā who was from Seville and is described as a learned jurist. The second funeral was of Abī Muḥammad ibn Yaḥyā al-Daqqāq (a flour merchant), who is characterised as 'the most illustrious master among the trans-

[77] Musabbiḥī, 9–10, 63.
[78] Ibn Muyassar, 49, 120, referring to the family history in 1144.
[79] Musabbiḥī, 39, 41.

mitters of traditions and historians who transmitted the history and events of Egypt [*akhbār* and *ḥawādith*]'. He was a scion of a learned family and left a large and diverse library.[80] These two men were distinguished members of the learned class towards whom the supreme cadi most likely was personally obliged. This class was made up of people who pursued different intellectual interests and the supreme cadi must have been involved with many of them on different levels.

In other funerals the presence of the supreme cadi and his prayers for the dead were more a courtesy and a social obligation than the expression of personal commitment. The supreme cadi, for example, performed the prayers at the funeral of a woman belonging to Jawhar's extended family. In August 1024, Qāsim, the brother of a high-ranking Shīʿī notable of the Husaynid line, who was notorious for his obnoxious character and immorality, died, but all state dignitaries attended his funeral. In this case, the Husaynid lineage more than the personality of the deceased was honoured and the presence of the upper echelon of the state was a mere formality. A sense of ceremonial obligation rather than personal involvement is also evident in two other funerals attended by the supreme cadi: on 25 Jumada I 414/15 August 1023, an unnamed woman died who is identified only through the names of other people. She is referred to as 'the daughter of', 'the wife of' and 'the mother of'. Her son was a court witness and her slave girl a singer with ties to several royal women. The main participants at her funeral were eunuchs of the court. A few days later, the supreme cadi and the most powerful man in the state at that time, the black eunuch Miʿḍād, attended the funeral of a *kātib* (clerk, secretary) at the Treasury.[81]

Other events brought the supreme cadi into the close circle of the ruler. As might be expected, during prayers on the Day of The Breaking of the Fast of Ramaḍān, the supreme cadi was seated on the pulpit behind the ruler. He was also present at sad events that involved the ruling family: during 1023–4 three of al-Ẓāhir's children died, a three-year-old girl, a boy and an heir apparent. They were buried in the family tomb of the Fatimid *imāms*, and the person responsible for the ritual washing of the corpses and

[80] Musabbiḥī, 92.
[81] Musabbiḥī, 92–3.

prayers was the supreme propagandist Qāsim ibn ʿAbd Allāh al-Nuʿmān though the supreme cadi Ibn Abī l-ʿAwwām was also present. One can hardly imagine two persons with more different backgrounds: one was a scion of a veteran Ismāʿīlī family in the service of the Fatimids and the other a Ḥanafī jurist with strong local ties.[82] It seems that it was the traditional role of the supreme propagandist to perform burial rites for members of the extended royal family. On the death al-Muʿizz's son the emir ʿAbd Allāh in 974, the corpse was washed by al-Qāḍī al-Nuʿmān and the prayers at the funeral were performed by al-Muʿizz himself. During the time period reflected by Musabbiḥī's chronicle it can be said that the supreme propagandist and the supreme cadi moved in different social circles, and that of the supreme cadi was wider and more diversified than that of the supreme propagandist.

Musabbiḥī's chronicle also offers an insight into two problems that would dominate legal debates during the twelfth century: the application of the Fatimid law of inheritance and seizure of estates by the state. In two accounts Musabbiḥī relates how the inheritance of an unnamed woman, the daughter of Abī ʿAbd Allāh Ḥusayn ibn Aḥmad ibn Naṣr, was handled. She was married to Jaʿfar, the son of Qā'id al-Quwwād (the supreme commander) al-Ḥusayn ibn Jawhar and died on 23 Ṣafar 415/6 May 1024. Her unnamed daughter had been married to the son of her cousin Ibn Abī Jaʿfar, the son of Qā'id al-Quwwād. Her funeral was attended by Miʿḍād and other eunuchs of the court while the prayers were conducted by the supreme cadi. She left a huge estate, including rented properties in Fusṭāṭ that yielded a monthly income of 600 *dīnārs*. The whole estate went to her daughter. On 24 Rabiʿ I 415/5 June 1024, however, Miʿḍād, accompanied by the vizier al-Jarjarā'ī and Muḥsin ibn Badūs, the person in charge of the Treasury, went to the house of Ibn Naṣr and registered and sealed the estate in question. The gist of the account lies in the explanation they provided for their conduct, claiming that a third of the estate belonged to the authorities (*sulṭān*, a term vaguely referring to the ruler/government/state), since 'the origin of the Jawhar family was as a slave of the dynasty (*wa-an aṣl Ibn*

[82] Musabbiḥī, 66, 71, 104–5, 106–7, 110–11; Maqrīzī, *Ittiʿāẓ*, I, 217–18. Actually, in 1024–5 two people held the position of chief propagandist. See Musabbiḥī, 81.

Jawhar ʿabd li-l-dawla)'.[83] Musabbiḥī was not present at the second event, and the sentence attributed to the state dignitaries is his rationalisation of their conduct. These facts do not undermine the validity of his explanation, but offer no clue as to how the term/expression 'a slave of the dynasty' should be understood. In the case of the Jawhar family the term can be understood as referring to the status of the founder of the family, who rose to eminence from servitude. If correctly understood, the concept 'a slave of the dynasty' was applied in the case of a woman married to the third generation of a family of such origins.[84]

In another case, the conduct of the state seems to have been even more outrageous. On 28 Dhū l-Qaʿda 415/31 January 1025 a pious poet (*mastūr*) died whose sister lived in Tyre. One would expect the cadi to make an effort to secure the rights of the absent sister, but the estate was seized by the authorities. In yet another case the conduct of the state was more in line with the concept of inheritances without legal heir. This case involved the murder of an unnamed homosexual broker whose considerable estate was taken by the authorities.[85]

Two other cases fall squarely under the concept of 'a slave of the dynasty' and involved servile women at the palace. Musabbiḥī records the death of ʿĀ'isha, the slave girl of the emir ʿAbd Allāh, al-Muʿizz's son. She is described as one of the noble old wise women of the palace and her estate, worth 400,000 *dīnārs*, was seized. She was buried in the domestic tomb of her master at his feet and the prayers were conducted by the supreme propagandist. No different was the fate of the estate of Taqarrub, the slave girl of al-ʿAzīz's wife, who later was in the service of the princess Sitt al-Mulk. She bequeathed her estate to al-Malīḥa, another slave girl of Sitt al-Mullk, but, as Musabbiḥī remarks, 'her money was brought to the palace'.[86]

83 Musabbiḥī, 32–3, 92–3.

84 According to Idrīs ʿImād al-Dīn, the letter of *amān* issued by Jawhar was on behalf of Jawhar al-Qā'id al-Kātib, *ʿabd* of the Commander of the Faithful (673, 677). While the terms *qā'id* and *kātib* must be understood as titles referring to military and administrative authority, *ʿabd* conveys the meaning of a servant, or a slave. For Jawhar al-Ṣaqlabī, al-Manṣūr's freedman, see Halm, *The Empire of the Mahdi*, index; Brett, *The Rise of the Fatimids*, index, under Jawhar al-Ṣiqlabī, al-Kātib.

85 Musabbiḥī, 104, 110.

86 Musabbiḥī, 105, 111; Maqrīzī, *Ittiʿāẓ*, II, 173. For these women, see Cortese and Calderini, *Women and the Fatimids*, 118, 151. Very little is known about emir ʿAbd Allāh, al-Muʿizz's heir

De-Ismailisation of the Fatimid Administration of Justice

When reading Musabbiḥī, the unavoidable conclusion is that although the conduct of the Fatimid state was governed by law, it was also shaped by administrative concepts, expediencies and greed. It can be argued that the Fatimid state was not different from any other contemporary state, but the question of what is meant by de-Ismailisation must be asked, and one may wonder whether full Ismailisation of the judicial system was ever achieved. In 990, following the death of the vizier Ibn Killis, members of the Nuʿmān family held the posts of the supreme cadi and supreme propagandist, and it can be argued that they were at the pinnacle of their power and that any obstacles (internal and external) to full Ismailisation of the judicial system were removed. The way the Nuʿmāns implemented Ismailisation was through the integration of outsiders in key judicial positions, and the nomination of Mālik ibn Saʿīd al-Fāriqī as cadi of Cairo is only one example. This trend is also exemplified by the renowned Shāfiʿī jurist and historian al-Quḍāʿī (d. 1062), the author of many works on a wide range of topics. In 1036, he was deputed to serve as cadi of Fusṭāṭ by the supreme cadi Aḥmad ibn Qāsim ibn ʿAbd al-ʿAzīz ibn al-Nuʿmān. Whether there was a clear-cut division of responsibilities between the two in the capital is unclear, but twice a week Aḥmad ibn Qāsim used to hold sessions with his witnesses in Cairo outside the palace's Nile Gate (Bāb al-Baḥr). He claimed that only people authorised by the *imām* are allowed to attend those sessions.[87] The familiar pattern of the integration of outsiders was dramatically transformed, however, with the rise to power of al-Yāzūrī (1049–58). Al-Yāzūrī was from a rural background in Palestine and his father served as cadi of Yāzūr while the son's first significant position was cadi of Ramla, an assignment he lost in unclear circumstances. In order to regain the appointment he went to Cairo and tried to make his way into the corridors of power through the personnel of the office of Sayyida Raṣad, mother of the reigning *imām*-caliph al-Mustanṣir and the real authority behind the throne. His initial efforts were blocked by the supreme

apparent. He fought the Carmathian invasion of Egypt and died during al-Muʿizz's reign. See al-Anṭākī, 142; Bianquis, 'Prise du pouvoir', 99–102, 104.

[87] Maqrīzī, *Kitāb al-Muqaffā*, III, 367–8, V, 710–12.

cadi and propagandist Aḥmad ibn Qāsim, who, in 1049, was dismissed from his posts, which he held during his second term in office for almost fourteen years.

Al-Yāzūrī succeeded him to the post of supreme cadi, and the rather modest title 'al-Qāḍī al-Ajall Khaṭīr al-Mulk' was bestowed on him. Upon his nomination al-Yāzūrī deputed his son to serve as cadi and bestowed on him a fabulous, though unspecified, salary. In 1050, he was appointed vizier and his titles were vastly expanded to also include the titles of supreme cadi and supreme propagandist.[88] With all these powers in his hand he never relinquished his position as the head of the office of al-Mustanṣir's mother, reflecting an acute awareness of the true disposition of political power in the state.[89] Whether al-Yāzūrī had any real power over Fatimid propaganda remains vague. As a civilian vizier with no independent power base he had no leverage against the Ismāʿīlī palace establishment. What is striking in his career is the integration of a total outsider, not to say stranger, into the top power structure of the Fatimid state and the combination of the posts of supreme cadi and vizier. As is clearly borne out by the letter of appointment of the vizier al-Jarjarā'ī, in 1027, the traditional Fatimid policy was to keep the post of vizier and judicial responsibilities apart.[90]

In 1058, following al-Yāzūrī's downfall, the state was plunged into administrative havoc, with a fast turnover in the posts of vizier and supreme cadi, which were occasionally combined and occasionally separated. Al-Yāzūrī's immediate successor in the post of cadi was Aḥmad ʿIlm al-Dīn, the son of the cadi al-Fāriqī, but he held the position for only a few months. In 1061, he was reappointed again for a few months, while his third nomination as vizier and the supreme cadi, in 1062, lasted for a few days only. Following this experience he gave up his administrative career and received permission to retire to Jerusalem.[91] Administrative disarray deteriorated into disastrous civil war, which brought the Fatimid state to the brink of collapse. The regime

88 Ibn Muyassar, 9, 11; Maqrīzī, *Kitāb-Muqaffā*, III, 374–5, 376, V, 550.

89 For al-Yāzūrī's extensive biography, see Maqrīzī, *Kitāb al-Muqaffā*, III, 363–408, and *Ittiʿāẓ*, II, 197–236; Ibn Muyassar, 16–17; Brett, 'The Execution of al-Yāzūrī', 15–27. For Sayyida Raṣad and her involvement in politics, see Cortese and Calderini, *Women and the Fatimids*, 110–14.

90 Ibn al-Qalānisī, 80–2, provides the full text of the document; Lev, *Saladin in Egypt*, 70.

91 Maqrīzī, *Kitāb al-Muqaffā*, I, 453–4, 502–3, referring to the equally turbulent career of the brother.

was saved through the military intervention of Badr al-Jamālī, the governor of Acre, who in a ruthless campaign restored order and established military dictatorship, rendering the Fatimid *imām*-caliph powerless.

Badr al-Jamālī's rise to power in the Fatimid state bears no resemblance to earlier patterns of the inclusion of outsiders in the Ismāʿīlī fold and Fatimid politics. There are no commonalities between him and his predecessors like Ibn Killis, Ibn Abī l-ʿAwwām or al-Yāzūrī in terms of background and integration into state's ruling circles. Badr al-Jamālī was a Muslim Armenian, a military man with considerable political-military experience, who prior to his arrival to Egypt served as governor of Damascus and, most significantly, had at his disposal a private military cohort.[92]

Badr al-Jamālī's total control of the cadi institution and the Ismāʿīlī *daʿwa* is reflected by his titles Protector (*kāfil*) of the Cadis of the Muslims and Guide (*hādī*) of the Propagandists of the Believers. Furthermore, he established hereditary military dictatorship by transferring his powers to his son al-Afḍal, who easily overcame the Ismāʿīlī palace establishment and, upon the death of al-Mustanṣir, in 1094, manipulated the succession to his advantage. He quashed the Nizārī rebellion in Alexandria and killed the Ismāʿīlī propagandist who invested al-Mustanṣir's son Nizār with the title Imām. No different was the fate of the cadi of Alexandria Abū ʿAbd Allāh Muḥammad of the Banū ʿAmmār, a long-serving veteran Ismāʿīlī family, who supported Nizār. Al-Afḍal took advantage of the disagreement between the cadi and his court witnesses who refused to swear allegiance to Nizār and reshaped the judicial system in the town by appointing a new cadi, Abū l-Ḥasan Zayd ibn al-Ḥasan of the Sunnī Ḥadid family of Andalusi origin, loyal to him. His son, the cadi al-Makīn al-Dawla Abū Ṭālib ibn Ḥadīd (1069–1134), became de facto ruler of the town, but nevertheless transferred payments to the state.[93] He also maintained his position after the assassination of al-Afḍal in 1121 since the Fatimids preferred to work with him, recognising his unique position in the town.[94]

The rise of the cadis of the Ḥadīd family was an important stage in the

[92] For his period as governor of Damascus, see Bianquis, *Damas*, II, 629–34.

[93] Maqrīzī, *Ittiʿāẓ*, III, 13–15; *Kitāb al-Muqaffā*, I, 505.

[94] Ibn Ẓāfir, ed. Ferré, 83–4, provides a list of the cadis of the Ḥadīd family.

crystallisation of the Sunnī character of twelfth-century Alexandria and the rise of Abū Bakr al-Ṭurṭūshī (1059–1126) to eminence in the town. He settled in Alexandria around 1096 and built his authority from below, being unpopular with both al-Afḍal and the Ḥadīd family, which owed its position to an official appointment. Al-Ṭurṭūshī's meeting with the vizier al-Ma'mūn in 1122 (alluded to earlier in this chapter) is important for understanding the position of Fatimid law during the twelfth century. Al-Ṭurṭūshī complained that the court's trustees who handled orphans' money took exaggerated remuneration for their services, but the key issue was the application of the Fatimid law of inheritance and the state's claims to legacies without legal heirs. The vizier answered that the prevailing situation was in line with the principle established by Badr al-Jamālī and known as *bi-l-madhhab al-dārij*, meaning that every inheritance case is handled according to the *madhhab* affiliation of the deceased.

If the drift of Maqrīzī's account is properly understood, it seems that the jurist urged the vizier to gain a divine reward and to scrap altogether the Fatimid law of inheritance. Al-Ma'mūn reminded him that he was the vizier of a Shīʿī *imām*-caliph and bluntly said that both Ismāʿīlīs and Sunnīs claim that what they do is the right interpretation of the Koranic verses, meaning the inheritance verses. Concerning one issue the vizier took immediate action: he prohibited the court's trustees from drawing any income from inheritances with no heirs, and he also promised to discuss the broader issue of inheritances with the caliph. The text suggests that the vizier, even prior to consulting the caliph, made one very substantial promise: to cancel the seizure of undivided shares of inheritance by the Treasury, which, according to his statement, was authorised neither by the Koran nor by the Prophet. The purport of the vizier's promise remains vague, since Qāḍī al-Nuʿmān envisioned the possibility of undivided parts of an inheritance being allotted to the Treasury.[95]

The vizier's promise also seems strange on the practical level, since al-Afḍal had amended state conduct concerning inheritances with no legal

[95] Maqrīzī, *Kitāb al-Muqaffā*, VII, 410–11; Cilardo, *The Early History of Ismāʿīlī Jurisprudence*, 58. For shifts in Abbasid policies concerning inheritances with no legal heirs, see Sourdel, *Le Vizirat*, I, 342–3.

heirs. The historian Ibn Muyassar (d. 1278) praises al-Afḍal for his policy of keeping the money of inheritances with no heirs separate from other funds. He claims that the supreme cadi Thiqat al-Mulk Abū l-Fatḥ Musallam ibn ʿAlī ibn al-Rasʿanī informed al-Afḍal that he had moved 100,000 *dīnārs* of long-unclaimed inheritances to the Treasury. Al-Afḍal was furious: he ordered the cadi to concern himself with his judicial obligations and not to deal with matters which are of no concern for him. At the time of al-Afḍal's assassination there were 130,000 *dīnārs* from unclaimed inheritances in the cadi's depository (*mawdaʿ al-ḥukm*). Perhaps facts and fabrication are mixed together in this tale, which Ibn Muyassar uses as an illustration in a very appreciative account of al-Afḍal's rule and justice towards the population.[96]

Ostensibly, al-Ṭurṭūshī's complaints were groundless, but perhaps after al-Afḍal's demise the state changed his policies and reverted to the indiscriminate seizure of inheritances. In any case al-Ma'mūn kept his word about consulting the caliph, and Maqrīzī provides lengthy, though somewhat disconnected, fragments of a decree issued by both the caliph and vizier in 1123. The stated purpose of the decree is to take care of the Muslims, to safeguard the circumstances of all of them and to act responsibly for the welfare of both worldly needs and the requirements of religion. Without referring to the principle *bi-l-madhhab al-dārij*, the decree restates in detail the practice of handling inheritances according to the *madhhab* affiliation of the deceased and his beliefs (*iʿtiqād*). The Shīʿī women's share is dealt with in accordance with the Koranic injunction (8:75): 'But kindred by blood (*wa ūlū l-arḥām*) have prior rights against each other in the Book of God, God has full knowledge of all things.'[97] The possibility that some inheritance shares would be allotted to the Treasury is restated and the authority of the *imāms* (i.e. the Fatimid rulers) to interpret the Koran reaffirmed. The *imāms* are referred to as the *kuramā'* of the Koran on whose guidance the Ismāʿīlī believers rely, conducting their affairs accordingly.[98]

At this point understanding of Maqrīzī's text becomes problematic,

[96] Ibn Muyassar, 83–4.

[97] The translation follows both Cilardo ('From Qur'an to Fiqh', 288) and Abdel Haleem (*The Qur'an*, 115). For the implementation of Koran 8:75 by Qāḍī al-Nuʿmān, see Fyzee, 'The Fatimid Law of Inheritance', 62, 66.

[98] Maqrīzī, *Kitāb al-Muqaffā*, VII, 411.

since it refers to the dissatisfaction of the Commander of the Faithful with the 'groundless, remote from the truth and unsubstantiated belief (*qāʿida*)', whose nature remains unspecified. The text says, however, that it is the wish of the Commander of the Faithful to return to the conduct of his pure ancestors and he therefore commands the vizier to warn his deputy al-Qāḍī Thiqat al-Mulk to discontinue a certain unspecified renewed practice (*al-sunna al-mujaddadah*), a reference that adds new difficulty to our understanding of the text. The text alludes to the hierarchy of judicial authority in the state: the vizier Ma'mūn al-Baṭā'ḥī, like his predecessors Badr al-Jamālī and al-Afḍal, officially held the highest judicial authority in the state and the supreme cadi was answerable to him. Therefore, the vizier is ordered to convey the edict's massage to the supreme cadi and through him to cadis, deputies and court witnesses (referred to as *al-mustakhdimīn fī l-bāb/shuhūd al-ḥukm bi-bāb*) in the capital and the provinces.

Although never clearly spelt out, it seems that the section of Maqrīzī's text dealing with warnings to cadis actually warns them against unlawful seizure of inheritances under the pretext of being legacies with no legal heirs. The text addresses the question of under which circumstances seizure of an inheritance is permitted: 'If somebody dies with no legal heirs (*ḥasharīan*) neither present nor absent, than the whole estate [is] for the Treasury, according to sound rulers and prevailing known laws. Unless he had a spouse or a confirmed debt.' The text goes on to describe what should be done in the case of an absent heir and how their rights should be confirmed. The last section of Maqrīzī's text deal with the remuneration of the court's witnesses/trustees responsible for orphans' money and inheritances, and the supreme cadi is ordered to make the text of the document (referred to as an open decree and rescript [*manshūr* and tawqīʿ]) known to all in the capital and provinces.

Although Maqrīzī's text is not an original Fatimid document in the strict sense of the term, he quotes the final lines of the document concerning its registration in the Office of the Chamber (*dīwān al-majlis*), and al-Āmir's Office of the Privy-Purse (*dīwān al-khāṣṣ al-Āmirī*). Following the registration of the document, its final deposition (*li-yukhllada*) was supposed to be in the archive (*majlis al-ḥukm*) of the supreme cadi.[99]

[99] Maqrīzī, *Kitāb al-Muqaffā*, VII, 412–13. For the registration of Fatimid documents, see Stern,

At this point in the discussion, the position of Fatimid law in the state prior to and after the rise of the military viziers of the Jamālī family must be re-examined. The starting-point is the explicit statement which claims that Jawhar and al-Muʿizz ordered cadis to apply the Fatimid law of inheritance, and the cadi Ibn Abī Thawān implemented the order. Irrespective of the cadi's mishandling of the policy, the question remains whether al-Muʿizz's order became state policy and whether the Fatimid law of inheritance ran supreme and replaced the Sunnī legal systems in these cases. Though not corroborated directly by the sources, the answer should be positive: this indeed was the state policy. How widely and how successfully it was applied outside Cairo, the bastion of Ismailism, remains controversial. Although Badr al-Jamālī's policy that inheritance cases should be handled according to the *madhhab* affiliation of the deceased revoked state policy, it was a realistic and reasonable measure which reflected the reality. The edict published by al-Āmir and the vizier Ma'mūn only vindicated Badr al-Jamālī's policy.

What the position was of Fatimid law after the assassination of al-Āmir in 1130 by the Nizārī Ismāʿīlīs is unclear. The political fortunes of the Fatimid dynasty only deteriorated, and most of the time the Fatimid rulers had no grip on real political power in the state. One of their lowest points was in 1131, during the half-year rule of the vizier Abū ʿAlī al-Kutayfāt, the sole survivor of the massacre committed against al-Afḍal's extended family. He declared himself Imāmī Shīʿī, but abolished the Shīʿī formula for the call to prayer introduced by the Fatimids and, more significantly, appointed four new cadis belonging to the Shāfiʿ, Mālikī, Ismāʿīlī and Imāmī schools of law. They were supposed to apply the laws of inheritance according to their legal affiliations, but nothing else is known about their activities. In 1132, following the declaration of al-Ḥāfiẓ as *imām*-caliph in his own right, Kutayfāt's policies were revoked. A new supreme cadi was appointed, and he also served as supreme propagandist.[100] It seems that the eminent position of Fatimid law was somewhat restored. The evidence, however, is contradictory.

Fatimid Decrees, 166–75. For a reference to *dīwān al-ḥukm* in an eleventh-century marriage contract from Palestine, see Khan, *Arabic Legal and Administrative Documents*, doc. 34.

100 Ibn Muyassar, 115–16, 118; Maqrīzī, *Ittiʿāẓ*, III, 142, 143–4, 146; *Kitāb al-Muqaffā*, I, 394–9. For critical examination of the account and the names of the cadis alluded to, see Allouche, 'The Establishment of Four Chief Judgeships', 317–20.

In 1139, following the death of the supreme cadi, the post was vacant for three months and eventually offered to the Mālikī jurist ʿAbd Allāh ibn al-Ḥuṭay'a (1085–1166), whose legal skills were minimal. He was an expert on the canonical readings of the Koran and well-versed in literature and language, but refused to earn money by reciting the Koran. He can be described as a socially oriented mild ascetic who had a wife and family and earned a living as a copyist. The Fatimids offered this humble person the post of cadi, but he rejected the demand to apply the Fatimid law (*madhhab al-dawla*). For the present discussion the demand is more significant that his refusal of the post, which was accepted by someone else.[101] Although the names of cadis during the period 1140–71 are known, and occasional references indicate the continuation of Ismāʿīlī teaching in Cairo, the position of Fatimid law in the state is vague.[102] In any case, the significance of the issue must have been overshadowed by wars and political events, and the discussion is complicated by the fact that during the twelfth century the term *qāḍī* acquired the function of an honorific title, having nothing to do with the post of cadi. It is difficult, therefore, to distinguish between people who actually held the post of cadi and others. In 1145, for example, responsibility for the state offices, the Turkish troops and various treasuries was conferred on al-Qāḍī al-Muwaffaq Abī l-Karam Muḥammad ibn Maʿṣūm, who was dismissed several months later, and al-Qāḍī al-Murtaḍā al-Muḥannak was reappointed as supervisor of the state offices. Al-Qāḍī al-Murtaḍā al-Muḥannak, who died in 1154, is better-known as a historian of Egypt.[103] The impression is that these people never served as cadis, and this is certainly true for Qāḍī al-Fāḍil (1135–1200), a Fatimid administrator who became a member of Saladin's inner circle. He is the best-known twelfth-century personality to have held the title *qāḍī* as an honorific, never serving as cadi.[104]

[101] Ibn Muyassar, 131; Maqrīzī, *Kitāb al-Muqaffā*, I, 491, 510–12; Lev, 'Piety and Political Activism', 310–11, with additional sources for Ibn al-Ḥuṭay'a's life.

[102] Ibn Muyassar, 132, 139, 145, 152–3.

[103] Ibn Muyassar, 136; Maqrīzī, *Ittiʿāẓ*, III, 180, 182, 223. All the people alluded to in the last reference are referred to as *qāḍī*. For other people referred to, or titled , *qāḍī*, see 219–20.

[104] While the title *qāḍī* became honorific, no less enigmatic is the term *walīy al-dawla* associated with the Qāḍī Abū l-Barakāt Ibn Abī Yaʿlā (1072–1161), who served as *muʿaddil*. His father served as a supreme cadi, but no judicial appointment is mentioned in connection with the son. See Maqrīzī, *Kitāb al-Muqaffā*, V, 610–11.

Qāḍī al-Fāḍil is the author of a letter of appointment bestowed on the cadi al-Mu'taman al-Amīn ʿAlam al-Dīn during the reign of al-ʿĀḍid (1160–71). It is a huge document, six pages long in modern print and, typically of Qāḍī al-Fāḍil's writings, characterised by excessive verbosity. It is a curious document which bears no resemblance to the earlier-quoted fragments of Fatimid letters of appointment, and offers no insight into the position of Fatimid law in the Fatimid state during its long twilights. Sifting through the phraseology we find that the cadi was entrusted with responsibility for *sikka*, meaning the minting of coins, *daʿwa* and the muezzins at the palace, mosques and shrines. These spheres of responsibility were in line with earlier Fatimid letters of appointment, but in Qāḍī al-Fāḍil's letter no judicial responsibilities are mentioned and the cadi is referred to only by his titles. The cadi's other duties involved supervision of the supplies of clothes to the caliph's general and private wardrobes, and storing the caliph's private Treasury.[105]

Another way to approach the question of the position of Fatimid law in the Fatimid state during its final years is to examine the deeds of Saladin when he dismantled it. Saladin's policy was marked by caution, and the same applies to his policy of de-Ismailisation. The key event in Saladin's seizure of power in Egypt was the Battle of the Blacks (21–3 August 1169) fought in Cairo against Fatimid black slave infantry and Armenian archers, but Saladin's approach remained cautious even after his victory in the battle. In 1170, the Shīʿī formula for the call to prayer was abolished and, by the end of year, a new supreme cadi was appointed by the Fatimid ruler. In a parallel move, Saladin made two key judicial appointments: he nominated ʿĪsā al-Hakkārī cadi of Cairo and Ibn Kāmil cadi of Fusṭāṭ. The pace of Saladin's actions intensified during 1171 and involved several decisive steps: the establishment of law colleges in Fusṭāṭ, the replacement of the newly-appointed supreme cadi by the Shāfiʿī jurist Ṣadar al-Dīn ʿAbd al-Mālik ibn Durbās (1117–1208), and the abolishing of the sessions of Ismāʿīlī teaching at the Azhar mosque. These and other actions culminated in the pronouncing of the Friday sermon at the mosques in the name of the Abbasid caliph and the death of al-ʿĀḍid on 13 September 1171. In his capacity as supreme cadi Ibn

[105] Qalqashandī, X, 351–6, esp. 353, 354. For the caliph's private and general wardrobes, see Lev, 'Tinnīs', 87–8.

Durbās purged the whole judicial system and replaced the judicial personnel of the Fatimid period with new Shafiʿī appointees. One of these deputies was the Shafiʿī jurist Abū l-Ḥasan (1118–93), whose family came from Ramla.

Abū l-Ḥasan served as Ibn Durbās's deputy in Fusṭāṭ, for twenty years. Maqrīzī claims that Shafiʿi and Mālikī predominance in Egypt goes back to that period.[106] The deeds of Saladin and his supreme cadi, who, like ʿĪsā al-Hakkārī, was Saladin's confidant, indicate that the Ismāʿīlī character of the Fatimid state embodied by the teaching of Ismailism and the service of Ismāʿīlī cadis persisted until the very end of the state. One must assume that these Ismāʿīlī cadis applied Fatimid law, but how widespread the phenomenon was remains unknown, and, most likely, these Ismāʿīlī cadis were Sunnī jurists who applied Fatimid law in inheritance cases.

Twelfth-century Paradoxes

How the administration of justice was carried out in Fusṭāṭ-Cairo during the civil war of the 1060s and early 1070s is impossible to ascertain. Documentary sources, however, offer a rare insight into the provincial realities of the 1060s. A marriage document dated to 1068–9 from Ashmūnayn illustrates that the practice of granting extensive responsibilities to cadis continued. Grave though the situation in the Fatimid state during that period was, the cadi of Ashmūnayn and its district (Abū l-Ḥasan Masarra ibn ʿAbd Allāh) is referred to as responsible for jurisdiction (*ḥukm, qaḍāʾ*), the *maẓālim* court, and the performance of prayers and sermons in the mosques. The document was drafted by his deputy.[107] Who these two cadis were and what their affiliation to Ismailism, if any, could have been remains an open question. The document is entirely in line with Fatimid state policies, and it can be argued that the supreme cadi used to delegate some of his responsibilities to provincial cadis. Other documents, however, indicate that the role of provincial cadis involved responsibilities which were not mentioned in literary sources and were, in a way, unprecedented.

Receipts emanating from the Fayyūm of the early eleventh century place

[106] Maqrīzī, *Ittiʿāẓ*, III, 317, 318, 319–20. For people associated with Ibn Durbās either as scholars or as deputies and witnesses, see Maqrīzī, *Muqaffā*, V, 480, 577, 586, VI, 94, 102 (referring to Abū Ḥasan), 278, VII, 25.

[107] Al-Mudarris, *Papyrologische Untersuchungen*, doc. 50, ll, 13–15 (text and trans.).

the cadi in the context of the tax collection system. These documents record tax instalments (*ḍamān*) paid by Abū l-Ḥasan ibn Wahb, the manager of a rural estate in the Fayyūm, and were written by a cashier (*jahbadh*). The context for these documents has been elucidated by Khan, and the role of the cadis was supervisory, to confirm the sums rendered and recorded. In nineteen receipts spanning the period 29 March 1012 to 27 March 1015 the cadi Abī l-Ḥasan ibn Yaḥyā ibn Bahār is mentioned. He is titled al-Qāḍī al-Saʿīd al-Rashīd Thiqat al-Mulk Makīn al-Dawla wa-Amīnuha (the Auspicious, the Rightly Guided, the Trustworthy of the Kingdom, the Trusted Upholder of the Dynasty), and referred to as the protégé (*ṣanīʿa*) of the Commander of the Faithful. His son Abū ʿAlī al-Ḥasan ibn Yaḥyā ibn Bahār, who served as his deputy and was titled the Trusted (al-Mu'taman), is also mentioned. The phrase 'protégé of the Commander of the Faithful' is significant and illuminates direct relations of the cadi with the ruler which bypass the supreme cadi, and is in stark contrast to letters of appointment issued to supreme cadis. In the case of Abī l-Ḥasan ibn Yaḥyā ibn Bahār these were special exclusive personal relations between him and al-Ḥākim, which others did not enjoy. In a receipt from 17 December 1012, deposition of money in the Glorious Storehouse is recorded. It took place in the presence of the cadi Abū l-Faḍl Jaʿfar ibn Ibrāhīm ibn Sulaymān, whose responsibility was to record and keep safe the money received. His titles were simply al-Qāḍī Fakhr al-Dawla (Glory of the Dynasty), and he did not enjoy the status of protégé.[108] It seems that every stage in the movement of tax money in the Fayyūm was supervised by cadis, but Abī l-Ḥasan ibn Yaḥyā ibn Bahār's special relations with al-Ḥākim escape conceptualization, and the question of whether this was a special case or a wider phenomenon remains unanswered.

Musabbiḥī's narrative and the documents discussed in this section shed light on what might be called a methodological paradox: Fatimid letters of appointment bestowed on the supreme cadis were both empowering and declarative documents. They reveal the state's intentions and declare policies, but not the full framework within which the supreme cadi operated. If possible, they must be corroborated or disproved by other evidence.

From methodological paradoxes we can move to those which marked

[108] Khan, *Arabic Legal and Administrative Documents*, docs 140–59.

Fatimid twelfth-century history. The administrative-political vision of the role of the supreme cadi as administrator fully integrated within the state's administrative fabric was not limited to the person at the top of the judicial hierarchy: it pervaded the cadi institution. This point is exemplified by a document published and translated by Khan, which records the lease of a plot of land from a state office by Efrayim ibn Eli, the Jew (July 1115). It is a very long, complex and well-preserved document whose main significance is for Fatimid economic history, especially that of the capital city. Efrayim requested the lease (in Khan's translation) from 'the office of prosperous Friday and neighbourhood mosques, in al-Muʿizziya Cairo, the guarded, and Fusṭāṭ and legacies with no legal heirs and of the auspicious granaries', which was headed by the cadi Abū l-Ḥasan Muḥammad ibn Hibatallāh ibn al-Ḥasan. The person who actually handled the lease was the supervisor (*mushārif*) of the office.[109]

The Fatimid political tradition of investing the supreme cadi with sweeping responsibilities continued during the twelfth century. In 1122, for example, Abū l-Ḥajjāj Yūsuf ibn Ayyūb al-Maghribī al-Andalusī (d. 1127) was appointed supreme cadi and his responsibilities resembled those given to the chief cadis of the Nuʿmān family decades ago. These included the supervision of preaching and prayers at the mosques and responsibility for the office of pious endowments and the mint. He also used to attend sessions of the *maẓālim* court held by the vizier and was vested with managing the economic interests of the ruler (*wakālat al-khalīfa*), but he refused to be responsible for state offices.[110] At the inception of the Fatimid rule in Egypt, on their own initiative the Nuʿmāns came to control vital state economic interests. A century and half later, in completely different political circumstances, the state entrusted its supreme cadi with responsibility for the ruler's personal economic interests.

[109] Khan, *Arabic Legal and Administrative Documents*, doc. 23, ll, 2, 6–7 (text and trans.); see also Khan's commentary, 164–5.

[110] Maqrīzī, *Ittiʿāẓ*, III, 93, 119–20. For the agent (*wakīl*) of the vizier al-Ma'mūn and the vizier's *dār al-wakāla* built in 1123 in Cairo, see Ibn Muyassar, 91–2. The term *wakālat al-khalīfa* can be understood as having a broad meaning, referring to the caliph's economic interests or denoting a caravanserai (*dār al-wakāla*). For the expression and its meanings, see Goitein, *Med. Soc.* I, 187–8, alluding to both a *dār al-wakāla* built in Fusṭāṭ during Badr al-Jamālī's period and al-Afḍal's *dār al-wakāla*.

It may be claimed that Abū l-Ḥajjāj Yūsuf's nomination came about because he was the tutor of the vizier's brother, but he must have had some judicial experience too, since he had served as cadi of Gharbiyya before being nominated supreme cadi. Generally speaking, career patterns of twelfth-century cadis are little-known, but the combination of non-judicial and judicial assignments was not rare. The cadi Abū l-Ḥajjāj Yūsuf, for example, was born in Jerusalem in 1091, and arrived as a child in Egypt after the fall of the town to the Franks in 1099. In 1130, he was appointed supervisor of the palace treasury of books and, in 1131, as cadi of Fuwa and its district.[111] The career of Abū Jaʿfar al-Afṭasī (1070–1124) falls within the same pattern. He was a Shīʿī poet and man of letters from Tripoli (Syria), who earned fame for his eulogies of rulers. In 1109, he finally settled in Egypt and entered al-Afḍal's circle. Between 1116 and 1117 he served as cadi of Ascalon, although his legal education is never mentioned. In 1121, he served as head of the office of pious endowments and inheritance in Fusṭāṭ and Cairo. This appointment illustrates, if any further evidence is required, the fact that inheritances were a legal issue with wide administrative ramifications. His next three mentioned appointments were: cadi of Gharbiyya and Maḥalla, person responsible for the *niqāba al-ashrāf*, and preacher at a mosque completed by the vizier al-Ma'mūn. Whether these appointments were consecutive or simultaneous remains unclear.[112]

These twelfth-century biographies illustrate that throughout its long history the Fatimid state served as a vehicle for the integration of Sunnīs into its judicial system and administration. To put it differently, the state never developed its own uniquely distinctive human resources – an Ismāʿīlī-trained cadre – needed for the running of its civilian institutions.

Ibn Ḥajar's biography of the cadi Ibn Durbās sheds light on a second twelfth-century paradox: lingering Fatimid legacy about the nature of the post of Supreme Cadi into the Ayyubid period. Ibn Durbās served as Supreme Cadi for the whole period of Saladin's reign, and during this period he was also entrusted with judicial authority for many regions of Syria, where he appointed deputies. In addition he served as supervisor of pious endowments

[111] Maqrīzī, *Ittiʿāẓ*, III, 255.
[112] Maqrīzī, *Kitab al-Muqaffā*, VII, 96–8.

and deputed his brother to serve as cadi. Ibn Durbās was dismissed from his post following bitter disagreement with his deputy in Fusṭāṭ, in which the sultan al-ʿAzīz ʿUthmān was also involved (1193–8). Although the dismissal did not end Ibn Durbās's career, he never again enjoyed long and uninterrupted term in office. He was re-appointed in 1198, for several months, then dismissed and re-appointed again. During his third term in office, in the best tradition of the Fatimid concept of the nature of the post of Supreme Cadi, he became responsible for preaching in the mosques, pious endowments, supervision of the markets, and the mint. For Ibn Durbās, his third term in office, in spite of the new responsibilities vested in him, must have been a difficult period marked by a painful severance of relations with his brother over (unspecified) theological issues.[113]

The history of the administration of justice during the Ayyubid and Mamlūk periods is yet to be written. One can say, however, that the Fatimid legacy, and the appointment of Ibn Durbās, at the beginning of the Ayyubid period, have their continuation in the appointment of Ibn Khallikān as Supreme Cadi of Syria in 1261. He was given a free hand to appoint deputies on his behalf and was vested with authority for the pious endowments and *maṣāliḥ* (administration/maintenance) of all mosques, hospitals and law colleges. In addition, he was appointed professor of law (*tadrīs*) at seven law colleges in Damascus. Although Ibn Khallikān is better known as the author of the biographical dictionary of the luminaries of medieval Islam, prior to his nomination in 1261 he had a career as cadi in Egypt. He served as deputy on behalf of the Supreme Cadi Badr al-Dīn Yusūf ibn Ḥasan.[114] It seems that the paradox of lingering Fatimid legacies went beyond the cadi institution and is a potentially promising line of research.

[113] Ibn Ḥajar, ed. ʿUmar, 252–3.
[114] Abū Shāma, 215; Ibn Wāṣil, 313–14.

PART TWO

JUDICIAL INSTITUTIONS OUTSIDE THE PALE OF ISLAMIC LAW

4

Criminal Justice and the Police

The Enigma of the Shurṭa

Although the term *shurṭa* is frequently referred to by Kindī, the nature of this body and its functions are never explained. The history of the institution in Fusṭāṭ goes back to the first and second governorship of ʿAmr ibn al-ʿĀṣ when the command of the *shurṭa* was in the hands of Khārija ibn Ḥudhāfa. Following the reference to Khārija ibn Ḥudhāfa, Kindī systematically lists the names of the people who were appointed to command the *shurṭa*. These appointments were made by the governors of Egypt, and one is left to conclude that it was sort of a military formation, a garrison or a police force.[1]

The meaning of the *shurṭa* is better understood in the context of Kūfa and Baṣra, and scholars such as Donner, Lecker and Michael Ebstein have discussed many of its aspects. Lecker and Donner have drawn attention to *shurṭat al-khamis*, which, in the Kūfa of ʿAlī's time, constituted an elite military force.[2] The military role of the *shurṭa* in the Umayyad period is well-attested, and in Baṣra it was responsible for maintaining order and fighting crime. In 665, for example, the governor of Baṣra with the help of the *shurṭa* took draconian measures to restore safety in the town.[3] It has been

[1] Kindī, 10, 31; Maqrīzī, *Kitāb al-Muqaffā*, III, 719–20; Tyan, *Histoire de l'organisation judiciaire*, 577.

[2] Lecker, 'Shurṭat al-Khamīs and Other Matters', 278–9; Donner, 'The Shurṭa in Early Umayyad Syria', 250–2.

[3] Ebstein, 'Shurṭa Chiefs in Baṣra', 108–16, esp. 113. The post of chief of police also existed in Kūfa of the 740s. See Tillier, *Les cadis d'Iraq*, 355. For the securing of the roads in southern Iraq during the Umayyad period (with no police involvement), see Al-Qāḍī, 'Security Positions under the Umayyads', 253–83.

suggested by Crone that the evolution of the *shurṭa* from military force to urban police took place in Baghdad, and the *ṣāḥib al-shurṭa* (the chief of the police) became involved in the administration of justice. In tenth-century Baghdad, the *shurṭa* was a sizeable force, 9,000-strong, that consisted of both cavalry and infantry.[4]

The range of duties of the chief of the police is specified in an anonymous mid-tenth-century text (*Siyāsat al-Mulūk*) from Buyid Baghdad, and these included patrolling the city, maintaining order and the administration of criminal justice. According to the text, legal education was not a qualification required in order to become a chief of police. It was enough for him to be knowledgeable about the scale of punishments laid down by God (*ḥudūd*), and he was advised to study texts such as Jāḥiẓ's *Book of Brigands* and other unspecified works (*kutub aṣḥāb al-shurūṭ wa-siyar al-mulūk*).[5]

One can follow Crone and assume that in Fusṭāṭ also the *shurṭa* evolved into a police force, which became to be known as the Lower Police (*al-shurṭa al-suflā*). During the Tulunid period, the term 'Upper Police' (*al-shurṭa al-ʿulyā*, or *fawqāniyya*) referred to the police force in ʿAskar, which was established immediately after the Abbasid takeover of Egypt. Balawī, Aḥmad ibn Ṭūlūn's biographer, writes that commanders of both police forces were military men (*quwwād*, officers) and that Aḥmad ibn Ṭūlūn's instructions to them were quite different. While the chief of the Lower Police was urged to be lenient and just with the population and to attend to the people's needs, the commander of the Upper Police was instructed to inspire awe. In any case, Aḥmad ibn Ṭūlūn warned them that he would personally supervise how they execute their duties. Perhaps the authority of the Upper Police in ʿAskar was extended to also include al-Qaṭāʾiʿ, the palace city of the ruler inhabited by the army and administrators. It can be argued that these two

4 Crone, *Slaves on Horses*, 248, n. 474; Kennedy, *The Armies of the Caliphs*, 163. The perception of the *shurṭa* in Baghdad as police is common in the literature. See Sourdel, *Le vizirat abbaside*, index, under police/préfecture de – à Bagdad; Tillier, *Les cadis d'Iraq*, esp. 120, 230, 334, 337, 459–60, 568, 569, 603. For the warning that one must not understand *shurṭa* as police in the modern sense of the term, see Tyan, *Histoire de l'organisation judiciaire*, 589. There were neither institutional nor functional links between the *ḥaras* and *shurṭa*. See Perlman, 'The Bodyguard of the Caliphs', 323–4, 326–7.

5 Sadan, 'A New Source of the Buyid Period', 370. 371–2. For other aspects of the text, see Sadan and Silverstein, 'Ornate Manuals or Practical Adab', 339–55.

different sets of instructions reflected two different populations: the civilian society of Fusṭāṭ, served by the Lower Police, and al-Qaṭā'iʿ, over which the Upper Police had extended duties. Except for Aḥmad ibn Ṭūlūn's mosque, al-Qaṭā'iʿ was destroyed in the Abbasid invasion of Egypt in 905, while ʿAskar became integrated into Fusṭāṭ.[6] Although barely alluded to, there was also a police force in Cairo and a jail for criminals (known as the *ḥabs al-maʿūna* in Cairo), which is described as a horrendous place.[7]

It seems that during the late eleventh century, especially after the civil war, a shift in the nomenclature referring to the police took place: the term *maʿūna* replaced the term *shurṭa*, while the term *mutawallī* replaced the term *ṣāḥib*, which referred to the chief of police.[8] The most explicit manifestation of this double shift is to be found in the account referring to the publication of a decree mourning the killing of al-Afḍal which was to be read at the Ancient Mosque by the *al-amīr mutawallī l-maʿūna bi-Miṣr*.[9] As has been pointed out by Sayyid, the term *wālī* is attested only in sources for the late Fatimid period. It seems that this term also appeared in the post-civil war period and perhaps reflects a deeper institutional change: the appearance of the posts of governors of Fusṭāṭ and Cairo. In 1097, for example, Dhakhīra al-Mulk in his role as *wālī* of Cairo quelled riots that erupted on the day of ʿĀshūrā', while in 1122 he was appointed on *wilāyat al-Qāhira wa-l-ḥisba*, meaning that he served as both governor and *muḥtasib* of Cairo. This appointment must be seen as a variation on the earlier practice of combining the posts of chief of police and

6 Abbasid development of ʿAskar involved the building of a *dār al-imāra* and a mosque, and the establishment of a police force. See Ibn Taghrī Birdī, I, 412–13; Balawī, 205–6, 234, referring to Mūsā ibn Ṣāliḥ, who was in charge of both police forces. For the Upper Police in ʿAskar and its history, see Sayyid, *La capitale de l'Égypte*, 30–2. For police in pre-Fatimid Fusṭāṭ, see Guest, 'Relations between Persia and Egypt', 167–8; Tyan, *Histoire de l'organisation judiciaire*, 579. For the Fatimid period, see Maqrīzī, *Ittiʿāẓ*, I, 144, 150, 216; Musabbiḥī, 47. When reading Guest's and Tyan's accounts one must remember that neither Maqrīzī's *Ittiʿāẓ* nor *Kitāb al-Muqaffā* were available to them. Both made extensive use of Maqrīzī's *Khiṭaṭ* (at that time editions with no indexes), but the unavailability of *Ittiʿāẓ* is very noticeable.

7 Musabbiḥī, 88; Maqrīzī, *Ittiʿāẓ*, II, 17, 116; *Khiṭaṭ*, III, 599.

8 Although the term *maʿūna* became dominant during the twelfth century, it is a common term also used in earlier sources. Balawī (195), for example, refers to *ʿāmil al-maʿūna bi-l-Jīza* as an official with supervisory and executive powers.

9 Ibn al-Ma'mūn, 18, 99; Maqrīzī, *Ittiʿāẓ*, III, 69. The *maʿūna* in Fusṭāṭ was demolished by Saladin and replaced by a law college. For *mutawallī l-maʿūna* in Geniza documents in the meaning of chief of police, see Goitein, *Med. Soc.* II, 609, n. 44. The term *shurṭa* is rarely attested in the Geniza documents. See Goitein, *Med. Soc.* II, 368, 607, n. 26.

muḥtasib. The terms *wālī Miṣr* and *wālī al-Qāhira* are mentioned in several accounts pertaining to events that occurred in both towns during the years 1121–3.[10]

Although the police as a state organ are frequently referred to, policemen are rarely alluded to. Ibn Zūlāq refers to a policeman as *shurṭī* and policemen as *aʿwān al-shuruṭ*. In other accounts policemen are referred to as *aṣḥāb al-shuruṭ*.[11] The most frequent term referring to policemen is, however, *raqqāṣūn*, which appears twice in Musabbiḥī's *Akhbār Miṣr* and is also common in the Geniza documents.[12] In Geniza, however, the term has a wider range of meanings and also designates an unskilled labourer and an errand boy in the service of any official.[13] One can possibly infer that policemen were recruited from the lower urban classes.

The realities reflected by the anonymous Buyid-period text are also relevant for the early Fatimid period in Egypt, the fundamental problem being incongruity between the way police functioned and Islamic law. The feeling that the criminal justice administrated by the chief of police was outside the pale of Islamic law must have motivated al-Muʿizz to install two jurists at the headquarters of the Fusṭāṭ police in 975, but they were removed after a short period of time. Similar measures were taken by al-Ḥākim when two court witnesses were installed at the police in the capital and other cities, their task being to approve the punishments meted out by the chief of police that felt under the category of *ḥudūd*.[14] Although representing the idiosyncrasies of al-Ḥākim's reign, the most revealing report about the chief of police's sphere of responsibilities comes from 1011 and must not be ignored. In August 1011, the Kutāmī general Muḥammad ibn Nizāl was appointed chief of the two police forces in Fusṭāṭ. He was ordered to impose the ban on the

[10] Ibn al-Ma'mūn, 27, 47, 69, 90, 98; Maqrīzī, *Ittiʿāẓ*, III, 20–1, 55, 100, 101; *Khiṭaṭ*, II, 515; Sayyid, *Al-Dawla al-Fāṭimmiya*, 335, 336–9. Goitein, however, understands the term *wālī* as meaning the chief of police. See *Med. Soc.* II, 250, 368. The ambiguity of the term *wālī* is not unique. For the double meaning of the term *shiḥna* as governor and chief of police in the Seljukid period see Lange, *Justice, Punishment*, 48–50, 51–4.

[11] Ibn Zūlāq, *Kitāb Akhbār Sībawaihi*, 24, 52; al-Anṭākī, 133; Ibn Ẓāfir, ed. Ferré, 54.

[12] Musabbiḥī, 73, 74. For the expression *raqqāṣīn al-wālī* in a letter from 1143, see Goitein, *Med. Soc.* II, 528, n. 57; Gil, *Documents of the Jewish Pious Foundations*, index, under *raqqāṣ*.

[13] Goitein, *Med. Soc.* I, 94, II, 370.

[14] Maqrīzī, *Ittiʿāẓ*, I, 224; al-Anṭākī, 205. For an enigmatic reference to the supreme cadi al-Fāriqī forbidding the chiefs of police to infringe on the *sharīʿa*, see Ibn Ḥajar, ed. Guest, 604.

production of wine, and he also regulated and limited the sale of raisins. Several witnesses were posted at the police headquarters to assist him with the task. Maqrīzī, in one of his writings, describes the task delegated to Muḥammad ibn Nizāl as involving implementation of the Koranic dictum of 'commanding right and forbidding wrong'. In another work, Maqrīzī writes that Muḥammad ibn Nizāl's task was to prevent *munkarāt* (reprehensible/blameworthy deeds), and he also supervised the conduct of the Christians during their festivals. The question that must be asked is whether Maqrīzī reliably reflects al-Ḥākim's mindset or whether the explanations he provides are his own rationalisation of the situation, which appears more to blur the lines between the spheres of responsibilities of the *ḥisba* and those of the *shurṭa*. Whatever the conceptual framework governing Muḥammad ibn Nizāl's actions might have been, he executed his task well and was promoted to serve as governor of Damascus.[15]

Al-Muʿizz must have been familiar with the institution and its problems, since police existed in Mahdiyya, the Fatimid capital city in Tunisia, and in Egypt he bestowed command over the police forces in Fusṭāṭ on a Kutāmī veteran of the Fatimid cause, Jabar ibn al-Qāsim (d. after 985), whose career also included the governorship of key towns such as Tinnīs and Damietta.[16] The names of certain chiefs of police in the Fatimid period are known, and these appointments throw indirect light on the nature of the institution. In some cases the people appointed as chiefs of police, like cadis, deputed others to carry out the day-to-day duties of the post. In 1024, for example, the chief of police in Fusṭāṭ and Cairo was Sāmī al-Dawla Abū Ṭāhir ibn Kāfī al-Kutāmī. He held the appointment on behalf of the black eunuch Badr al-Dawla Nāfidh, who eventually appointed Ibn Kāfī al-Kutāmī governor of Tinnīs and Damietta. When this happened, Ibn Kāfī al-Kutāmī appointed his brother Jalāl al-Dīn as chief of both police forces, but this delegation of powers was quickly quashed since Badr al-Dawla Nāfidh appointed his black eunuch Bakī al-Khādim to the police forces in Fusṭāṭ. For how long

[15] Maqrīzī, *Kitāb al-Muqaffā*, V, 433–4; *Ittiʿāẓ*, II, 89.

[16] For a short allusion to police in Mahdiyya, see *Sīrat al-Ustādh Jawdhar*, 125 (text), 122 (trans.). For Jabar ibn al-Qāsim, see Ibn al-Ṣayrafī, 24; Maqrīzī, *Kitāb al-Muqaffā*, III, 12. Although the names of the chiefs of police in 973 and 974 are known, they cannot be identified. See Maqrīzī, *Ittiʿāẓ*, I, 144, 216.

this appointment lasted remains unknown. In December 1024, Ibn Kāfī al-Kutāmī served (again) as chief of the Lower Police in Fusṭāṭ, on behalf of Badr al-Dawla Nāfidh (*khalīfat Badr al-Dawla Nāfidh fī l-shurṭā al-suflā*), who continued to wield overall responsibility for the two police forces.[17]

The nature of Badr al-Dawla Nāfidh's overall responsibility for the policy is illustrated during the famine riots that erupted in Fusṭāṭ during February 1025, when the town was threatened by famine-stricken black slave infantry (*ʿabīd*) and criminals. The police force in Fusṭāṭ had to be reinforced by troops deployed at the palace. On 23 Dhū l-Ḥijja 415/25 February 1025, Badr al-Dawla Nāfidh, with white-skinned military slaves (*ghilmān*) and other infantry units (*rajjāla*), descended from Cairo to defend Fusṭāṭ and declared, in the name of the ruler, that the population was allowed to kill the *ʿabīd* who menaced them. Badr al-Dawla Nāfidh's force fought the *ʿabīd* and later was assisted by another force dispatched from Cairo.[18] A few days later, the inhabitants complained to the chief of the Lower Police that actually they had been robbed not by the *ʿabīd* but by mobsters living in Kūm Dīnār. The chief of police took severe measures and punished the suspects by flogging, and returned the plundered grain to its owners. Famine riots also swept Cairo, but there order was restored by one of the palace eunuchs.[19]

The available information indicates that during the late tenth and early eleventh centuries the chiefs of police were nominated from two specific groups: white-skinned and black eunuchs of the ruler, and free-born Berbers of the Kutāma. In 1008, Ghālib ibn Mālik was appointed commander of the two police forces in Fusṭāṭ and as *muḥtasib*, and his responsibilities are described as *al-naẓar fī l-balad*. His letter of appointment was read both at the Ancient Mosque and at Aḥmad ibn Ṭūlūn's Mosque.[20] During al-Ḥākim's rule, two of his high-ranking eunuchs, Muẓaffar al-Ṣaqlabī, the bearer of the ceremonial parasol, and Ghayn al-Khādim, were given authority over the police forces and entrusted with the supervision of the markets, and such combination of posts was not exceptional. Reliance on Kutāma and eunuchs typifies the political and ethnic changes associated with Fatimid rule, while in

[17] Musabbiḥī, 44, 47, 68, 70, 71, 90; Halm, *Die Kalifen von Kairo*, 143, 315.
[18] Musabbiḥī, 87.
[19] Musabbiḥī, 87–8, 89.
[20] Maqrīzī, *Ittiʿāẓ*, II, 73.

early Abbasid Fusṭāṭ chiefs of police were drawn from Arab tribal groups and *mawālī*.[21] A typical chief of police was Badr al-Dawla Abū l-Futūḥ Mūsā ibn al-Ḥasan, who served as chief of the Lower Police, but in 1021 was appointed governor of Upper Egypt. His next two assignments were as head of the Chancery and *wisāṭa* (office of intermediary, meaning between the ruler and the people), an office replacing that of the vizier. He held this position for nine months and was executed in early 1023. It is said that the staggering sum, must likely highly exaggerated, of 620,000 *dīnārs* was found following his demise.[22] The combination of administrative (Chancery) and executive (police, governorship) assignments was highly unusual.

The inner world of the people appointed as chiefs of police during the Fatimid period remains hidden from us and is never alluded to in the sources. An exceptional indirect glimpse is offered by the biography of the grammarian Muḥammad ibn Barakāt (1029–1126). Maqrīzī writes that in 1068 he was studying grammar with a teacher who lived in seclusion on the roof of the Ancient Mosque, immersed in worship. Apparently, Muḥammad ibn Barakāt made a living as tutor to the children of the chief of police in Fusṭāṭ and also dined at his table. He used to receive two loaves of bread: one he regularly gave to his teacher and the other he sold on the market for fourteen *dirhams*. He used the money to bribe the attendants of the palace's library to provide him with books. Fascinating though Maqrīzī's biography of Muḥammad ibn Barakāt is, it also sheds some light on the unnamed chief of police.[23] He certainly was not a eunuch. As for any other member of the elite, the education of his children was for him a priority, and he survived well the early years of the disastrous great calamity and was also able to provide for the teacher of his children.

[21] For two brief obituary notes about Kutāmī chiefs of the police in Fusṭāṭ, see Musabbiḥī, 101, 108. For Muẓaffar al-Ṣaqlabī's appointment in 1004, see Maqrīzī, *Ittiʿāẓ*, II, 48, and for Ghayn's career between 1011 and 1013, see 89, 91, 100, 102. For pre-Fatimid Fusṭāṭ, see ʿAbd al-Ẓāhir, 'Aṣḥāb Shurṭat Miṣr', 5–6.

[22] Maqrīzī, *Ittiʿāẓ*, II, 128–9. The post of *wisāṭa* was created at the inception of al-Ḥākim's reign. See Halm, *Die Kalifen von Kairo*, 172.

[23] See *Kitāb al-Muqaffā*, V, 426–31, esp. 428.

A Criminal Chronicle, Fusṭāṭ 1023–1025

The history of crime in medieval Islam bears on many interwoven sociological, legal and institutional aspects.[24] There is a considerable body of literature on these topics devoted either to specific social groups such Banū Sāsān or to hashish addicts or to specific cities such as ninth- to twelfth-century Baghdad or Mamlūk Cairo.[25] This section reflects the multi-dimensional nature of any discussion of crime, but is narrowly focused, which, I would argue, has its advantages. It allows us to focus on the question of how criminal justice was administered in a specific urban and historical context which is quite well-known.

The nomination of eunuchs as chiefs of police indicates that it was a post of paramount significance for the ruler. The importance of the police is also indicated by the efforts of the Fatimid propagandists, who were active in Fusṭāṭ on the eve of the Fatimid conquest, to win the loyalty of the chief of police of that time. Their efforts were successful and the co-operation of the police proved instrumental immediately after the conquest.[26] The nomination of eunuchs also accentuates the question of how criminal justice could have been administered by them when left unsupervised by jurists. Owing to the surviving fragments of Musabbiḥī's chronicle we have for the first time an opportunity to answer some of these questions. Musabbiḥī had an interest in people from all walks of life and his narrative is an important source for the social history of Fusṭāṭ and Egypt, but the months covered by his history were marked by famine and this had a direct impact on how the grain market and market supervisor functioned. It seems, however, that no impact of the famine is discernible in reports about crimes. The lack of a direct correlation between the two (except when Fusṭāṭ was attacked by the *ʿabīd*) is a reflection of the slow and complex way the famine had evolved (see Chapter 5).

[24] For criminal offences and their prescribed punishments see Reinfandt, 'Crime and Punishment in Early Islamic Egypt', 655–6.

[25] For these social groups and their relations with the normative society and state institutions, see Bosworth, *The Mediaeval Islamic Underworld*, I, 13–16; Rosenthal, *The Herb. Hashish versus Medieval Muslim Society*, 127–30. Frequently, social protest turned violent and involved criminal behaviour. See Sabari, *Mouvements populaires*, ch. 2; Lapidus, *Muslim Cities*, ch. 5; Petry, *The Criminal Underworld*, esp. ch. 9; Elbendary, *Crowds and Sultans*, esp. ch. 6.

[26] Al-Anṭākī, 133; Maqrīzī, *Ittiʿāẓ*, I, 102, 110, 117. The commander of the police who co-operated with the Fatimids was Ḥusayn ibn Lu'lu', but he was replaced shortly after the conquest. The name Ḥusayn ibn Lu'lu' is unusual; Lu'lu' (pearl) is mostly a name of white-skinned eunuchs.

The first report to be discussed refers to events that took place on 22 Jumādā II 414/11 September 1023, when Ṣabūḥ al-Ṣaqlabī, the chief of police, apprehended a man and his wife, flogged them, displayed them publicly, and ordered it to be proclaimed that this was a punishment for one who had pimped his female family member to Jews and Christians.[27] About a year later (24 Rajab 415/1 October 1024), two Christian men were found in the company of two Muslim women, and Musabbiḥī provides two different accounts of the event. In the annalistic section of his chronicle he writes that all of them were flogged and paraded in Fusṭāṭ, while in the obituaries for the years 1024–5 he adds that the two Christians were put to death.[28] These accounts are complementary. Perhaps the execution took place later on, and the full account is therefore narrated in the obituary section of the text.

Two other reports also refer to cases involving sexual mores. On 9 Shawwāl 415/14 December 1024, Ibn Kāfī al-Kutāmī flogged and paraded a hermaphrodite (*mukhannath*), asserting that he had served as a pimp for five women in his house. A few days later, on 12 Shawwāl 415/17 December 1024, the murder of another *mukhannath*, a broker originally from Baghdad, became known. He was a very wealthy person who dealt with merchandise, especially precious gems. He was a singer with a pleasant voice who kept singing slave-girls in his house but was also inclined towards beardless boys. It was said that he was murdered by the son of the cadi Ibn Manhāl, who was his lover, and that they used to meet at the house of Ibn Marzubān, the gambler. For four days his whereabouts were unknown, meaning, apparently, that he was last seen on 14 December. The police took no action, but the government seized his house and took the money, property and the singing slave-girls.[29] These are the only reports concerning illicit sexual conduct, while other reports refer to criminal cases that involved theft and murder.

[27] Musabbiḥī, 12. Prostitution was not a crime punished by *ḥudūd*, see Petry, *The Criminal Underworld*, 150. For prostitution and pimping in Mamlūk towns, see Martel-Thoumain, *Délinquance et ordre social*, index under prostitution/racolage, and for whorehouses, 51–2.

[28] Musabbiḥī, 50, 98.

[29] Musabbiḥī, 68, 104. For legal attitudes towards hermaphrodites, see Sanders, 'Gendering the Ungendered Body', 74–99. For other episodes of interaction between hermaphrodites and the society and its institutions, see Petry, *The Criminal Underworld*, 157. For gambling and gamblers, see Rosenthal, *Gambling in Islam*, esp. index under *q.m.r.* Shmuel Moreh understands the term *mukhannath* as referring to somebody involved in live performances. For example, he refers to the murdered broker in Musabbiḥī's account as an 'entertainer'. See *Live Theatre*, 25–7, esp. 26.

Several reports describe criminal cases with no allusion to violence. On 24 Muḥarram 415/7 April 1024, for example, a robber (*liṣṣ*) was caught and it was established (*wujida*) that he had robbed a shop. He was flogged, paraded through the town and returned to prison. On the same day a group of people were accused of robbing shops at al-Ṣaffayan (literary the Two Rows or a Colonnade, which, according to Goitein, served as 'an exchange in which all kinds of transactions were made'); some of them were flogged and some imprisoned. A search was mounted in the town to recover the money robbed from the merchants.[30]

On 29 Ṣafar 415/12 May 1024, a mystic stole a silver object from a Turk in Fusṭāṭ. He was apprehended by Ibn Kāfī al-Kutāmī and brought to the police headquarters for interrogation. He confessed about his (in modern parlance) criminal record and said that in the past he had stolen only two objects: one of silver and the other of metal. He was flogged and paraded, but his request to avoid the Great Market, where he might have been seen by his family, was granted. A few months later, on 29 Shaʿbān 415/5 November 1024, a person who had stolen two copper objects was severely flogged at the Lower Police, paraded with the two items and returned to prison.[31]

In Shaʿbān in 415/October 1024, a burglary took place in a warehouse located near the port of Tinnīs in Fusṭāṭ (to where goods from Tinnīs were shipped). A man from a rural area (*rīf*) found lodgings in a room on the upper floor of a warehouse (*ṭibāq al-makhzan*) and broke into the apartment of Abū l-Ḥusayn ibn Abī l-Qurqūbī, where he stored his goods and conducted business. The burglary took place on a Friday when al-Qurqūbī was at the Qarāfa (cemetery) and the burglar stole 1,200 *dīnārs* from the apartment. Al-Qurqūbī became aware of the theft only the next day, and the agent (*wakīl*) in charge of the warehouse was interrogated at the Lower Police, but he knew nothing about the man who had stayed at the warehouse. A search was mounted and information came that the perpetrator stayed in a village in Lower Egypt. The Qarāfiyya (i.e. al-Qurqūbī's companions, whom he used to befriend in the cemetery) arranged to fetch the

[30] Musabbiḥī, 19. For the wide range of meanings associated with the term *liṣṣ* (pl. *luṣūṣ*), see Martel-Thoumian, *Délinquance et ordre social*, 355.

[31] Musabbiḥī, 30, 61.

burglar, who was brought to the police and interrogated. He confessed to his crime and returned 300 *dīnārs*, while another 400 *dīnārs* were recovered from his sister to whom he had given 500 *dīnārs*. A man from the village brought 100 *dīnārs*, but 400 *dīnārs* remained unaccounted for. The burglar remained in prison, but his fate is not alluded to. The Qarāfiyya also appear in another report about criminal activity: on 8 Dhū l-Qaʿda 415/11 January 1025, a person who had stolen money from them was brought to the Lower Police and his right hand was amputated. He was paraded and brought back to the prison, where he died, but he was granted a proper burial. Although no explanation is offered for the severity of the punishment, the Qarāfiyya must have been a highly esteemed social group and a crime against them was perceived as a grave offence.[32]

Another report also refers to non-violent crime, but of a particularly heinous nature. On 28 Rajab 415/5 October 1024, a person who had exhumed a grave in the Muqaṭṭam desert was caught and later executed in the Qarāfa, where his body was put on display.[33] The severity of the punishment indicates the outrageous nature of the crime.

On 4 Ramaḍān 415/9 November 1024, a person was flogged, paraded and forced to ring two bells, loudly crying 'This is double punishment for somebody who stole on such a day'. This peculiar form of punishment was applied because the person was a jailer who used to ring bells on prisoners at the Banān Jail. The gist of the account is that he was shamed in the way he used to shame other inmates at the jail. On 5 Ramaḍān 415/10 November 1024, a person was found sitting drunk at the Textile Covered Market (Qayṣāriyyat al-Bazz) in Fusṭāṭ. He was jailed at the Lower Police jail. Although Musabbiḥī expresses his indignation that the crime took place in 'such an exalted month', the offender was punished mildly.[34]

In another case, the severity of the punishment directly reflects the

[32] Musabbiḥī, 58, 71, 107. The population that lived in the Qarāfa in 1526 is estimated at 10,000–12,000. See Taylor, *In the Vicinity of the Righteous*, 22–3. The term *qarāfiyya* must be understood as referring to a close-knit group of worshippers.

[33] Musabbiḥī, 98.

[34] Musabbiḥī, 62, 63. The reading Qayṣāriyya al-Burr, Wheat Covered Market, suggested by the editors, cannot be sustained. The term *qayṣāriyya* appears in the context of the textile trade. See Musabbiḥī, 103. The terms *tashīr* and *tajrīs*, meaning punishment by shaming, are interchangeable. See Tyan, *Histoire de l'organisation judiciaire*, 650; Lange, *Justice, Punishment*, 79–80.

gravity of the crime. On 26 Rajab 415/3 October 1024, a violent robbery took place at the Ancient Mosque in Fusṭāṭ. A money-changer who conducted his business at the Ḥammām al-Fār came to the mosque for evening prayers. He was watched by a person from the Delta, who saw him carrying a purse with money and attacked and stabbed him, but was unable to grab the purse. Although he fled from scene of the crime, he was caught by the public and brought to the headquarters of the Lower Police and imprisoned there. The mortally wounded money-changer was carried on a stretcher to his house accompanied by two witnesses sent by the chief of police in order to ensure the safe delivery of the purse to his family. The chief of police was authorised to execute the robber and the body was publicly displayed. The same account is repeated in the obituary section of Musabbiḥī's text, with one important addition: the money-changer recovered from his wounds and returned to do business in his shop. In this case the additional information reflects the time that lapsed between the crime, recorded in the annalistic section of the text, and the recovery of the money-changer.[35]

Apparently, as two other cases show, execution of offenders who committed murder regularly took place. On 29 Jumādā II 415/7 September 1024, a person strangled a woman who had raised him and looted the belongings she had at home. He was apprehended by the chief of the night patrol (*mutawallī l-ṭūf laylān*), who also recovered the looted goods. Next morning the body of the dead woman was discovered and the criminal was executed and his body put on public display in the cemetery. Another violent crime was committed on 1st Dhū l-Qaʿda 415/4 January 1025, the victims being Abū l-Ḥasan al-Sūsnajardī, a respected elderly merchant, and his young servant. They were slain in their house by gang of robbers. A search was mounted and one of the robbers was caught. The chief of the Lower Police was authorised to put him to death and he ordered that the execution be carried out. In another case, however, the fate of the perpetrators of a murder remains unknown. On 18 Shaʿbān 415/25 October 1024, a frail woman who lived in seclusion, described as a chaste woman who practised long fasts, was found strangled. She had a young servant who used to operate an oven next to her

[35] Musabbiḥī, 52–3, 98.

house. He and others were caught with the stolen property and brought for interrogation.[36]

The number of cases reported by Musabbiḥī is too small to allow us to understand why in some cases the police vigorously investigated crimes and pursued the criminals while in other cases they took no action. The police's passivity in the case of Ibn Abī l-Qurqūbī was not exceptional. The same happened in the case of Darī, a textile merchant. His stabbed body was found at the edge of the desert on 27 Dhū l-Qaʿda 415/30 January 1025. He had been robbed of his money and some of his clothes. Although the body was brought on a stretcher to the Lower Police, no investigation into the crime is reported.[37]

A crime of a completely different nature is reported under the entry for 9 Muḥarram 415/23 March 1024. A group of Koran reciters at the Ancient Mosque brought Abū Zakariyya to the Lower Police and testified against him. Abū Zakariyya was a Christian who had converted to Islam, and, upon his conversion, collected many prophetic traditions, read the Koran, stayed at a mosque and performed the pilgrimage to Mecca. Eventually he apostatised, and his execution was authorised directly by the *imām*-caliph (*al-ḥaḍra al-muṭahhara*, the Noble Presence) and carried out by the chief of the Lower Police.[38]

Additional details about the case and crucial background facts are provided by al-Anṭākī. Towards the end of al-Ḥākim's reign a dramatic reversal of anti-*dhimmī* policies occurred. It involved the rebuilding of destroyed churches, the return of their *awqāf* lands, and permission for Christians who had adopted Islam under duress to return to Christianity. In a symbolic gesture marking their return to *dhimmī* status, Christians who relinquished Islam wore the distinctive clothes typical of non-Muslims, known in Muslim law as *ghiyār*. All were aware (i.e. Al-Ḥākim and the Christians who solicited him to relinquish Islam) that this shift in policies might be considered apostasy (*irtidād*). Al-Ḥākim therefore ordered the police to protect the Christians

[36] Musabbiḥī, 97, 101, 106. For the night watch, or patrol, as part of the police functions, see Tyan, *Histoire de l'organisation judiciaire*, 590.

[37] Musabbiḥī, 110. Crime and punishment in a provincial setting is a little-researched topic, see Reinfandt, 'Crime and Punishment in Early Islamic Egypt', 633–40.

[38] Musabbiḥī, 90.

who had reverted to Christianity.[39] The whole situation must have been highly volatile, and al-Anṭākī avoids both the term *irtidād* and any reference to Koran 9:60: 'There is no compulsion in religion.' Following al-Ḥākim's demise, under the rule of al-Ẓāhir (1021–36), the reversal of al-Ḥākim's anti-*dhimmīs* policies intensified: more Christians relinquished Islam, *ghiyār* regulations were eased, churches were rebuilt and their endowments restored. Most significantly, there was no public backlash either against the regime or against the Christians who had publicly returned to Christianity. Therefore, one must see the accusations against Abū Zakariyya as personal: he was singled out.

According to al-Anṭākī, Abū Zakariyya was among those who were granted permission to relinquish Islam. The question is whether the permission was granted personally or, more likely, collectively. The accusations levelled against him were because of his immersion in Islam and therefore the case was handled as *irtidād*, but due legal process was maintained. Al-Anṭākī claims that the execution took place following ten days during which Abū Zakariyya was given the opportunity to repent his apostasy.[40]

Al-Anṭākī s accounts provide the clue for understanding another case reported by Musabbiḥī, which concerns a young unnamed Christian who had converted to Islam and lived as a Muslim. He performed the pilgrimage and raised two daughters as Muslims. Because of his immersion in Islam his return to Christianity was considered apostasy and he was executed on 7 Sha'bān 415/14 October 1024.[41] Judging from the police involvement in Abū Zakariyya's case, one would assume that the police were also involved in this case.

Musabbiḥī's avoidance of the term *irtidād* when reporting on crimes against religion is unexplained, especially as al-Ẓāhir's regime provided the legal framework for accommodating the policy of allowing widespread renunciation of Islam. At the inception of his rule, al-Ẓāhir published a decree that dealt with a range of issues, including a reference to claims of adopting Islam under duress. The decree referred to the Koranic dictum 'There is no compul-

39 Al-Anṭākī, 231–2.
40 Al-Anṭākī, 238.
41 Musabbiḥī, 99.

sion in religion' and, therefore, relinquishing Islam would not be considered *irtidād*. The regime also took practical steps to forestall any accusations of *irtidād*. Christians who relinquished Islam, including those who returned from exile in Byzantium, had to pay the poll tax for the period during which they had adopted Islam up until the time they had relinquished it.[42] Having successfully provided the declarative and practical cover for its policies, the regime also remained attentive to demands coming from below concerning specific cases that were perceived as *irtidād* and could not have been accommodated within the framework created to handle this specific issue.

In Abū Zakariyya's case the cadi played no role. Ibn Ḥajar reports, in a somewhat incoherent way, an earlier case of apostasy that was examined by the cadi Muḥammad ibn al-Nuʿmān and involved an eighty-year-old Christian who had converted to Islam and committed *irtidād*. He was asked to repent, but refused. The case was brought to the attention of al-ʿAzīz, who handed the offender to the chief of police and ordered the cadi to send four witnesses to urge the man to repent (again?). Al-ʿAzīz also promised the offender 100 *dīnārs* if he repented but upon his refusal authorised his execution. The body was thrown into the Nile.[43]

Another case of *irtidād* took place during the rule of al-Mustanṣir and, as in Abū Zakariyya's case, the cadi was not involved. The people who apprehended the apostate at the market brought him directly to the custody of the chief of police. The case is known only from a Coptic source and has been discussed by Johannes den Heijer. In this case, the final authorisation to execute the apostate, who actively sought martyrdom, was granted by the vizier.[44]

[42] Al-Anṭākī, 237–8, 239. The conversion of *dhimmīs* to Islam under duress during al-Ḥākim's rule was also noted by the geographically and chronologically distant Ibn al-Athīr (1160–1233). Perhaps his interest in the case was driven by his hostility to the Fatimids, since he emphasises the permission given to them to renounce Islam. See VIII, 40. Sibṭ ibn al-Jawzī (d. 1256), another historian with no sympathy for the Fatimids, states (37) that those who renounced Islam committed *irtidād* and should have been executed.

[43] Ibn Ḥajar, ed. Gottheil, 246 (text), 277 (trans.). For a brief allusion to a case of apostasy handled, apparently, by ʿAlī ibn al-Nuʿmān, see 243. It seems that caliphs were always involved in cases of *irtidād* and their authorisation was necessary for the execution of the offender. In 856, the caliph al-Mutawakkil was involved in such a case. The apostate was asked to repent his *irtidād* and, when he refused, he was put to death. Ibn al-Jawzī, VI, 3184.

[44] See 'The Martyrdom of Bifām Ibn Baqūra al-Ṣawwāf', 452–84, esp. 470–1. Another case, dated to 978, took place in Damīra and involved a Muslim who converted to Christianity and sought

The question of who authorised the execution of apostates has wider ramifications, and one can ask who held the ultimate coercive powers in the state. In many cases it was the de jure or de facto ruler who applied them directly, bypassing the judicial bodies, be they the cadi or the chief of police. The first years of Fatimid rule in Egypt are well-documented through Maqrīzī's quotations of Ibn Zūlāq and were marked by determined efforts by the new regime to establish law and order and to fight local and foreign enemies. Highwaymen were executed by Jawhar in 970, and others, described as being engaged in lawless activities, were put to death in 973. High-ranking commanders and soldiers of the former Ikhshidid regime were also executed but more harmless unruly protesters (an old blind woman) were imprisoned. In 973, Jawhar also backed up the market supervisor who took punitive actions against money-changers, but the regime was quite restrained when dealing with them. The Berber troops that made up Jawhar's and al-Muʿizz's armies also proved to be an unruly element; they clashed with and robbed people in Fusṭāṭ in 972 and in 974. The regime made an effort to return the looted goods and arrested some of them.[45]

The regime also handled in a highly authoritative way issues pertaining to its religious identity. In 979, the regime proclaimed, most likely in the form of an edict, that swearing in the name of the Commander of the Faithful was forbidden, only oaths taken in the name of God being allowed. The wording of the proclamation was menacing; subjects were threatened with forfeiting their *dhimma* (protection). The only possible explanation is that, in the regime's perception, what was at stake was its conservative Ismāʿīlī identity, which maintained that the *imām*-caliph should not be presented as equal to God. Other measures were taken against Sunnī opponents or challengers. In 991, a person who kept a copy of Mālik's *Muwaṭṭa'* was flogged and paraded, a type of punishment usually inflicted by the chief of

martyrdom. The case is known from a Christian source and the crowd played a dominant role in the unfolding events. Although the cadi and governor are mentioned, the people were the driving force behind the execution of the martyr. See Swanson, 'The Martyrdom of Jirjis (Mazāḥim)', 431–51, esp. 432–4.

45 Maqrīzī, *Ittiʿāẓ*, I, 120, 122, 128, 130–1, 132, 139, 148. For the involvement of Abbasid caliphs in the execution of a murderer and highwaymen in 871 and 933, see Ibn al-Jawzī, VII, 3345, VIII, 3843.

police. In 995, in the midst of preparations for a military campaign, a person claiming to be a Sufyānī was executed.[46]

The Police and the Urban Society of Fusṭāṭ

The frequent use of verbs in the passive form in Musabbiḥī's reports about criminal events in Fusṭāṭ hinders understanding of the inner workings of the police forces in the town. Questions concerning how criminals were caught and by whom remain unanswered. The use of the passive also leaves the reader in the dark as to which government body was involved in the handling of the reported cases. Musabbiḥī, for example, reports that on 13 Muḥarram 415/27 March 1024 a woman in a market was knocked down and killed by the camel of a water carrier, who was apprehended and arrested. One would assume that the market supervisor would be involved in the case. However, if the offender had been caught by the public, he might have been brought either to the police or market supervisor. This report alludes to two real problems: regulations concerning how water carriers should handle their camels and, on another level, lack of clear demarcation lines between the bodies involved in the administration of justice in an urban society. Although each of these bodies had its own legal and institutional identity, the overlap between them was considerable and, as has been pointed out by Goitein, this baffled contemporaries.[47] The way Musabbiḥī writes also hinders our understanding of the incarceration powers vested with the chief of the police. It is clear that the chief of police had the authority to jail offenders. The existence of a jail under his authority in Fusṭāṭ is alluded to by the expressions *ḥabs al-maʿūna* and, more explicitly, *ḥabs al-maʿūna bi-Miṣr*, while emirs and other high-ranking people were imprisoned at the palace in *khizānat al-bunūd*.[48] A police headquarters was built in 846, south of the Ancient Mosque, and was known as Shurṭa. A gate of the mosque's compound leading to the Shurṭa was adorned with

[46] Maqrīzī, *Ittiʿāẓ*, I, 253, 273, 287. The possible explanation for the execution of the Sufyānī is that in apocalyptic *ḥadīth* a Sufyānī descendant appears as the opponent of the Mahdī.

[47] An edict regulating the water carriers' trade was published in 991. Maqrīzī, *Ittiʿāẓ*, I, 276; Musabbiḥī, 91; Goitein, *Med. Soc.* II, 371.

[48] Maqrīzī, *Khiṭaṭ*, II, 515.

a wooden inscription which referred to the edifice as al-Dār al-Hāshimiyya al-Mubāraka.[49]

Musabbiḥī's way of writing raises the question of how he got his information about events in Fusṭāṭ. The precise dating of the events would suggest that he derived information from written sources: a Lower Police logbook, for instance. On the other hand, it is also possible that he relied on oral information which he arranged in annalistic sequence. Another issue is the absence of references to crime in Cairo. Musabbiḥī lived in Fusṭāṭ but attended events at the palace; many of his obituaries are dedicated to members of the royal family and people of the court, but his knowledge of everyday events in Cairo must have been deficient.

Whatever the explanation may be for Musabbiḥī's use of the passive, his reports depict the police as a well-established body which enjoyed public approval and perhaps even some respect. People handed caught criminals in to the police, and turned to them requesting protection from criminals. Three reports deserve closer examination. When reading between the lines of the report about the violence committed against the money-changer at the Ancient Mosque, one must note that the robber was not lynched by the public but brought alive to the Lower Police. The police were also efficient in handing over the victim to the care of his family and ensured the safe delivery of the money in his purse. No less remarkable is the appeal to the chief of the Lower Police by the people robbed by criminals during the attack of the famished *ʿabīd* on Fusṭāṭ. The police who failed to protect them at the time were, nonetheless, quite effective in recovering the looted grain and returning it to its owners. The last point to be considered in this context is the choice made by the reciters of the Koran at the Ancient Mosque to bring Abū Zakariyya to the chief of police and not to the cadi, which reflects their perception of the relative strength of these two bodies. One would expect them to opt for the cadi, but this was not the case.

Whatever the relative strength of the police was among the different bodies involved in the administration of justice in the capital, their limitations in terms of motivation to act and capabilities are illustrated by the

[49] Musabbiḥī, 19, 52, 58, 71, see also 98 and 107; Maqrīzī, *Khiṭaṭ*, III, 598. For jails in Baghdad, see Tillier, 'Prisons et autorités urbaines', 399–406, 408. Occasionally, jails in Baghdad were attacked and the inmates set free by the population and the *ʿayyārūn*. See Sabari, *Mouvements populaires*, 66, 74.

Qurqūbī case. Only Qurqūbī's wider social network – the Qarāfiyya – proved instrumental in the recovery of two-thirds of the 1,200 looted *dīnārs*. They gathered information and brought the robber to the police for interrogation, and must have been involved in the partial recovery of the money. They did what the police should have done. The feeble response of the police in this case can be explained by the fact that the *shurṭa* was an urban institution and had no jurisdiction or ability to function outside the confines of Fusṭāṭ.

However, as illustrated by the case of the murdered hermaphrodite broker, even within the urban context the motivation of the police to act was selective. In this case their passivity can be explained by the lifestyle of the people involved in the event, no harm was done to the normative society, and the regime was quick to exploit the circumstances to its advantage. There was a considerable degree of tolerance for a deviant lifestyle, the broker was not ostracised and conducted his business undisturbed with the normative members of the society, but no one especially cared about his fate when a crime took place within the deviant group to which he belonged.

Social sensibilities are also illustrated through the prism of sexual crimes. Pimping and prostitution were punished, like the theft of objects of low value, by flogging and shaming. However, any sexual relations between Muslim women and non-Muslim men were illicit and even a suspicion of such relations bore grave consequences for the non-Muslim men. Social sensibilities also came to the fore in other cases. Theft of objects of low value was lightly punished except when the victims were the Qarāfiyya, when the punishment prescribed by Islamic law was applied. Why exactly the Qarāfiyya were held in such high esteem and who they were remains unknown. The reports discussed so far clearly indicate that the chiefs of police, whatever their social background, applied criminal justice that reflected social norms (respect for the Qarāfiyya, bigotry towards non-Muslims) more than strict legal requirements.

The Rulers and the Capital City

Al-Ḥākim used the police as a tool for the implementation of his edicts.[50] The regime's direct involvement in the life of the capital city, however, went

[50] For explicit references pertaining to the year 1012, see Maqrīzī, *Ittiʿāẓ*, II, 89, 91; *Kitāb al-Muqaffā*, V, 433.

beyond control of the bodies responsible for the administration of justice. Actually, as the riots of the famished *ʿabīd* show, the police were not a body strong enough to maintain order in cases perceived by the regime as threating its wider economic interests or security. Three further cases of different backgrounds must also be discussed. The first case illustrates the ruler's intervention in events that took place in the capital through administrative channels, while the second illustrates the use of troops deployed at the palace to restore order in the capital. The third case illustrates the scope and might of the regime's coercive powers when the army was mobilised to deal with internal security threats.

In May 984, a foreign merchant was murdered and robbed at the Ikhshīd Qayṣariyya in Fusṭāṭ, frequented by textile merchants. Rashīq, the slave of Maymūn al-Dubbah, chief of the Lower Police, made several arrests, including the sons of the murdered merchant. People, however, accused Rashīq of being behind the plot while arresting innocent people. A petition to this effect was submitted to al-ʿAzīz, who handed it to the vizier Ibn Killis. Maqrīzī, relying on Ibn al-Ṣayrafī (1071–1147), a well-known administrator and author of administrative manuals, quotes fragments of al-ʿAzīz's letter concerning the petition. Al-ʿAzīz expresses dismay that such a crime could have happened in a secure precinct, in a place inhabited by Muslims. He is especially concerned that it occurred 'under our wings in our city', and the vizier is urged 'to cleanse this disgrace from our dynasty and [the] grief it has caused to it'. The strong letter stands in contrast to the feeble response of the vizier, who merely dismissed Rashīq from his post but took no action against Maymūn al-Dubbah. It must be pointed out that in al-ʿAzīz's letter the two people responsible for the police are referred to as 'having no fear of God', which alludes to both the chief of police and his deputy.[51] Undoubtedly, Ibn al-Ṣayrafī's intention was to glorify both the ruler and the vizier as attentive to people's grievances, but police corruption was a problem that the regime found difficult to rectify.

On Friday, 24 Rabīʿ II 386/16 May 996, large-scale riots erupted in Fusṭāṭ and 107 Amalfitan merchants who stayed in Dār al-Mānak were

[51] Maqrīzī, *Ittiʿāẓ*, I, 263–6. Abū Saʿīd Maymūn al-Dubbah is mentioned as a high-ranking courtier at the death of al-ʿAzīz. See Ibn Muyassar, 174.

killed. At the time of the riots al-ʿAzīz ws staying at a military camp outside Cairo, supervising preparation for a military campaign to Syria to fight the Byzantines. The riots followed a fire that broke out and consumed several warships under construction at the Arsenal in Maqs. The sailors and the common people blamed the foreign merchants staying at Dār al-Mānak near the arsenal for setting the fire and stormed their dwelling place, killing 107 people and looting merchandise worth 90,000 *dīnārs*. Other foreign merchants were imprisoned at the Arsenal. The riots spread beyond Maqs and several churches were also looted. The police failed to quell the riots at the time, and the regime had to deal with the consequences of these events. Cairo, as far as can be ascertained, was not affected by these events.

Three people of the ruling establishment were involved in restoring order in the city: ʿIsā ibn Nestrious, the Christian vizier (or chief administrator) of the Fatimid state, Abū l-Ḥasan Yānis al-Ṣaqlabī, described as in charge of Cairo during al-ʿAzīz's intended campaign in Syria, and Masʿūd al-Ṣaqlabī, the chief of police. They went to the Arsenal to secure the safety of the foreigners imprisoned there, and the police (*aṣḥāb al-shuruṭ*) proclaimed a harshly worded decree ordering the return of the goods looted from the foreign merchants. Many arrests were made and the offenders were flogged and paraded through the town accompanied by armed troops and torch-bearers while heralds proclaimed: 'This is the punishment for those who provoke disorder and rob those protected by the Commander of the Faithful, and those who watch should learn a lesson. [And this] cannot be considered a slip [on their part], and their tears invoke no mercy.' On 8 Jumādā II 386/28 June 996, executions were carried out by Abū Aḥmad Jaʿfar, an associate of Yānis. In order to forestall any hostile reaction to this display of state violence, the private regiment of Yānis was brought to Fusṭāṭ and the police were reinforced by a unit, or units, of naphta-hurlers. It must be pointed out that the punishments meted out were decided by a lottery in which each offender drew his lot.[52]

[52] Maqrīzī, *Khiṭaṭ*, III, 619–20, quoting Musabbiḥī. For the looting of churches during the riots, see al-Anṭākī, 178–9. Although the fate of the offenders was decided by drawing lots, the standard terminology associated with the practice is not employed. The texts by Musabbiḥī/Maqrīzī and al-Anṭākī state that they drew a *ruqʿa* (a piece of paper) on which their fate either to be flogged or to be executed was written. For a broader discussion of the casting of lots, see Rosenthal, *Gambling in Islam*, ch. 2; Crone and Silverstein, 'The Ancient Near East and Islam: The Case of

When the broader picture of Fatimid trade with its European partners (Italians and Byzantines) is considered, it becomes apparent that the Fatimid effort at damage control was successful and the authorities managed to convince the European trading nations that what happened was an exception to the rule and that the regime would continue to protect them. The internal repercussions of these events are also well-known. ʿIsā ibn Nestrious was not directly involved in punishing the rioters; he focused on rebuilding the navy and his efforts were successful. Al-ʿAzīz died at the military camp, and the intended campaign came to a halt. Following the coronation of al-Ḥākim, the new men in power in Cairo made ʿIsā ibn Nestrious a scapegoat for the way the regime had handled the riots and put him to death and paid compensation to the families of those executed for participating in the riots. Yānis's career was unaffected by his involvement in quelling the riots. Following the death of al-ʿAzīz he was entrusted with responsibility for the palaces and, in 998, nominated as governor of Barqa and rewarded with 5,000 *dīnārs*.[53]

In 1124, the vizier al-Ma'mūn envisioned a threat against the caliph's and his own life and took measures to prevent the infiltration of the country by agents of the Assassins of Alamūt. His first step was to replace the governor of Ascalon and to ensure that all state employees (*arbāb al-khidam*) in the town were native people known to the authorities. The focus on Ascalon and the inland routes must have been motivated by the fall of Tyre, the last Muslim port on the Eastern Mediterranean, to the Franks (7 July 1124). Ascalon became an important gateway to Egypt from the Muslim East, and merchants arriving to the town were closely inspected and registered. The same precautions were applied to the camel owners who brought merchants and other people to the town.

The measures taken in the capital were equally extensive. The governors of Cairo and Fusṭāṭ were ordered to impose a curfew and register the names of people and their occupations in order to identify the strangers who had arrived from Persia (*bilād al-ʿAjam*). The next step involved sending the army to arrest suspects according to prepared lists. One must assume that the

Lot-Casting', 423–50. For the location of Maqs, the Arsenal and Dār al-Mānak, see Sayyid, *La capitale de l'Égypte*, 143–4, 603.

[53] See *Khiṭaṭ*, III, 46–7.

army was also involved in imposing the curfew. To what extent the regime was really able to carry out the operation on the scale described remains an open question. The accounts glorifying the vizier for the achievement seem over-enthusiastic.[54] The three accounts discussed above point out that when the overall coercive resources of the Fatimid state are examined, the *shurṭa* was indeed an urban police force intended to fight crime, but was too small to maintain law and order in the capital.

[54] Ibn Muyassar, 97–9; Maqrīzī, *Ittiʿāẓ*, III, 108–9; Sayyid, *Al-Dawla al-Fāṭimiyya*, 341–2. For the fall of Tyre, see Halm, *Kalifen und Assassinen*, 158–60, and for the attempts to discover Alamūt's agents, 152–3, including translations of the relevant accounts.

5

The Law of the Market

Ḥisba Manuals

There is a long Middle Eastern tradition of regulating and supervising commerce and market life embodied in the post of market supervisor known in Greek, Persian, Aramaic and Hebrew as *agoranomos*, *vazarbad*, *rabb shūk* and *baʿal ha-shūk*. One can argue that practice in Late Antiquity continued under the guise of Islam, and in the Egyptian context, one of the earliest references alluding to such continuity is from the eighth century. The jurist Ḥarmala ibn ʿImrān ibn Qurrād, known as Abū Ḥafṣ (699–776), was appointed in charge of *sūq Miṣr*, meaning a market supervisor in Fusṭāṭ. In ninth-century documentary sources the term *ṣāḥib al-sūq* appears. One document is a letter addressed to the *ṣāḥib al-sūq*, concerning the delivery of vinegar to a certain person and his six companions. In late literary sources the term *muḥtasib* is widely used, and Maqrīzī, for example, refers to the jurist Abū Muzāḥim (d. 818) as *muḥtasib*. What the range of the *ṣāḥib al-sūq*'s/*muḥtasib*'s duties could have been is perhaps reflected by the responsibilities held by Ḥasan ibn ʿAlī ibn Mūsā al-ʿAddās (d. 935), who was in charge of *ḥisba*, *daqīq* (flour) and *sūq Miṣr*.[1] The account should not be understood as indicating three different posts, since the term *ḥisba* subsumes supervision of the markets and the grain/bread trade.

[1] Ibn Yūnus, I, 112–13, 121–2; Maqrīzī, *Kitāb al-Muqaffā*, III, 260–1; VII, 424; Grohmann, *Arabic Papyri*, V, 152–3. I owe the last reference to the kindness of one of the anonymous readers on behalf of EUP. In Kūfa in the first half of the eighth century, responsibility for *ḥisba* also included the supervision of measures and weights. See Chalmeta, 'La ḥisba en Ifriqiya et al-Andalus', 89, 91. For references to *ḥisba* in Baghdad during al-Ma'mūn's reign, see Tyan, *Histoire de l'organisation judiciaire*, 623.

The epigraphic evidence is essential for the early history of the *ḥisba* institution, since both terms, *ṣāḥib al-sūq* and *muḥtasib*, appear on glass weights and measures issued by officials in late Umayyad and early Abbasid Egypt. The earliest appearance of the title *ṣāḥib al-sūq* cannot be securely established, but the title *muḥtasib* is engraved on a stamp inscription of a *wuqiyya* weight from the time of the governorship of ʿAlī ibn Sulaymān (786–7). Alexander H. Morton has suggested a link between this epigraphic reference to a *muḥtasib* and the characterisation of ʿAlī ibn Sulaymān as a governor who followed the 'commanding right and forbidding wrong' doctrine, which eventually became the motto of the *ḥisba* institution. Other stamp inscriptions on glass weights which bear the names of governors and *muḥtasibs* are from the second half of the ninth century.[2]

When the wider institutional and conceptual context is considered, the notion that early Islam was a direct heir of Late Antiquity should be cautiously approached. The assumption that Islamic *muḥtasib* is a derivative of *agoranomos* has been questioned by Benjamin R. Foster, while Crone has suggested that the terms *ṣāḥib al-sūq/muḥtasib* were borrowed from Hebrew, stating: 'the *muḥtasib* tells us more about the relationship between the Arab conquerors and Judaism than it does about that between Greek, Roman and Islamic law.'[3] Any study of genetic links between Late Antiquity and Islamic towns and urban institutions is fraught with many difficulties, and another approach to understanding the Islamic market supervisor is to survey the early *ḥisba* manuals.

A *ḥisba* manual from ninth-century Ṭabaristān (ruled by the Zaydī *imāms* from 864) offers an insight into the perception of the institution and its underlying principles. R. S. Serjeant attributes the text to the Imām al-Nāṣir li-Ḥaqq Ḥasan ibn ʿAlī al-Uṭrūsh (d. 917) and, most likely, it reflects the socio-economic realities of the capital city of Āmul. The text is cast in the literary form of sayings of the Imām, who explains what a *muḥtasib* ought to know for proper execution of his duties. The post is presented as a required urban institution which owes its existence to the collective agreement of

2 See 'Ḥisba and Glass Stamps', 21–4.

3 Foster, 'Agoranomos and Muḥtasib', 128–44; Crone, *Roman, Provincial and Islamic Law*, 108. For an argument in favour of Arab roots of the *ḥisba* institution, see Ghabin, *Ḥisba*, 17–31.

the Shīʿī religious sages (*ʿulamāʾ ahl al-bayt*). Its deeper ideological underpinnings are, however, derived from the Koranic dictum of 'commanding right and forbidding wrong'. The example of ʿAlī is also invoked, and the Imām states that the *muḥtasib* should be versed in the affairs of the market and must emulate ʿAlī, who every morning inspected the markets.[4]

When the content of the manual is examined, it becomes clear that the range of duties entrusted to the *muḥtasib* also included supervision of the urban public sphere and the interaction between various social groups that took place there.[5] The *muḥtasib* was expected to secure the sacredness of the mosques by prohibiting trade and removing non-Muslims and storytellers from their precincts. The appearance of women in the public sphere and segregation between the sexes was also one of his duties. Illuminating though this text is, it offers no hint as to how the *muḥtasib* was expected to carry out his duties and what were the coercive powers vested in him and which legal and punitive principles governed his actions. In any case, the text alludes to the merger between the doctrine of 'commanding right and forbidding wrong' and the *ḥisba* institution.

The chapter devoted to the *ḥisba* in the anonymous text from the Buyid period makes no links between the institution and the 'commanding right and forbidding wrong' doctrine. It is impossible to properly evaluate the absence of such a linkage. Is it merely a reflection of the fragmentary preservation of the text, or a more significant indication of the slow development of such a correlation, which, perhaps, initially evolved at the geographical and socio-religious fringe of the Muslim world? The Buyid text, however, alludes to the position of *ḥisba* within the wider context of the administration of justice in the state: the appointee has to be knowledgeable in jurisprudence and be drawn from the ranks of the jurists. The text maintains that the task has its complexities and that some unnamed books of *ḥisba* should be studied.[6]

Moving from prescriptive literature to institutional realities, it can be

[4] Serjeant, 'A Zaydī Manual', 11. For a review of the *ḥisba* literature, see Shatzmiller, *Labour in Medieval Islam*, 71–80.

[5] It can be argued that this aspect of the Zaydī manual became a standard topic in the *ḥisba* literature and came to typify the range of the duties entrusted to a *muḥtasib*. See Klein, 'Between Public and Private', 41–62.

[6] Sadan, 'A New Source of the Buyid Period', 373, 376.

seen that the range of responsibilities entrusted to a *muḥtasib* in Baghdad of the second half of the tenth century was very broad. It included supervision of weights and measures, prices and the public sphere, including the way women and non-Muslim should dress.[7] The final merger between the *ḥisba* and public morals epitomised by the 'commanding right and forbidding wrong' concept was achieved by Ghazzālī (1111), and late medieval *ḥisba* manuals reflect the fusion between the institution and the concept.[8]

The public image of the *ḥisba* institution and the relations between *muḥtasibs* and the urban population rarely come to the fore in literary sources. For what it is worth, Sībawayhi was deeply antagonistic to *muḥtasibs*. He kept a grudge against many other people in positions of power, however, and mostly got away with his criticisms of them. In an encounter with a *muḥtasib* accompanied by guards (*aḥrās*), he launched a verbal attack on them and on the practice of ringing bells (*ajrās*) to shame offenders. He accused the *muḥtasib* of taking bribes (*barāṭīl*), and was equally critical of the (unnamed) person responsible for his nomination. Another of Sībawayhi's outbursts was against the *muḥtasib* Muḥammad ibn Jaʿfar ibn Salām, who, most likely, inflicted punishment on one of his neighbours. Sībawayhi complained to the vizier Jaʿfar ibn al-Furāt about the appointment of unworthy persons to the post.[9] What can be learnt from these anecdotes remains unclear.

The Grain Economy of Fusṭāṭ-Cairo

The functional aspects of the *ḥisba* institution are better reflected in the literary sources, which offer abundant information on the *muḥtasib*'s supervision of the grain and bread trade, aspects discussed neither by the Zaydī *ḥisba* manual nor by the anonymous Buyid-period text. Any meaningful discussion of the *muḥtasib*'s involvement in these aspects of the life of Fusṭāṭ-Cairo requires a brief explanation of the yearly Nile cycle, the typology of famines and the grain/bread trade market mechanism.

7 Sabari, *Mouvements populaires*, 30–1. For a broader discussion of the *ḥisba* institution in Baghdad, including the Seljukid period, see Lange, 'Changes in the Office of Ḥisba under the Seljuks', 157–81.

8 Cook, *Commanding Right*, 427–59, esp. 427, 435, 447.

9 Ibn Zūlāq, *Akhbār Sībawayhi al-Miṣri*, 29, 53. For Sībawayhi's complaints to Kāfūr about the market supervisor and the chief of police, see Maqrīzī, *Kitāb al-Muqaffā*, VII, 322.

The agricultural life of medieval Egypt was governed by the Nile and the Coptic calendar. The Nile's annual rise used to begin during the month of Ba'unah (8 June–7 July) and intensified during Abib (8 July–6 August), and took place first in Upper Egypt. The Nile usually reached plentitude (i.e. sixteen cubits as measured at the Fusṭāṭ Nilometer) during Misra (7 August–5 September), while the new agricultural year began during Tut (11/12 September–9/10 October). During Tut the seeds needed for the planting of wheat and barely were delivered to the fellahin, but the actual sowing began in Upper Egypt during Babah (11/12 October–9/10 November), and in other parts of the country during Kiyah (10/11 December–8/9 January). The agricultural cycle ended shortly before the beginning of the new rise of the Nile in Ba'unah and was marked by the distinction between winter crops, which included basic foods such as grain and beans as well as flax, and other cash crops such as cotton, sugar cane and watermelons, which were part of the summer crops.[10]

The typology of famines in medieval Egypt is rather simple, since famines occurred either as a result of the speculative withholding of supplies or as a result of the Nile not rising enough. Simple though this typology is, it determined what the regime could or could not do, and any assessment of the regime's actions must be directly related to the type of shortage that occurred. It must be emphasised that, in the case of shortages caused by insufficient inundation of the Nile, the wheat harvest and shipments of grain to the capital during the year in which the Nile failed ('the current year') were determined by the rise of the river in the preceding year, which could have been quite normal. Knowledge about a shortage in the next year created a buyers' market in 'the current year', leaving wide room for government intervention in both Fusṭāṭ-Cairo's grain market and the supply of bread. When, in the year following 'the current year', the full impact of grain shortage hit Fusṭāṭ-Cairo, the ability of the government to intervene and to alleviate the situation was quite limited.

The grain market of Fusṭāṭ-Cairo was influenced by two parallel events: the observation of the rise of the Nile and the arrival of freshly-harvested

[10] This section is based on late medieval agricultural calendars. These texts have been collected, translated into French and annotated by Pellat, *Cinq calendriers Égyptiens*.

wheat to the grain ports of the capital, where it was taxed. The size of the crop was determined by the rise of the Nile the previous year, but the volume and intensity of demand for the freshly harvested wheat were determined by the progress in the rise of the Nile in 'the current year', which indicated the fortunes of the next agricultural year. Famines did occur in 'the current year' because of predictions of a bad harvest in the next year, which created a buyers' market and drove prices up beyond the reach of many.

Furthermore, the capital's grain market was torn between the household grain economy of the regime and the commercial urban grain market. In Cairo, the regime stored grain and fodder and provided for the court, employees of the state, the army and navy, and special institutions such as the Royal Guest House. The commercial urban market operated in parallel with the regime's household grain economy but was influenced by it. The regime sold surplus grain on the urban market, but, in times of crisis, diverted and confiscated grain shipments intended for the commercial urban market to its granaries.[11]

The majority of the population bought bread on a daily basis and were dependent on oven owners (*farrānūn*) and bread vendors (*khabbāzūn*) for their purchases. The *farrān* served mostly the lower middle class and baked bread for customers who brought him dough, but he also baked bread from his own dough. The bread vendor served the working class and the vast urban underclass. Both professions are widely mentioned in twelfth- to fourteenth-century Egyptian *ḥisba* manuals, which provide sets of rules but do not discuss the economic aspects of these professions.[12] Literary sources clearly indicate that access to the various professional groups involved in the grain/bread trade was class-related, and the vast majority of the population were exposed to sharp price fluctuations and food insecurity.

The provision of the capital city and maintainance of affordable prices were a constant concern of the market supervisor. The basic tools at his disposal

[11] The basic distinction between the household grain economy of the regime and the commercial urban grain market has been put forward by Lapidus, 'The Grain Economy of Mamluk Egypt', 12–14, and is applicable to the Fatimid period too. See Maqrīzī, *Musawwadat Kitāb al-Mawāʿiẓ*, 246–8.

[12] One of the issues dealt with in the *ḥisba* literature is how to ensure that the fuel used for operating the ovens is neither human nor animal waste. Al-Shayzarī, 22–3; Ibn Bassām, 21–3, 61–2; Ibn al-Ukhūwah, 91–2.

were close control and supervision of the market, but minor problems with bread supplies are never properly explained in the sources. For example, a crisis erupted at the beginning of Rabīʿ II 359/end of January–February 970; whether it was related to the death of the serving *muḥtasib* remains unknown. Jawhar appointed Sulaymān ibn ʿAzza al-Maghribī market supervisor, and he imposed strict personal supervision over the grain port and grain merchants and flogged and paraded eleven millers. Quite possibly the violence he applied brought about his dismissal, but the difficulties in supply continued. He was reinstated in Dhū l-Qaʿda/September and resumed the same method of strict supervision over grain supplies, focusing on the brokers.[13] It must have been a minor crisis which did not necessitate the intervention of higher authorities.[14]

More serious were the events that took place in 1006 which began because of the insufficient rise of the Nile. In 1007 the full impact of the Nile's failure to reach plentitude a year earlier was fully felt. Moreover, for the second consecutive year the Nile's rise during Muḥarram 398/October 1007 was below optimum. Bread supply was gravely affected and punishments were inflicted on bread vendors. Maqrīzī's reports about these events are terse and the full gravity of the situation remains hidden from us. In July 1008 the government abolished taxes (*mukūs*) levied on grain and rice and invested Ghālib ibn Mālik (also referred to as Ghālib ibn Hilāl) with command of the two police forces and the *ḥisba* and with overall responsibility for the city (*naẓar fī l-balad*, meaning Fusṭāṭ). Reports about outbreaks of diseases in September 1008, March 1009 and October–November 1009 must be understood as indicating a famine and food shortages. We know very little about how the *muḥtasib* dealt with the crisis, but, perhaps less surprisingly, Ghālib ibn Mālik was executed in 1010.[15]

[13] Maqrīzī, *Ittiʿāẓ*, I, 117, 120, 122. In eighth- to ninth-century Kairouan the supervision of the markets was confounded with the post of *wālī*, while under the Aghlabids the post was combined with the *maẓālim* function. See Dachraoui, *Le califat fatimide*, 419–21.

[14] Maqrīzī, *Ittiʿāẓ*, II, 31; *Kitāb al-Muqaffā*, III, 9–10, referring to events of 1000. For the killing of a *muḥtasib* who, in the official version of the events, overstepped his authority and harmed people, see Maqrīzī, *Ittiʿāẓ*, II, 43, referring to events of 1001.

[15] Maqrīzī, *Ittiʿāẓ*, II, 70, 71, 73, 74, 76, 78, 79, 81, 83. Al-Ḥākim's policies were idiosyncratic and marked by investing some individuals with extensive administrative responsibilities. The eunuch Abū ʿAlī Manṣūr al-Jawdharī, for example, was entrusted with responsibility for pious endowments, *ḥisba*, the slave market and the grain ports. See Maqrīzī, *Musawwadat Kitāb al-Mawāʿiẓ*, 352; *Khiṭaṭ*, III, 12; Halm, *Die Kalifen von Kairo*, 38. Between Rajab 408/November 1017 and

The *Muḥtasib* and the Famine of 1024–1025

While our knowledge about the shortages during al-Ḥākim's rule is derived from Maqrīzī's brief summaries of the sources available to him, for the 1024–5 famine we have the original surviving fragments of Musabbiḥi's chronicler. His first record of the rise of the Nile is from Friday, 11 Jumādā II 414/5 September 1023, the height of the Nile being fourteen cubits and one finger. On that day the Coptic New Year was celebrated and the rise of the Nile took its normal course and, on Thursday, 13 Jumādā II/2 September, the Cairo Canal (Khalij) was opened. However, on Sunday, 23 Jumada II/12 September the Nile massively receded. This was an unprecedented event that led people to perform public supplicatory prayers and had a devastating effect on the grain market since it drove prices up, supplies ceased and a black market emerged. The price of bread also went up.[16] This was a panic response driven by the inner logic of the grain market mechanism. Up until that day everything had gone smoothly: the supply was regular (due to a good harvest determined by the rise of the Nile during the previous year) and the prices of wheat and bread affordable. However, in anticipation of a shortage the next year, those who could were buying more wheat than usual or withholding sales of their stocks; consequently, prices went up. Eventually, those who had stocks stopped selling in order to protect themselves from the anticipated next-year's shortage. The rising prices of wheat also pushed up the price of bread, which was prepared and baked on a daily basis. In social terms, it can be said that large purchases of wheat by the 'haves' (the urban upper class) drove prices up, immediately affecting the urban poor and the lower middle class, if such terms can be applied to a medieval society.

Another way of discussing the social consequences of the evolving crisis

his execution in Shawwāl/February 1018, Ja'far ibn al-Falāḥ was entrusted with administrative and fiscal responsibilities, including governorship of towns on the Mediterranean coast and the *ḥisba* and police in the capital. See Ibn al-Ṣayrafī, 31–2. The sphere of the *muḥtasib*'s responsibilities was flexible. Al-'Azīz's mother, for example, entrusted the *muḥtasib* al-Ḥusayn ibn 'Abd Allāh al-Farsī with the building of her numerous projects in the Qarāfa. See Maqrīzī, *Khiṭaṭ*, II, 580.

[16] Musabbiḥī, 10–11, 12–13. For the geography of the Cairo Canal, see Cornu, *Atlas*, map X; Halm, *Die Kalifen von Kairo* ch. 2, esp. 64–8, who provides extensive discussion of the Nile's geography and other aspects pertinent to the river's flow and rise. The fluctuations of prices during the 1024–5 famine has been extensively dealt with by Bianquis ('Une crise frumentaire', 65–101, esp. 74–5), and therefore the issue is left out of my discussion.

is to employ the terms 'structural poor' (meaning the permanent poor) and 'conjunctural poor' (meaning the temporary poor). Both terms are frequently used by historians of medieval and early modern Europe and were introduced into Middle Eastern studies by Mark R. Cohen. The 'structural poor' were the truly destitute who eked out a living on a daily basis, while the 'conjunctural poor' were people who usually lived on the verge of subsistence. The term applies to a diverse range of social groups, including artisans and small shopkeepers. These classes frequently fluctuated between poverty and subsistence and any rise in bread prices affected them immediately as bread was their staple food, which they bought on a daily basis. [17] We are completely in the dark about the wider social ramifications of the crisis, and about the lot of other groups disadvantaged because of age or gender, such as infants, orphans, widows and elderly men and women.

The regime's response to the evolving crisis was restrained and focused on the replacement of the market supervisor. The post of *muḥtasib* of Fusṭāṭ was offered to al-Abū Saʿīd al-ʿAmīdī, an administrator in charge of the Office of Payments, who declined it, claiming that it constituted a demotion relative to his current assignment which brought him into close contact with the ruler.[18] The post was accepted by Yaʿqūb ibn al-Dawwās al-Kutāmī (appointed on Sunday, 5 Rajab 414/23 September 1023), who was entrusted with the *ḥisba* in Fusṭāṭ, the markets and grain ports. Musabbiḥī's text requires close reading: the post offered was *ḥisba bi-Miṣr*, clearly indicating that Cairo was not affected by the crisis at that moment. The palace and the people living there relied on the 'household grain economy' and bread prices in Cairo must have been different. There was a link, nevertheless, between the twin cities of Fusṭāṭ and Cairo in the form of the grain ports through which Cairo got its supplies. Actually, without holding the post of *muḥtasib* of Cairo, Yaʿqūb ibn al-Dawwās was also responsible for the grain supplies of Cairo.

Yaʿqūb ibn al-Dawwās's first action was to punish by beating the bread vendors and floor merchants. Musabbiḥī asserts that these deeds brought

[17] See *Poverty and Charity*; 33–72; *The Voice of the Poor*, 31–46.

[18] Musabbiḥī, 13–14. By training al-ʿAmīdī was a grammarian and possibly attended *ʿilm* sessions convened by the ruler. For his nomination in 1041 to the Chancery, see Maqrīzī, *Kitāb al-Muqaffā*, V, 294. For some of his literary output, see Sanders, 'A New Source for the History of Fatimid Ceremonial', 127–31.

about the renewal of the bread supply and people calmed down. The effect of these punitive actions against the professional groups involved in the more narrow mechanism of bread production and supply was short-lived. On Wednesday, 8 Rajab/26 September, the bread shortage intensified and new steps were taken to deal with the situation. These involved the forcible opening of grain stores (*makhāzin*) belonging to people of the ruling establishment (*rijāl al-dawla*) and delivery of grain from the grain ports of the capital.[19] Some bread vendors were flogged because they raised the price of bread, and the millers were ordered to assume responsibility for the supply of bread instead of the bread vendors.

The actions aimed at increasing the supply of grain at the expense of the better-off players in the market proved effective and, for eight months (i.e Rajab 414–Rabīʿ I 415/September 1023–May 1024), the wheat and bread markets functioned in an orderly fashion. This statement must be qualified as it relies on the only source available to us. It can be argued that the text does not necessarily fully reflect events during these eight months. Although such an argument is valid, no alternative account can be offered. We can conjecture that during all those months the market was a buyers' market and that, eventually, it collapsed under the pressure of excessive demand for grain. Musabbiḥī reports on rising prices of grain and bread during Rabīʿ I 415/May–June 1024 as the situation was getting more and more desperate. Owing to a good harvest the previous year grain continued to arrive in the capital, but, towards the end of Rabīʿ II/end of June, a shipment intended for the grain port of Fusṭāṭ was diverted to Maqs to supply one of the palaces. The regime was hoarding grain in preparation of the impending famine.[20]

On 17 Jumadā II 415/26 August 1024, al-Ẓāhir participated in the ceremonies for the opening of the Canal and two days later the New Year (Nawrūz) was celebrated. Yaʿqūb ibn al-Dawwās proclaimed an edict that the slaughter of cattle was forbidden and stated that offenders would forfeit their life and property. The butchers claimed that the cattle designated for slaughter were unfit for agricultural work and incurred expenses for fodder while the ban deprived them of expected incomes. Eventually, for

[19] Musabbiḥī, 14, 15–16.
[20] Musabbiḥī, 32, 39.

three days the slaughter of animals was permitted and banned again on the fourth day.[21] Enigmatic as this account is, the rise of the Nile in Rajab 415/end of August–September 1024 was above the optimal level and the next agricultural year looked promising, but the current realities were harsh and the situation volatile. For some inexplicable reason a new market inspector was appointed, and his one day in office (4 Rajab 415/11 September 1024) proved disastrous since he announced maximum prices (*tasʿīr*) for both good-quality white bread and ordinary bread. This decree brought the grain market and the sale of bread to a complete standstill. The *muḥtasib* who disrupted the market was the black eunuch Baqī, the slave of Badr al-Dawla Nāfidh, who was appointed chief of the police forces and market supervisor. The regime's reaction was swift: Baqī was dismissed after a day in office and Yaʿqūb ibn al-Dawwās reinstated. He partially revoked the disastrous policy of his immediate predecessor. He allowed the bread vendor to sell bread at the market price, but imposed a maximum price for the bread baked and sold by the oven owners. Musabbiḥī maintains that a new price pattern emerged: top-quality bread (*samid*) was sold at twice the price of other breads.[22]

Fascinating and detailed though Musabbiḥī's chronicle is, we must read between the lines. His accounts of the three months Rajab, Shaʿbān and Ramaḍān 415/end of September, November and December 1024 depict a fully functioning regime and an orderly society living its life under the long shadow of a food shortage. Rarely in these accounts is the gloomy situation of the masses (*al-ʿamma*) reflected, especially the fact that prices went up during Rajab/September and the shortage became more acute. In Shawwāl/December 1024–January 1025 the situation deteriorated; the grim presence of famine suddenly comes to the fore of Musabbiḥī's narrative and, except for the inner core of the ruling elite, no one was immune. People invited to the palace for the traditional feast of The Breaking of Ramaḍān – a wide, privileged circle of the ruling class – looted food and sweets offered at the banquet. Outside the confines of the palace the prices of grain and bread continue to rise and the famine exacted a death toll. Musabbiḥī's references to mortality caused by the famine are more implied than explicit. The first

[21] Musabbiḥī, 46.
[22] Musabbiḥī, 47, 48. For types of bread, see Lewicka, *Food and Foodways*, 156–7.

allusion appears in the account of the events of Dhū l-Qaʿda/January 1025, when the caliph realised that many people had died and had been buried without ritual washing or shrouds. He was quick to provide shrouds and money for their proper burial. Eventually, the famine comes to dominate Musabbiḥī's narrative.[23]

The whole entry referring to Friday, 13 Dhū l-Qaʿda/16 January 1025 is devoted to the deaths of the poor and the fate of the starving who were reduced to eating grass. The caliph who traversed the town in a procession was confronted by shouts of: 'Hunger, oh Commander of the Faithful, hunger. Nor your father neither you grandfather did such a thing to us. [We implore] God, He [is responsible for] our being [*amr*].' The town was on the verge of violence and Yaʿqūb ibn al-Dawwās lost his grip on the situation. For all his experience and reasonable handling of affairs up until then, his deeds only aggravated the misery of the people. On mid-Dhū l-Qaʿda/18 January, he went to Fusṭāṭ accompanied by infantry (*rajjāla*) and the Saʿdiyya cohort, and flogged a group of porters who carried grain to stores and brokers and asked them to provide a list of grain stores in Fusṭāṭ. The list specified 150 stores of grain, which he sealed, forbidding any selling of grain from them. The decree had a catastrophic effect and the danger of violence hung about the town, while one person in the service of the vizier disobeyed the order. He sold grain from his store at the price prevailing before the proclamation of the decree, and there were buyers able and willing to buy at that price. The next day, 16 Dhū l-Qaʿda/19 January, Yaʿqūb ibn al-Dawwās was summoned to the palace and accused of mishandling the situation and held responsible for the death toll that the famine was exacting and for fermenting anti-government feelings in the town. His interlocutors alluded to a document in his handwriting which testified that he had farmed out the town's supply (*ʿimāra*) of bread and grain until the arrival of the new harvest.[24]

The account provides a rare insight into the situation. Yaʿqūb ibn al-Dawwās was a market supervisor and private entrepreneur, with vested interests in the business he was also supposed to supervise. Apparently, the

[23] Musabbiḥī, 52, 66–7, 71.

[24] Musabbiḥī, 74; Halm, *Die Kalifen von Kairo*, 319–20. The Saʿdiyya served as al-Ḥākim's henchmen, but the name of the cohort endured into 1058. See Maqrīzī, *Ittiʿāẓ*, II, 127, 242.

combination of the two roles was not that unusual. In 993, for example a Christian official was reinstated as *muḥtasib* and he also farmed out taxes on the grain ports. Supposedly, his direct predecessor in 992 was also involved in the tax-farming system, and on immense scale: he offered 300,000 *dinars* for the supply of fodder.[25]

The events of 19 January are reported in great detail by Musabbiḥī. Immediately after the harsh conversation at the palace, Yaʿqūb ibn al-Dawwās changed his policy and permitted grain from grain stores to be sold to the millers for a fixed price, and he also set maximum prices for bread. Towards the end of that day the *muḥtasib* came from Cairo with a decree abolishing all of the taxes (*mukūs*) levied at the grain ports. This tax rescission was presented as a favour granted by the Commander of the Faithful to his people. The decree also abolished price fixing and stated that commerce should be conducted according to God's will (*bi-ma aṭʿama Allāhu wa-razaqa bi-ghayr tasʿīr*).[26]

The edict announcing the lifting of the custom duties on grain reflects not only the entrenched division between the 'household grain economy' of the regime and the grain market of Fusṭāṭ, but also the fact that the regime levied taxes on grain arriving at Fusṭāṭ's grain ports. Rescinding the grain tax at this point proved to be too little too late and the *muḥtasib* punished floor merchants by beating, shamed them by parading them, and imprisoned them because of price rises and adulteration of the purity of their floors.[27] At the height of the famine also the 'household grain economy' of the regime failed in providing for the army, especially the black infantry. This failure might reflect the vast expansion of the black infantry corps that took place during al-Ḥākim's reign. The black infantry lived in military quarters outside the walls of the palace city of Cairo and posed a danger to Fusṭāṭ, forcing the regime to defend the population from starving troops who went on the rampage. The failure of the regime was even deeper: hunger encroached on the palace and some of those who directly depended on the regime for their daily supplies went hungry. Musabbiḥī's chronicle stops at this point, and we are left in dark concerning the immediate and long-term effects of the famine.

[25] Maqrīzī, *Ittiʿāẓ*, I, 276, 277.
[26] Musabbiḥī, 74–5.
[27] Musabbiḥī, 72–3, 75–6.

The legal underpinnings (if any) of the *muḥtasib*'s involvement in the supply of grain and bread are hazy at best. The same can be said about the declaration of maximum prices for bread, which was mostly unpractical and was legally disputed. Daniel Gimaret has offered a detailed discussion of price fixing. Generally speaking, Sunnī sages who adhered to the doctrine of predestination rejected the practice, arguing that prices are in the hand of God, whereas the Muʿtazilites allowed human intervention in the fixing of prices.[28] Turning away from theology to day-to-day realities and beliefs, we see that the notion that prices and livelihood are in the hands of God was widely held by both Muslims and Jews, and was expressed by the stock phrase '*bi-mā qasama Allāhu wa-razaqa*' and its variants. The notion, and the phrase, were invoked by the regime, under the worst of circumstances, at the height of the 1025 famine.[29] A dissonance can be discerned between theology and policies. Fixing of prices was the rulers' first choice when dealing with food shortages, or, to put it differently, rulers did not take their cue from theology. They handled food shortage at the political level, and their *muḥtasibs* responded to concrete situations and imposed their policies irrespective of doctrines, unleashing violence as a first resort.[30] Their involvement in the mechanism of the market was actually two-pronged, since they tried to regulate both supply and prices or, more precisely, regulate prices through supply. None of these issues is dealt with by twelfth-century *ḥisba* manuals, which focus exclusively on the quality of flour and bread and the ethics of the grain and bread trade rather than its economics.[31]

Institutional Aspects of the *Ḥisba*

The Persian traveller and late convert to Ismailism Nāṣir-i Khusraw, who visited Egypt during 1047–8, was greatly impressed by the honesty of Fusṭāṭ's merchants, which was enforced by public shaming of offenders. Nāṣir-i

[28] See 'Les théologiens musulmans devant la hausse des prix', 330–8. A twelfth- to fourteenth-century *ḥisba* manual forbade the *muḥtasib* to set maximum prices. See Stilt, *Islamic Law in Action*, 152–4.

[29] Musabbiḥī, 75; Goitein, *Med. Soc.*, I, 185–6; Goitein and Friedman, *India Traders*, 63–5.

[30] For the flogging of millers in Rabīʿ I 359/January–February 970, see Maqrīzī, *Ittiʿāẓ*, I, 120. For violence unleashed against people who stored grain (*khazzānūn*), and bread vendors in 1008, see Maqrīzī, *Ittiʿāẓ*, II, 71; Ibn al-Dawādārī, VI, 277.

[31] Al-Shayzarī, 223–5; Ibn al-Bassām, 297–301.

Khusraw does not specify which institution the *ḥisba* or police inflicted these punishments.[32] The vagueness of his report is typical, since the organisational and institutional aspects of the *ḥisba* remain mostly hidden from the eye. This is true even when documents concerning the *ḥisba* institution are reproduced in literary sources. Qalqashandī (1355–1418), for example, provides an undated letter of appointment issued by Qāḍī al-Fāḍil during the late Fatimid period, but it offers little. On the one hand, the letter states that the appointed was entrusted with the command of the police (*maʿūna*) and *ḥisba* in Fusṭāṭ, Jazīra and Qarāfa. On the other hand, at the beginning of the letter the assignment is presented as *wilāyat madinat Miṣr*. The terms *muḥtasib* or *mutawallī l-maʿūna* are not mentioned in the document, and one is left to understand that *wilāyat madinat Miṣr* subsumes *maʿūna* and *ḥisba* in Fusṭāṭ, Jazīra and Qarāfa. The main significance of the document is in providing clear evidence that both police and *ḥisba* were judicial institutions, part of the state system for the administration of justice. The nominee is urged to dispense 'God's laws [*aḥkām*] among God's beings' and to treat all people equitably. He is also required to provide justice for the oppressed and to subdue the oppressor. The notion of 'commanding right and forbidding wrong' is only alluded to, without use of the full phrase that indicates the doctrine.[33]

Some glimpses of the structure of the *ḥisba* force can be gained from the writings of Ibn al-Ṭuwayr (1130–1220), which reflect the late Fatimid period. He asserts that it was a religious post occupied by respected Muslims and had branches in both Cairo and Fusṭāṭ and Egypt's provinces. He compares the organisation of the *ḥisba* network to the judicial institution. The *muḥtasib* held session on alternate days in the congregational mosques of both Cairo and Fusṭāṭ, while his deputies (*nuwwāb*) made their rounds at the markets. Whether the Dikkat al-Ḥisba (the Bench of the Ḥisba) that he mentions can be considered the Fusṭāṭ headquarters of the force remains unclear.[34]

The financial aspects involved in the way the *ḥisba* operated are revealed by two decrees. That from 993 forbade the people serving with the *ḥisba*

[32] See *Book of Travels*, 55.
[33] Qalqashandī, X, 356, 358, 359.
[34] See *Nuzhat al-Muqlatayn*, 116.

force, simply referred to as *aʿwān* (helpers), to take things from people. Most probably, the aim of the edict was to end the informal illegal collection of dues by members of the force. Another edict from 1012 abolished the dues (*mukūs*) collected by the *muḥtasib*, indicating perhaps that people who served on the *ḥisba* force, including the *muḥtasib*, lived off the merchants whom they were supposed to supervise.[35]

Although Maqrīzī's accounts depicting the daily life of Fusṭāṭ-Cairo during the Fatimid period refer to frequent intervention by the authorities in the life of subjects, allusions to the *muḥtasib* are rare. One of these rare accounts is from 8 Dhū l-Ḥijja 415/10 February 1025 and reflects a core concern of the *ḥisba* manuals. On that day the owner of a clean candy shop, at the very heart of Fusṭāṭ (*ʿala bāb Zuqāq al-Qanādīl*), was flogged because of defective weights.[36] Beginning with the Zaydī *ḥisba* manual, the emphasis on maintaining correct weights and measures pervades this literature. Another case, which also reflects a typical sphere of the *muḥtasib*'s responsibilities, was the dispute between the *muḥtasib* and money-changers in Fusṭāṭ in 971.[37]

Opposite cases of close co-operation between the people of the *ḥisba* force and merchants are also known. In 1053, for example, the *ʿarīf* (the head of the profession) of the *khabbāzūn* secured the co-operation of the *muḥtasib* to curb reduction in the price of bread sold by one of the vendors, which was considered by the *ʿarīf* as unfair. Only the intervention of the vizier al-Yāzūrī, who rebuked the *muḥtasib* and dismissed the *ʿarīf*, restored competition.[38] Any conclusions whether the *ḥisba* institution was antagonistic to merchants or co-operative and furthered their interests are, at the current state of knowledge, beyond our reach.

In cases in which one would expect the involvement of the *muḥtasib*, he is not mentioned. In 975, an edict ordering the change of (the glass) *riṭāl* weights to lead weights was published by al-Muʿizz but which authority the

35 Maqrīzī, *Ittiʿāẓ*, I, 277; II, 96.
36 Musabbiḥī, 78.
37 Maqrīzī, *Ittiʿāẓ*, I, 132
38 Maqrīzī, *Ittiʿāẓ*, II, 224–5. The relations between *muḥtasibs* and *ʿarīfs* of various professions remain obscure. See Tyan, *Histoire de l'organisation judiciaire*, 627, 636, 640; Ghabin, *Ḥisba*, 176–8.

ḥisba, *shurṭa* or the cadi, was supposed to oversee its implementation remains unspecified. The same applies to edicts that dealt with issues such as how the water carriers should handle their mules and camels and what arrangements for extinguishing fires should be taken in Fusṭāṭ and Cairo.[39] The reports leave the impression of very centralised and authoritative Fatimid regime directly involved in the day-to-day life in the capital. In 975, for example, on the occasion of Nawrūz (the Persian New Year), theatrical performances (*laʿba*) by masked actors (*samajāt*) were forbidden and people were arrested. The report conveys the impression that al-Muʿizz was behind the ban since attempt was made to bring the performances that began in Fusṭāṭ to Cairo too.[40] In 1025, the masked actors had a decree (*sijill*) that allowed them to perform with no hindrance and they brought their performances to Cairo. The performances went on for two weeks and were organised by people of fourteen different markets in Fusṭāṭ who were handsomely rewarded by the ruler.[41] Whether the *sijill* was written by the *muḥtasib* or higher authority remains unspecified.

In cases which involved separation between the sexes in the public domain, the vizier is depicted as the keeper of public morals since other authorities have failed to do so. The vizier al-Ma'mūn used to receive, from the chief of police, a daily report about events that took place in Fusṭāṭ, but he failed to report a complaint of a merchant against the owner of a wedding hall who watched women during weddings. The *muḥtasib* is not mentioned as involved in these events.[42] Abuse of power by people who held the post of *muḥtasib* and/or chief of police is sometimes reported. The most notorious case involved Dhakhīra al-Muluk, who, in 1097, served as *wālī* of Cairo, and in 1115 was also nominated as *muḥtasib* (see Chapter 4). In his role as *wālī*, he used to inflict unheard-of punishments on criminals (meaning most likely sadistic ones), and he also constructed a mosque, using forced labour, which became known as the 'godless mosque'. Maqrīzī writes that God smote him

[39] Maqrīzī, *Ittiʿāẓ*, I, 224, 276, 277, 280, 283; II, 44, 93. The instructions for how to prevent fires in the capital were published by the vizier in 1123, while their implementation was entrusted to the governors of Cairo and Fusṭāṭ. See Maqrīzī, *Khiṭaṭ*, II, 515.

[40] Maqrīzī, *Ittiʿāẓ*, I, 224.

[41] Musabbiḥī, 42–3. For an English translation of Musabbiḥī's account, see Moreh, 'Live Theatre in Medieval Islam', 572; for *laʿba*, see 582–3.

[42] Maqrīzī, *Ittiʿāẓ*, III, 100–1.

with a rare disease of which he died, and people refused to take part in his funeral and accord him last prayers.[43]

Kristen Stilt's book on *ḥisba* and market supervisors in the Mamlūk period, entitled *Islamic Law in Action*, begs the question of whether the *ḥisba* law can be regarded as Islamic law. A partial answer lies in the book's subtitle, *Authority, Discretion, and Everyday Experiences in Mamlūk Egypt*, which places the *ḥisba* jurisdiction in the realm of discretion. Stilt explains that the position of the *muḥtasib* 'has a place in the domains of both *fiqh* and *siyāsa*, straddling the two sources of authority and guided theoretically and practically by the jurists and the rulers'.[44] Whether *ḥisba* manuals can be described as a part of Islamic law remains an open question. For another perspective on the question, one must go back to Tyan's remarkable quotation from Māwardī, which places the *ḥisba* law in the realm of customary law. Māwardī's discussion of the *ḥisba* is complex and begins with setting the institution in the unmistakable Islamic context of 'commanding right and forbidding wrong'. It can be argued that al-Māwardī's discussion offers a historical perspective on the way *ḥisba* jurisdiction had evolved. Although the technical aspects of the *muḥtasib*'s supervision of the markets fall outside the pale of the *sharīʿa*, the Islamic concept of 'commanding right and forbidding wrong' had been grafted onto these aspects. This mechanism provided an Islamic aura for the m*uḥtasib*'s supervision of the public sphere in which he imposed Muslim religious and cultural values.

[43] Ibn Muyassar, 65; Maqrīzī, *Ittiʿāẓ*, III, 55; *Kitāb al-Muqaffā*, III, 39.

[44] *Islamic Law in Action*, 37.

6

The Ruler's Justice: The *Maẓālim* Institution

The *Maẓālim* Institution and its Functions

In the ancient Middle Eastern political tradition the monarch was perceived as a lawgiver and dispenser of justice, while petitioning the ruler for justice was a common practice. The monarch's legal functions also symbolised his legitimacy, and these traditions were very much alive in the medieval Middle East. The quest for direct access to the ruler/state in search of justice and personal and communal favours embodies the *maẓālim* institution. It was, however, a complex institution, with which modern scholars have grappled with some difficulty since it combined both judicial and administrative functions and escapes a neat definition of its true nature. The most extensive discussion of the *maẓālim* has been offered by Tyan and this, as pointed out by Tillier, relied on the literary sources that were available at the time he wrote. Furthermore, in the case of Egypt, some of the most important of Maqrīzī's writings were not available to Tyan.[1]

Notwithstanding modern difficulties in defining the *maẓālim* institution, it was a typical medieval institution which reflects a hazy distinction between administrative and judicial spheres and overlapping institutional responsibilities. Furthermore, it was an institution that functioned in states characterised by disproportionately powerful regimes and weak societies dependent on their rulers politically and economically on both personal and communal levels. People and communities petitioned rulers for almost every-

[1] See Chapter 4, n. 6. For Tyan's discussion of the *maẓālim* institution, see *Histoire de l'organisation judiciaire*, 434–525. For Tillier's review of the *maẓālim* in modern literature, see 'The Maẓālim in Historiography', 1–25.

thing: justice, confirmation and maintenance of privileges and livelihood. They also brought their squabbles not only before judicial institutions but also to people of authority, trying to make sense of the intricate maze of power relations characterised by mighty political brokers and governmental institutions. The dependence of people on rulers played into their hands and enhanced their governability. It was in a ruler's/state's interest to respond to people's complaints and requests and politically emasculate them. From the point view of the rulers, so important was this channel of communication that maintaining the *maẓālim* institution became an attribute of good governance. This complex web of relations is highlighted by both literary and non-literary sources and is well-documented for the Fatimid period.

In mid-Rabīʿ I 364/3 December 974, when al-Muʿizz's sickness, to which he eventually succumbed, intensified, it became clear that many petitions concerning *zulāmāt* and *ḥawāʾij* were being left untreated. When asked about the matter, al-Muʿizz conferred the task on his heir apparent Nizār, the future *imām*-caliph al-ʿAzīz. Although Maqrīzī's report is not first-hand information, it does reflect the intensity of the situation and how vital this aspect of taking care of people's complaints (*zulāmāt*) and needs (*ḥawāʾij*) was for the proper running of the state. Having assumed responsibility for petitions, Nizār received the oath of allegiance from members of his family and people of the court, and a delegation representing the religious (Sunnī) elite of Fusṭāṭ, made up of the cadi, court witnesses and jurists, paid him a visit.[2] Other reports clearly indicate that the *maẓālim* institution, or taking care of *zulāmāt wa-ḥawāʾij al-nās*, was an administrative institution headed by a top-ranking administrator. In 993, for example, the task was entrusted to Abū Muḥammad al-Ḥasan ibn ʿAmmār, who was in charge of the state finances (*tadbīr al-amwāl*) and auditing of state offices (*muḥasaba arbāb al-dawānīn*). He was replaced by Faḍl ibn Ṣāliḥ, who shared these responsibilities with the cadi Muḥammad ibn al-Nuʿmān.[3] Concern with the proper handling of petitions also typified al-Ḥākim's reign throughout the whole period of his rule, both as a minor under the tutelage of the white eunuch Bajawān and during his long independent reign of terror. In 997, Barjawān conferred

[2] Maqrīzī, *Ittiʿāẓ*, I, 228.
[3] Maqrīzī, *Ittiʿāẓ*, I, 277.

responsibility for petitions on his Christian secretary Fahd ibn Ibrāhīm, and both of them brought cases to al-Ḥākim, whose decisions were transferred to the relevant state offices. The petitions are described as containing both personal requests and redress for justice.[4]

As was exemplified by the killing of Barjawān on 16 Ṣafar 390/27 January 1000, the need to maintain political stability pervaded the thoughts and actions of the main actors on the political scene. The new man in charge of state affairs (*tadbīr al-mamlaka*) was Ḥusayn ibn Jawhar, whose responsibilities also involved 'the affairs of the people [*umūr al-nās*]', the rendering of justice to the oppressed and the issuing of *sijills*. The actual handling of the petitions was in the hands of Fahd ibn Ibrāhīm, and both kept a low public profile, used simple titles and made every effort not to eclipse al-Ḥākim's prominence. The caliph initiated a policy of allowing free access to himself, and he personally dealt with petitions.[5] The events described so far took place at the Fatimid palace and in Cairo in general, and one can wonder who exactly were 'the people' who submitted their petitions and requests to the Fatimid rulers. The 'free access' policy continued throughout al-Ḥākim's rule and, as the reign of terror intensified, became a prominent feature of the ruler's conduct. On his frequent outings al-Ḥākim received petitions, which he examined himself or handed to subordinates. The years 1014–15 were marked by executions and attention to state affairs while new rules for the submission of petitions were announced: Sunday was designated for the Kutāma and the Maghribis, Monday for the Easterners and Thursday for other people. Petitions requesting redress for justice (*maẓālim*) were handed to the heir apparent, lawsuits (*daʿāwā*) to the supreme cadi, and difficult cases were brought to al-Ḥākim's personal attention.[6]

In many ways this account provides the key for understanding the *maẓālim* institution: indeed it was an administrative-judicial institution geared to handling a wide range of issues concerning the relation between subjects and the state, requests from subjects to rulers and problems that

[4] Maqrīzī, *Ittiʿāẓ*, II, 14–15. Eighteen *maẓālim* cases are described in tenth- to eleventh-century Abbasid historiography; three of these contain requests for financial support. See van Berkel, 'Embezzlement and Reimbursement', 714.

[5] Maqrīzī, *Ittiʿāẓ*, II, 29, 30.

[6] Maqrīzī, *Ittiʿāẓ*, II, 105, 106, 109–10.

subjects could not solve internally. The term *maẓālim* stood for administrative justice while legal matters were subsumed under the term *daʿāwā*, which also might indicate appeals on rulings made by cadis. The account also raises the question of how inclusive the *maẓālim* institution was. The regime was attentive to the socio-military groups it relied upon (the Kutāma, Maghribis and Easterners), heavily concentrated in the capital. One might ask to what extent other social groups, even in the capital, not to say throughout the country, had access to the *maẓālim* institution.

The political dimension of the *maẓālim* institution explains why rulers who presided over *maẓālim* sessions are frequently mentioned in the literary sources, although no explanations about the nature of the institution are provided.[7] Undoubtedly, the institution was well-understood by contemporaries. On one level, *maẓālim* sessions were a ritual that symbolised political power and, on another level, this was a political mechanism that bound people to their rulers in a web of expectations, dependence and gratitude, when their pleas were answered.

Subjects Approaching the State

Complaints against the state

One way of discussing the question of how inclusive the *maẓālim* institution was is to examine the nature of the petitions submitted to the Fatimid rulers, which fall under three major categories: complaints against state offices and personnel, personal requests and communal requests. The first petition to be discussed pre-dates the Fatimid period; it was submitted by monks living in a monastery in Asyūṭ and is dated to the ninth century. It is tempting to see the document as proof that the *maẓālim* institution was an inclusive institution open to all, including to non-Muslims living in Upper Egypt. The petition is addressed to a high-ranking emir (possibly the governor) and consists of a complaint against abusive treatment of monks by a lower-ranking emir and

[7] For references to people in charge of the *maẓālim* sessions in Egypt of the late 830s, see Ibn Taghrī Birdī, II, 251, 259–60. For Muḥammad ibn Ṭughj's sessions of *maẓālim*, see Ibn Saʿīd, 39; for Kāfūr, see Maqrīzī, Kitāb al-Muqaffā, V, 255; for al-Mahdī, see al-Anṭākī, 108; and for Jawhar, see Maqrīzī, *Ittiʿāẓ*, I, 117, 128.

his men.[8] Such petitions are rare, however, and the document can only be regarded as an indication that the *maẓālim* concept and institution indeed became an integral part of the state machinery in the capital and provinces. The petition also highlights a completely separate aspect: the self-image of the monastic community and its function in the society. The monks state that they have no means of production and live at subsistence level ('bread is our nourishment'), but offer hospitality to everybody. They describe themselves, using the standard Koranic terms *ḍuʿfāʾ wa-masākīn*, as poor people who rely on 'the charitable support of our nation (*milla*)'. Their tribulations began when they admitted the men of the (lower-ranking) emir to their monastery, and subsequently they were arrested and brought to the emir, who beat them and impose a fine on them.

They appealed to the justice of the (higher-ranking) emir and boldly referred to the other emir as a tyrant and oppressor to whom they used to pay a quarter and one sixth of a *dīnār* each month. How the petition was handled and whether they received any redress for their grievances remains unknown.[9] Most likely some actions were taken by the higher-ranking emir, since commitment to justice and condemnation of oppression appear as administrative guidelines early on in the history of Muslim rule in the Middle East. Writing in the 680s, a high-ranking financial official in southern Palestine reminded his appointee that 'God dislikes oppression and corruption', using the Koranic terms *ẓulm* and *fasād*. In his letters Qurra ibn Sharīk emphasised that the duties of a provincial governor are to collect taxes justly and dispense justice to people.[10] Important though the letters of officials at the top of the tax collection system are, it must always be borne in mind that medium- and low-level officials had many means of shunning accountability and evading complaints levelled against them. An eighth-century trilingual document tells the story of a complaint about taxation submitted by the people of Akhmīm against ʿAmr ibn al-ʿAttāsh and his staff. Yazīd ibn ʿAbd Allāh, however,

[8] The distinction between high- and lower-ranking emir is my addition; the text refers to both of them by the term 'emir'.

[9] Rex Smith and al-Moraekhi, 'The Arabic Papyri', doc. 11. For an improved edition accompanied by a French translation, see Vanthieghem, 'Violences et extorsions', 189–92.

[10] Hoyland, 'The Earliest Attestation of Dhimma of God', lines 4, 13, 15 (text and trans.); Bell, 'Translation of the Greek Aphrodito Papyri', no. 1,356.

who was in charge of Akhmīm and Ṭhāṭā on behalf of the emir (meaning most likely the local governor), coaxed the leading personalities in Akhmīm to acquit the officials of the charges brought against them and threated them with a fine if the accusations were repeated. The acquittal document was signed by no fewer than 93 people, bearing Arab-Muslim and Christian names.[11]

Another monastic community, the St Catherina monastery on Mount Sinai (Ṭūr Sīnā), is well-represented in the published record of petitions from the Fatimid period. Stern has published a number of documents of the open decree (*sijill manshūr*) type, issued as a response to petitions and delivered to petitioners who, equipped with the state response, went to seek justice for their case. One of these documents was an open decree issued in reply to a petition submitted by ʿAbd al-Masīḥ, supervisor of one of the monastery's pious endowments, against provincial officials who had appropriated the endowment revenues. The state granted the request and ordered townspeople and nomads not to harm the monastery in any way. The document also echoes the much-repeated monks' claim that they extended hospitality to travellers in the area.[12] Although the monks of the Mount Sinai monastery enjoined extensive privileges from the Fatimid state, they, like the monks of the Asyūṭ monastery, presented themselves as maintaining reciprocal relations with the local society, and alluded to having a function within the wider social matrix, and therefore they deserved state protection. The state accepted the self-view promulgated by the monks. In 1158, for example, the Fatimid vizier, in an open decree to the military governor of al-Ṭūr, described the monks as pious men who live in seclusion and take care of travellers and pilgrims in the area. The governor was instructed to attend to the monks' welfare, to protect them and to abolish new taxes imposed on them.[13] In another petition from the late Fatimid period, the monks asked the vizier to order the military governor of the province's emir Ibn al-Faramāwī not to take up residence in the monastery since they feared that such a move would result in Bedouins entering the monastery's compound. They claimed that they had noble documents

[11] Grohmann, *Arabic Papyri*, III, doc. 167.
[12] See *Fatimid Decrees*, doc. 3, and 85–90, for a discussion of the open decree type of document.
[13] Stern, *Fatimid Decrees*, doc. 9.

(*sijallāt sharīfa kārima*) forbidding the military governors and the Bedouins from entering the monastery and seizing their possessions (*amwāl*). Their request was granted.[14]

The petitions discussed above belong to a category of documents in which specific officials are referred to. Such documents are quite rare. In the first half of the twelfth century, for example, a petition was submitted against the Head of the Arsenal by someone who claimed that the official in question had unjustly demanded from him that he pay a debt incurred by his brother. The petitioner asked to hand him a rescript (*tawqīʿ*), instructing the official to cease molesting him.[15] This was a clear case of a state official using his powers to secure a personal interest while abusing a subject.

In another petition from 1151 the official against whom the complaint was submitted is explicitly alluded to: the chief of police in Fusṭāṭ (*mutawallī l-maʿūna bi-Miṣr*). The petition highlights a frequently mentioned issue: overlap between administrative and judicial spheres of responsibilities and competition among state officials for power, not to say questionable grabbings of authority. The document is a draft of an intended petition written in Judaeo-Arabic and tells the story of a seizure of property by the chief of police accompanied by two witnesses. The broader context for the affair was the death of a Jewish merchant who, as the document repeatedly reassures its reader, had no dealings whatsoever with the state and whose death was registered with the supreme cadi. A brother of the petitioner, described as an abjectly poor man, served as a clerk in a state office and became entangled in a bitter struggle with Abū Zikrī but was absolved of any financial obligations he had undertaken, following the death of Abū Zikrī. The chief of police was quick to take advantage of the situation for the state, and/or himself, and the petitioner appealed to the dynasty's justice and mercy and asked for the restoration of his family's rights to the seized properties.[16] The perennial problem alluded to in the document was the claim by the rulers to the inheritances of

[14] Richards, 'A Fatimid Petition and 'Small Decree', 140–58, esp. lines 8–13 (text and trans.).

[15] Khan, *Arabic Legal and Administrative Documents*, doc. 83. In 1025, the state intervened against another abuse of power by the Head of the Arsenal, who demanded two *dīnārs* from the families of people drowned in the Nile wanting to bury their relatives (the payment is described as *ḥaqq al-Baḥr*, Nile's due). See Musabbiḥī, 95.

[16] Khan, *Arabic Legal and Administrative Documents*, doc. 79.

people employed by state and the fact that the state co-opted merchants to collect taxes on its behalf. For this reason, the document firmly asserts that the dead merchant was known as a trader who did not farm out taxes from the state and had no dealings with state offices.[17]

Many petitions in the category 'complaints against the state' are of a judicial nature and refer to cadis and the courts. The question of whether the *maẓālim* institution can be regarded as an appellate court on the rulings of cadis is extensively discussed by Tillier in his review of the literature on the *maẓālim* institution, including the question of what is meant by an appeal.[18] Judging from the inner logic of the *maẓālim* one could certainly complain about a cadi, but, as the following case shows, such appeals were carefully worded so that the complaint was more implicit than explicit. The reason was that the cadi and the state claimed to be dispensers of justice and any claim against a cadi could have been perceived as a criticism of the state which undermined one of its claims to legitimacy. These subtleties are illustrated by a petition addressed to al-Āmir by the Jewish merchant Mūsā ibn Ṣadaqa. He complained against a cadi, identified only by his titles as Jalāl al-Mulk Tāj al-Dīn, who had seized merchandise he had brought under *commenda* contract from India and Yemen. The seizure is alluded to only as inappropriate, and the petitioner failed to convince the cadi of the rightfulness of his case. He therefore asked for a rescript instructing the cadi to accept his arguments. In modern terms, the petition can be described as an appeal against the cadi's judicial-administrative decision. Although the full text of the document is preserved, the complaint against the cadi is tersely phrased and one must venture a speculation about the events behind the petition. Most likely, Mūsā ibn Ṣadaqa was sued by his partner (or partners) to the *commenda* contract and the cadi ruled against him.[19]

Perhaps the clearest case of an appeal to a higher judicial authority is the petition submitted to the supreme cadi in Damascus during the Fatimid

[17] For an illuminating discussion of how merchants were co-opted to work for the state, see Udovitch, 'Merchants and Amīrs', 53–73.

[18] See 'The Maẓālim in Historiography', 1–25.

[19] Stern, 'Three Petitions of the Fatimid Period', 174–8; Khan, *Arabic Legal and Administrative Documents*', doc. 77. Stern and Khan offer a slightly different interpretation of the possible background events behind the petition.

period. The petition is remarkable for its simple structure. The petitioner presents himself in the *tarjama* as Ṣakhr, *al-mamlūk*, and immediately after the *basmala* he addresses the supreme cadi saying 'I report to [*yunhī ilā ʿilm*] our Master the Eminent Cadi, the Imām, the Learned, the Pillar of Religion, Murtaḍā al-Islām, the Supreme Cadi'.[20] The substance of the plea concerns litigation that had taken place the previous day at the court (*bi-majlis al-ḥukm*) before an unnamed cadi, referred to as *al-majlis al-sāmī* (the lofty seat). The litigation was between Ṣakhr and the husband of his sister, who was granted the right to her dowry. Ṣakhr's appeal to the supreme cadi is phrased as a request to be granted the benefaction (*inʿām*) of having the proofs presented by his litigant in order to establish the truth of the matter.[21]

Personal requests from the state

While specific complaints submitted against state officials are not that common, requests from rulers to 'do something' are far more numerous. This category includes complex issues which partly remain obscure. In the second half of the eleventh century, for example, an unnamed petitioner who invoked 'the justice of the prophetic dynasty' submitted a rather strange request to an unknown Fatimid dignitary titled ʿAmīd al-Dawla. He asked the dignitary to order the office dealing with military affairs in Palestine (*dīwān jund Filasṭīn*, the Office of the Army in Palestine) to take possession of lands belonging to him and stop harassing him on the matter. The issues alluded to in the petition remain unclear: the status of the lands (described as desolate), how the petitioner came to own or control them, and why previous petitions had failed to resolve the affair. Apparently, failure in petitioning the state directly brought the petitioner to seek the mediacy of a powerful dignitary, and one can only hope that the choice was wise and brought results.[22] Although the *maẓālim* institution enabled the people to seek direct redress for grievances caused by the state, dignitaries were important political players in medieval states and people sought their mediacy in order to advance their causes when petitioning the state. Thus the choice of ʿAmīd al-Dawla as a power broker

[20] For the terms *tarjama* and *mamlūk*, see the next section.
[21] Mouton, Sourdel and Sourdel-Thomine, *Mariage et séparation à Damas*, doc. 23.
[22] Khan, *Arabic Legal and Administrative Documents*, doc. 94.

can be regarded as typical of how people approached the state when seeking justice and solutions to their problems. The same scenario is repeated in another petition submitted during al-Mustanṣir's reign by a father who asked that the murder of his son and a travel companion be investigated. The two lads were merchants who sailed on the Nile with 500 *dīnārs* and merchandise and were murdered by the captain of a boat and its crew. The petitioner asked the ruler to issue a rescript to the deputies (*khulafā'*) of the emir al-Muwaffaq Sinān al-Dawla to apprehend the perpetrators and confirm the truthfulness of the complaint.[23] Most probably the emir was a military man in charge of a garrison stationed in the Delta (the two merchants were headed for Alexandria) whose range of responsibilities, if they were ever precisely defined, remains obscure.

Although petitions that can be described as appeals against rulings by cadis are rare, many other petitions are of a judicial nature and deal with a variety of issues that lack a common dominator. Two petitions addressed to al-Āmir were requests for rescripts to order cadis to 'do something'. One of these petitions was from a woman who submitted a request that the cadi, referred to only by his titles, be ordered to take possession of the inheritance of a deceased woman who owed the creditor the very substantial sum of 241 *dīnārs*. Although the creditor submitted to the cadi's court (*majlis al-ḥukm al-sharīf*) a document stating the amount of the debt, she felt the need to support her claim by a royal rescript.[24] In another petition submitted to al-Āmir, a Muslim who lived in the village of Sindiyūn in Lower Egypt requested the cadi be ordered to register the house he had inherited from his mother as his property.[25]

In a petition submitted during the twilight years of Fatimid rule, the petitioner asked the vizier to order the cadi to accept his plea. The petition is remarkable for several reasons: the petitioner (Abū ʿAbd Allāh ibn Yaḥyā) turned to the vizier without presenting his case first to the cadi,

[23] Stern, 'Three Petitions of the Fatimid Period', 172–8, with extensive discussion of the geography of the failed commercial trip and the type of boat used for the journey; Khan, *Arabic Legal and Administrative Documents*, doc. 74.

[24] Khan, 'A Petition to the Fatimid Caliph al-Āmir', 44–54.

[25] Khan, 'A Petition to the Fatimid Caliph al-Āmir concerning an Inheritance', 177, lines 9–11 (text and trans.). For the location of Sindiyūn (between Fuwa and Rashīd), see Cornu, *Atlas*, 106, map X.

and he alluded to his low social status by describing himself as a poor baker (*al-farrān*) with a family and children.[26] The gist of the petition consists of Abū ʿAbd Allāh ibn Yaḥyā's admission that he owes a debt to ʿAbd al-Bāqī ibn Wardar, who pressed him hard for paying the money, which was beyond his means. He asked for an order to be issued to the person in charge of the jurisdiction (*mutawallī l-ḥukm al-ʿazīz*) to look into the matter and to pay the debt in instalments. The petition was endorsed by the clerks of both the fine and the thick pen. These two short texts are invaluable, and make it clear that the expression *mutawallī l-ḥukm al-ʿazīz* stands for the cadi. The Fatimid officials instructed the cadi, referred to by highly deferential titles, to deal with the petition according to the law and the public interest, provided that the poverty of the petitioner was established in the customary way in which such requests were handled.[27] The main interest in the baker's petition is that everyone involved in the case accepted the circumvention of the cadi as a normative procedure, but whether the petition can be regarded as typical or atypical remains an unsettled issue.

Another aspect of the petition that must be discussed is the use of the term *mutawallī*, which is taken from administrative terminology. It can be argued that in the eyes of the petitioner there was no difference between the cadi and any other state office. The adjective *al-ʿazīz* (the noble) indicates, however, that there was a difference, and that *ḥukm* was a higher function than those performed by state *dīwāns* headed by *mutawallīs*.

Other petitions of a judicial nature were submitted to cadis and allude to executive powers wielded by them. For example, in one petition submitted to a cadi during the Fatimid period concerning a debt, the cadi was asked to exercise his executive powers. The petitioner, the broker (*samāsir*) ʿUmar ibn Ibrāhīm, reported to a cadi that he had a warrant (*tarsīm*) issued by a court for a period of two years against a debtor who owed him seven and a half *dīnārs*. He asked the cadi to issue an order preventing the debtor from leaving

[26] The term *farrān* can also be understood as an owner or operator of an oven. Perhaps the petitioner was not as poor (*ṣuʿlūk*, pauper) as he described himself.

[27] Stern, 'Three Petitions of the Fatimid Period', 182–6; Khan, *Arabic Legal and Administrative Documents*', doc. 85; Rustow, 'The Legal Status of ḏimmī-s in the Fatimid East', 320. For how petitions were handled by the state and the functions of the clerks of the fine and thick pen, see Khan, *Arabic Legal and Administrative Documents*, 303–5.

without paying the debt. Why ʿUmar ibn Ibrāhīm was afraid that the debtor might leave, or would be forced to leave with others, remains unclear.[28]

Petitioning a cadi for a rescript which orders others to do, or acknowledge, something was quite common. These documents extend our understanding of the cadi's functions within the state structure: the cadi also wielded executive powers. These came in addition to the fiscal and administrative responsibilities he had acquired during the long evolution of the institution. This amalgam of functions is reflected by an eleventh-century petition submitted by Ibn ʿAbd al-Jabbār. He identified himself as a Muslim and refers – 'in a rather convoluted manner', to quote Khan – to a pious endowment established by him in favour of his deceased wife Khulla, in the Fayyūm. The endowment consisted of shops, and Ibn ʿAbd al-Jabbār claimed that actually Khulla, during her lifetime, had taken no actions concerning them and they remained in his hands.[29] The cadi was presented with verified documents issued by jurists authorised (or qualified) to issue legal opinions. Although the request for a rescript appears twice in the text of the document, the nature of the plea is clarified only by the endorsement attached to the petition and addressed to court witnesses in the town of Fayyūm (i.e. the capital of Fayyūm province). The cadi instructed them to take notice of the *mudraj* issued by him, which was based on the legal opinion presented (or submitted) to him. It is quite possible that the document is actually a petition submitted to the supreme cadi in Cairo and includes the rescript issued by him concerning a pious endowment case that had been debated at the court in the town of Fayyūm. Furthermore, one can assume that Ibn ʿAbd al-Jabbār asked the court in the Fayyūm to nullify the endowment since his wife had taken no legal action concerning it, but the local court hesitated, or refused, to grant the request.[30] If this assumption can be sustained, the petition is actually an appeal submitted to the supreme cadi relating to a decision of the provincial court, or, at least, a request to intervene in a case that was adjudicated at a provincial level.

The cases discussed in this section consist of complaints against state

[28] Khan, *Arabic Legal and Administrative Documents*, doc. 98b.
[29] Khan, *Arabic Legal and Administrative Documents*, doc. 95, line 15 (text and trans.).
[30] Khan, *Arabic Legal and Administrative Documents*, doc. 95, line 17 (text and trans.).

officials and requests that the state fulfil the wishes of the petitioners as presented by them. The cases discussed in next section consist of a sub-category of requests to the state and include requests for personal benefits (fiscal and others), representing a wide range of *ḥawāʾij al-nās*.

The notion that court documents and petitions are literary artifacts has become deeply embedded in the modern scholarly discussion on the subject. When this line of inquiry is followed, the texts of petitions are perceived as stylised and shaped by scribes who used a range of stock phrases, meaning that petitions are not personal but rather structured formulaic documents.[31] As Krakowski and Rustow have powerfully emphasised, the formulaic features of both petitions and documents issued by the state endowed them with potency and made them instruments of power.[32] These insights are highly relevant for the discussion in this section, which also suggests viewing these petitions as a kind of a dialogue between subjects and state.

My departure point is that, in the world of medieval people living in Egypt and Syria, the state's presence was overwhelming. The state collected a staggering amount of taxes, waged wars, regulated the life of subjects, persecuted opponents and imprisoned people. The Fatimid dynasty was the biggest employer in the state, and on its payroll were the military, administrators, cadis and religious functionaries and privileged groups. Other people were indirectly employed by the dynasty through pious endowments set up by members of the royal family and dignitaries. The payments rendered to state employees involved salaries, and the yearly distribution of clothes, grain allowances and *iqṭāʿ* grants to the military. Requests to maintain the benefits distributed by the state figure prominently in petitions of a personal nature submitted to Fatimid rulers, viziers and other top-ranking dignitaries. The published record of petitions reflects petitioners of diverse backgrounds and status who faced the state alone, outside the protective shield of patron–client relationships, which somewhat mitigated the crushing impact of state power.

[31] As is widely recognised, discussion of the literary form of petitions is inspired and informed by the work of Natalie Zemon Davis. See Bryen, 'Visibility and Violence in Petitions from Roman Egypt', 181–3. The bibliography on the subject is extensive and the following references reflect personal preferences; see Fournet, 'Entre document et littérature', 61–75; Kovelman, 'From Logos to Myth', 135–52.

[32] See 'Formula as Content', 116.

The dependence of people with, or without, connections to the state on rulers is vividly illustrated by many petitions, and a convenient starting point is the one recently published and discussed by Rustow. This petition was submitted by a preacher at a congregational mosque endowed by the princess Sitt al-Mulk. He, like other members of the staff, drew his salary from the proceeds of the endowment, which, however, were declining since the tenants living in the *waqf* properties endowed for the mosque deferred paying the rents they owed. The endowed mosque served the purpose of spreading Ismailism, and the preacher asked the princess to order the district administrators to help in recovering the payments withhold by the tenants. The petition combines a personal plea to maintain a livelihood with an appeal to the self-interest of the princess to preserve the function of the endowment, and to achieve both of these ends the princess's help in coercing the provincial administrators to render their services was needed.[33]

The main problem a petitioner faced was what he could realistically expect from the state. It seems that rulers could easily accommodate petitions requesting financial support, or 'the needs of the people', since their resources were vast. Petitions requesting redress for wrongdoings posed a problem, and the question was to what extent the state would turn on its officials and administrators. Unsurprisingly, perhaps, the single explicit reference to the dismissal of an official following a complaint comes from the reign of al-Ḥākim, who in 1017–18 dismissed the governor of Damascus following a petition, but such accounts are rare and al-Ḥākim ruled through a reign of terror.[34] In order to be heard, not to say successful, the petitioner had to create 'common ground' with the state and to craft the petition so as to appeal to this. The precondition for creating the 'common ground' was the admission of petitioner's humble status and dependence on the state. This was the function of the *tarjama*, that is, the introductory formula written at the top left corner of a petition, which consists of the petitioner's name preceded by the word 'slave'.

For example, in a petition submitted to al-Āmir, Mūsā ibn Ṣadaqa,

[33] See 'A Petition to a Woman at the Fatimid Court', 1–27.

[34] Sibṭ ibn Jawzī, 136. See van Berkel's cautious remarks about the Abbasid approach to the disciplining of officials who abused subjects, 'Embezzlement and Reimbursement', 716.

a Jewish Indian Ocean merchant identified himself as a slave (*al-ʿabd al-mamlūk*). In the text he presents himself as *mamlūk*, using the unmistakable term for a slave, preferring it over the more ambivalent *ʿabd*. The fact that he was a Jew and introduced himself as such (although no one could mistake him for a Muslim) is, in this case, irrelevant.[35] The term *ʿabd* was also used by Muslim petitioners.[36] Although the *tarjama* of the petition submitted to the princes Sitt al-Mulk is missing, the petitioner repeatedly refers to himself as her 'slave' and, as was befitting for a slave, omits his name.[37] It can be convincingly argued that in this case *ʿabd* signifies a loyal servant rather than a slave, but the choice of the term is telling. The petitioner was a free-born person of some standing, and his petition aimed both at safeguarding his interests as a beneficiary of the princess's pious endowment and at ensuring its future and the functions it fulfilled. In other words, these things were in Sitt al-Mulk's self-interest as patroness of the foundation. Emphasising a mutually shared interest was, however, an unthinkable approach.

The approach medieval people adopted was to be self-effacing while glorifying the rulers. Any document submitted to the ruler included blessings on the reigning *imām* and his titles, while the petitioner presented himself as *ʿabd*, or *mamlūk*, and frequently used both terms. This approach is adopted in all types of documents submitted to the state, including reports about events in which the formula 'prophetic dynasty' or 'prophetic presence' is also employed. During times when political power in the Fatimid state rested with military viziers, the documents reflect this situation and properly address the Fatimid ruler, the vizier and any other dignitary mentioned. Civilians and military men addressed rulers in the same way and the ubiquitous terminology of a slave reporting to a master is used.[38]

Self-abasement before rulers is powerfully attested by an Arabic draft of a

[35] Stern, 'Three Petitions of the Fatimid Period', 179; Khan, *Arabic Legal and Administrative Documents*, doc. 77.

[36] The *tarjama* of the petition of the villager from Sindiyūn contains the terms *al-ʿabd al-mamlūk* and the name of the person, Manṣūr ibn Salāma. In the text he uses the term *mamlūk*. Khan, 'A Petition to the Fatimid Caliph al-Āmir concerning an Inheritance', 176–7, lines 5 and 7.

[37] Rustow, 'A Petition to a Woman at the Fatimid Court', 26–7, lines 7, 11 (text and trans.).

[38] Khan, *Arabic Legal and Administrative Documents*', docs 108, 109, 110 (reports to al-Ẓāhir, al-Āmir and al-Afḍal), and docs 111 (a report on fighting the Franks), 113 (a petition by a military man to al-Ḥāfiẓ).

petition intended for submission to al-Mustanṣir by the Rabbinite Jews concerning their dispute with the Karaites. Their request is phrased as follows: 'The Jews [*al-ʿabīd*] ask for a favour [charity] to be granted to them by issuing an exalted order to one of the Muslim *al-ʿabīd* of the *dawla* [dynasty/state] to open their synagogue.' The term *ʿabīd* is repeated many times throughout the document.[39] Although this document was about Jews appealing to the state, the pervasive influence of state practices also shaped the way Hebrew administrative documents were written during the eleventh century. The adoption of *ʿabd* as a self-reference by a lower-ranking person writing to a higher-ranking one became common.[40]

While a subject who beseeched the ruler or reported to him adopted a self-effacing approach, the state's responses were phrased in a more dignified way, and addressed the subjects by titles bestowed on them or allusions to their professional and occupational backgrounds. An emir who was granted a book from the royal library is addressed by his titles and referred to as one of the distinguished (*khawāṣṣ*) affiliates of the 'exalted prophetic presence'; others are alluded as *al-qāḍī al-faqhī*, as merchants and ship-owners. Given the huge disparity between the Fatimid rulers who claimed to be 'God's deputies on earth' and their subjects, the state could afford politeness when addressing subjects.[41] The terminology adopted in documents issued by the state also reflects a perception of the society as divided into groups and professions, and subjects are categorised accordingly.

Although it was a prerequisite, admission of submission was not enough to create 'common ground', since it only reconfirmed the obvious. 'Common ground' was mainly created by admitting and restating the rulers' claims for political legitimacy. This is the function of the *basmala* section following the *tarjama*, which consists of three elements: blessings on the ruler, listing of his titles that signify claims of legitimacy, and references to Fatimid dynastic ideology and rulers' self-perception as those who dispense justice.[42] The most

[39] For two readings of the document, with many variants, see Gil, *Palestine during the First Muslim Period*, II, doc. 196; Khan, *Arabic Legal and Administrative Documents*, doc. 73.

[40] Rustow, 'The Diplomatics of Leadership', 306–51.

[41] Khan, *Arabic Legal and Administrative Documents*, doc. 120 line 7 (text and trans.). For the way the state alluded to subjects, see docs 116, 117, 118, 119.

[42] For various variants of the blessing formula, see Khan, *Arabic Legal and Administrative Documents*, 307–9.

revealing example is the petition submitted to al-Mustanṣir by the father of a slain young merchant who travelled in a boat on the Nile. The *tarjama* is missing and the text begins with the *basmala*, which consists of blessings on the ruler, his titles, and the petitioner's statement that 'He takes refuge in God's exalted name and in the justice of the prophetic dynasty'. There are several variants on the theme of the 'prophetic dynasty' and acknowledgement of the Fatimid rulers as *imāms* (i.e. God-guided infallible rulers). In the petition of Mūsā ibn Ṣadaqa, for example, immediately after the blessing on al-Āmir, he refers to him as 'Our lord and master *imām* of our epoch and time al-Imām al-Āmir bi-Aḥkām Allāh, Commander of the Faithful'. His position vis-à-vis the ruler is encapsulated in a powerful phrase which, in Khan's translation, is as follows: 'The *mamlūk* kisses the ground before the pure and noble prophetical presence, may God double its light and exalt its beacon, and give victory to its armies, banners and helpers.'

The phrasing of the petitions was standard, and not related to the identity of the petitioner, be he a Jew or a Muslim. For example, the *tarjama* of the baker's petition introduces him as 'The *mamlūk* Bū ʿAbd Allāh ibn Yaḥyā *al-farrān* in Fusṭāṭ'. The text continues in the familiar way by blessing the ruler and listing his titles, including the phrase 'The *mamlūk* kisses the ground', followed by the titles of the vizier to whom the petition was addressed.

The effort to create 'common ground' can be also perceived as the petitions' subtext, in which the petitioner says to the ruler: 'You are indeed the legitimate God-guided infallible *imām* and in your name and the justice of the prophetic dynasty, I ask for justice.' To put it differently, the petitioner was actually saying: my acceptance of your political claims entitles me to your justice and/or magnanimity. This strategy necessitated acute awareness of changing political ideologies and also testifies to how successful regimes were in disseminating their claims of political legitimacy. A petition submitted by a Jew to Saladin begins with the *tarjama* 'The *mamlūk* ʿAbd al-Bāqī ibn Yaḥyā, resident of Malīj', and continues with the *basmala*, followed by a short blessing formula and a full list of the ruler's titles: 'May God, the exalted, make eternal the rule of the exalted and lofty seat, the mighty lord, al-Malik al-Nāṣir, the uniter of the world of faith, the conqueror of the slaves of the cross, Ṣalāḥ al-Dunyā wa-l-Dīn, Sulṭān of Islam and the Muslims, reviver of the dynasty of the Commander of the Faithful, cause his power to endure and exalt his word.'[43] Three key elements of Saladin's claims for legitimacy are reflected by these carefully listed titles: adherence to Sunnī Islam ('the uniter of the world of faith'), achievements in the holy war and commitment to the Abbasid cause ('reviver of the dynasty of the Commander of the Faithful').

Other petitions to Saladin that came from the ranks of the military, however, reflect a completely different mindset, which perhaps can be described as the comradeship of fighting men and which is typified by a sense of closer relations between the sultan, who led his armies in the field, and the troops. For example, the *tarjama* of a petition dated to 1174 presents the petitioner as 'The *mamlūk* Akhwājā Iqbāl, the eunuch'. The main body of the text begins with 'In the name of God, the merciful and compassionate', and continues '[he] kisses the ground before our master al-Malik al-Nāṣir Ṣalāḥ al-Dunya wa-l-Dīn, may God perpetuate his rule. [He] reports his situation [by stating that he is] a poor stranger from the town of Ashmūnayn.' The substantive section of the text which presents the request begins with '[he] asks for an *in'am* [benefaction] [to be conferred on him]'. The same simplified version of a petition by a military man to his sultan is also attested by the slightly later petition of a free-born Kurdish emir addressed to Saladin.[44]

Leaving aside the formulaic aspects of petitions written by the military to Saladin, which have no direct bearing on my argument, 'Abd al-Bāqī ibn Yaḥyā's petition reflects the fact that while political fortunes were changing, values remained constant. This brings me to the secondary device used to create 'common ground': appeal to a set of commonly shared socio-religious values. Subjects presented themselves as normative meritorious people and, therefore, as deserving of compassion on the part of the rulers no matter whether they were Fatimid *imāms* or Ayyubid sultans. 'Abd al-Bāqī ibn Yaḥyā asked Saladin for a rescript to be issued to the state collectors of the poll tax (in his place of residence) asking them not to force him to collect the poll tax for them. The practice of co-opting subjects to work for the state endured no matter which regime was in power. What is significant for this discussion, however, are the arguments 'Abd al-Bāqī ibn Yaḥyā presented in

[43] Khan, *Arabic Legal and Administrative Documents*, doc. 87, lines 6–9 (text and trans.).
[44] Mouton, Sourdel and Sourdel-Thomine, *Gouvernance et libéralités de Saladin*, docs 2 and 3.

support of his request. He alludes to himself as a poor person (*ṣaʿlūk*) with a family and children who makes a living among Muslims in his native town, pays the obligatory poll tax and quarrels with nobody. In other words, he is the model subject, whose sole request is to maintain his way of life, and as such he deserves compassion. In practical terms, he asked for a rescript to be given to him 'as a benefaction (*inʿām* [to be conferred]) on him and a benevolence (*iḥṣān* [to be granted]) to him'. The notion of the model subject exemplified by the petition comprised family life, a humble existence and peaceful conduct. References to family life and care of a family also appear in other petitions from the Fatimid period. In another case, a person who petitioned al-Mustanṣir did not dispute the rightfulness of his detention at the palace jail, but appealed for mercy in the name of his family, his children and a crippled mother.[45]

The petitioners repeatedly alluded to their requests as a favour (*ṣadaqa*, charity) to be granted them as a benefaction and as benevolence (*inʿām* and *iḥṣān*). The standardised use of these three terms was a convention, while references to values are implicit. The difference between the two is epitomised by a long, well-preserved twelfth-century collective petition submitted, most likely, to al-Afḍal.[46] The *tarjama* presents the petitioners as '*Al-ʿabīd al-mamālik*, the family of Ḥabīb, the servant'. Ḥabīb was employed as a servant at the Office of the Chamber and was imprisoned for nine months because of the disappearance of Nādir, a young slave. In the petition the aforementioned slaves introduce themselves as the female family members of Ḥabīb, state that they live in seclusion, stricken with poverty and illness, and enumerate the family members dependent on Ḥabīb as his children, an orphan, elderly parents who have lost their eyesight, a blind child and young girls. They complain that there is no one to shield them from the tribulations of the world and appeal for the release of Ḥabīb, whom they describe as a person who has performed good deeds in his *dhimmī* (Jewish) community: that is, he not only cared for his family but also lived according to the noble

[45] Khan, *Arabic Legal and Administrative Documents*, docs 75 and 85.

[46] Although (in the petitions) the terms *ṣadaqa*, *iḥṣān* and *inʿām* are used as stock phrases, they have deep socio-religious meanings and appear in a variety of socio-political contexts in Muslim and Jewish societies. See Rustow, 'Benefaction (Niʿma), Gratitude (Shukr)', 365–90.

principle of dispensing charity.[47] The petition ends with an unusually long but understandable plea for mercy, which, indeed, was heeded and the release of Ḥabīb ordered.[48]

The incapacitating effect of illness which prevented the breadwinner from making a living and brought his family to starvation is told in another petition, which asked for a rescript against the state collectors of the poll tax. The petitioner states that he pays a poll tax of one and a third *dīnārs* and four dirhams; usually he is dependent on the help of the Jewish community for the payment, but his situation has deteriorated because of illness and imprisonment by the tax collectors. Actually, he asks for an exemption, but the request is not phrased in the name of the legal framework that governed the collection of the poll tax, which envisioned a progressive tax and made provisions for exemptions. Instead he boldly contrasts pretentious Fatimid dynastic claims for justice with the conduct of the tax collectors, putting this in a carefully phrased inoffensive statement: 'Exceptionally, for the justice of these glorious days . . . a blind person having nothing is required to pay the poll tax and is disgracefully treated by the tax collectors.' The petitioner ends his plea in the customary way, stating, in Khan's translation: 'The *mamlūk* kisses the ground again and humbly asks for the issuing of an exalted rescript, may God increase its efficacy.'[49]

While appeals that invoked family life and care for the family were used by all, petitioners from specific backgrounds appealed to other values too. A trooper who submitted a petition to the vizier Ibn Salār (1149–53) described his dire situation and his need to care for a family and mentioned his exemplary military service in fighting the enemy (Franks) in Ascalon.[50] Only a fragment of the petition has survived and the nature of the request remains unknown, but, most likely, it was for financial support justified by his model life, loyalty, and the fulfilment of his duty to fight the holy war.

Although the identity of the 1153–4 petitioner who submitted a request to the vizier al-ʿAbbās is unknown, the content of the request is clearly

47 For the significance of this assertion, see Rustow, 'Benefaction (Niʿma), Gratitude (Shukr)', 388.

48 Khan, *Arabic Legal and Administrative Documents*, doc. 98.

49 Khan, *Arabic Legal and Administrative Documents*, doc. 86, including discussion of the poll tax during the Fatimid–Ayyubid period.

50 Khan, *Arabic Legal and Administrative Documents*, doc. 80.

stated. He asked to keep receiving his yearly allowance of grain. The state used to pay his employees in both cash and grain, but the petitioner refers to the allowance not as his due by rather 'as a benefaction and a benevolence'.[51] While this petition was a personal plea for the maintaining of a privilege, another twelfth-century petition highlights the vested interests of the jurists as a privileged class in the state. Jurists and other religious functionaries such as Koran reciters and muezzins were on the payroll of the Fatimid state and, in 1015–16, payments to these people in Fusṭāṭ and Cairo amounted to 71,733 *dīnārs* per annum. This system of payments must have collapsed during the civil war of the 1060s, and in 1123–4 the payments rendered by the state amounted to merely 16,000 *dīnārs*.[52] The gist of the twelfth-century petition consists of a complaint that unspecified state office had reduced the monthly payments rendered to the jurists, which were financed from two types of taxes, the fifth (*khums*) and the poll tax (*jawālī*). The reference to these taxes is not incidental and reflects a perennial problem: the jurists' susceptibility to the charge that most state income came from illegal taxation. The scope of the taxation authorised by the law was too narrow to sustain the needs of the state, and jurists who enjoyed state money were at pains to ensure that payments rendered to them came from legal sources such as the fifth, levied on foreign merchants, or the poll tax collected from non-Muslims.[53]

Communal requests from the state

The phrase 'communal requests from the state' refers to petitions submitted by non-Muslim communities which deal with a range of issues such as requests for the restoration of seized religious institutions, pleas for preserving privileges granted by the state, and requests for the state to intervene in the internal affairs of non-Muslim communities and reaffirm the position of serv-

[51] Khan, *Arabic Legal and Administrative Documents*, doc. 82.

[52] Maqrīzī, *Itti'āẓ*, II, 112; Ibn al-Ma'mūn, 70. The list according to which these payments were made is referred to as *istīmār*.

[53] Khan, *Arabic Legal and Administrative Documents*, doc. 84. For a wider discussion of the jurists and their demands from the Fatimid state, see Lev, 'Piety and Political Activism', 292–300. For the fifth collected from foreign merchants at the Mediterranean ports during the Fatimid period, see Rabie, *The Financial System*, 90–2.

ing *dhimmī* leaders.[54] These petitions are unique, since they reflect aspects of the state's relations with non-Muslim communities that are rarely mentioned in the literary sources, which mostly refer to *dhimmī* officials in the service of the state and violent outbursts against non-Muslims.

A petition dated to 1031–2 requested the return of a church seized during the persecution of non-Muslims by al-Ḥākim. The document explicitly refers to the reversal of policy and to documents issued to that effect. The events, as mentioned in Chapter 4, were complex and not all churches and monasteries seized during al-Ḥākim's persecutions were returned to their owners. Buildings and lands that were granted as fiefs to soldiers and Bedouins were not returned. These grants were handled by the Office of Fiefs.[55] The petition was submitted against the Office of the Reclaimed Fiefs, which did not comply with the official policy, and a rescript was requested to order the office to pay a sum of money or to return a church to the Christians of an unnamed district.[56] This office must have been either a new bureau created to deal with Christian claims for the return of properties or a sub-office of the Office of Fiefs. The petitioner presented a bill, so to speak, to the state, implying that the church received an income of six *dīnārs* per annum from its endowed properties, described as shops and a press, and that a first payment of twenty-four *dīnārs* was supposed to be paid in 1030. It was a bold petition, since literary sources point out that the princess Sitt al-Mulk, who is described as responsible for the downfall of her brother al-Ḥākim and for installing his son al-Ẓāhir on the throne, cancelled much of the largesse bestowed by al-Ḥākim on various people. She also tried to extract taxes and dues from the pious endowments returned by al-Ḥākim to churches, and the people who submitted the petition must have been aware of that.[57]

It can certainly be argued that, in the context of Fatimid history, al-Ḥākim's persecutions of non-Muslims were an aberration, and a completely different tenor in relations between the state and the *dhimmīs* is revealed by the open decree documents published by Stern. Petitions that requested reconfirmation

[54] Rustow, 'The Legal Status of ḏimmī-s in the Fatimid East', 310. Petitions requesting investiture are discussed in Chapter 7.

[55] Al-Anṭākī, 204, 228–30.

[56] Khan, *Arabic Legal and Administrative Documents*, doc. 70.

[57] Al-Anṭākī, 237.

of privileges were regularly submitted to the Fatimid rulers by the monks of the Mount Sinai monastery. These privileges included exemption from providing military assistance to the local authorities and exemption from duties levied on supplies delivered to the monastery. The state also declared that monks outside the monastery should be protected and must not be harmed. A major worry of the monks concerned their securing safe use of the revenues, in cash and kind, generated by their extensive pious endowments in Fusṭāṭ, Alexandria, Damietta and Tinnīs. The protection of the monastery's food stores was another worry of the monks, and one of the open decree documents instructed the local military governor and others not to tamper with these stores in any way. The monks also asked the state to rescind new taxes imposed on them by the military governors of al-Ṭūr province and the state complied with these requests. The open decree documents reprimanded the governors for their actions and reminded them that the state's policy was to protect the monks. The St Catherine monastery, like any other monastic community, was vulnerable but relatively well-off. Being situated in a region of meagre resources the monastery's productive lands and stores were coveted by both the local population and by Fatimid governors and administrators whose opportunities for self-enrichment while serving in this region were limited. The problems the monastery faced were structural and long-term, and state protection was indispensable and constantly needed.[58]

Requests for state intervention in the internal affairs of the Rabbinite Jews and their quarrels with the Karaites were made several times throughout the Fatimid period. During the years 1039–42 the Rabbinite community was torn apart by a fierce struggle between Solomon ben Judah and Nathan ben Abraham, who was proclaimed by his supporters Head of the Palestinian Academy (*yeshiva*) in Jerusalem, and excommunicated by Solomon, the presiding Head of the Academy. The scuffle between the two factions took place in Ramla and led to the closure of one of the two synagogues in the town by Fatimid officials, most likely by the chief of police. Stern has published and discussed several drafts of petitions intended for submission by the partisans

[58] For these perennial problems, see Stern, *Fatimid Decrees*, docs 1, 4, 5, 6, 7, 8, 9 and 10, spanning the years 1024–1169. Stern has provided extensive discussion of Fatimid political history as reflected by some of these documents.

of Solomon in Fusṭāṭ. The state's involvement in such matters was motivated by ideological as well as practical reasons. The Fatimid rulers portrayed themselves as responsible for all their subjects and the *dhimma* status of the non-Muslim communities facilitated – actually, required – state supervision of their affairs. On the practical level state policies were always conservative, and maintaining law and order was a high priority.

The drafts mention the previous involvement of the state in the dispute and the appointment of a go-between, who, however, failed in his mission. The request to the state was simple but quite amorphous: that the factions be treated equally. One of the drafts alluded to the Karaite Faḍl ibn Sahl al-Tustarī, whose support of Nathan proved most valuable. The petitioners must have realised, however, that criticising a powerful administrator and power broker was counterproductive and that the state would not turn on such a powerful figure, and therefore his name is omitted in other drafts. Another draft fragment in Arabic and Judaeo-Arabic contains a more realistic request that a certain emir (most likely, as Stern has suggested, the governor of Ramla) be ordered to reopen the synagogue.[59] Another draft fragment in Arabic, published by Khan, offers a brief summary of the conflict and alludes to the help that Nathan received from Karaites in his bid to be recognised as the Head of the Academy. The document requests the reopening of the synagogue and refers to emir Munjiz al-Dawla as the person who had ordered its closure. According to Khan, the synagogue was in Fusṭāṭ, not in Ramla.[60] When considered from the point of view of what could realistically have been expected of the state, the request to reopen the synagogue was entirely in line with the logic of petitioning, since requests that deeds of officials and administrators be reversed was the essence of the *maẓālim* institution.

Amān and *Dhimma*: State Perception of Subjects

The silent dialogue between subjects and the state, as reflected in the way petitions were written and phrased, must be seen within the wider context of the state's perceptions of its subjects. The issue is elusive and never directly addressed in the sources, but diverse reports indicate that the state's attitude

[59] Stern, 'A Petition to the Fatimid Caliph al-Mustanṣir', 203–22.
[60] Khan, *Arabic Legal and Administrative Documents*, doc. 73.

towards its subjects was governed by the notion of protection (*amān/dhimmi*, the boundaries of which were defined by the state. What was at stake is revealed by the events that took place in 972 in Tinnīs.

The Fatimids gained control of Tinnīs in 969 by employing a former Ikhshidid military commander, who overcome local resistance and sent 150 captives to Jawhar in Fusṭāṭ. Later, the commander, whose name is uncertain, rebelled, fled to Syria and was captured and imprisoned by Jawhar. Tinnīs, however, remained under Fatimid control until 972, when a popular anti-Fatimid rebellion erupted in this island town: 'And the people [*ahl*] of Tinnīs rebelled. They changed political recognition and displayed black, and the army fought them.' The recapture of Tinnīs was Jawhar's priority and further troops were sent there. The rebellion ended in a settlement between Jawhar and a group of *ahl Tinnīs* (Dhū l-Ḥijja 362/September 973), which involved the payment of one million *dirhams* as wergild money for the 'Maghāriba which were killed at your place'. Jawhar's original demand was for 200,000 *dīnārs*. Maqrīzī's use of the term *ahl Tinnīs* is somewhat loose, since he states that prior to that agreement *ahl Tinnīs* had actually repelled a sea-borne Carmathian attack on the island.[61] The chain of events discussed so far is quite clear, but what sparked off the popular anti-Fatimid rebellion remains unknown. In the fighting Fatimid soldiers were killed, and the fact that later the population helped to fight the Carmathians was not considered a mitigating factor. Subjects had to obey their rulers and rebellions bore consequences.

The way the Fatimids dealt with the aftermath of the Tinnīs rebellion stands in sharp contrast with the way they treated political opponents and rebels. In 972, a rebellion led by ʿAbd al-ʿAzīz ibn Ibrāhīm al-Kalābi erupted in Upper Egypt and was quickly quashed. The leader and other rebels were captured and displayed, but no wergild money was demanded.[62] These were political adversaries, not subjects under protection and obligation to their rulers, and against political adversaries a variety of means were employed, ranging from violence to attempts at wining them over. This contrasting approach towards the population and political adversaries goes back to the first years of the Fatimid rule in Egypt. The Fatimid conquest was intended to

[61] See Maqrīzī, *Ittiʿāẓ*, I, 120, 122, 130, 142.
[62] Maqrīzī, *Ittiʿāẓ*, I, 131.

be peaceful, and Jawhar's letter of safety is presented as God's comprehensive *amān* which promised to end oppression and establish justice.[63] On one level, the acceptance of the *amān* by the Sunnī elite of Fusṭāṭ served them as a personal guarantee of their safety, while on another level the elite represented the people and acted on their behalf. The Fatimids kept their promise to both the elite and the people; they made every effort to maintain law and order and contained clashes between their North African foreign troops and the population of the capital. The troops of the former Ikhshdid regime who rejected the offer were fought, killed, captured, executed and imprisoned and their property was expropriated, but many were also won over.

The notion that the population's life is governed by the *amān/dhimma* concept was powerfully illustrated during al-Ḥākim's reign of terror. In 1004–5, fear-struck state employees and common people traversed Cairo on their way to one of the palace's gates to submit a petition requesting pardon. The petition was brought to al-Ḥākim's attention, and they were reassured by a verbal message about their safety. Next day, three different versions of a formal edict granting safety were issued, to Muslims, Christians and Jews, indicating that the recipients were state clerks and administrators. The spectacle of groups of people approaching the ruler through the mechanism of the *maẓālim* institution in search of personal safety became contagious. Many military groups and the palace's eunuchs asked for and received similar documents. The trend spread and engulfed the population; eventually, a hundred letters of safety were issued to various professional groups at the markets. These letters invoked the name of God (*amān Allāh*) and the Prophet, while the authority which granted the safety was the ruler (*amān* of the Commander of the Faithful). Similar letters of safety to individuals and groups were also issued during the years 1009, 1010 and 1011.[64]

Al-Ḥākim's rule, although an atypical aberration in Fatimid history, illustrates the *amān/dhimma* concept, which was the term of reference during the whole period. People were threatened with loss of their *dhimma* if they did not obey state edicts, and people were punished for rioting, which was

[63] Maqrīzī, *Itti'āẓ*, I, 106, referring to God's *amān*. For other clauses of the document, see 103–5, and for its implementation, 110.
[64] Maqrīzī, *Itti'āẓ*, II, 54–5, 56, 57, 77, 82, 83, 84, 85.

perceived as a breach of their *dhimma*. In unusual circumstances, people were authorised to protect themselves against troops on the rampage as exceptional extension of their *dhimma*. However, Fatimid *amāns* were not only about safety: they also promised justice, and justice was claimed through the *maẓālim* institution. In the wider context of the state's relations with its subjects, the *maẓālim* institution was a bridging institution between the two, which also offered a mechanism for how to perform the bridging.[65]

[65] Unauthorised approaches to rulers could be perilous. Once, when Muḥammad ibn Ṭughj came out of an orchard on the outskirts of Fusṭāṭ, he was approached with a complaint by an elderly shaykh, Masʿūd al-Ṣābūnī. The emir, however, ordered that the shaykh be beaten and thrown to the ground, sensing an evil omen emanating from him. The shaykh did not survive the ordeal and died, while the emir postponed the trip and retired to the orchard. Eventually, the very substantial sum of 300 *dīnārs* was paid to the family and the public honoured the shaykh with a massive funeral, which also symbolised the popular outcry at the incident. Ibn Saʿīd, 31–2.

PART THREE

THE ADMINISTRATION OF JUSTICE IN NON-MUSLIM COMMUNITIES

7

Judicial Autonomy: Medieval Realities and Modern Discourse

Judicial Autonomy and the Jewish Communities

The pre-Fatimid history of Jews in Muslim Egypt is little-known and Arabic sources offer only a few bits of information. Jews and Christians, for example, alongside Muslims, participated in the prayers for the recovery of Aḥmad ibn Ṭūlūn during his final illness.[1] Jews lived in the former Byzantine fortified town (Qaṣr al-Shamʿ), which was engulfed by the expanding town of Fusṭāṭ. Immigration from Iran and Iraq (Hebrew Bavel [Babylonia]) that began in the second half of the ninth century was an important factor in the growth of Egyptian Jewry, and it shaped its spiritual orientation towards the Iraqi academies (*yeshivot*) of Sura and Pumbeditha and the Palestinian *yeshiva* in Jerusalem. In Fusṭāṭ there were two Jewish congregations and synagogues, Palestinian and Babylonian, which constituted the Rabbinite community, while the Karaites (Bible readers or Scripturalists, who disapproved of the teaching of the Talmud) were a separate community with complex relations with the Rabbinite Jews. The Palestinian and Babylonian synagogues were located along the Zuqāq al-Yahūd in Qaṣr al-Shamʿ. Although the Samaritans seceded from mainstream Judaism during the Second Temple, there was interaction between them and the Rabbinite community and, in the eyes of the Fatimid rulers, they were part of the subject Jewish population.

[1] Balawī, 330. For a ninth-century prison log, referring to a Jewish debtor who owed the quite substantial sum of forty *dīnārs* to a Jewish creditor, see Tillier and Vanthieghem, 'Un registre carcéral', 3–4 (text and trans.).

The size of the Jewish community in Fusṭāṭ and Cairo during the eleventh century has been estimated by Goitein at 4,000 (3,600 Rabbinites and 400 Karaites). The Jewish community of Cairo, however, is barely attested by the Geniza documents or the Arabic sources. It had apparently existed since the foundation of the town and was gravely affected by al-Ḥākim's persecutions, though it subsequently recovered.[2] The second-biggest Jewish community was in Alexandria, but Jewish communities were also found in the Delta and Upper Egypt and individual Jews lived in many places all over the country.[3]

The *yeshivot* were institutions of learning headed by the *gaon* and also had judicial functions and served as a court. The title *av beth din* (head of the court) was preserved for the president of the *yeshiva* court, who was also heir apparent to the post of *gaon*. Provincial judges (dayyānim/*shōfeṭīm*) derived their authority from the *geonim* who appointed them.[4] The *geonim* also received legal queries from local courts and bestowed honorific titles on the *yeshiva*'s supporters and benefactors. Many of the *dayyānim* in Fusṭāṭ during the Fatimid period bore the title *ḥave*r bestowed on them by the Palestinian *yeshiva*, which indicated affiliation and symbolic membership of the institution, while a few of them also held the title *alluf* bestowed by the Babylonian academies.

Considering the broader context of relations between non-Muslims and the Islamic state, Goitein has stated: 'Nothing is so characteristic of the position of the non-Muslim minorities under classical Islam as their judicial organization.'[5] The conceptual framework he alludes to is the notion of personal rather than territorial law that prevailed in medieval Islam and the tension between communal autonomy and governmental interference.[6] Because of the inseparable link between law and religion in both Judaism and Islam,

[2] Maqrīzī, *Musawwadat Kitāb al-Mawā'iẓ*, 352–3; *Khiṭaṭ*, III, 12.

[3] For a lucid overview, see Stillman, 'The Non-Muslim Communities', 198–210, with ample references to sources and literature, esp. 202, n. 7, referring to the debate about the size of the Fusṭāṭ-Cairo community. For Alexandria, see Frenkel, 'Medieval Alexandria', 29–30. For the geography of Jews and Jewish communities, see Golb, 'The Topography of the Jews of Medieval Egypt', esp. 148–9.

[4] The title *av beth din* was also bestowed on communal leaders. According to Goitein, the biblical Hebrew term *shōfeṭ* is equivalent to Arabic *ḥākim*, while *dayyān* refers to a 'professional judge'. See *Med. Soc.* II, 28, 314, 315.

[5] See *Med. Soc.* II, 311.

[6] See *Med. Soc.* II, 402–7.

one cannot envision a Jewish community able to conduct its life and internal affairs without its own court. In Judaism, as in Islam, the law encompassed a whole spectrum of private and socio-economic life.

Terms such as 'communal autonomy/judicial autonomy' or 'self-rule' are, however, modern constructs which stand for complex medieval realities and when used need qualification. Mikhail, for example, has argued that the notion of the legislative and communal autonomy of non-Muslim communities in medieval Islam 'presumes a degree of independence and self-governance never fully realized by any *dhimmī* community'.[7] In the medieval Middle East, communal boundaries were both rigid and fluid, especially in economic life. The tiny Jewish minority in the Fatimid capital city and in Egypt as a whole was fully integrated into the economic life of the Muslim majority and its material culture. Integration meant having Muslim customers in day-to-day market life and Muslim partners in commercial ventures. The community in Fusṭāṭ-Cairo also enjoyed access to the corridors of power at the Fatimid court and involved the rulers in its internal politics and squabbles. Taking into account how vigorous Jewish life in medieval Egypt was, one must view communal/judicial autonomy as a construct having a certain core meaning and dynamic shifting boundaries.[8]

In contrast to the elaborate modern discourse about autonomy/self-rule, the Fatimids' perception of their Jewish subject population is reflected by al-Ẓāhir's decree issued in 1024 addressed to the military commander in Palestine. The decree states that the Rabbinite and Karaite Jews should live according to their own customs, and both communities are referred to in an offhand manner as being sheltered by the *dhimma* of the *milla* (the protection of Islam, or the Muslim nation), and as enjoying justice, repeating the Fatimids' self-perception as rulers who upheld justice for all.[9]

Another factor that must be taken into account is that the *dhimmī* judicial autonomy in medieval Islam was more a default than a granted right. Gideon Libson's studies have shown that its existence and scope were extensively debated by the founders of Islamic legal schools and in the legal literature in

[7] See *From Byzantine to Islamic Egypt*, 150.

[8] Rustow, 'At the Limits of Communal Autonomy', 133–59, which offers both an overview and a detailed discussion of certain events.

[9] Stern, *Fatimid Decrees*, doc. 2, lines, 35–7.

general. Because of differences in the marriage laws of the three monotheistic religions, the authority of the *dhimmī* courts in these matters was perceived by Abū Ḥanīfa and Muḥammad al-Shaybānī as a necessity. Their pragmatic approach dictated that as long as the *dhimmīs* conducted their marriages in their courts they were outside the purview of Islamic law.[10]

Whatever might have been the legal underpinnings which allowed the existence of *dhimmī* courts in medieval Islam, the court was a crucial institution in the life of the Jewish community during the Fatimid–Ayyubid period. Goitein, for example, has reconstructed a list of 32 Jewish *dayyānim* who served in Fusṭāṭ-Cairo between 965 and 1265.[11] The authority that the Jewish courts wielded during the Fatimid period was a reflection of the relationships between the Fatimid *imāms*-caliphs, their viziers, the Palestinian *yeshiva* and the Egyptian Jewry. This complex web of ties is attested by several fragmentary Geniza texts. The most illustrative is perhaps the Judaeo-Arabic draft of a petition intended for submission to al-Ẓāhir, in which the *gaon* of the Palestinian *yeshiva* argues against the attempt made by Yūsuf al-Sijilmāsī of the Babylonian congregation to appoint judges and officials on his behalf in Palestine. What renders the document significant is that it represents the *gaon*'s self-perception of his position and how he perceived his relations with the caliph. The main drive of the *gaon*'s argument is that only one authority should be recognised, while a multiplication of authorities would lead to sedition and anarchy (*fitan*). Most likely, such an argument would have found favour with a medieval autocrat, and the *gaon* pushed the argument to its limit by stating that recognition of any additional authority would invalidate the benefaction conferred on him by the caliph. He also warned that it might have practical implications, since in such a case no one would be able to obtain any dues (*ḥaqq*), not even from the humblest man. This was a rather strange assertion, or warning, since there are no indications that the *gaon* had any tax-collection powers, unless he perceived donations to the *yeshiva* as its institutional right (*ḥaqq*). The *gaon*'s additional argument was that according to the percepts (*qanūn*) of the Jewish religion (*madhhab*), Jerusalem and its head (*ra'īs*) are vested with supreme authority and disobedience of the head is disobedience of God, as is confirmed by the

[10] See 'Legal Autonomy', 334–93, esp. 365–6.
[11] See *Med. Soc.* II, Appendix D.

Torah. The *gaon* stated that, just as a body cannot exist with two heads, there is no learning in a town with two cadis (*qāḍyan*). In the context of the present discussion, leaving aside the wider ramifications of the document, the *gaon* claimed a single spiritual and legal authority.[12]

Insights into the extent of Jewish self-rule and the ability to maintain courts are offered by another undated Arabic Geniza fragment which is considered to be a draft of a petition sent in 1036 by the *gaon* of Jerusalem to his supporters in the capital Fusṭāṭ-Cairo, asking them to submit the final version to the caliph. The authors of the document state that they had been asked to provide testimony about the community (*ṭā'ifa*) known as the rabbinic Jews and their head, known as the head of the academy, and his son, whom they ought to obey, and accept the appointments he makes (in every town and region [*aqlīm*]). The text touches upon an issue that can be termed the scope of the *gaon*'s authority or, more broadly, the scope of Jewish self-rule, and refers to judicial rulings, marriage contracts and divorces, maintainance of religion and learning, the commanding of right and forbidding of wrong, the imposition of bans, and the appointment of cantors, slaughterers and *dayyānim*.[13] Another Geniza fragment which is considered by Goitein to be a draft of a petition to be submitted to the Fatimid rulers belongs to the same context. The authors asked for the appointment of Joseph ben Yeshūʿā as *muqaddam* (head of community) and *dayyān* in Alexandria (c. 1036). His judicial responsibilities are described as involving marriages and divorces and his administrative authority included the appointment of cantors and other officials as he saw fit. The post of *muqaddam* was for life and hereditary, but leadership in the Jewish community was ill-defined, involved several officials and lacked a clearly structured hierarchy. The *muqaddam* was engaged in a range of communal and charitable activities such as the collection of ransom money to free captured Jews brought to Alexandria by pirates or those imprisoned during the wars of the Crusades.[14]

12 Goitein, 'Congregation versus Community', 301–2 (text and trans.). For a discussion of the document and its terminology, see Rustow, 'The Legal Status of ḏimmī-s in the Fatimid East', 316–18.

13 Goitein, *Palestinian Jewry*, 57 (text and Hebrew trans.), 58– 60, with extensive discussion of the document's content.

14 The document is written in the third person plural: 'their *aḥkām* (law/rulings) and their marriages and their divorces, according to the tradition (*sunan*) of their religion (*madhhab*).' Goitein,

Important though the formal relations between the Fatimid state and the Jews were, intra-Jewish tensions generated by conflicting loyalties to Palestine and Babylonian *yeshivot* had significant political and legal repercussions. During the early 1060s a new office, the Head of the Jews (*ra'īs al-Yahūd*, also known by the Hebrew term *nagid*), had emerged.[15] The first attested appearance of the title *nagid* is from 1064, when it was bestowed on the physician and communal leader Judah ben Saadya.[16] The political scene in the Fatimid capital of the early 1060s was overshadowed by the first two rounds of internal fighting between the various military corps of the Fatimid army (1062 and 1066), which deteriorated into a full-scale civil war during 1068–72 that engulfed the whole country. Order was restored by Badr al-Jamālī, who usurped power from the caliph and established a hereditary military dictatorship (1073–1121). During the rule of Badr al-Jamālī (1073–94), the Coptic patriarch moved permanently to Cairo and became involved in state politics. Cohen sees parallels between the close association between the Coptic Church and state and the emergence of the *nagid* institution, an innovation described by Cohen as 'promoted by a coterie of Jewish notables in Fusṭāṭ-Cairo that included the first heads of the Jews, themselves'.[17] The events that took place within the Jewish community in Fusṭāṭ-Cairo were also influenced by the moving of the Palestinian *yeshiva* from Jerusalem, under the rule of the Turcomans, to Tyre (around 1076–89). In a parallel move during the 1070s, the Karaite leader in Jerusalem, the *nāsī*, left for Egypt.[18] The political history of Palestine during the second half of the eleventh century was a significant factor behind the waning authority of the Palestinian *yeshiva* over the Jewish community in Egypt. During the first *nagidim* the judicial authority of the *gaon* was still acknowledged, but eventually, the appointment of *dayyānim* became the *nagid*'s prerogative. The power wielded by twelfth-century *nagidim* is illustrated by the deeds

Palestinian Jewry, 77–8. For the Yosef ben Yeshuah family and its role in the Jewish community of Alexandria, see Frenkel, *'The Compassionate and Benevolent'*, 47–74.

15 Cohen, 'Administrative Relations between Palestinian and Egyptian Jewry', 113–35, with reference to earlier studies and reinterpretation of sources.

16 Cohen, *Jewish Self-Government*, 160.

17 Cohen, *Jewish Self-Government*, 98.

18 The document referred to in n. 44 indicates the presence of the Karaite *nāsī* in Fusṭāṭ already in 1055.

of the *nagid* and *gaon* Nathanal ha-Levy, who, in 1160, coerced Meir ben Hillel ben Ṣādōq into leaving Fusṭāṭ and accepting the post of *dayyān* in Alexandria. Although the post was paid, Meir was bitter and unhappy about his forced stay in Alexandria.[19]

The Working of the Jewish Courts

Having provided a short overview of background topics pertaining to the way Islamic law perceived *dhimmī* courts and the internal structure of the Jewish communities in Egypt and their relations with the Fatimid rulers, this section deals directly with the subject matter of the chapter: the legal authority of the Jewish court and the way it conducted its business. Prior to the full consolidation of the authority of the *nagid*, the legal authority of the Jerusalem academy was acknowledged by the Jewish court in Fusṭāṭ and is explicitly stated in legal documents. In 1032, for example, a complex divorce case was adjudicated, the document issued by the court stated: 'Sa῾īda the daughter of David appeared before the permanent [*qavu῾a*] court in Fusṭāṭ (Mitzrayim) which derives its authority from the great court.'[20] A variant phrase refers to 'a case [*ma῾aseh*, a happening] that took place before us at the permanent court which derives its authority from the great court'. These declarations were sometimes reduced to simpler phrases which state the names of a man or a woman who 'came before us at the permanent court in Fusṭāṭ'.[21] The

[19] Frenkel, *'The Compassionate and Benevolent'*, 109–13, including references to legal documents signed and written by him. For the reference to pay involved with the post of *dayyān*, see doc. 92. For other foreigners appointed as *dayyānim* in Alexandria during the twelfth and thirteenth centuries, see 12–33, 135–7.

[20] The phrase 'the permanent court' stands for the court in Fusṭāṭ. See Bareket, *The Jews of Egypt*, doc. 67 (text and Hebrew trans.). Oded Zinger points out that the term *qavu῾a* means 'situated in' since it is always followed by a name of a locality (personal communication).

[21] For these phrases, see See Bareket, *The Jews of Egypt*, docs 87, 88, 97, and 104, spanning the years 1038–50. A shorter, less formal reference to the court in Fusṭāṭ appears in a document from 1034, which simply states 'the court here'. See Ben-Sasson, *The Jews of Sicily*, doc. 43. To what extent the full phrase referring to the court in Fusṭāṭ that invokes the authority of the Jerusalem *yeshiva* was unique to that court is an open question. A document written on 16 December 1046 at 'the permanent court in Fusṭāṭ' refers to a person who appeared before the court with a legal document signed at 'the permanent court in the town of Qayrawān'. See Ben-Sasson, *The Jews of Sicily*, doc. 94, ll. 3, 11, 12 (text and Hebrew trans.). For other reference to Jewish courts, see the opening line of a document from 21 April 1020, which states: 'A case that took place before us, we the community of Syracuse, at court session.' See Golb, 'A Judaeo-Arabic Court Document', 119–21 (text and trans.); republished in Ben-Sasson, *The Jews of Sicily*, doc. 19.

standard court procedure would be to convene at the Palestinian synagogue with three *dayyānim* in session. The phrase 'In the presence of the three permanent *dayyānim* in the town of Cairo and Fusṭāṭ in Egypt' is common in court documents.[22]

The daily business of the court in Fusṭāṭ is reflected by the documents written by two of its most renowned scribes Hillel ben Eli (dated documents spanning the years 1067–1108), who also served as cantor of the Palestinian synagogue, and his son-in-law and disciple Ḥalfōn ben Manasse (1100–38). These documents have been studied and edited by Gershon Weiss and include several types of deeds (*sheṭārōt*, formularies). The court was involved in every aspect pertinent to the personal status of the Jewish population and the two scribes wrote betrothal and marriage contracts, amendments of marriage contracts, bills settling marriage strives, bills of divorce, deeds of gift, wills and deathbed declarations. Other documents issued by the court pertained to the socio-economic life of the community and involved bills of partnership, releases and indebtedness, acknowledgement of debts, sale and purchase documents concerning houses and slaves and leases of houses and shops.[23] Another insight into the everyday business of the Jewish courts can be gained through court archives, or record books, of which the most extensive (still unpublished) consists of 28 folios that comprise 66 items written by the *dayyān* Mevōrākh ben Nathan during April–August 1156.[24] A shorter book of record of the Palestinian court in Fusṭāṭ (from the end of 1026 to mid-1028) written by Yefet ben David (1007–57) has been published by Elinoar Bareket and sheds light on how complicated disputes could be concerning the annulment of betrothal contracts, marriage contracts, inheritance cases or Levirate marriage.[25]

22 According to Goitein, the phrase refers to the two professional judges (*dayyānim*) in Fusṭāṭ and the one in Cairo. See *Med. Soc.* II, 314. For the talmudic roots of the concept that financial matters should be considered by three *dayyānim*, see Gil, *Documents of the Jewish Pious Foundations*, 40.

23 Weiss, *Documents Written by Hilel ben Eli*, 29–88; *Legal Documents Written by the Court Clerk Halfon ben Manasse*, Part 1, ch. 9.

24 Goitein, *Med. Soc.* II, 343–4.

25 Levirate marriage involved the marriage of a man to his late brother's childless widow. In the case of either of the parties refusing to perform the marriage, both were required to go through a ceremony known as *ḥaliẓah*, which symbolised the renunciation of their obligations. Bareket, 'Books of Records of the Jerusalemite Court', 1–65; *Fusṭāṭ on the Nile*, 53–62, referring to other cases dealt with by the court.

Following Goitein, Weiss, in his study of Hillel ben Eli, has stated: 'The members of the Jewish court were, as a rule, personally known to the parties from the synagogue or otherwise.'[26] He provides prosopographical details about twenty-four people whose names appear as signatories of the court, of whom six are described as permanent *dayyānim*, but full biographical details are not available. Learning was of course a factor that promoted people to the rank of *dayyānim*, and equally important were ties with the Palestinian *yeshiva*. These findings are enhanced by Miriam Frenkel's study of the Jewish elite of medieval Alexandria, which clearly shows a correlation between elite status and service as *dayyān*.[27]

Another group of people mentioned in countless Geniza legal documents are the elders. Goitein perceived the elders as a social institution and as a permanent body of people who were involved in communal affairs and played a role in the deliberations of the court. The elite status of the elders and their reputation for probity are also attested in the context of the social and legal life of the Jewish community of Kairouan.[28] Emphasis on the elite status of the elders should not obscure the fact that in a traditional society, with its short life expectancy, age was an important social marker that ideally would be augmented by belonging to the elite. For example, during the time Anatoli bar Joseph served as communal leader and *dayyān* in Alexandria (1199–1228), a young member of the rival Alʿmani family was appointed *dayyān*. The elders were split over the nomination since some members of the community were hostile and claimed that the new *dayyān* was beardless and unmarried, and thus unfit for the position.[29] The term 'the elders' must have conveyed a sense of meritorious seniority, while probity and elite status were acquired qualities.

This complex web of social norms must be taken into consideration when reading the statute (*taqqānā*), published most likely in 1044, which set up a body of ten elders to assist Efraim ben Shemarya (1020–47), the

[26] See *Documents Written by Hillel ben Eli*, 23. He goes on to point out that Jewish law requires two witnesses to validate a writ, and Weiss has discovered that 88% of the documents he studied were signed by two or three witnesses, while 3% of the documents were signed by four witnesses and 9% by five. For Goitein's original statement, see *Med. Soc.* II, 312.

[27] Weiss, *Documents Written by Hillel ben Eli*, 23–8.

[28] Goitein, *Med. Soc.* II, 109–11; Ben-Sasson, *The Emergence of the Local Jewish Community*, 326–9.

[29] Frenkel, *'The Compassionate and Benevolent'*, 132–3.

communal leader and *dayyān*, in the execution of his duties. The justification for the proclamation of the statute was religious and reflects not only the linguistic and cultural acculturation of Jews into the dominant Arab culture but also internalisation of Muslim discourse on God and the Koran. The document states that the *taqqānā* of the rabbinic community in Fusṭāṭ (Miṣr) was published in conjunction with Efraim ben Shemarya and motivated by the 'wish of all of them to obey God, blessed and extolled, and the resolution to maintain the norms [*sunan*] of the religion [*dīn*] as imposed by God on them in His Torah that descended from the heaven'. They also proclaimed their determination to execute the obligations (*ḥuqūq*) laid on them and to establish 'ten elders among the community who would sit with Efraim ben Shemarya at the court room and will share with him the burden of the community needs and help him to carry out the *ḥuqūq* and execute commanding right and forbidding wrong. With him they will remove what is impermissible by the *shar*ʿ [the religious law].' They also undertook to assist Efraim ben Shemarya with implementation of the letters of the *gaon* while the community undertook to honour him and to accept his judgments (*aḥkām*, rulings) as it was religiously obliged to do. The issue of incomes from the slaughter house (i.e. the slaughter house that provided the community with meat slaughtered in accordance with the Jewish law) is also mentioned.[30] Like any judge, Muslim or Jewish, Efraim ben Shermarya needed social acceptance and enlisted the help of the elite in carrying out his duties and enforcing his rulings. In political terms, he actually shared powers with the elite and this co-operation was presented as instrumental in the implementation of God's laws and social norms.

The co-operation between the *dayyānim* and the elders highlights the social function of the court and its role in the dispute resolution process. Goitein has pointed out that formal judgments are rarely found in the Geniza, but he also states: 'It would be entirely wrong to assume that the courts acted merely as boards of arbitration, without having recourse to statutory law.'[31] The issue has been re-examined by Philip I. Ackerman-Lieberman,

[30] Goitein, *Palestinian Jewry*, 109–11. For the adoption of the terminology of the Muslim religious discourse by the Jews, see Erder, 'The Split between the Rabbanite and Karaite Communities', 337.

[31] See *Med. Soc.* II, 334.

who points out that Goitein's use of the term 'arbitration' should be revised, since the court's preferred method of dispute resolution was mediation rather than arbitration.[32]

The emphasis laid on the similar social milieu in which the cadi and *dayyān* operated should not obscure the institutional differences in how the cadi's court and the Jewish court operated. One of these differences – a single cadi in contrast to three *dayyānim* – has already been mentioned. Furthermore, the elite status of both the *dayyān* and the cadi should not obscure the fact that a *dayyān*, in contrast to a cadi, wielded no administrative-financial responsibilities for orphans or pious endowments. Jewish communities managed these affairs differently. Although the court had supervisory powers, there was no direct personal involvement of the *dayyānim* in these affairs.

The Jewish pious endowment institution (*heqdesh/qōdesh*) of the Fusṭāṭ community evolved and expanded in the course of the eleventh to thirteenth centuries, and the lion's share of the revenues was used for communal needs such as supporting scholars, and paying community officials and the teachers of orphaned and poor boys. Only 10 per cent went to charity, which was also financed by other communal means. The most significant critical remarks about the Jewish endowment documents published by Gil have been made by Haim Gerber, who points out that these involve lists of rents, expenditures and repairs and 'contain no legal terms at all'. His main conclusion is that the documents reflect Jewish endowment custom rather than the Muslim *waqf* institution. No matter from what angle these documents are approached, one can confidently conclude that there was no Jewish parallel to the Muslim *waqf ahlī* and that the *parnāsim* were mostly involved in management of the *heqdesh* and in collecting the dues from the renting of its properties.[33]

Parnāsim were chosen from the mercantile elite of the community, and up until the mid-twelfth century received no remuneration for their services.[34] In line with the typical medieval lack of distinction between the public and

[32] See 'Commercial Forms and Legal Norms', 1,032, 1,034–5.

[33] Goitein, *Med. Soc.* II, 118; Gil, *Documents of the Jewish Pious Foundations*, 477–8. Gerber, *Crossing Borders*, 160–2, esp. 160.

[34] For the involvement of the *parnasim* in the managing the properties of the pious endowment, see the summary of *heqdesh* documents published by Goitein, *Med. Soc.* II, Appendix A, docs 25–36, 101, spanning the years 1180–95. For a broader discussion of the *parnasim*, see Goitein, *Med. Soc.* II, 78–80; Gil, *Documents of the Jewish Pious Foundations*, 47–52.

private spheres of activity of state officials or communal leaders, *parnāsim* lived in the properties of the pious endowment that were under their management and farmed out the collection of rents from these properties.[35] *Parnāsim* are mentioned in many deeds and their names appear as signatories on countless court documents. Furthermore, certain *parnāsim* also served as trustees of the court (sing. *ne'emān bēth dīn*) and were involved in communal charitable affairs. Management of the Jewish pious endowment was, however, flexible and other communal officials such as collectors (*gabbai*, Arabic jābī), cantors and the synagogue beadle (*shammāsh*, literally attendant, Arabic *khādim*) were also involved. Goitein and Gil have pointed out that from the mid-twelfth century the officials involved in the collection of rents from the pious endowment properties received a fee of 10 per cent, which was approved by the court and appears in accounts submitted to the court for authorisation. Although the court supervised the work of the various communal officials involved with the management of pious endowments, the *dayyānim* were not personally involved in the affairs of the *heqdesh*.[36]

A similar type of supervisory involvement was exercised by the court in the case of orphans. Goitein has extensively discussed orphanage in the Jewish society of the Geniza period and the lot of orphans, and has stated: 'We read too much about the sufferings of the orphans and their widowed mothers.'[37] He provides a long and detailed explanation for this state of affairs, but this section deals only with the court's involvement in this aspect of private and communal life. The Biblical assertion that God is the father of orphans and judge of widows (Psalms 68: 6) has been understood in the geonic period in terms of the court's responsibility for the welfare of orphans, and the court's involvement began with the execution of wills and/or deathbed declarations.[38] The court used to appoint an executor or executors, who acted as guardians for minor orphans, and a supervisor over the executors. In cases where the father made these appointments the court used to confirm the people he had chosen. The potential intricacies of such cases are illustrated by the will of the Andalusī merchant Samuel ha-Levi ben Abraham, extensively discussed by

[35] Gil, *Documents of the Jewish Pious Foundations*, 51–2, doc. 53.
[36] Goitein, *Med. Soc.* II, 80; Gil, *Documents of the Jewish Pious Foundations*, 42–5, 52–4.
[37] See *Med. Soc.* III, 312.
[38] Cohen, *Poverty and Charity*, 236–7.

Goitein. New documents from the court of Efraim ben Shemarya indicate that Samuel had appointed two guardians for his minor son and a supervisor. Those were appointments of trust since the guardians were granted freedom of action and exemption from oaths. The father had also stipulated that when the son reached maturity and was able to conduct business of his own the whole estate would be given to him. The case (dated documents span the years 1019–25) got ugly and complicated when the orphan, upon reaching maturity, demanded that his guardians produce accounts of the transactions they had conducted while executing their task. A cadi (referred to al-Shaykh al-Jalīl ʿImād al-Dawla) also became involved, but how the affair ended remains unclear.[39]

More examples of the smooth or problematic execution of duties by the trustees of the court and other communal officials can be given, but, so far as I am aware from the published record of Geniza documents and the literature, there was no Jewish equivalent of the Muslim fund known as *amwāl al-yatāmā*. In the Jewish context, the danger of gross misuse of money belonging to orphans, as happened during the term in office of the supreme cadi Muḥammad ibn al-Nuʿmān, was slim or non-existent. This was due to a different approach to how funds of this type were handled. The Jewish community was perhaps not especially successful in alleviating the plight of orphans and widows, but through a decentralised system supervised by the court it minimised abuses of trust by those involved.

In Goitein's view, 'Only when the deep decline of Egyptian Jewry set in around the turn of the thirteenth century did the Jewish judge, like the Muslim *qāḍī*, become administrator of the public funds, making each and every decision'. Goitein assumes that around half of the Jewish population in Fusṭāṭ was wiped out during the famine and plague of 1200–2, and though communal institutions survived, the way they functioned have changed.[40] It can be argued that the community, which dwindled in size, also lost its elite social group from which officials who dealt with pious endowments and orphans' properties were recruited. These changes are illustrated by the

39 Goitein, *Med. Soc.* III, 293–5. Additional documents have been published by Bareket, *The Jews of Egypt*, docs 79 and 80; 'The Affair of Abraham b. Samuel ha-Sepharadi', 124–37.

40 See *Med. Soc.* II, 103, 141, V, 488. For the short- and medium-term consequences of the 1200–2 famine, see Lev, 'Saladin's Economic Policies', 343–7.

documents pertaining to Elijah ben Zechariah (born c. 1165, died after 1241), *dayyān* and communal leader in Fusṭāṭ. Aryeh Leo Motzkin describes him as deeply involved with charitable services in his capacity as *dayyān*, as well as on a personal level.[41]

While the existence of the rabbinic court is a straightforward issue, the evidence for the existence of a Karaite court is more complex and difficult to interpreter. A decree published during al-Ḥākim's reign stated that the Karaite community was separate from the rabbinic Jews. Undoubtedly, the decree was published in response to a petition submitted by the Karaites, and the text states that the decree is in line with the policy of justice pursued by the Imām al-Ḥākim bi-Amr Allāh, the servant of God and His friend, and takes into consideration differences in law (*aḥkām*) and in the perception of what is permitted (*ḥalāl*) and forbidden (*ḥarām*) between the two communities. The decree also declared that the Karaites are no longer under the jurisdiction of the rabbinic judge (*qāḍī*). It can be argued that one of the decree's consequences was the need to set up a separate Karaite judicial system. Alternatively, it can be argued that the decree granted independence to the Karaite court, if it existed.[42]

In tenth-century Iraq the Karaites had their own courts, and the existence of Karaite courts under the Fatimids is taken for granted by Judith Olszowy-Schlanger.[43] The evidence stemming from the Karaite marriage documents she has published is, however, more implicit than explicit, since the usual terms *bēth dīn* (court) and judges (*dayyānim*/*shōfeṭīm*) do not appear in these documents.[44] In these documents there are, however, references to the Karaite *nāsīim* (communal leaders) and elders. The title *nāsī* (prince) was bestowed on the descendants of ʿAnan ben David, the supposed founder of Karaism, who claimed descent from King David. A Karaite *nāsī* also had a judicial role and presided over the court, at least occasionally. The standard phrases in the various types of Karaite marriage documents refer to testimonies being

[41] See 'Elijah ben Zechariah', 339–48. See the huge entry on him in the index of Goitein, *Med. Soc.* VI, 33.

[42] Khan, *Arabic Legal and Administrative Documents*, doc. 115; Olszowy-Schlanger, 'Karaite Legal Documents', 262. For a broader context of the decree, see Rustow, *Hersey and the Politics of Community*, 164–9; Erder, 'The Split between the Rabbanite and Karaite Communities', 340–1.

[43] See *Karaite Marriage Documents*, 41, 60, 61.

[44] For a broader discussion of this issue, see Zinger, 'A Karaite–Rabbanite Court Session', 98–100.

given 'before the *nāsī* and before the elders' and, more frequently, 'before the elders'. However, the drafting of a marriage document did not necessarily require the conveyance of the court. On the other hand, the Karaite court played a greater role in divorce cases. Olszowy-Schlanger has pointed out that beginning with the eleventh-century Karaite law envisaged the possibility of granting a woman a bill of divorce by the court in cases where her husband had adamantly refused to do so.[45]

Going beyond the question of the existence of separate Karaite courts, we can observe mounting evidence and academic literature indicating Karaite patronage of rabbinic institutions, including the court. This was also true on the political level, since Karaites were involved in rabbinic politics and Karaite dignitaries facilitated access to Fatimid rulers and viziers while, on a personal level, inter-denominational Karaite–Rabbinite marriages did take place. Karaites made used of the rabbinical courts for drawing up bills of agency and release, and the use of these courts was facilitated by the fact that Rabbinite scribes were versed in writing Karaite legal formularies.[46] Legal co-operation between the two groups at the highest communal level is attested by what Oded Zinger describes as a joint Karaite–Rabbinite court session, which took place on 13 July 1055. Eli ben ʿAmram, a prominent Rabbinite leader in Fusṭāṭ, came to the Karaite *nāsī* to examine an inheritance case which involved a mixed Karaite–Rabbinite marriage. The document also illustrates another factor that could potentially undermine the judicial *dhimmī* autonomy: the possibility that one of the parties might bring the case 'to the court of the Gentiles' is explicitly stated.[47]

Jews and the Muslim Courts

Ignoring for a moment the broader legal framework that allowed the existence of *dhimmī* courts in medieval Islam, the supremacy of the cadi as judicial institution was never questioned. The involvement of a cadi in the

[45] See 'Karaite Legal Documents', 262–6, where she adduces further evidence for the existence and regular working of the Karaite courts.

[46] For a Karaite *kātib* employed by the Fatimid state in some unclear capacity who, in 1073, made use of the rabbinic court in Mahdiyya for drawing a power of attorney, see Harry and Rustow, 'Karaites at the Rabbinical Court', 9–35.

[47] See 'A Karaite–Rabbanite Court Session', 95–7, 102–7, Text B. lines 4–5 (text and trans.).

judicial affairs of non-Muslim subjects goes back to Khayr ibn Nuʿaym's term in office (738–45, d. 754). He served as cadi and storyteller and is described as the foremost jurist of his time, and many reports in both Kindī and Ibn Ḥajar refer to various cases adjudicated by him. What strikes the reader of Kindī's narrative is its implicit tenor that Jews and Copts brought their cases to him. Possibly this was due to the fact that he spoke Coptic and used the language to converse with litigants at his court, but this does not explain why Jews turned to his court. The account must be seen as testimony that the supremacy of Muslim institutions for the administration of justice was evident to *dhimmīs* already during the formative period of Islamic law at a time when the procedures at the cadi's court were still evolving.

Kindī's account is quite informative as to how Khayr ibn Nuʿaym treated non-Muslim litigants at his court. The cadi held court at a mosque for Muslim litigants, but, after the afternoon prayer, he held court for non-Muslims on the steps leading to the edifice. The cadi also used to hold court at a small kiosk (*majlis*) in front of the entrance to his house, overlooking the street. Perhaps there both Muslim and non-Muslim litigants were admitted. While serving as cadi for non-Muslims Khayr ibn Nuʿaym applied the procedural practices of a Muslim court. In line with these practices, he accepted the testimonies of Jews and Copts in cases that involved them, and he enquired about the probity and piety (*ʿadāla*) of the non-Muslim witnesses among their co-religionists.[48] A cadi could not function without establishing the *ʿadāla* of witnesses testifying at his court. Khayr ibn Nuʿaym, for example, in cases that involved injuries among young Muslim boys, accepted the testimony of one specific brother of a boy's mother over that of another of his mother's brothers. These testimonies were accepted only when the *ʿadāla* of the maternal brother was verified. Khayr ibn Nuʿaym applied the conceptual and procedural norms of the Muslim court when adjudicating disputes among non-Muslims. He could do so because of a shared system of values about what honesty and piety (religiosity and scrupulous performance of religious rites) meant. This shared Muslim–*dhimmī* moral outlook made it easier for

[48] Kindī, 351; Tillier, *Histoire des cadis*, 108–9; Ibn Ḥajar, ed. Majīd, I, 228, 231–2; Maqrīzī, *Kitāb al-Muqaffā*, III, 839, 840; El-Shamsy, 'The Logic of Excluding Testimonies in Early Islam', 13.

non-Muslims to bring their disputes to a cadi, whose superior institutional position was taken for granted.

The use of the cadi's court by *dhimmīs* became a reality and the cadi Muḥammad ibn Masrūq (793–800) allowed intra-*dhimmī* litigation to take place at the mosque. Muḥammad ibn Masrūq was, however, an exceptional cadi who feared neither the authorities nor public opinion and he went a step beyond other cadis in his actions.[49]

Geniza documents show that Jews frequently approached the cadi for a variety of reasons and legal needs, such as registration of debts and transfer of real estate. This regular use of Muslim courts is extensively discussed by Menahem Ben-Sasson in the context of the Jewish community of Kairouan. In many cases the Muslim judicial institutions are referred to by the enigmatic term *sulṭān* or its Hebrew equivalents *shilton* (authority) and *malkhūt* (kingdom). Ben-Sasson explains that the trend was driven by the search for enforceability since the Jewish court found it difficult to enforce its decisions as executive powers were in the hands of Muslim authorities (loosely referred to by the Hebrew terms *sulṭān/shilton/malkhūt*).[50] A new aspect of the problem has been illuminated by Zinger's findings that Jewish women frequented the cadi's court and many others threatened to do so. Zinger offers a multi-dimensional discussion of the issue and makes a distinction between upper-class Jewish women who actually brought their cases to the cadi and lower-class women who just threatened to do so. He perceives the appeal to the cadi as an expression of female resentment against male communal dominance.[51]

The terms *sulṭān/shilton/malkhūt* appear in many documents studied by Zinger, and he understands them as meaning a separate, or additional, venue of justice from that of the cadi. Consequently, he translates these terms as 'government justice'.[52] The term *sulṭān* appears in Ibn Ḥawqal's description of the Delta in the meaning of a government official or agency, but not in the context of the administration of justice. Arabic sources contemporary with

[49] Kindī, 390–1; Tillier, *Histoire des cadis*, 156; Dridi, 'Christian and Jewish Communities', 110–13.

[50] See *The Emergence of the Local Jewish Community*, 321–3.

[51] See 'She Aims to Harass Him', 160, 165–6, 170, 179, 182.

[52] See 'She Aims to Harass Him', 168–9.

Geniza documents between 1000 and 1250 contain no allusions to 'governmental justice'. These terms must be understood in a general way as alluding to various Muslim officials who were involved in, or meddled in, Jewish communal life and affairs. One must remember that terms were used both loosely and precisely and that contemporary people well understood each specific meaning which frequently eludes us today. In *c.*1020, for example, a letter was sent from the *shōfet* and the elders of Rafaḥ to the *gaon* about an inheritance case adjudicated by them. They had ruled on who the legal heirs of ʿĀ'isha, the daughter of Joseph ben Sudayk, were, but some of the heirs took the case to the cadi, who confirmed the ruling of the Jewish court. The second round of litigation involved the *shōfet* Solomon, and members of the community went to the cadi who (again) confirmed the ruling of the Jewish court. At this stage things got really complicated and the text leaves us wondering which officials in Rafaḥ were approached. Some of the heirs approached '*al-shilton*' (the precise meaning remains elusive), which, apparently, ordered them to relinquish items and money of the inheritance they kept. The losing side argued against the cadi, who kept the money to which they claimed to be entitled. At this point the letters contains a fascinating phrase, expressing the despair of the Jewish court with the case and, especially, the new claims against the cadi: 'as if the *shilton* is not just [*ʿādil*] and the *qāḍī* righteous [*munṣif*], shall God make better the rewards of our master the *qā'id* [referring to a person holding a military title or rank] and our lord the *qāḍī*. We made for them communal supplicatory prayers in Jerusalem with *shaykh* Sālim ibn Saʿīd and the Torah [in gratitude] for their good deed and their support of justice [*ḥaqq*].' The letter ends by naming the people against whom the Jewish court imposed a ban until they should return the parts of the inheritance they kept to the rightful owners, and declares that other people have to approach the Jewish great court in order to present their claims there. The letter also threatens them with a ban if they did not comply.[53]

The first thing that strikes the reader here is that the cadi and other Muslim officials involved in the case upheld the ruling of the Jewish court and left the implementation to the *shōfet*. The impression given is that the Jewish court was an arm of the Muslim system of administration of justice and the

[53] Gil, *Palestine during the First Muslim Period*, doc. 43, with Hebrew trans.

term *shilton* refers to Muslim officials (the *qā'id*) who were approached by the Jews following the appeal to the cadi. This nuanced interplay between Jewish and Muslim courts, which involved a considerable degree of independence and subordination of Jewish judicial institutions to their Muslim counterparts, also had an additional aspect: the drafting of a document that would be accepted as valid at the cadi's court. Ackerman-Lieberman has drawn attention to the fact that it was a common practice of Muslim scribes to produce documents that would be accepted by cadis of various legal schools, and Rustow has pointed out that in mixed Rabbinite–Karaite communities scribes were able to draw up marriage contracts to the satisfaction of both sides.[54] Preservation of identity and an acute awareness of diversity that had to be functionally bridged were powerful factors within both the Jewish world and Jewish–Muslim relations.

The term *shilton* exemplifies the range of interaction between the Jewish minority and Muslim society and its institutions and, like many other medieval terms, it had a broad range of meanings and was loosely issued. These complexities are illustrated in a letter of 1094 sent from Alexandria which recounts a case of inheritance handled according to the Jewish law. Challenging the ruling of the Jewish court, a cadi (*shōfeṭ*) and a governor (*ʿāmil*) were approached. Following this turn of events, the Jewish court and the elders somehow modified their first ruling taking into consideration the possibility of appeal to the *shilton*, whoever they meant by that.[55] The myriad Muslim officials to whom the term might have been applied is alluded to in a letter of a communal leader in Alexandria of Saladin's time, who writes about two communal cases he had handled. The first case concerned a Jew who had said something highly offensive against the religion or his co-religionists and was beaten on the spot. The writer considered approaching the authorities, but was at loss as to whom the case should be submitted: the *wālī*, the *nā'ib*, the cadi or the *muḥtasib*. He preferred the *muḥtasib*, assuming that the offender would be leniently treated by him. The *muḥtasib*'s messengers, accompanied by *aṣḥāb al-arbāʿ* (the quarter's supervisors) who came to fetch

[54] Ackerman-Lieberman, 'Legal Pluralism', 81, 82, 85; Rustow, *Heresy and the Politics of Community*, ch. 10.

[55] Frenkel, *'The Compassionate and Benevolent'*, doc. 9.

the offender, decided, however, that the he must be brought before the *wālī al-kābir* (the terms *wālī* and *wālī al-kābir* must be considered synonymous), who punished him by a shaming parade through one of the town's quarters. The writer emphasises his agony over the case, stressing that he was personally acquainted neither with the *wālī* nor the *nā'ib*, nor had he seen the *muḥtasib*. His address to the authorities is phrased in general terms: 'the slave kisses the ground'.[56] The term *shilton* is not mentioned in the letter, but the officials mentioned wielded administrative-judicial powers and had authority over Muslim and Jewish subjects alike. It seems that the medieval Hebrew term *shilton*, like the modern one, meant authorities in the wider sense.

Geniza documents reflect both the ease with which Jews, out of self-interest, brought their cases to the cadi and communal efforts to resist the trend which undermined communal identity, its privileges, and the position of its leaders and dignitaries. This tension between the individual and the community is repeatedly illustrated and powerfully illuminated by a document written in Fusṭāṭ on behalf of Efraim ben Shemarya, which makes it clear that he had been forcibly brought for litigation to the cadi court. The document recounts events which took place between 4 and 9 January 1016 and which began when three slaves of ʿAmrūn ben Aliya of Palermo dragged Efraim ben Shemarya to the *shurṭa* because, allegedly, he was unwilling to go to the Jewish court to settle a lawsuit concerning a debt. Efraim ben Shemarya denied the accusation and said to ʿAmrūn: 'Sir, this is a lie, things are not like that. We are Jews, however, and have our judges who will find time to examine our case.'[57] Given the nature of the document, which intended to ward off any suspicion that Efraim ben Shemarya went to the court of the cadi willingly, one can consider the phrase 'We are Jews . . . and have our judges' as merely a literary expression written at the behest of Efraim ben Shemarya. Other documents, however, offer further light on the drive led by communal leaders to bolster the exclusive position of the Jewish court.

A letter sent in 1032 from Ṣahrajt in Lower Egypt to Efraim ben Shemarya, in his capacity as *dayyān* in Fusṭāṭ, tells the story of Saʿīda, who

56 Frenkel, *'The Compassionate and Benevolent'*, doc. 29. For quarter supervisors, see Goitein, *Med. Soc.* II, 369–70.

57 Ben-Sasson, *The Jews of Sicily*, doc. 2.

brought her divorce case to the cadi against the wish of her husband. The cadi granted her a divorce and ordered the husband to pay alimony, and he did so for three months. Those who wrote the letter characterise her as one who 'refused to adhere to the laws of Israel'. They also describe how they dealt with her by publicly exposing her shameful behaviour, as 'is fit for an evil daughter which can be brought back to probity only by prohibition'. They also claimed that their conduct brought peace to the community. The second document pertinent to this case is a court record written in Fusṭāṭ, which tells a complicated story that bears little resemblance to the letter written from Ṣahrajt to Efraim. The document tells Saʿīda's version of the events and relates her claim that it was her husband who brought the case to the cadi, while she describes herself as unjustly treated (*maẓlūma*). An eye witness testified that the couple willingly brought their divorce case to the cadi, and the Jewish court in Fusṭāṭ declared any dealings with the case suspended until the facts were clearly established.[58]

The superior position of the cadi and *dhimmīs*' access to his court are only one aspect of the so-called '*dhimmī* judicial autonomy; the other aspect is the subjection of non-Muslims to Islamic law in certain cases. Although it is uncorroborated by other authorities, Ibn Taghrī Birdī (1409–70) writes that Ḥafṣ ibn al-Walīd, the governor of Egypt (741–7), ordered that *dhimmī* inheritance cases be handled according to Islamic law.[59] The logic behind the decree was that in certain cases Jewish and Muslim inheritance laws differed. For example, according to Jewish law a daughter inherits the whole estate of her father while in Muslim law she inherits only half. In the absence of other heirs the undivided half can be claimed by the authorities, providing an incentive to apply Muslim law in such cases. Ibn Taghrī Birdī's statement must not be taken too literally; the subjection of non-Muslims to the Muslim law of inheritance was neither comprehensive nor systematic, but the problem was perennial and state officials were rapacious. In a letter written in 1135 from Fusṭāṭ to Alexandria the sender (Maḥrūz) warns Abū Zikrī Kohen that his business partner is dying and that the officials of the *dīwān al-mawārīth*

[58] Bareket, *The Jews of Egypt*, doc. 67. For a partial English translation of these documents, see Zinger, 'She Aims to Harass Him', 177. Briefly referred to by Krakowski, *Coming of Age in Medieval Egypt*, 78, n. 28.

[59] See I, 374–5.

are about to seize his inheritance at a warehouse in Alexandria. Maḥrūz warns Abū Zikrī Kohen to move all his belongings from the warehouse, fearing that the officials might seize the properties of other people too. Apparently, the dying man had no heirs of the first degree, and the state officials gathered information and made preparations to seize the inheritance.[60]

Another aspect of the so-called '*dhimmī* judicial autonomy' concerns the role of Jewish law in the economic life of Jews, especially in their partnership agreements. This issue is at the heart of Cohen's recent publications devoted to the adoption of Islamic commercial law and judicial procedures by the *geonim* and Maimonides (1138–1204) in order to meet the demands of the mercantile economy of the high Middle Ages (eleventh–thirteenth centuries). The flexibility of the Jewish sages was also instrumental in bolstering Jewish judicial autonomy and limiting the use of Muslim courts by Jews in cases of commercial disputes.[61] The Jews' recourse to Islamic and Jewish law touches upon the central theme of the book: to what extent law governed the lives of people at individual and communal levels. The issue is also highlighted through Krakowski's discussion of child marriage, which is permitted in both Jewish and Islamic law. In medieval Jewish society in Egypt, however, an aversion to child marriages developed, which explains '[t]he low proportion of child marriages documented in the Geniza'.[62] The unavoidable conclusion is that individuals and societies lived comfortably with only partial congruence between law and social norms and practices, without undermining their identities.

60 Goitein and Friedman, *India Traders*, 487–8.

61 The most comprehensive discussion of these topics is offered in Cohen's *Maimonides and the Merchants*. For earlier publications see Cohen, 'A Partnership Gone Bad', 218–63, which deals with the incorporation of agency relations (*ṣuḥba*) into contractual law; 'The "Custom of the Merchants" in Geonic Jurisprudence', 86–111, which discusses the permissibility of *suftaja* (an order of payment) in the Jewish *halakha*; 'Defending Jewish Judicial Autonomy', 13–33, for the concept of *ḥukm al-tujjār* (law of the merchants) in gaonic responsa and Maimonides' writings. Philip I. Ackerman-Lieberman has argued, however, that Jewish law played an important role in the economic activities of Jews, especially in their partnership agreements. See 'Commercial Forms and Legal Norms', 1,010, 1,011, 1,023, 1,047; 'Contractual Partnership in the Geniza', 652, 665, 669.

62 See *Coming of Age in Medieval Egypt*, ch. 3, esp. 128. For the duality between law and social norms and the meaning of Jewish identity in Muslim environment, see 19–24.

The Copts: Complex Realities and the Limits of Evidence

The information available for the judicial history of the Jewish communities in medieval Egypt greatly exceeds anything available for the Copts. Before the subject matter of this section is addressed, two background topics are discussed: the legal situation in late Byzantine and early Muslim Egypt is set out, and a brief allusion made to the debate about the emergence of Coptic identity during the first centuries of Muslim rule.

The administration of justice in Byzantine Egypt was complex and involved both civilian and military office holders. During the rule of Justinian (527–65), Egypt was divided into seven provinces and each governor held court. There is considerable scholarly agreement that imperial law (i.e. the codex of Justinian, first proclaimed in 529 and revised in 534) was known and applied in Egypt.[63] On the local level, civil cases up to the value of 300 *solidi* were referred to the *defensores civitatis* (defenders of the municipality) while military commanders were entrusted with judicial authority and were also approached by civilians. Extra-judicial settlement of civil disputes through various forms of mediation or arbitration was also practised and ecclesiastical adjudication of civil litigation was common. However, in the words of Bernhard Palme:

> from the last one hundred years of Roman rule in Egypt there is not a single piece of direct documentary evidence for the work of gubernatorial courts. Despite the well-known methodic principle that 'absence of evidence is not evidence of absence', this has been interpreted as being indicative of the end of gubernatorial, i.e. state jurisdiction.[64]

The attempt to explain the gap in the evidence is at the heart of Palme's article, and he alludes to a problem discussed in the Introduction to this volume: the uneven geographical distribution of the papyrological findings and the accidental nature of this type of source material. He also, however, offers a closer look at the evolution of contracts and petitions as legal tools

[63] Palme, 'Law and Courts in Late Antique Egypt', 58–9; Keenan, 'Law in the Byzantine Period', 25–6.

[64] See 'Law and Courts in Late Antique Egypt', 68.

with which to approach state officials and their ability to provide justice in criminal, civil and administrative cases, and points out that the evidence should not be interpreted as indicating a collapse of the state jurisdiction.[65]

The question of how the administration of justice was conducted becomes even more complicated when the issue of Coptic law is discussed. Mikhail, for example, has pointed out that the Copts 'lacked any officially sanctioned law code'.[66] Tonio Sebastian Richter has drawn attention to the usefulness of the concept put forward in the late 1930s of 'the law of Coptic documents' as an alternative paradigm to the concept of Coptic law. He also points out that only after the Arab conquest were private legal documents drawn up in Coptic.[67] Another way to approach the issue is through the perspective of scribal practice alluded to earlier, which was influential in shaping real-life practice in the legal arena. Esther Garel and Maria Nowak, for example, have pointed out that the schema of late Roman wills was modified in wills written in Coptic (fourth to seventh centuries). These changes were introduced through local scribal practice and the Arab conquest had no impact on the way these documents were written.[68]

Richter's allusion to developments taking place during the early Muslim period must be seen within a broader context of the evolving identity of the Coptic Church and of the Copts as a people, and of how both processes are relate to the administration of justice. Addressing the socio-religious and linguistic realities of the seventh to eighth centuries, Jacques van der Vliet has written:

> To put it strongly, in the seventh century there were *no* Copts. There were Egyptians, long Christianised, who used two distinct written codes, Greek and Coptic. These same Egyptians were deeply divided ecclesiastically. The official 'Chalcedonian' church had to compete with strong 'anti-Chalcedonian' opposition that was itself much divided.[69]

[65] See 'Law and Courts in Late Antique Egypt', 72, 73–6. For a broad overview of administrative, military and judicial institutions in Byzantine Egypt, see Palme, 'The Imperial Presence', 271–88.

[66] See *From Byzantine to Islamic Egypt*, 150, 151.

[67] See 'The Law of Coptic Legal Documents', 29–30.

[68] See 'Garel and Nowak, 'Monastic Wills', 108–28, esp. 115, 118–20.

[69] See 'Coptic Documentary Papyri', 193.

This statement summarises and amplifies the extensive literature dealing with the crystallisation of Coptic identity during the first three centuries of Muslim rule, and the same can be said about the formation of the Coptic Church. How the anti-Chalcedonian Monophysite Church had evolved and how it became the Coptic Church has been discussed by Arietta Papaconstantinou, who summarises the process as follows:

> The Egyptians, speakers of the Coptic language, thus turned into the Copts, the indigenous population of the Valley and members of the Coptic, that is to say anti-Chalcedonian, Church. Thus, the terms defining the group acquired a meaning that was simultaneously religious and ethnic.[70]

The formation of new identities among the indigenous population was also accompanied by slow and patchy Islamisation. Any attempt to correlate these profound changes that took place among the Coptic population and the system of administration of justice is marred by many difficulties since most of the information about judicial institutions outside Fusṭāṭ is derived from the documentary sources. Reliance on papyri has its problems, and Upper Egypt is better known than the Delta. Bruning, for example, has noted the introduction of the Arab legal system in Upper Egypt during the seventh century. He also has pointed out that there were no visible changes in the way justice was administered in seventh-century Edfū, which involved the *pagarch*, the *dux* and arbitration by local rural chiefs and clergymen.[71]

A direct link is discernible between Palmer's discussion and Tillier's re-examination of Qurra ibn Sharīk's judicial letters. The first thing that strikes the readers is that Christian inhabitants of Ishqūh/Aphrodito had direct access to the governor of Egypt and brought their cases to his attention. Qurra ibn Sharīk sent his instructions to Basilios, the *pagarch* of Ishqūh/Aphrodito, how he should handle the cases. If we assume that those judicial letters were typical of Qurra ibn Sharīk's overall correspondence, than much of his time was taken by judicial matters. His devotion to judicial matters stemmed from his declared commitment to justice and remonstrations against oppression.[72]

[70] See 'Historiography, Hagiography', 72.
[71] See *The Rise of a Capital*, 135.
[72] Tillier, 'Dispensing Justice in a Minority Context', 133–57.

Other Muslim officials known through the papyri were also involved in judicial matters. One letter in the corps of 39 documents pertaining to Najīd ibn Muslim, a mid-eighth century administrators, has judicial content. The letter is addressed to Najīd ibn Muslim's subordinate administrator ʿAbd Allāh ibn Asʿad and instructs him to restore the rights of a petitioner which had been violated by others. These documents lack geographical context, but higher-ranking administrators must have been regularly approached by plaintiffs who sought justice.[73]

Although any discussion of how justice was administered in Coptic villages and provincial towns to their homogeneous Coptic and mixed Coptic–Muslim populations is limited by insufficient evidence, documentary sources indicate the dominance of Islamic law by the second half of the tenth century. How the process had evolved remains unknown, but its end result is well-attested. Two sale contracts of residential properties from the village of Ṭuṭūn in the Fayyūm, dated 962 and 963, have been discussed in detail by Frantz-Murphy. These documents are in Arabic but originated in a Coptic milieu and include the phrase that the transactions are according to Islamic stipulations of sale (*sharṭ bayʿ al-Islām*) and its contracts (*ʿahd*). Both documents also state that the text was read in Arabic and explained to the sellers in a foreign language (*ʿajamiyya*, i.e. Coptic), while the witnesses bore Arabic and Coptic names.[74] Frantz-Murphy has concluded that already during the two first decades of the eighth century the wording of the Coptic contracts of sale had changed to fit the Arabic formulary model, and the change is related to Kindī's report that, at that time, Coptic village heads were replaced by Muslims.[75] The origins of Arabic formularies are traced by Frantz-Murphy to Middle Eastern Semitic and south Arabic legal traditions.[76]

The phrase stating that a sale of a residential property was done according

[73] Sijpesteijn, *Shaping a Muslim State*, doc. 21.

[74] See 'A Comparison of the Arabic and Earlier Egyptian Contract Formularies, Part I', 209, ll. 12, 15; 216, ll. 11, 13–14 (text and trans.).

[75] See 'A Comparison of the Arabic and Earlier Egyptian Contract Formularies, Part II', 100, 101, including references to earlier literature. Frantz-Murphy's findings are summarised in her 'Settlement of Property Disputes in Provincial Egypt', 95–105, esp. 98–9, concerning phrases in documents emanating from the Coptic milieu which demonstrate adoption of Muslim preferences for oral testimonies.

[76] See 'A Comparison of the Arabic and Earlier Egyptian Contract Formularies, Part III–V', 105, 112; 269, 279; 99, 102, 107, respectively.

to Islamic law also appears in other tenth-century documents from the village of Buljusūq in the Fayyūm which emanated from a Coptic milieu. Three such documents, dated 1037, 1043 and 1058, are written in Arabic by one of the witnesses, while other witnesses bear Arabic/Islamic names. The sellers and the buyers were Copts who, apparently, understood Arabic well enough and needed no translation. The phrase stating that the sale was carried out according to Islamic law is also mentioned in two documents from the town of Ashmūnayn (1067).[77]

It can be argued, however, that the notion of the dominance of Islamic law among Copts engaged in buying and selling properties is overstated and not supported throughout the papyrological record. The archive of the Bifām family of the Damūya al-Lahūn village in the Fayyūm, for example, includes twenty-seven documents of sale of properties and land spanning the years 992–1030. The Copts involved in these transactions needed no translation of the Arabic text, and many of the documents were written by Muḥammad ibn Aḥmad, preacher at the local mosque. The witnesses bore Arabic/Islamic names and in many documents the name appears of Ḥusayn, muezzin at the local mosque. No statement assuring conformity with Islamic law appears in these documents. The reason for this might have been that Muḥammad ibn Aḥmad's involvement with jurisdiction (*ḥukm*) in al-Lahūn, on behalf of the cadi Abū l-Ḥusayn Rustam ibn Aḥmad ibn Rustam, rendered the phrase spurious.[78]

Intriguing though the identification of the local preacher with judicial matters is, it provides no clue as to how justice was administrated in this village or the Fayyūm in general. The exact religious make-up of the population of the Fayyūm, village by village, is unknown, and, it can be argued, we are at the limit of what the sources have to offer. In sharp contrast to the abundant information on the administration of justice in Fusṭāṭ, the urban and rural world outside the capital is poorly attested and the deadlock remains insurmountable.

[77] Grohmann, *Arabic Papyri*, I, doc. 62, ll. 9, 17; doc. 63, ll. 1, 9–10, 11; doc. 67, ll. 1–2, 13–14, 21–2; doc. 70, ll. 22–3; doc. 71, ll. 29, 39 (text and trans.). See also doc. 72, from 1068, of unknown provenance, ll. 12–13, 16 (text and trans.).

[78] Gaubert and Mouton, *Hommes et villages du Fayyoum*, doc. 23, lines 1–2 (text and trans.). For the legal aspects of sale documents and the role of the witnesses, see 28–30, 32–3.

Conclusions

Goitein's statement 'Nothing is so characteristic of the position of the non-Muslim minorities under classical Islam as their judicial organization' has the rare quality of being fundamental and overstated, if not somewhat misleading. The supremacy of the cadi was a fact of life, and cadi's justice was one of the options available. If the phrase 'legal shopping' has any meaning, it reflects the range of choices that Jewish men and women had at certain junctures of their lives when they had to decide to whom to turn: the *dayyān*, or the cadi. Furthermore, the scope of so-called 'dhimmī judicial autonomy' was limited since there were no *dhimmī* equivalents to Muslim institutions such as the *shurṭa* and *ḥisba*. In practical terms this meant that in criminal cases, and when trading on the market, or even frequenting it, *dhimmīs* found themselves under the jurisdiction of Muslim officials, rendering Jewish legal precepts irrelevant.[79] In a paraphrase of Goitein's statement, I would say that nothing is so characteristic of the position of the non-Muslim minorities in medieval Islam as their desire to preserve their separate religious identity. This drive is powerfully illustrated by the differences in how justice was administrated at the cadi's court and by the *dayyānim*. The tiny Jewish minority in Fusṭāṭ-Cairo, and elsewhere in the medieval Muslim world, managed its communal affairs related to pious endowments and orphans strikingly differently from the Muslim majority. These differences bring us back to the question of communal autonomy, which in its core meaning involved the attempt to preserve religious identity and distinctive culture in terms of how things are done and institutions run. Judicial institutions were vital and instrumental for preserving identity. On the other hand, notwithstanding Ackerman-Lieberman's revision as to what extent Jewish law was applied in contractual partnership agreements, the law and scribal practice must have been flexible enough to facilitate economic integration with the life of the majority.

[79] As is clearly borne out by Tillier and Vanthieghem's study ('Un registre carcéral'), Muslim, Christian and Jewish debtors were treated in the same way by the penitentiary system.

8

The Administration of Justice in a Broader Perspective

A View from Ottoman Cairo

The medieval Islamic system of the administration of justice had emerged and taken root during the seventh to ninth centuries, before and in parallel with the formation of Islamic law. Its basic structure persisted into the Ottoman period, and we can truly speak about *longue durée* trends. The scholarship of James E. Baldwin and his publications on the judicial institutions in Ottoman Cairo provide the natural comparative framework. Baldwin describes the judicial institutions in Ottoman Cairo as consisting of the cadi's *sharʿī* court, the governor's tribunal (*dīwān al-ʿalī*), and military officers who were involved in policing and regulating the markets, while some notables dispensed justice among their clients. The imperial council in Istanbul (*dīvān-i hümāyūn*) presided over by the Grand Vizier was also approached by litigants from Egypt and accepted petitions from all Ottoman territories. In addition, in Ottoman Cairo there were also Jewish and Christian courts, but the supremacy of the cadi and his court were taken for granted.[1]

The way justice was administrated in Ottoman Cairo is largely a continuation of medieval realties. The system was made up of several bodies, or agencies, and the question can be asked, to what extent did the governor's tribunal, officers and notables dispense *sharʿī* justice? Untypical of the medieval administration of justice, the system described by Baldwin was marked by the involvement of powerful individuals, or the privatisation of justice. This

[1] See *Islamic Law and Empire*, ch. 1.

seems to be a legacy of the Mamlūk period rather than a reflection of seventh- to twelfth-century realities. The history of the administration of justice during the Ayyubid and Mamlūk periods is yet to be written, and emphasising *longue durée* trends does not mean that systems were static. Nonetheless, the appointment of Ibn Khallikān as supreme cadi in Syria in 1261 (see Chapter 3) is significant and should be re-examined. As mentioned earlier, he was entrusted with responsibility for the management and maintenance of pious endowments and was appointed teacher of law in several law colleges. When approached from the *longue durée* perspective, two aspects of the nomination stand out. In 801, the Mālikī cadi al-Umarī rejected the notion, allegedly supported by Mālik ibn Anas, that maintenance of *waqf*'s properties is not necessarily the obligation of the *waqf*'s supervisor (see Chapter 1). Long before 1261 the issue had been settled: maintenance of *waqf*'s properties was one of the duties of the *waqf* supervisor. He was also given authority to exchange unprofitable properties for better ones, a legal-economic mechanism known as *istibdal*. Another aspect of the 1261 appointment touches upon lingering Fatimid legacy. In Fatimid times, the supreme cadi was also perceived as an authority on doctrine (*daʿwa*) and law. The Sunnī version of the concept closely followed the Fatimid precedent: the supreme cadi was both judicial authority and officially appointed professor of law.

The gap in the literature pertaining to the Ayyubid–Mamlūk period prevents more meaningful discussion of the evolution of the administration of justice from the medieval to the Ottoman period, and the following sections revert to discussion of the medieval system and its characteristics.

The Medieval Cadi Institution

The loss of the original historiography of the Fatimid period hampers any attempt to give a comprehensive picture of the medieval cadi institution and *sharʿī* justice. Authors such as Ibn Zūlāq, Musabbiḥī, Quḍāʿī and al-Muḥannak wrote histories of Egypt from the Muslim conquest to their own times.[2] Musabbiḥī's *History of Egypt*, for example, contained 13,000 folios

[2] Sayyid, 'Lumières nouvelles', 1–41. For the loss of works of the *Khiṭaṭ* type, see Sayyid, 'L'évolution de la composition', 77–93. For short quotations from al-Muḥannak, see Ibn Ẓāfir, ed. Ferré, 89, 92. For reports derived from Musabbiḥī's *History of Egypt*, spanning the years 885–959, see Sayyid, 'Nuṣūṣ Ḍā'iʿh', 7–11.

and was divided into 40 parts. Yāqūt (1179–1229) praised it and used it, but only fragments of the original have survived, and how rich the work was is mirrored in Chapters 3, 4 and 5.[3] Nonetheless, the survival of a number of ninth- to tenth-century texts offers information about and insights into the evolution of the cadi institution during the eighth century, which was characterised by two contradictory trends. On the one hand, the post of cadi acquired a separate judicial identity and the augmentation of other functions for the post ceased. On the other hand, cadis extended the sphere of their authority to also include various fiscal supervisory and administrative roles. These developments took place between 705 and 810 and involved the extension of the cadi's authority over the monies of orphans, control of funds belonging to absent people and legacies with no legal heirs, and supervision and management of *waqfs*.

From the beginning the cadi was a key state official, but, in a process largely hidden from our eyes, the post became imbued with respectability and moral authority. State tutelage, and the fact that cadis were paid state officials, did not affect their ability to shape proceedings at their courts. During the eighth century cadis gained the authority to choose their clerks, controlled the appointment and dismissal of witnesses, recorded their judicial decisions and maintained an archive.

State tutelage was one thing and the integration of cadis into the rulers' orbit another. As is exemplified by the personalities and conduct of cadis such as Ibrāhīm ibn Isḥāq, al-Ḥārith ibn Miskīn and Bakkār ibn Qutayba, state tutelage left a wide margin for personal and institutional conduct. These were atypical, fiercely independent cadis. Al-Dhuhlī's career illustrates the full meaning of state tutelage: a cadi could keep his professional integrity but also had to be flexible and politically savvy to secure appointments from Abbasid caliphs or rulers like Kāfūr. Al-Dhuhlī was also the first in a long line of Sunnī jurists who made the amendments necessary to flourish under the Fatimids.

Integration into the rulers' orbit, as in the case of the cadi Ibn Ḥarb's close association with the Tulunid rulers, meant total identification with the regime and its fortunes. This was the case with the cadis of the Nuʿmān family. On the one hand, this was a special case of a veteran Ismāʿīlī family

[3] See *Muʿjam al-Udabāʾ*, VI, 2,567–8.

closely associated with the Fatimid rulers on both personal and state levels. On the other hand, the Fatimids had a clear vision of the cadi institution and, especially, of the position of the supreme cadi. The cadi was not only the state's judicial functionary; he was part of the state's administrative machinery and, as exemplified by the case of the twelfth-century supreme cadi Abū l-Ḥajjāj Yūsuf ibn Ayyūb al-Maghribī al-Andalusī, this perception was enduring in spite of changes in personal and political circumstances. The employment of cadis as supervisors of the movement of tax money from one depository to another in the Fayyūm must be seen in this context. Cadis in the Fatimid period wielded judicial, supervisory and executive powers. Their executive powers are alluded to in the petitions submitted to them asking them 'to do something' or to order others to take certain actions. The discussion so far has emphasised the powers the cadis wielded, but they were not the highest-ranking state officials. The cadi's exact position within the state's administrative hierarchy remains unknown, but certainly cadis, including the supreme cadi, were subordinate to the vizier. This is reflected by petitions circumventing cadis or requesting higher-ranking state officials to order them 'to do something'. This issue notwithstanding, from the *longue durée* perspective the Fatimid vision of the cadi's function is a Fatimid legacy in the judicial-administrative sphere.

Law and Society

Important though the institutional character of the post of cadi might be, this book has attempted to investigate to what extent Muslim law was applied in medieval Islamic states and whether its precepts governed the lives of people and the conduct of society. If indeed, as argued by Schacht, 'Islamic law is the epitome of Islamic spirit', then the law was the cadi's remit and entailed, first and foremost, personal and contractual law. It can be argued that the cadi also embodied the application of the Koranic ethics through his care for orphans and supervision/management of *waqfs*, which came to signify the Koranic notion of charity. The cadi institution played a crucial role in the lives of Muslims and shaped their identity, but it had its limitations too.

In contrast to the *ḥisba* and *shurṭa*, the cadi's role was reactive: he responded to cases brought to his court. The cadi's court consisted of a single judge with no clearly structured appellate hierarchy above him. In the absence of formal arrangements as to how to challenge a cadi's decisions, people approached the *maẓālim* institution with requests for rescripts ordering a cadi 'to do something'. In other cases people submitted requests to the *maẓālim* court as first choice in their 'legal shopping'. In a case discussed in Chapter 6, the *maẓālim* court headed by the vizier reverted the case back to the cadi and empowered (or instructed) him to establish the facts and to deal with the case according to the law and public interest (*maṣlaḥa*). How typical circumvention of the cadi through direct appeal to the *maẓālim* was remains unknown. One must assume that some dialogue between the two institutions did take place, but the *maẓālim* court was not a judicial institution in the strict sense of the term. It was an institution instrumental in defusing tension between the state and subjects, aimed at winning subjects' gratitude by granting their requests and providing redress for abuses by state officials.

While the *maẓālim* court was an administrative institution with judicial functions but without clear legal underpinnings, *ḥisba* law was not a jurist's law. *Ḥisba* manuals represent the Islamisation of various local market laws upon which the Koranic ethics of commanding right and forbidding wrong was grafted. In the Fatimid period market supervisors came from the second tier of the ruling circles and their actions were driven by practical considerations even when their policies of price regulation had deeper theological meaning.

The *shurṭa* is an enigmatic institution, but in evolutionary terms, like the *ḥisba* it represents the phase when the administration of justice preceded the development of Islamic law. The *shurṭa* dealt with crime, but how exactly criminal justice was dispensed remains vague and attempts to involve jurists in the way the chief of the police carried out his duties were short-lived.

In conclusion, one might say that the medieval system of the administration of justice was an Islamic system governed by Islamic law developed by jurists and Islamised customary law, with a grey area of criminal law. As an abstraction, Schacht's statement 'Islamic law is the epitome of Islamic spirit' can be accepted, but law was only one component of what defined an individual and society as Muslim. Consequently, I would argue for a more limited role of law in what defined individual and collective identities in medieval Middle Eastern societies and support my claim by examining the position of the Jews in medieval Islam.

In line with Schacht's statement, one can argue that Jewish law (*halakha*) is the epitome of Jewish spirit. *Halakha*, nevertheless, played a narrow role in the life of Jews in the medieval Muslim world. Jews turned to the cadi court even in cases of personal law and were subjected to the jurisdiction of the market supervisor and chief of police in other matters. Jews used the *maẓālim* institution since it was an administrative agency of the state, and took advantage of its amorphous legal role when having difficulties with state officials, including the cadi, the market supervisor or the chief of police. Although Jews did not and could not live their lives fully according to the *halakha*, this did not undermine their Jewish identity since adherence to law was only one element in their personal and collective identity.

Bibliography

Abbreviations

AI	*Annales islamologiques*
BEO	*Bulletin d'études orientales*
BSOAS	*Bulletin of the School of Oriental and African Studies*
E.I. 2	*Encyclopedia of Islam*, 2nd edn
Goitein, *Med. Soc.*	Goitein, S. D., *A Mediterranean Society. The Jewish Communities of the Arab World as Portrayed in the Documents of the Cairo Geniza* (Berkeley and Los Angeles, 1967–93), 6 vols
IEJ	*Israel Exploration Journal*
ILS	*Islamic Law and Society*
IOS	*Israel Oriental Studies*
JAOS	*Journal of the American Oriental Society*
JESHO	*Journal of the Economic and Social History of the Orient*
JJP	*Journal of Juristic Papyrology*
JNES	*Journal of Near Eastern Studies*
JQR	*Jewish Quarterly Review*
JRAS	*Journal of the Royal Asiatic Society*
JSAI	*Jerusalem Studies in Arabic and Islam*
JSS	*Journal of Semitic Studies*
Maqrīzī	*Khiṭaṭ Al-Mawāʿiẓ wa-l-Iʿtibār fī Dhikr al-Khiṭaṭ wa-l-Athār*, ed. Ayman Fu'ād Sayyid (London, 2002–5), 5 vols
ME	*Medieval Encounters*
SI	*Studia Islamica*

Documentary Sources

Balogh, E. and Kahle, P. E., 'Two Coptic Documents Relating to Marriage', *Aegyptus*, 33 (1953), 331–41.

Bareket, Elinoar, *The Jews of Egypt 1007–1055. Based on Documents from the 'Archive' of Efraim ben Shemarya* (Jerusalem, 1995) [in Hebrew].

Bareket, Elinoar, 'The Affair of Abraham b. Samuel ha-Sepharadi', in *Mas'at Moshe. Studies in Jewish and Islamic Culture Presented to Moshe Gil*, ed. Ezra Fleischer and others (Tel Aviv, 1998), 124–37 [in Hebrew].

Bareket, Elinoar, 'Books of Records of the Jerusalemite Court from the Cairo Geniza in the First Half of the Eleventh Century', *Hebrew Union College Annual*, 69 (1998), 1–65 [in Hebrew].

Bell, H. I., 'Translation of the Greek Aphrodito Papyri in the British Museum', *Der Islam*, 2 (1911), 269–83.

Ben-Sasson, Menahem, *The Jews of Sicily 825–1068. Documents and Sources* (Jerusalem, 1991) [in Hebrew].

Bruning, Jelle, 'Developments in Egypt's Early Islamic Postal System (with an Edition of P. Khalili II 5)', *BSOAS*, 81 (2018), 25–40.

Frantz-Murphy, Gladys, 'A Comparison of the Arabic and Earlier Egyptian Contract Formularies', Parts I–V, *JNES*, 40 (1981), 203–25, 355–6; 44 (1985), 99–114; 47 (1988), 105–112, 269–80; 48 (1989), 97–107.

Frenkel, Miriam, *'The Compassionate and Benevolent'. The Leading Elite in the Jewish Community of Alexandria in the Middle Ages* (Jerusalem, 2006) [in Hebrew].

Gaubert, Christian and Mouton, Jean-Michel, *Hommes et villages du Fayyoum dans la documentation papyrologique arabe (Xe–XIe siècles)* (Geneva, 2014).

Gil, Moshe, *Documents of the Jewish Pious Foundations from the Cairo Geniza* (Leiden, 1976).

Gil, Moshe, *Palestine during the First Muslim Period (634–1099). Cairo Geniza Documents* (Tel Aviv, 1983), 3 vols.

Goitein, S. D., *Palestinian Jewry in Early Islamic and Crusader Times. In the Light of the Geniza Documents* (Jerusalem, 1980) [in Hebrew].

Goitein, S. D., 'Congregation versus Community. An Unknown Chapter in the Communal History of Jewish Palestine', *JQR*, XLIV (1953–4), 291–304.

Golb, Norman, 'A Judaeo-Arabic Court Document of Syracuse, A. D. 1020', *JNES*, 32 (1973), 105–23.

Grohmann, Adolf, *Arabic Papyri in the Egyptian Library* (Cairo, 1934–62), 6 vols.

Guest, Rhuvon, 'An Arabic Papyrus of the 8th Century', *JAOS*, 43 (1923), 247–8.

Hary, Benjamin and Rustow, Marina, 'Karaites at the Rabbinical Court: A Legal Deed from Mahdiyya Dated 1073 (T-S 20.187)', *Ginzei Qedem*, 2 (2006), 9–35.

Hoyland, Robert G. (with an Appendix by Hannah Cotton), 'The Earliest Attestation of the Dhimma of God and His Messenger and the Rediscovery of P. Nessana 77 (60s AH/680s)', in *Islamic Cultures, Islamic Contexts. Essays in Honor of Professor Patricia Crone*, ed. Behnan Sadeghi and others (Leiden, 2015), 51–72.

Khan, Geoffrey, *Arabic Legal and Administrative Documents in the Cambridge Genizah Collections* (Cambridge, 1993).

Khan, Geoffrey, *Bills, Letters and Deeds. Arabic Papyri of the 7th to 11th Centuries* (Oxford, 1993).

Khan, Geoffrey, 'A Petition to the Fatimid Caliph al-Āmir', *JRAS* (1990), 44–54.

Khan, Geoffrey, 'An Early Arabic Legal Papyrus', in *Semitic Papyrology in Context*, ed. Lawrence H. Schiffman (Leiden, 2003), 227–37.

Khan, Geoffrey, 'A Petition to the Fatimid Caliph al-Āmir from the Cairo Genizah concerning an Inheritance', in *Orientalistische Studien zu Sprache und Literature. Festgabe zum 65. Geburtstag von Werner Diem*, ed. Ulrich Marzolph (Wiesbaden, 2011), 175–86.

Khoury, Raif Georges, *Chrestomathie de papyrologie arabe. Documents relatifs à la vie privée, sociale et administrative dans les premiers siècles islamiques* (Leiden, 1993).

Khoury, Raif Georges, *Papyrologische Studien: Zum privaten und gesellschaftlichen Leben in den ersten islamischen Jarhunderten* (Wiesbaden, 1995).

Marmer, David, 'Patrilocal Residence and Jewish Court Documents in Medieval Cairo', in *Judaism and Islam Boundaries, Communication and Interactions*, ed. Benjamin H. Hary and others (Leiden, 2000), 67–83.

Mouton, Jean-Michel, Sourdel, Dominique and Sourdel-Thomine, Janine, *Mariage et séparation à Damas au Moyen Âge. Un corpus de 62 documents juridiques inédits entre 337/948 et 698/1229* (Paris, 2013).

Mouton, Jean-Michel, Sourdel, Dominique and Sourdel-Thomine, Janine, *Gouvernance et libéralités de Saladin d'après les données inédites de six documents arabes* (Paris, 2015).

Al-Mudarris, Abdulbary, *Papyrologische Untersuchungen zur arabischen Diplomatik anhand von Eheurkunden aus den ersten islamischen Jarhunderten* (Wiesbaden, 2009).

Olszowy-Schlanger, Judith, *Karaite Marriage Documents from the Cairo Geniza* (Leiden, 1998).

Rāġib, Yūsuf, *Marchands d'étoffes du Fayyoum au IIIe/IXe siècle. D'après leurs archives (actes et lettres)*, vol. 1. *Les actes des Banū ʿAbd al-Muʾmin* (Cairo, 1982).

Rāġib, Yūsuf, 'Une ère inconnue d'Égypte musulmane: l'ère de la juridiction des croyants', *AI*, 41 (2007), 187–207.

Rāġib, Yūsuf, 'Un papyrus arabe de l'an 22 de l'hégire', in *Histoire, archéologies, littératures du monde musulman. Mélanges en l'honneur d'André Raymond*, ed. Ghislaine Alleaume and others (Cairo, 2009), 363–70.

Richards, Donald S., 'A Fatimid Petition and "Small Decree" from Sinai', *IOS*, III (1973), 140–58.

Rustow, Marina, 'A Petition to a Woman at the Fatimid Court (413–414 A.H./ 1022–23 C.E.)', *BSOAS*, 73 (2010), 1–27.

Sijpesteijn, Petra M., *Shaping a Muslim State. The World of a Mid-Eighth Century Egyptian Official* (Oxford, 2013).

Sijpesteijn, Petra M., 'Profit Following Responsibility. A Leaf from the Records of a Third/Ninth Century Tax-Collecting Agent', *JJP*, XXXI (2001), 91–132.

Sijpesteijn, Petra M., 'Army Economics: An Early Papyrus Letter Related to ʿAṭāʾ Payments', in *Histories of the Middle East, Studies in Middle Eastern Society, Economy and Law in Honor of A. L. Udovitch*, ed. Roxani Eleni Margariti and others (Leiden, 2011), 245–67.

Sijpesteijn, Petra M., 'An Early Umayyad Papyrus Invitation for the Ḥajj', *IJNES*, 73 (2014), 179–90.

Sijpesteijn, Petra M., 'Making the Private Public: A Delivery of Palestinian Oil in Third/Ninth-Century Egypt', *Studia Orientalia Electronica*, 2 (2014), 74–91.

Sijpesteijn, Petra M., 'A Ḥadīth Fragment on Papyrus', *Der Islam*, 92 (2015), 321–31.

Sijpesteijn, Petra M., 'Delegation of Judicial Power in Abbasid Egypt', in *Legal Documents as Sources for the History of Muslim Societies, Studies in Honour of Rudolph Peters*, ed. Maaike van Berkel and others (Leiden, 2017), 61–84.

Smith, G. Rex and al-Moraekhi, Moshalleh, 'The Arabic Papyri of the John Rylands University Library of Manchester', *Bulletin of the John Rylands University Library of Manchester*, 78 (1996), 5–229.

Stern, Samuel M., *Fatimid Decrees. Original Documents from the Fatimid Chancery* (London, 1964).

Stern, Samuel M., 'Three Petitions of the Fatimid Period', *Oriens*, 15 (1962), 172–209.

Stern, Samuel M., 'A Petition to the Fatimid Caliph al-Mustanṣir concerning a

Conflict within the Jewish Community', *Revue des études juives*, 128 (1969), 203–22.

Thung, Machael H., 'Written Obligations from the 2nd/8th to the 4th/10th Century', *ILS*, 13 (1996), 1–12.

Tillier, Mathieu, 'Deux papyrus judiciaires de Fusṭāṭ (IIe/VIIIe siècle)', *Chronique d'Égypte*, LXXXIX (2014), 412–45.

Tillier, Mathieu and Vanthieghem, Naïm, 'La rançon du serment. Un accord à l'amiable au tribunal fatimide de Ṭalīt', *Revue des mondes musulmans et de la Méditerranée*, 140 (2016), 53–72.

Tillier, Mathieu and Vantieghem, Naïm, 'Un registre carcéral de la Fusṭāṭ abbasside', *ILS*, 25 (2018), 1–40.

Vanthieghem, Naïm, 'Violences et extorsions contre des moines dans la région d'Assiout. Réédition de P. RyL. Arab. II 11', *Journal of Coptic Studies*, 18 (2016), 185–96.

Vida, Levi Della G., 'A Papyrus Reference to the Damietta Raid of 853 A.D.', *Byzantion*, 17 (1944–5), 212–21.

Zinger, Oded, 'A Karaite–Rabbanite Court Session in mid-Eleventh Century Egypt', *Ginzei Qedem*, 13 (2017), 95–116.

Epigraphy

Cytryn-Silverman, Katia, 'The Fifth Mīl from Jerusalem: Another Umayyad Milestone from Southern Bilād al-Shām', *BSOAS*, 70 (2007), 603–10.

Elad, Amikam, 'The Southern Golan in the Early Muslim Period. The Significance of Two Newly Discovered Milestones of ʿAbd al-Malik, *Der Islam*, LXXVI (1999), 33–88.

Ghabban, ʿAlī ibn Ibrāhīm and Hoyland, Robert, 'The Inscription of Zuhayr. The Oldest Islamic Inscription (24 AH/AD 644–645)', *Arabian Archaeology and Epigraphy*, 19 (2008), 210–37.

Green, Judith and Tsafrir, Yoram, 'Greek Inscriptions from Hammat Gader', *IEJ*, 32 (1982), 77–96.

El-Hawary, Hassan Mohammad, 'The Most Ancient Islamic Monument Known Dated A.H. 31 (A.D. 652)', *JRAS* (1930), 321–33.

El-Hawary, Hassan Mohammad, 'The Second Oldest Islamic Monument Known Dated A.H. 71 (A.D. 691)', *JRAS* (1932), 289–93.

Hirschfeld, Yizhar and Solar, Giora, 'The Roman Thermae at Hammat Gader', *IEJ*, 31 (1981), 197–219.

Hoyland, Robert, 'New Documentary Texts and the Early Islamic State', *BSOAS*, 69 (2006), 395–416.

Imbert, Frédéric, 'Califes, princes et compagnons dans les graffiti du debut de l'Islam', *Romano-Arabic*, XV (2015), 59–78.

Khamis, Elias, 'Two Wall Mosaic Inscriptions from the Umayyad Market Place in Bet Shean/Baysān', *BSOAS*, 64 (2001), 159–76.

Lecker, Michael, 'The Estates of ʿAmr B. al-ʿĀṣ in Palestine: Notes on a New Negev Arabic Inscription', *BSOAS*, 52 (1989), 24–37.

Meimaris, Yiannis, 'The Arab (Hijra) Era Mentioned in Greek Inscriptions and Papyri from Palestine', *Graeco-Arabica*, III (1984), 177–89.

Miles, George C., 'Early Islamic Inscriptions Near Ṭā'if in the Ḥijāz', *JNES*, 7 (1948), 236–42.

Morton, Alexander H., 'Ḥisba and Glass Stamps in Eighth- and Early Ninth-Century Egypt', in *Documents de l'Islam médiéval*, ed. Yūsuf Rāġib (Cairo, 1991), 19–42.

Répertoire chronologique d'épigraphie arabe, ed. Ét. Combe, J. Sauvaget and G. Wiet (Cairo, 1931–1956), vol. I.

Sharon, Moshe, 'An Arabic Inscription from the Time of the Caliph ʿAbd al-Malik', *BSOAS*, 39 (1966), 367–72.

Sharon, Moshe, 'A New Fatimid Inscription from Ascalon and Its Historical Setting', *Atiqot*, XXVI (1995), 61–86.

Literary Sources

ʿAbd al-Ẓāhir, Ḥisām, 'Aṣḥāb Shurṭat Miṣr fī l-ʿAṣr al-ʿAbbāsī l-Awwal (132–232 H/ 749–847CE)', *AI*, 36 (2002), 1–22.

Abdel Haleem, M. A. S., *The Qur'ān. A New Translation* (Oxford, 2010).

Abdullah, A. A., 'A New Definition of Waqf', *Journal of Islamic and Comparative Law*, 7 (1978), 57–73.

Abū Zurʿa, ʿAbd al-Raḥmān, *Kitāb al-Ta'rīkh*, ed. Laṭīf Maḥmūd Manṣūr (ʿAmmān, 2008), 2 vols.

Abū Shāma, Shihāb al-Dīn, *Tarājim Rijāl al-Qarnayn al-Sādis wa-l-Sābiʿ* (Beirut, n. d.).

Ackerman-Lieberman, Phillip I, 'Contractual Partnership in the Geniza and the Relationship between Islamic Law and Practice', *JESHO*, 54 (2011), 646–76.

Ackerman-Lieberman, Phillip I, 'Commercial Forms and Legal Norms in the Jewish Community of Medieval Egypt', *Law and History Review*, 30 (2012), 1,007–52.

Ackerman-Lieberman, Phillip I, 'Legal Pluralism among the Court Records of Medieval Egypt', *BEO*, 63 (2014), 79–112.

Agapius, Bishop of Manjib, *Kitāb al-ʿUnwān*, ed. Louis Cheikho (Paris, 1912).

El-Ali, Saleh, A., 'Muslim Estates in Hidjaz in the First Century A.H.', *JESHO*, II (1959), 247–61.

Allam, Schafik, 'Islamic Foundations (Waqf) in Egypt (Back into Pharaonic Times)', *Journal of the American Research Center in Egypt*, 44 (2008), 105–13.

Allouche, Adel, 'The Establishment of Four Chief Judgeships in Fatimid Egypt', *JAOS*, 105 (1985), 317–20.

Amedroz, H. F., 'The Office of Kadi in the Ahkam Sultaniyya of Mawardi', *JRAS* (1910), 761–96.

Amedroz, H. F., 'The Mazalim Jurisdiction in the Ahkam Sultaniyya of Mawardi', *JRAS* (1911), 635–74.

Amedroz, H. F., 'The Hisba Jurisdiction in the Ahkam al-Sultaniyya of Mawardi', *JRAS* (1916), 287–314.

Al-Anṭākī, Yaḥyā ibn Saʿīd, *Taʾrīkh*, published as a continuation of Eutychii Patriarchae Alexandrini, *Annales*, ed. Louis Cheikho and others (Paris, 1906).

Anthony, Sean W., 'The Domestic Origins of Imprisonment: An Inquiry into an Early Islamic Institution', *JAOS*, 129 (2009), 571–96.

Anthony, Sean W., 'The Prophecy and Passion of al-Ḥāriṯ al-Kaḏḏāb: Narrating a Religious Movement from the Caliphate of ʿAbd al-Malik b. Marwān', *Arabica*, 57 (2010), 1–29.

Armstrong, Lyall R., *The Quṣṣāṣ of Early Islam* (Leiden, 2017).

Ashtor, Eliyahu, *Histoire des prix et des salaires dans l'Orient médiéval* (Paris, 1969).

Athamina, Khalil, 'Arab and Muhajirun in the Environment of the Amsar', *SI*, LXVI (1987), 5–25.

Aykan, Yavuz, *Rendre la justice à Amid* (Leiden, 2016).

Bacharach, Jere L., 'Marwanid Umayyad Building Activities: Speculations on Patronage', *Muqarnas*, 13 (1996), 27–44.

Bacharach, Jere L., 'Signs of Sovereignty: The Shahāda, Qur'ānic Verses, and the Coinage of ʿAbd al-Malik', *Muqarnas*, 27 (2010), 1–30.

Balādhurī, Aḥmad ibn Yaḥyā, *Kitāb Futūḥ al-Buldān*, ed. M. J. De Goeje (Leiden, 1968) (reprint).

Balawī, *Sīrat Aḥmad ibn Ṭūlūn*, ed. Muḥammad Kurd ʿAlī (Damascus, 1939).

Baldwin, James E., *Islamic Law and Empire in Ottoman Cairo* (Edinburgh, 2017).

Bareket, Elinoar, *Fusṭāṭ on the Nile. The Jewish Elite in Medieval Egypt* (Leiden, 1999).

Barnes, J. R., *An Introduction to Religious Foundations in the Ottoman Empire* (Leiden, 1987).

Ben-Sasson, Menahem, *The Emergence of the Local Jewish Community in the Muslim World. Qayrawān, 800–1057* (Jerusalem, 1996) [in Hebrew].

Berkel, Maaike van, 'Embezzlement and Reimbursement. Disciplining Officials in Abbasid Baghdad (8th–10th Centuries AD)', *The International Journal of Public Administration*, 34 (2011), 712–19.

Bernheimer, Teresa, *The ʿAlids* (Edinburgh, 2014).

Bianquis, Thierry, *Damas et la Syrie sous la domination fatimide (359–468/969–1076)* (Damascus, 1986–9), 2 vols.

Bianquis, Thierry, 'La prise du pouvoir par les fatimides en Égypte (357–363/968–974)', *AI*, XI (1972), 49–109.

Bianquis, Thierry, 'L'acte de succession de Kāfūr d'après Maqrīzī', *AI*, XII (1974), 263–9.

Bianquis, Thierry, 'Une crise frumentaire dans l'Égypte fatimide', *JESHO*, 23 (1980), 65–101.

Bligh-Abramski, 'The Judiciary (Qāḍīs) as a Governmental-Administrative Tool in Early Islam', *JESHO*, XXXV (1992), 40–71.

Bonner, Michael, 'Ibn Ṭūlūn's Jihād: The Damascus Assembly of 269/883', *JAOS*, 130 (2010), 573–605.

Booth, Phil, 'The Muslim Conquest of Egypt Reconsidered', in *Constructing the Seventh Century*, ed. Constantin Zuckerman, *Travaux et Mémoires*, 17 (2013), 639–71.

Borsch, Stuart J. *The Black Death in Egypt and England. A Comparative Study* (Austin, 2005).

Bosworth, Clifford Edmund, *The Mediaeval Islamic Underworld. The Banū Sāsān in Arabic Society and Literature* (Leiden, 1976), 2 vols.

Bouderbala, Sobhi, 'Les aḥbās de Fusṭāṭ aux deux premiers siècles de l'hégire: entre pratiques socio-économiques et normalisation juridique', *Médiévales*, 64 (2013), 37–56.

Bouderbala, Sobhi, 'Les māwālī à Fusṭāṭ aux deux premiers siècles de l'Islam et leur intégration sociale', in *Les dynamiques de l'islamisation en Méditerranée centrale et en Sicile: nouvelles propositions et découvertes récentes*, ed. Annliese Nef and others (Roma–Bari, 2014), 141–51.

Boyce, M., 'On the Sacred Fires of the Zoroastrians', *BSOAS*, XXXI (1968), 52–68.

Boyce, M., 'The Pious Foundations of the Zoroastrians', *BSOAS*, XXXI (1968), 270–89.

Brett, Michael, *The Rise of the Fatimids. The World of the Mediterranean and the Middle East in the Tenth Century* CE (Leiden, 2001).

Brett, Michael, 'The Execution of al-Yāzūrī', in *Egypt and Syria in the Fatimid, Ayyubid and Mamluk Eras*, vol. II, ed. Urbain Vermeulen and Daniel De Smet (Leuven, 1998), 15–27.

Breydy, Michel, 'La conquête arabe de l'Égypte', *Parole de l'Orient*, VIII (1977–8), 379–97.

Brockopp, Jonathan E., 'The Formation of Islamic Law. The Egyptian School (750–900)', *AI*, 45 (2011), 123–40.

Bruning, Jelle, *The Rise of a Capital. Al-Fusṭāṭ and Its Hinterland, 18/639–132/750* (Leiden, 2018).

Bruning, Jelle, 'A Legal Sunna in Dhikr Ḥaqqs from Sufyanid Egypt', *ILS*, 22 (2015), 352–74.

Brunschviq, Robert, 'Fiqh fatimide et histoire de l'Ifrīqiya', in *Mélanges d'histoire et d'archéologie de l'Occident musulman. Hommage à Georges Marçais* (Algiers, 1957), II, 13–20.

Bryen, Ari Z., 'Visibility and Violence in Petitions from Roman Egypt', *Greek, Roman, and Byzantine Studies*, 48 (2008), 181–200.

Bryer, David R. W., 'The Origins of the Druze Religion', *Der Islam*, 53 (1976), 5–27.

Butler, A. J. *The Treaty of Miṣr in Ṭabarī. An Essay in Historical Criticism* (Oxford, 1919).

Cahen, Claude, 'Réflexions sur le waqf ancien', *SI*, XIV (1961), 37–56.

Calasso, Giovanna, 'Récits de conversion, zèle dévotionnel et instruction religieuse dans les biographies des "gens de Baṣra" du Kitāb al-Ṭabaqāt d'Ibn Saʿd', in *Conversions islamiques*, ed. Mercedes García-Arenal (Paris, 2001), 19–47.

Canbakal, Hulya, *Society and Politics in an Ottoman Town. ʿAyntab in the 17th Century* (Leiden, 2007).

Chalmeta, Pedro, 'La ḥisba en Ifrīqiya et al-Andalus: étude comparative', *Les cahiers de Tunisie*, 18 (1970), 87–105.

The Chronicle of Zuqnīn (Parts III and IV, A.D. 488–775), trans. and annotated by Amir Harrak (Toronto, 1999).

Cilardo, Agostino, *The Early History of Ismāʿīlī Jurisprudence* (London, 2012).

Cilardo, Agostino, 'Some Peculiarities of the Law of Inheritance. The Formation of Imāmī and Ismāʿīlī Law', *Journal of Arabic and Islamic Studies*, 3 (2000), 127–37.

Cilardo, Agostino, 'From Qur'ān to Fiqh: Sunnī and Shīʿī Tafsīr on the Inheritance Verses and the "Named Cases" (al-Masā'il al-Mulaqqaba)', in *The Meaning of the Word. Lexicology and Qur'ānic Exegesis*, ed. S. R. Burge (Oxford, 2015), 283–318.

Cohen, Mark R., *Jewish Self-Government in Medieval Egypt* (Princeton, 1980).

Cohen, Mark R., *Poverty and Charity in the Jewish Community of Medieval Egypt* (Princeton, 2005).

Cohen, Mark R., *The Voice of the Poor in the Middle Ages. An Anthology of Documents from the Cairo Geniza* (Princeton, 2005).

Cohen, Mark R., *Maimonides and the Merchants. Jewish Law and Society in the Medieval Islamic World* (Philadelphia, 2017).

Cohen, Mark R., 'Administrative Relations between Palestinian and Egyptian Jewry during the Fatimid Period', in *Egypt and Palestine. A Millennium of Association (868–1948)*, ed. Amnon Cohen and Gabriel Baer (Jerusalem, 1984), 113–39.

Cohen, Mark R., 'A Partnership Gone Bad: Business Relationships and the Evolving Law of the Cairo Geniza Period', *JESHO*, 56 (2013), 218–63.

Cohen, Mark R., 'The "Custom of the Merchants" in Gaonic Jurisprudence and in Maimonides Mishneh Torah', in *The Festschrift Darkhei Noam. The Jews of Arab Lands*, ed. Carsten Schapkow and others (Leiden, 2015), 86–112.

Cohen, Mark R., 'Defending Jewish Judicial Autonomy in the Islamic Middle Ages', in *Law and Religious Minorities in Medieval Societies: Between Theory and Praxis*, ed. Ana Echevarria and others (Turnhout, 2016), 13–35.

Cook, Michael, *Commanding Right and Forbidding Wrong in Islamic Thought* (Cambridge, 2000).

Cooperson, Michael, *Classical Arabic Biography. The Heirs of the Prophets in the Age of al-Ma'mūn* (Cambridge, 2000).

Cornu, Georgette, *Atlas du monde arabo-islamique à l'époque classique IXe–Xe siècles* (Leiden, 1985).

Cortese, Delia, 'Voices of the Silent Majority: The Transmission of Sunnī Learning in Fāṭimī Egypt', *JSAI*, 39 (2012), 345–67.

Cortese, Delia and Calderini, Simonetta, *Women and the Fatimids in the World of Islam* (Edinburgh, 2006).

Coulson, Noel J., *A History of Islamic Law* (Edinburgh, 1964).

Coulson, Noel J., 'Doctrine and Practice in Islamic Law. One Aspect of the Problem', *BSOAS* (1956), 211–26.

Crone, Patricia, *Slaves on Horses. The Evolution of the Islamic Polity* (Cambridge, 1980).

Crone, Patricia, *Roman, Provincial and Islamic Law* (Cambridge, 1987).

Crone, Patricia and Hinds, Martin, *God's Caliph. Religious Authority in the First Centuries of Islam* (Cambridge, 1986).

Crone, Patricia and Silverstein, Adam, 'The Ancient Near East and Islam: The Case of Lot-Casting', *JSS*, LV (2010), 423–50.

Dachraoui, Farhat, *Le califat fatimide au Maghreb (296–362/909–973). Histoire politique et institutions* (Tunis, 1981).

Darling, Linda T., 'The Vicegerent of God, from Him We Expect Rain': The Incorporation of Pre-Islamic State in Early Islamic Political Culture', *JAOS*, 134 (2014), 407–29.

Donner, Fred M., 'The Shurṭa in Early Umayyad Syria', in *The Fourth International Conference on Bilad al-Shām during the Umayyad Period*, ed. M. Adnan Bakhit and Robert Schick (Amman, 1989), 246–62.

Donner, Fred M., 'The Formation of the Islamic State', *JAOS*, 106 (1986), 283–92.

Donner, Fred M., 'Umayyad Efforts at Legitimation: The Umayyad's Silent Heritage', *in Umayyad Legacies. Medieval Memories from Syria to Spain*, ed. Antoine Borrut and Paul Cobb (Leiden, 2010), 185–212.

Donner, Fred M., 'Introduction', in *The Articulation of Early Islamic State Structures*, ed. Fred M. Donner (Farnham, 2012), XIII–XLIV.

Donner, Fred M., 'Arabic Fatḥ as "Conquest" and Its Origin in Islamic Tradition', *Al-ʿUṣūr al-Wusṭā*, 24 (2016), 1–14.

Donner, Fred M., 'Talking about Islam's Origins', *BSOAS*, 81 (2018), 1–23.

Donner, Fred M., 'ʿUmar ibn al-Khaṭṭāb, ʿAmr ibn al-ʿĀṣ, and the Muslim Invasion of Egypt', in *Community, State, History and Changes. Festschrift for Ridwan al-Sayyid on His Sixtieth Birthday* (n.p., n. d.), 67–85.

Dridi, Audrey, 'Christian and Jewish Communities in Fusṭāṭ: Non-Muslim Topography and Legal Controversies in the Pre-Fatimid Period', in *The Late Antique World of Early Islam: Muslims among Christians and Jews in the East Mediterranean*, ed. Robert G. Hoyland (Princeton, 2015), 107–33.

Drory, Rina, 'The Abbasid Construction of Jāhiliyya: Cultural Authority in the Making', *SI*, 83 (1996), 33–49.

Duggan, T. Mikail P., 'Some Reasons for the Currency Reform of A.H. 77/696–7 A.D.', *Mediterranean Journal of Humanities*, IV (2014), 1–24.

Ebstein, Michael, 'Shurṭa Chiefs in Baṣra in the Umayyad Period: A Prosopographical Study', *Al-Qantara*, XXXI (2010), 103–47.

Elad, Amikam, *Medieval Jerusalem and Islamic Worship. Holy Places, Ceremonies, Pilgrimage* (Leiden, 1995).

Elbendary, Amina, *Crowds and Sultans. Urban Protest in Late Medieval Egypt and Syria* (Cairo, 2015).

Erder, Yoram, 'The Split between the Rabbanite and Karaite Communities in the Geonic Period', *Zion*, LXXVIII (2013), 321–49 [in Hebrew].

Ergene, Bogac A., *Local Court, Provincial Society and Justice in the Ottoman Empire. Legal Practice and Dispute Resolution in Çankırı and Kastamonu (1652–1744)* (Leiden, 2003).

Fasawī (or Basawī), Yaʿqūb ibn Sufyān, *Kitāb al-Maʿrifa wa-l-Taʾrīkh*, ed. Akram Ḍiyāʾ al-ʿUmarī (Beirut, 1981), 3 vols.

Forand, P. G., 'The Status of the Land and Inhabitants of the Sawād during the Two First Centuries of Islam', *JESHO*, XIV (1971), 25–37.

Foss, Clive, 'Egypt under Muʿāwiya Part I: Flavius Papas and Upper Egypt'; 'Part II: Middle Egypt, Fusṭāṭ and Alexandria', *BSOAS*, 72 (2009), 1–24, 259–78.

Foster, Benjamin R., 'Agoranomos and Muḥtasib', *JESHO*, XIII (1970), 128–44.

Fournet, Jean-Luc, 'Entre document et littérature: la pétition dans l'Antiquité tardive', in *La pétition a Byzance*, ed. Denis Feissel and Jean Gascou (Paris, 2004), 61–75.

Frantz-Murphy, Gladys, *The Agrarian Administration of Egypt from the Arabs to the Ottomans* (Cairo, 1986).

Frantz-Murphy, Gladys, 'A New Interpretation of the Economic History of Medieval Egypt', *JESHO*, XXIV (1981), 247–97.

Frantz-Murphy, Gladys, 'Settlement of Property Disputes in Provincial Egypt: The Reinstitution of Courts in the Early Islamic Period', *Al-Masaq*, 6 (1993), 95–105.

Frantz-Murphy, Gladys, 'The Economics of State Formation in Early Islamic Egypt', in *From al-Andalus to Khurasan*, ed. Petra M. Sijpesteijn and others (Leiden, 2007), 101–14.

Frenkel, Miriam, 'Medieval Alexandria – Life in a Port City', *AL-Masaq*, 26 (2014), 5–35.

Friedman, Mordechai A., see Goitein, S. D., *India Traders of the Middle Ages: Documents from the Cairo Geniza*.

Fyzee, Asaf A. A., 'Qāḍī an-Nuʿmān the Fatimid Jurist and Author', *JRAS* (1934), 1–32.

Fyzee, Asaf A. A., 'The Fatimid Law of Inheritance', *SI*, 9 (1958), 61–9.

Garcin, Jean-Claude, *Un centre musulman de la Haute-Égypte médiévale: Qūṣ* (Cairo, 1976).

Garel, Eshter and Nowak, Maria, 'Monastic Wills: The Continuation of Late Roman

Legal Tradition?', in *Writing and Communication in Early Egyptian Monasticism*, ed. Malcom Choat and Maria Chiara Giordi (Leiden, 2017), 108–28.

Gascoigne, Alison, *The Impact of the Arab Conquest on Late Roman Settlement in Egypt*, Ph. D. dissertation (University of Cambridge, 2002), 2 vols.

Gascou, Jean, 'Arabic Taxation in the Mid-Seventh Century Greek Papyri', in *Constructing the Seventh Century*, ed. Constantin Zuckerman, *Travaux et Mémoires*, 17 (2013), 671–9.

Gerber, Haim, *Crossing Borders. Jews and Muslims in Ottoman Law, Economy and Society* (Istanbul, 2008).

Ghabin, Ahmad, *Ḥisba, Arts and Craft in Islam* (Wiesbaden, 2009).

Gibb, Hamilton A. R., 'The Fiscal Rescript of ʿUmar II', *Arabica*, 2 (1955), 1–16.

Gibb, Hamilton A. R., 'Arab–Byzantine Relations under the Umayyad Caliphate', *Dumbarton Oak Papers*, 12 (1958), 219–33, reprinted in his *Studies on the Civilization of Islam* (Cambridge, MA, 1968).

Gil, Moshe, 'The Earliest Waqf Foundations', *JNES*, 57 (1998), 125–40.

Gil, Moshe, 'The Flax Trade in the Mediterranean in the Eleventh Century A.D. As Seen in Merchants' Letters from the Cairo Geniza', *JNES*, 63 (2004), 81–96.

Gimaret, Daniel, 'Les théologiens musulmans devant la hausse des prix', *JESHO*, XXII (1979), 330–7.

Gleave, Robert, 'Deriving Rules of Law', in *The Ashgate Research Companion to Islamic Law*, ed. Rudolph Peters and Peri Bearman (Farnham, 2014), 57–73.

Goitein, S. D., *A Mediterranean Society. The Jewish Communities of the Arab World as Portrayed in the Documents of the Cairo Geniza* (Berkeley and Los Angeles, 1967–93), 6 vols.

Goitein, S. D. and Friedman, Mordechai A., *India Traders of the Middle Ages: Documents from the Cairo Geniza*, 'India Book' (Leiden, 2008).

Golb, Norman, 'The Topography of the Jews of Medieval Egypt', *JNES*, 24 (1965), 251–74; 33 (1975), 116–49.

Goldberg, Jessica L., *Trade and Institutions in the Medieval Mediterranean. The Geniza Merchants and Their Business World* (Cambridge, 2012).

Gottheil, Richard, 'A Distinguished Family of Fatimide Cadis (al-Nuʿmān) in the Tenth Century', *JAOS*, 27 (1906), 217–96,

Guessous, Azeddine, 'Le rescrit fiscal de ʿUmar b. ʿAbd al-ʿAzīz: Une nouvelle appréciation', *Der Islam*, 73 (1996), 113–84.

Guest, Rhuvon, 'Relations between Persia and Egypt under Islam up to the Fatimid Period', in *A Volume of Oriental Studies*, ed. T. W. Arnold and R. A. Nicholson (Cambridge, 1922), 163–74.

Haji, Amin, 'Institutions of Justice in Fatimid Egypt (358–567/969–1,171), in *Islamic Law and Historical Contexts*, ed. Aziz al-Azmeh (London, 1988), 199–214.

Haji, Othman Mohammad, 'Origin of the Institution of Waqf', *Hamdard Islamicus*, VI (1983), 3–23.

Haldon, John, 'Greater Syria in the Seventh Century: Context and Background', in *Money, Power and Politics in Early Islamic Syria*, ed. John Haldon (Farnham, 2010), 1–21.

Halevi, Leor, 'The Paradox of Islamization: Tombstone, Inscriptions, Qur'ānic Recitations, and the Problem of Religious Change', *History of Religion*, 44 (2004), 120–52.

Hallaq, Wael B., 'Uṣūl al-Fiqh: Beyond Tradition', *Journal of Islamic Studies*, 3 (1992), 172–202.

Hallaq, Wael B., 'Model Shurūṭ Works and the Dialectic of Doctrine and Practice', *ILS*, 2 (1995), 109–34.

Hallaq, Wael B., 'The Qāḍī's Dīwān before the Ottomans', *BSOAS*, 61 (1998), 415–36.

Hallaq, Wael B., 'From Regional to Personal Schools of Law? A Reevaluation', *ILS*, 8 (2001), 1–26.

Halm, Heinz, *The Fatimids and Their Traditions of Learning* (London, 1997).

Halm, Heinz, *Die Kalifen von Kairo. Die Fatimiden in Ägypten 973–1074* (Munich, 2003).

Halm, Heinz, *The Empire of the Mahdi. The Rise of the Fatimids*, trans. Michael Bonner (Leiden, 1996).

Halm, Heinz, *Kalifen und Assassinen. Ägypten und der Vordere Orient zur Zeit der ersten Kreuzzüge 1074–1171* (Munchen, 2014).

Heidemann, Stefan, 'The Evolving Representation of the Early Islamic Empire and its Religion on Coin Imagery', in *The Qur'ān in Context*, ed. Angelika Neuwirth and others (Leiden, 149–97.

Heijer, Den Johannes, 'The Martyrdom of Bifām ibn Baqūra al-Ṣawwāf by Mawhūb ibn Manṣūr ibn Mufarrij and Its Fatimid Background', *ME*, 21 (2015), 452–85.

Hennigan, Peter C., *The Birth of a Legal Institution. The Formation of the Waqf in Third-Century* A. H. *Ḥanafī Legal Discourse* (Leiden, 2004).

Hentati, Nejmeddine, ''Āqila, indice de survivance des relations tribales en Occident musulman médiéval?', *Revue Tunisienne des Sciences Sociales*, 127 (2004), 203–17.

El-Hibri, Tayeb, *Reinterpreting Islamic Historiography. Hārūn al-Rashīd and the Narrative of the Abbasid Caliphate* (Cambridge, 2006).

History of the Patriarchs of the Egyptian Church, known as *The History of the Holy Church*, by Sawīrus ibn al-Muqaffaʿ, Bishop of Ashmūnīn: vol. II, part I, ed. and trans. Yassā ʿAbd al-Masīḥ and O. H. E. Burmester; vol. II, part II, ed. and trans. Aziz Suryal Atiya and Yassā ʿAbd al-Masīḥ; vol. II, part III, ed. and trans. Aziz Suryal Atiya and Yassā ʿAbd al-Masīḥ (Cairo, 1943–59).

Hodgson, Marshall G. S., 'Al-Darazī and Ḥamza in the Origin of the Druze Religion', *JOAS*, 82 (1962), 5–20.

Hoyland, Robert G., *In God's Path. The Arab Conquest and the Creation of an Islamic Empire* (Oxford, 2015).

Hoyland, Robert G., 'Reflections on the Identity of the Arabian Conquerors of the Seventh-Century Middle East', *Al-ʿUṣūr al-Wusṭā*, 25 (2017), 113–40.

Hurvitz, Nomrod, Competing Texts. The Relationship between al-Māwardī's and Abū Yaʿlā's al-Ahkām al-Sulṭāniyya, *Occasional Publications Islamic Legal Studies Program*, Harvard Law School, n. 8, 2007.

Ibn ʿAbd al-Ḥakam, *Futūḥ Miṣr*, ed. Charles C. Torrey (New Haven, 1922) (New York, n.d.) (reprint).

Ibn ʿAbd al-Ḥakam, *Sīrat ʿUmar ibn ʿAbd al-ʿAzīz ibn Marwān*, published under the title *al-Khalīfa al-ʿĀdil ʿUmar ibn ʿAbd al-ʿAzīz*, ed. Aḥmad ʿUbayd (Cairo, n.d.).

Ibn ʿAsākir, ʿAlī ibn al-Ḥasan, *Taʾrīkh Madīnat Dimashq*, ed. ʿUmar ibn Gharāma al-ʿAmrawī (Damascus, 1997), vol. 53.

Ibn al-Athīr, ʿAlī ibn Muḥammad, *Al-Kāmil fī l-Taʾrīkh*, ed. ʿAlī Shīrī (Beirut, 2004), vol. VIII.

Ibn al-Bassām, Muḥammad ibn Aḥmad, *Nihāyat al-Rutba fī Ṭalab al-Ḥisba*, ed. Ḥasan Ismāʿīl and Farīd al-Mazīdī (Beirut, 2003).

Ibn al-Dawādārī, Abū Bakr ibn ʿAbd Allāh, *Kanz al-Durar*, ed. Ṣalāḥ al-Dīn al-Munajjid (Cairo, 1961), vol. VI.

Ibn Ḥabīb, ʿAbd al-Malik, *Kitāb al-Taʾrīkh*, ed. ʿAbd al-Ghanī Mastū (Beirut, 2008).

Ibn Ḥajar, al-Asqalānī, *Rafʿ al-Iṣr ʿan Quḍāt Miṣr*, ed. and trans. Richard Gottheil, 'A Distinguished Family of Fatimide Cadis (al-Nuʿmān) in the Tenth Century', *JAOS*, 27 (1906), 217–96, esp. 238–96 (text); ed. Rhuvon Guest as an appendix to his edition of Kindī (see under Kindī); ed. Ḥāmid ʿAbd al-Majīd and others (Cairo, 1957–61), 2 vols; ed. ʿAlī Muḥammad ʿUmar (Cairo, 1998).

Ibn Ḥawqal, *Kitāb Ṣūrat al-Arḍ*, ed. J. H. Kramers (Leiden, 1938, 2nd edn); French trans., Gaston Wiet, *Configuration de la terre* (Paris, 1964), 2 vols.

Ibn al-Haytham, *Kitāb al-Munāẓarāt*, ed. and trans. Wilfred Madelung and Paul E. Walker, *The Advent of the Fatimids* (London, 2000).

Ibn ʿIdhārī, al-Marrākushī, *Kitāb al-Bayān al-Mughrib*, ed. G. S. Colin and E. Lévi-Provençal (Leiden, 1948–51), 2 vols.

Ibn Isḥāq, *Taʾrīkh al-Khulafāʾ*, ed. and trans. Nabia Abbott, *Studies in Arabic Literary Papyri*, vol. 1, Historical Texts (Chicago, 1957).

Ibn al-Jawzī, Abū l-Faraj, *Al-Muntaẓam fī Taʾrīkh al-Mulūk wa-l-Umam*, ed. Sahīl Zakār (Beirut, 1995), vols VI–VIII.

Ibn Khallikān, Shams al-Dīn, *Wafayāt al-Aʿyān*, ed. Iḥsān ʿAbbās (Beirut, 1968–71), 8 vols.

Ibn Khayyāt, Khalīfa ibn Khayyāt, *Taʾrikh*, ed. Akram Ḍiyā al-ʿUmarī (Al-Najaf, 1967), 2 vols.

Ibn al-Maʾmūn, al-Baṭāʾiḥī, *Akhbār Miṣr*, ed. Ayman Fuʾād Sayyid (Cairo, 1983).

Ibn Muyassar, Yūsuf ibn Jalab Rāghib, *Akhbār Miṣr*, ed. Ayman Fuʾād Sayyid (Cairo, 1981).

Ibn al-Qalānisī, *Dhayl Taʾrīkh Dimashq*, ed. H. F. Amedroz (Leiden, 1908).

Ibn Saʿīd, *Kitāb al-Mughrib fī Ḥulā al-Maghrib*, ed. Knut L. Tallqvist (Leiden, 1898).

Ibn al-Ṣayrafī, Abū l-Qāsim ʿAlī, *Al-Ishāra ilā man Nāla al-Wizāra*, ed. ʿAbd Allāh Mukhliṣ in *Bulletin de l'Institut français d'archéologie orientale du Caire*, 25 (1924).

Ibn Taghrī Birdī, Abū l-Maḥāsin, *Al-Nujūm al-Zāhira fī Mulūk Miṣr wa-l-Qāhira* (Beirut, 1992), vols I–II.

Ibn al-Ṭuwayr, Abū Muḥammad al-Murtaḍā, *Nuzhat al-Muqlatayn fī Akhbār al-Dawlatayn*, ed. Ayman Fuʾād Sayyid (Beirut, 1992).

Ibn al-Ukhūwah, *Maʿālim al-Qurba*, ed. Reuben Levy (London, 1938).

Ibn Wāṣil, Jamāl al-Dīn, *Mufarrij al-Kurūb fī Akhbār Banī Ayyūb*, ed. ʿAbd al-Salām al-Tadmurī (Beirut, 2004), vol. VI.

Ibn Yūnus, ʿAbd al-Raḥmān ibn Aḥmad, *Taʾrīkh Ibn Yūnus al-Ṣadafī*, ed. Fatḥī ʿAbd al-Fattāḥ (Beirut, 2000), 2 vols.

Ibn Ẓāfir, al-Azdī, *Akhbār al-Duwal al-Munqaṭiʿa*; ed. A. Ferré (Cairo, 1972), ʿAlī ʿUmar (Cairo, 2001).

Ibn al-Zayyāt, Shams al-Dīn, *Al-Kawākib al-Sayyāra fī Tartīb al-Ziyāra* (Baghdad, n.d.).

Ibn Zūlāq, al-Ḥasan ibn Ibrāhīm, *Faḍāʾil Miṣr*, MS Paris, BnF Arabe 4727; MS Dublin, Chester Beatty Library 4683; ed. ʿAlī Muḥammad ʿUmar (Cairo, 2000).

Ibn Zūlāq, al-Ḥasan ibn Ibrāhīm, *Kitāb Akhbār Sībawayhi al-Miṣrī*, ed. Muḥammad Ibrāhīm Sa'd and Ḥusayn Dīb (Cairo, 1933).

Idrīs, 'Imād al-Dīn, *'Uyūn al-Akhbār*, published as *Ta'rīkh al-Khulafā' al-Fāṭimiyyin bi-l-Maghrib*, ed. Mohammed Yalaoui (Beirut, 1985).

Jany, János, *Judging in the Islamic, Jewish and Zoroastrian Legal Traditions* (Farnham, 2012).

Jany, János, 'Persian Influence on the Islamic Office of Qāḍī al-Quḍāt: A Reconsideration', *JSAI*, 34 (2008), 149–68.

Al-Jawdharī, Manṣūr al-'Azīzī, *Sīrat al-Ustādh Jawdhar*, ed. and trans. Hamid Haji (London, 2012).

Jeffery, Arthur, *The Foreign Vocabulary of the Qur'ān* (Leiden, 2007).

John, Coptic Bishop of Nikiu, *The Chronicle of John*, trans. Robert Henry Charles (London, 1916) (reprint Amsterdam, n.d.).

Jokish, Benjamin, *Islamic Imperial Law: Hārūn al-Rashīd's Codification Project* (Berlin, 2007).

Judd, Steven, 'Muslim Persecution of Heretics during the Marwanid Period (64–132/684–750)', *Al-Masaq*, 23 (2011), 1–14.

Judd, Steven, 'The Jurisdictional Limits of Qāḍī Courts during the Umayyad Period', *BEO*, LXIII (2014), 45–56.

Juynboll, G. H., A. *Muslim Tradition. Studies in Chronology, Provenance and Authorship of Early Ḥadīth* (Cambridge, 1983).

Kaegi, Walter E., 'Egypt on the Eve of the Muslim Conquest', in *The Cambridge History of Egypt*, vol. 1, *Medieval Egypt*, ed. Carl F. Petry (Cambridge, 1998), 34–61.

Keenan, J. G., 'Law in the Byzantine Period', in *Law and Legal Practice in Egypt from Alexander to the Arab Conquest*, ed. James G. Keenan and others (Cambridge, 2014), 23–8.

Kennedy, Hugh, *The Armies of the Caliphs* (London, 2001).

Kennedy, Hugh, 'Central Government and Provincial Élites in the Early Abbasid Caliphate', *BSOAS*, XLIV (1981), 26–38.

Khan, Geoffrey, 'Pre-Islamic Background to Muslim Legal Formularies', *Aram*, 6 (1994), 193–224.

Khan, Geoffrey, 'Remarks on the Historical Background and Development of Early Arabic Documentary Formulae', *Asiatische Studien/Études Asiatique*, LXII (2008), 885–906.

Kindī, Muḥammad ibn Yūsuf, *The Governors and Judges of Egypt*, ed. Rhuvon Guest (Leiden, 1912).

Klein, Yaron, 'Between Public and Private: An Examination of Ḥisba Literature', *Harvard Middle Eastern Islamic Review*, 7 (2006), 41–62.

Knost, Stefan, 'The Waqf in Court: Lawsuits over Religious Endowments in Ottoman Aleppo', in *Dispensing Justice in Islam. Qadis and Their Judgments*, ed. Muhammad Khalid Masud and others (Leiden, 2006), 427–51.

Kovelman, Arkady B., 'From Logos to Myth: Egyptian Petitions of the 5th–7th Cemturies', *Bulletin of the American Society of Papyrologists*, 28 (1991), 135–52.

Krakowski, Eve, *Coming of Age in Medieval Egypt. Female Adolescence, Jewish Law, and Ordinary Culture* (Princeton, 2018).

Krakowski, Eve and Rustow, Marina, 'Formula as Content: Medieval Jewish Institutions, the Cairo Geniza, and the New Diplomatics', *Jewish Social Studies*, 20 (2014), 111–46.

Kubiak, Władysław, *Al-Fusṭāṭ Its Foundation and Early Urban Development* (Warsaw, 1982).

Lalani, Arzina R., 'Judgment', *Encyclopaedia of the Qur'ān*, III, 64–8.

Lane, Edward William, *An Arabic–English Lexicon* (Beirut, 1980), 8 vols (reprint).

Lange, Christian, *Justice, Punishment and the Medieval Muslim Imagination* (Cambridge, 2008).

Lange, Christian, 'Changes in the Office of Ḥisba under the Seljuks', in *The Seljuks: Politics, Society, and Culture*, ed. Christian Lange and S. Mecit (Edinburgh, 2009), 157–81.

Lapidus, Ira Marvin, *Muslim Cities in the Later Middle Ages* (Cambridge, MA. 1967).

Lapidus, Ira Marvin, 'The Grain Economy of Mamluk Egypt', *JESHO*, 12 (1969), 1–15.

Lecker, Michael, 'Shurṭat al-Khamīs and other Matters: Notes on the Translation of Ṭabarī's Ta'rīkh', *JSAI*, 14 (1991), 276–88.

Lecker, Michael, 'A Pre-Islamic Endowment Deed in Arabic Regarding al-Waḥīda in the Ḥijāz', in *People, Tribes and Society in Arabia around the Time of Muḥammad* (Aldershot, 2005).

Lecker, Michael, 'Glimpses of Muḥammad's Medinan Decade', in *The Cambridge Companion to Muḥammad*, ed. Jonathan E. Brockopp (Cambridge, 2010), 61–83.

Legendre, Marie, 'Hiérarchie administrative et formation de l'État islamique dans la campagne Égyptienne pré-Ṭūlūnide', in *Les dynamiques de l'islamisation en Méditerranée centrale et en Sicile: nouvelles propositions et découvertes récentes*, ed. Annliese Nef and Fabiola Ardizzone (Rome, 2014), 103–19.

Legendre, Marie, 'Islamic Conquest, Territorial Reorganization and Empire

Formation: A Study of Seventh-Century Movements of Population in the Light of Egyptian Papyri', *in The Long Seventh Century. Continuity and Discontinuity in an Age of Transition*, ed. Alessandro Gnasso and others (Bern, 2015), 235–50.

Legendre, Marie, 'Neither Byzantine nor Islamic? The Duke of the Thebaid and the Formation of the Umayyad State', *Historical Research*, 243 (2016), 3–18.

Lev, Yaacov, *Saladin in Egypt* (Leiden, 1999).

Lev, Yaacov, *Charity, Endowments, and Charitable Institutions in Medieval Islam* (Gainesville, 2005).

Lev, Yaacov, 'Persecutions and Conversion to Islam in Eleventh-Century Egypt', *The Medieval Levant. Studies in Memory of Eliyahu Ashtor (1914–1984)*, *Asian and African Studies* (Haifa), 22 (1988), 73–93.

Lev, Yaacov, 'Tinnīs: An Industrial Medieval Town', in *L'Égypte fatimide son art et son histoire*, ed. Marianne Barrucand (Paris, 1999), 97–107.

Lev, Yaacov, 'Charity and Justice in Medieval Islam', *Rivista degli Studi Orientali*, LXXVI (2002), 1–16.

Lev, Yaacov, 'Piety and Political Activism in Twelfth Century Egypt', *JSAI*, 31 (2006), 289–324.

Lev, Yaacov, 'Saladin's Economic Policies and the Economy of Ayyubid Egypt', in *Egypt and Syria in the Fatimid, Ayyubid and Mamluk Eras*, vol. V, ed. Urbain Vermeulen and Kristof D'Hulster (Leuven, 2007), 307–48.

Lev, Yaacov, 'From Revolutionary Violence to State Violence: The Fatimids (297–567/909–1,171)', in *Public Violence in Islamic Societies*, ed. Christian Lange and Maribel Fierro (Edinburgh, 2009), 67–87.

Lev, Yaacov, 'The Discourse of Charity and Piety in Medieval Arabic Literary Sources', in *Caridad y compassíon en biografías islámicas*, ed. Ana María Carballeira Debasa (Madrid, 2011), 67–85.

Lev, Yaacov, 'Coptic Rebellions and the Islamization of Medieval Egypt (8th–10th Centuries): Medieval and Modern Perceptions', *JSAI*, 39 (2012), 303–45.

Lev, Yaacov, 'The Fatimid Caliphs, the Copts, and the Coptic Church', Non-Muslim Communities in Fatimid Egypt (10th–12th Centuries CE), *ME*, 21 (2015), 390–411.

Lewicka, Paulina B., *Food and Foodways of Medieval Cairenes* (Leiden, 2011).

Libson, Gideon, 'Legal Autonomy and the Recourse to Legal Proceedings by Protected People, According to Muslim Sources during the Gaonic Period', in *The Intertwined Worlds of Islam. Essays in Memory of Hava Lazarus-Yafeh*, ed. Nahem Ilan (Jerusalem, 2002), 334–93 [in Hebrew].

Lindstedt, Ilkka, 'Muhājirūn as a Name for the First/Seventh Century Muslims', *JNES*, 74 (2015), 67–73.

Macuch, Maria, 'Pious Foundations in Byzantine and Sasanian Law', in *La Persia e Bisanzio* (Rome, 2004), 181–96.

Madelung, Wilfred, 'The Sources of Ismāʿīlī Law', *JNES*, 35 (1976), 29–40.

Madelung, Wilfred, 'The Religious Policy of the Fatimids toward Their Sunnī Subjects in the Maghreb', in *L'Égypte fatimide son art et son histoire*, ed. Marianne Barrucand (Paris, 1999), 97–107.

Maghen, Zeev, *After Hardship Cometh Ease. The Jews as Backdrop for Muslim Moderation* (Berlin, 2006).

Magued, A. M., 'La fonction de juge suprême dans l'État fatimide en Égypte', *L'Égypte Contemporaine*, 51 (1960), 45–56.

Magued, A. M., 'De quelques juridictions fatimides en Égypte', *L'Égypte Contemporaine*, 52 (1961), 47–59.

Maqrīzī, Taqī al-Dīn, *Kitāb al-Muqaffā al-Kabīr*, ed. Mohammed Yalaoui (Beirut, 1991), 8 vols.

Maqrīzī, Taqī al-Dīn, *Ittiʿāẓ al-Ḥunafā' bi-Akhbār al-A'imma al-Fāṭimiyyin al-Khulafā'*, vol. 1, ed. Jamāl al-Dīn al-Shayyāl (Cairo, 1971), vols 2–3, ed. Muḥammad Ḥilmī Muḥammad Aḥmad (Cairo, 1973–6).

Maqrīzī, Taqī al-Dīn, *Al-Mawāʿiẓ wa-l-Iʿtibār fī Dhikr al-Khiṭaṭ wa-l-Athār*, ed. Ayman Fu'ād Sayyid (London, 2002–5), 5 vols.

Maqrīzī, Taqī al-Dīn, *Musawwadat Kitāb al-Mawāʿiẓ wa-l-Iʿtibār fī Dhikr al-Khiṭaṭ wa-l-Athār*, ed. Ayman Fu'ād Sayyid (London, 1995).

Margoliouth, David Samuel, 'Omar's Instructions to the Ḳāḍī', *JRAS*, 139 (1910), 307–27.

Marsham, Andrew, 'Public Execution in the Umayyad Period: Early Islamic Punitive Practice and Its Late Antique Context', *Journal of Arabic and Islamic Studies*, 11 (2011), 101–36.

Marsham, Andrew, 'The Pact (Amān) between Muʿāwiya ibn Abī Sufyān and ʿAmr ibn al-ʿĀṣ (656 or 658 CE): "Documents" and the Islamic Historical Tradition', *JSS*, LVII (2012), 69–96.

Martel-Thoumian, Bernadette, *Délinquance et ordre social. L'État mamlouk syro-égyptien face au crime à la fin du IXe–XVe siècle* (Paris, 2012).

Masud, Muḥammad Khalid, 'Procedural Law between Traditions, Jurists and Judges: The Problem of yamīn maʿ al-shāhid', *Al-Qantara*, XX (1999), 387–416.

Masud, Muḥammad Khalid, 'A Study of Wakīʿ's (d. 306/917) Akhbār al-Quḍāt', in *The Law Applied. Contextualizing the Islamic Shariʿa, A Volume in Honor of Frank E. Vogel*, ed. Peri Bearman and others (London, 2008), 116–27.

Masʿūdī, Abū l-Ḥasan ʿAlī, *Kitāb al-Tanbīh wa-l-Ishrāf* (Beirut, 1965) (reprint).

Māwardī, ʿAlī ibn Muḥammad ibn Ḥabīb, *Al-Aḥkām al-Sulṭāniyya*, ed. Muḥammad Jāsim al-Ḥadīthī (Baghdad, 2002).

Mayerson, Philip, 'The Port of Clysma (Suez) in Transition from Roman to Arab Rule', *JNES*, 55 (1996), 119–27.

Mayerson, Philip, 'The Role of Flax in Roman and Fatimid Egypt', *JNES*, 56 (1997), 201–7.

McCormik, Michael, *Origins of European Economy* (Cambridge, 2001).

McCormik, Michael, 'Toward a Molecular History of the Justinianic Plague', in *Plague and the End of Antiquity*, ed. Lester K. Little (Cambridge, 2007), 290–312.

Melchert, Christopher, 'Religious Policies of the Caliphs from al-Mutawakkil to al-Muqtadir, A.H. 232–295/A.D. 847–908', *ILS*, 3 (1996), 316–42.

Melchert, Christopher, 'Mawārdī, Abū Yaʿlά and the Sunnī Revival', in *Prosperity and Stagnation: Some Cultural and Social Aspects of the Abbasid Period*, ed. Krzystof Kościelnik (Cracow, 2010), 37–61.

Melchert, Christopher, 'The Life and Works of al-Nasāʾī', *JSS*, LIX (2014), 377–407.

Mikhail, Maged S. A., *From Byzantine to Islamic Egypt. Religion, Identity and Politics after the Arab Conquest* (London, 2014).

Mikhail, Maged S. A., 'Notes on Ahl al-Dīwān: The Arab-Egyptian Army of the Seventh through Ninth Centuries CE', *JAOS*, 128 (2008), 277–87.

Moreh, Shmuel, *Live Theatre and Dramatic Literature in the Medieval Arab World* (Edinburgh, 1992).

Moreh, Shmuel, 'Live Theatre in Medieval Islam', in *Studies in Islamic History and Civilization in Honour of Professor David Ayalon*, ed. Moshe Sharon (Jerusalem–Leiden, 1986), 565–611.

Morony, Michael G., 'For Whom Does the Writer Write? The First Bubonic Plague Pandemic According to Syriac Sources', in *Plague and the End of Antiquity*, ed. Lester K. Little (Cambridge, 2007), 59–86.

Motzki, Harald, 'The Muṣannaf of ʿAbd al-Razzāq al-Ṣanʿānī as a Source of Authentic Aḥādīth of the First Century A. H.', *JNES*, 50 (1991), 1–21.

Motzki, Harald, 'The Author and his Work in the Islamic Literature of the First Centuries: The Case of ʿAbd al-Razzāq's Muṣannaf', *JSAI*, 28 (2003), 171–201.

Motzkin, Aryeh Leo, 'Elijah ben Zechariah. A Member of Abraham Maimuni's Court: A Geniza Portrait', *Revue des études juives*, 128 (1969), 339–48.

Muḥammad, Tarek M., 'The Role of the Copts in the Islamic Navigation in the 7th and 8th Centuries: The Papyrological Evidence', *Journal of Coptic Studies*, 10 (2008), 1–31.

Muqaddasī, *Aḥsan al-Taqāsīm fī Maʿrifat al-Aqālīm*, ed. M. J. De Goeje (Leiden, 1967) (reprint).

Musabbiḥī, *Akhbār Miṣr*, ed. Ayman Fu'ād Sayyid and Thierry Bianquis (Cairo, 1978).

Nāṣir-i Khusraw, *Book of Travels (Safarnāma)*, trans. W. M. Thackston Jr (New York, 1986).

Nawas, John, 'A Client's Client: The Process of Islamization in Early and Classical Islam', *Journal of Abbasid Studies*, 1 (2014), 143–58.

Noth, Albrecht, *The Early Arabic Historical Tradition. A Source-Critical Study* (2nd edn, in collaboration with Lawrence I. Conrad), trans. Michael Bonner (Princeton, 1994).

Oberauer, Norbert, 'Early Doctrines on Waqf Revisited: The Evolution of Islamic Endowment Law in the 2nd Century A.H.', *ILS*, 20 (2013), 1–47.

Olszowy-Schlanger, Judith, 'Karaite Legal Documents', in *Karaite Judaism*, ed. Meira Polliack (Leiden, 2003), 255–73.

Opwis, Felicitas, 'Shifting Legal Authority from the Ruler to the ʿUlamāʾ: Rationalizing the Punishment for Drinking Wine during the Saljūk Period', *Der Islam*, 86 (2011), 65–92.

Pahlitzsch, Johannes, 'Christian Pious Foundations as an Element of Continuity between Late Antiquity and Islam', in *Charity and Giving in Monotheistic Religions*, ed. Miriam Frenkel and Yaacov Lev (Berlin, 2009), 125–53.

Palme, Bernhard, 'The Imperial Presence: Government and Army', in *Egypt in the Byzantine World, 300–700*, ed. Roger S. Bagnall (Cambridge, 2007), 244–70.

Palme, Bernhard, 'Law and Courts in Late Antique Egypt', in *Aspects of Law in Late Antiquity*, ed. Boudewijn Sirks (Oxford, 2008), 55–76.

Papaconstantinou, Arietta, 'Historiography, Hagiography, and the Making of the Coptic "Church of the Martyrs" in Early Islamic Egypt', *Dumbarton Oak Papers*, 60 (2006), 65–86.

Peirce, Leslie, *Morality Tales. Law and Gender in the Ottoman Court of Aintab* (Berkeley and Los Angeles, 2003).

Pellat, Charles, *Cinq calendriers Égyptiens* (Cairo, 1986).

Perikhanian, Anahit, *The Book of a Thousand Judgments (A Sasanian Law-Book)*, trans. Nina Garsoïan (Costa Mesa, 1997).

Perlman, Yaara, 'The Bodyguard of the Caliphs during the Umayyad and Early Abbasid Periods', *Al-Qantara,* XXXVI (2015), 315–40.

Peters, Frank E., 'The Roman Near East: The View from Below', in *Semitic Papyrology in Context,* ed. Lawrence H. Schiffman (Leiden, 2003), 187–201.

Petry, Carl F., *The Criminal Underworld in a Medieval Islamic Society. Narratives from Cairo and Damascus under the Mamluks* (Chicago, 2012).

Picard, Christophe, 'La Méditerranée centrale, un territoire de l'Islam', in *Les dynamiques de l'islamisation en Méditerranée centrale et en Sicile: nouvelles propositions et découvertes récentes,* ed. Annliese Nef and Fabiola Ardizzone (Rome, 2014), 37–47.

Picard, Christophe, *La mer des califes. Une histoire de la Méditerranée musulmane (VIIe–XIIe siècle)* (Paris, 2015).

Poonawala, Ismail K., 'Al-Qāḍī al-Nuʿmān's Work and the Sources', *BSOAS,* XXXVI (1973), 109–15.

Poonawala, Ismail K., 'A Reconsideration of al-Qāḍī al-Nuʿmān's Madhhab', *BSOAS,* XXXVI (1974), 572–80.

Poonawala, Ismail K., 'Al-Qāḍī al-Nuʿmān and Ismāʿīlī Jurisprudence', in *Mediaeval Ismāʿīlī History and Thought,* ed. Farhad Daftary (Cambridge, 1996), 117–45.

Poonawala, Ismail K., 'The Beginning of the Ismāʿīlī Daʿwa and the Establishment of the Fatimid Dynasty as Commemorated by al-Qāḍī al-Nuʿmān', in *Culture and Memory in Medieval Islam. Essays in Honour of Wilferd Madelung,* ed. Farhad Daftary and Josef W. Meri (London, 2003), 338–64.

Powers, David S., *Studies in Qur'ān and Ḥadīth. The Formation of the Islamic Law of Inheritance* (Berkeley and Los Angeles, 1986).

Powers, David S., 'Orientalism, Colonialism, and Legal History: The Attack on Muslim Family Endowments in Algier and India', *Comparative Studies in Society and History,* 31 (1989): 535–71.

Powers, Paul R., 'The Schools of Law', in *The Ashgate Research Companion to Islamic Law,* ed. Rudolph Peters and Peri Bearman (Farnham, 2014), 41–57.

Puin, Gerd-Rüdiger, *Der Dīwān von ʿUmar ibn al-Ḫaṭṭāb* (Bonn, 1970).

Al-Qāḍī al-Nuʿmān, Muḥammad al-Tamīmī, *Risalāt Iftitāḥ al-Daʿwa,* ed. Wadād al-Qāḍī (Beirut, 1970).

Al-Qāḍī, al-Nuʿmān, *Kitāb al-Majālis wa-l-Musāyarāt,* ed. Al-Ḥabīb al-Faqqī and others (Tunis, 1978).

Al-Qāḍī, Wadād, 'Population Census and Land Surveys under the Umayyads (41–132/661–750)', *Der Islam,* 83 (2006), 341–417.

Al-Qāḍī, Wadād, 'A Documentary Report on Umayyad Stipends Registers (Dīwān al-ʿAṭā') in Abū Zurʿa's Ta'rīkh', *Quaderni di Studi Arabi*, 4 (2009), 7–44.

Al-Qāḍī, Wadād, 'The Salaries of Judges in Early Islam: The Evidence of the Documentary and Literary sources', *IJNES*, 68 (2009), 9–30.

Al-Qāḍī, Wadād, 'Security Positions under the Umayyads: The Story of "Maʿbad al-Ṭuruq"', in *Differenz und Dynamik im Islam. Festschrift für Heinz Halm zum 70. Geburtstag* (Würzburg, 2012), 253–83.

Al-Qāḍī, Wadād, 'Death Dates in Umayyad Stipends Registers (Dīwān al-ʿAṭā')? The Testimony of the Papyri and the Literary Sources', in *From Bāwīṭ to Marw. Documents from the Medieval Muslim World*, ed. Andreas Kaplony and others (Leiden, 2015), 59–83.

Al-Qāḍī, Wadād, 'Non-Muslim in the Muslim Conquest Army in Early Islam', in *Christians and Others in the Umayyad State*, ed. Antoine Borrut and Fred M. Donner (Chicago, 2016), 83–129.

Al-Quḍāʿī, Muḥammad ibn Salāma, *ʿUyūn al-Maʿārif wa-Funūn Akhbār al-Khalā'if*, ed. ʿAbd al-Ḥamīd ʿAlī (ʿAmmān, 1997); Jamīl ʿAbd Allāh al-Maṣrī; *Ta'rīkh Al-Quḍāʿī (Kitāb ʿUyūn al-Maʿārif wa-Funūn Akhbār al-Khalā'if)* (Mecca, 1995); ed. ʿAbd al-Salām Tadmarī, *Kitāb al-Inbā' bi-Anbā' l-Anbiyā' wa-Tawārīkh al-Khulafā' wa-Wilāyāt al-Umarā'* [known as *Ta'rīkh al-Quḍāʿī*] (Beirut, 1998).

Rabb, Intisar A., 'The Curious Case of Bughaybigha, 661–883: Land and Leadership in Early Islamic Societies', in *Justice and Leadership in Early Islamic Courts*, ed. Intisar A. Rabb and Abigail Krasner Balbale (Cambridge, MA, 2017), 23–47.

Rabie, Hassanein, *The Financial System of Egypt* A.H. *564–741/*A.D. *1169–1341*, (London, 1972).

Rapoport, Yossef, *Marriage, Money and Divorce in Medieval Islamic Society* (Cambridge, 2005).

Raqīq al-Qayrawānī, Ibrāhīm ibn l-Qāsim, *Ta'rīkh Ifrīqiya wa-l-Maghrib*, ed. Muḥammad ʿAzab (Cairo, 1994).

Rebstock, Ulrich, 'A Qāḍī's Errors', *ILS*, 6 (1999), 1–37.

Redmount, Carol A., 'The Wadi Tumilat and the "Canal of the Pharaohs"', *JNES*, 54 (1995), 127–35.

Reinfandt, Lucian, 'Crime and Punishment in Early Islamic Egypt (AD 642–969): The Arabic Papyrological Evidence', in *Proceedings of the 25th International Congress of Papyrology*, ed. Traianos Gagos (Ann Arbor, 2010), 634–40.

Reinfandt, Lucian, 'Local Judicial Authority in Umayyad Egypt (41–132/661–750)', *BEO*, LXIII (2011), 127–46.

Reinfandt, Lucian, 'Arabic Papyrology and Early Islamic Egypt', in *JJP*, 43 (2013), 209–39.

Richter, Tonio Sebastian, 'The Law of Coptic Legal Documents', in *Law and Legal Practice in Egypt from Alexander to the Arab Conquest*, ed. James G. Keenan and others (Cambridge, 2014), 28–30.

Riḍā, Yūsuf Muḥammad, *Muʿjam al-ʿArabiyya al-Klāsīkiyya wa-l-Muʿāṣira* (Beirut, 2006).

Robinson, Chase F., *ʿAbd al-Malik* (Oxford, 2005).

Rosenthal, Franz, *The Herb. Hashish versus Medieval Muslim Society* (Leiden, 1971).

Rosenthal, Franz, *Gambling in Islam* (Leiden, 1975).

Rustow, Marina, *Heresy and the Politics of Community. The Jews of the Fatimid Caliphate* (Ithaca, 2008).

Rustow, Marina, 'At the Limits of Communal Autonomy: Jewish Bids for Intervention from the Mamluk State', *Mamluk Studies Review*, XIII (2009), 133–59, e-publication.

Rustow, Marina, 'Benefaction (Niʿima), Gratitude (Shukr), and the Politics of Giving and Receiving in Letters from the Cairo Geniza', in *Charity and Giving in Monotheistic Religions*, ed. Miriam Frenkel and Yaacov Lev (Berlin, 2009), 365–91.

Rustow, Marina, 'The Legal Status of ḏimmī-s in the Fatimid East: A View from the Palace in Cairo', in *The Legal Status of ḏimmī-s in the Islamic West (Second/Eight-Ninth/Fifteenth Centuries)*, ed. Maribel Fierro and John Tolan (Turnhout, 2013), 307–32.

Rustow, Marina, 'The Diplomatics of Leadership: Administrative Documents in Hebrew Script from the Geniza', in *Jews, Christians and Muslims in Medieval and Early Modern Times. A Festschrift in Honor of Mark R. Cohen*, ed. Arnold E. Franklin and others (Leiden, 2014), 306–52.

Sabari, Simha, *Mouvements populaires à Bagdad à l'époque abbasside IXe–XIe siècles* (Paris, 1981).

Sadan, Joseph, 'A New Source of the Buyid Period', *IOS*, IX (1979), 355–76.

Sadan, Joseph, 'A "Closed-Circuit" Saying on Practical Justice', *JSAI*, 10 (1987), 325–41.

Sadan, Joseph and Silverstein, Adam, 'Ornate Manuals or Practical Adab? Some Reflections on a Unique Work by an Anonymous Author of the 10th Century CE', *Al-Qantara*, XXV (2004), 339–55.

Saʿīd ibn Baṭrīq, *Kitāb al-Taʾrīkh*, published as Eutychii Patriarchae Alexandrini, *Annales*, ed. Louis Cheikho and others (Paris, 1906).

Sanders, Paula, 'Gendering the Ungendered Body: Hermaphrodites in Medieval Islamic Law', in *Women in Middle Eastern History*, ed. Nikki R. Keddie and Beth Baron (New Haven, 1991), 122–43.

Sanders, Paula, 'A New Source for the History of Fatimid Ceremonial: The Rasā'il al-ʿAmīdī', *AI*, XXV (1991), 127–31.

Sänger, Patrick, 'The Administration of Sasanian Egypt: New Masters and Byzantine Continuity', *Greek, Roman, and Byzantine Studies*, 51 (2011), 653–65.

Savant, Sarah Bowen, *The New Muslims of Post-Conquest Iran* (Cambridge, 2013).

Sayyid, Ayman Fu'ād, *La capitale de l'Égypte jusqu'à l'époque fatimide* (Beirut, 1998).

Sayyid, Ayman Fu'ād, *Al-Dawla al-Fāṭimiyya fī Miṣr. Tafsīr Jadīd* (Cairo, 2000, 2nd edn).

Sayyid, Ayman Fu'ād, 'Lumières nouvelles sur quelques sources de l'histoire fatimide en Égypte', *AI*, 13 (1977), 1–41.

Sayyid, Ayman Fu'ād, 'Nuṣūṣ Ḍāʿiʿh min Akhbār Miṣr li-Musabbiḥī', *AI*, 17 (1981), 1–54.

Sayyid, Ayman Fu'ād, 'L'évolution de la composition du genre de Khiṭaṭ en Égypte musulmane', in *The Historiography of Islamic Egypt (c.950–1800)*, ed. Hugh Kennedy (Leiden, 2001), 77–93.

Schacht, Joseph, *The Origins of Muhammadan Jurisprudence* (Oxford, 1950).

Schacht, Joseph, *An Introduction to Islamic Law* (Oxford, 1964).

Schacht, Joseph, 'Early Doctrines on Waqf', in *Mélanges Fuad Köprülü* (Istanbul, 1953), 143–52.

Schacht, Joseph, 'Pre-Islamic Background and Early Development of Jurisprudence', in *Law in the Middle East*, ed. Majid Khadduri and Herbert J. Liebesny (Washington, DC, 1955), 28–57.

Schneider, Irene, 'Imprisonment in Pre-Classical and Classical Islamic Law', *ILS*, 2 (1995), 153–73.

Serjeant, Robert B., 'A Zaidī Manual of Ḥisbah of the 3rd Century (H)', *Rivista degli Studi Orientali*, XXVIII (1957), 1–34.

Serjeant, Robert B., 'The Caliph ʿUmar's Letters to Abū Mūsā al-Ashaʿrī and Muʿawiyya', *JSS*, XXIX (1984), 65–79.

Shaddel, Mehdy, 'The Year According to the Reckoning of the Believers: Papyrus Louvre inv. J. David-Weil 20 and the Origins of the Hijrī Era', *Der Islam*, 95 (2018), 291–311.

El-Shamsy, Ahmed, *The Canonization of Islamic Law. A Social and Intellectual History* (New York, 2013).

El-Shamsy, Ahmed, 'The Logic of Excluding Testimonies in Early Islam', in *Justice and Leadership in Early Islamic Courts*, ed. Intisar A. Rabb and Abigail Krasner Balbale (Cambridge, MA, 2017), 3–16.

Shatzmiller, Maya, *Labour in the Medieval Islamic World* (Leiden, 1994).

Al-Shayzarī, ʿAbd al-Raḥman, *Nihāyat al-Rutba fī Ṭalab al-Ḥisba*, ed. Ḥasan Ismāʿīl and Farīd al-Mazīdī (Beirut, 2001).

Sheehan, Peter, *Babylon of Egypt. The Archeology of Old Cairo and the Origins of the City* (Cairo, 2010).

Sibṭ ibn al-Jawzī, *Mirʾāt al-Zamān fī Taʾrīkh al-Aʿyān*, ed. Juliette Rassi (Damascus, 2005).

Sijpesteijn, Petra M., 'New Rule over Old Structures: Egypt after the Muslim Conquest', in *Regime Change in the Ancient Near East and Egypt*, ed. Harriet Crawford (Oxford, 2007), 183–200.

Silverstein, Adam, J., *Postal Systems in the Pre-Modern Islamic World* (Cambridge, 2007).

Simonsohn, Uriel I., *A Common Justice. The Legal Allegiances of Christian and Jews under Early Islam* (Philadelphia, 2011).

Sourdel, Dominique, *Le vizirat abbaside de 749 à 936 (132 à 324 de l'Hégire)* (Damascus, 1959–60), 2 vols.

Stern, Gertrude H., 'Muḥammad's Bond with the Women', *BSOAS*, X (1939), 185–97.

Stern, Samuel M., *Studies in Early Ismailism* (Jerusalem, 1983).

Stewart, Devin J., 'Muḥammad B. Dāwūd al-Ẓāhirī's Manual of Jurisprudence: al-Wuṣūl Ilā Maʿrifat al-Uṣūl', in *Studies in Islamic Legal Theory*, ed. Bernard G. Weiss (Leiden, 2002), 99–161.

Stewart, Devin J., 'Muḥmmad B. Jarīr al-Ṭabarī's al-Bayān ʿan Uṣūl al-Aḥkām and the Genre of Uṣūl al-Fiqh in Ninth Century Baghdad', in *Abbasid Studies*, ed. James E. Montgomery (Leuven, 2004), 321–49.

Stillman, Norman A., 'The Non-Muslim Communities: The Jewish Communities', in *The Cambridge History of Egypt*, vol. I *Islamic Egypt, 640–1517*, ed. Carl F. Petry (Cambridge, 1998), 198–211.

Stilt, Kristen, *Islamic Law in Action. Authority, Discretion, and Everyday Experience in Mamluk Egypt* (New York, 2011).

Swanson, Mark N., 'The Martyrdom of Jirjis (Muzāḥim): Hagiography and Coptic Orthodox Imagination in Early Fatimid Egypt', *ME*, 21 (2015), 431–51.

Taylor, Christopher S., *In the Vicinity of the Righteous. Ziyāra and the Veneration of Muslim Saints in Late Medieval Egypt* (Leiden, 1999).

Theophanes Confessor, *The Chronicle of Theophanes Confessor. Byzantine and Near Eastern History* A.D. *284–813*, trans. and annotated by Cyril Mango and Roger Scott (Oxford, 1997).

Theophilus, bar Thomas of Edessa, *Theophilus of Edessa's Chronicle*, trans. and annotated by Robert G. Hoyland (Liverpool, 2011).

Tillier, Mathieu, *Vies des cadis de Misr 237/851–366/976* (Cairo, 2002).

Tillier, Mathieu, *Les cadis d'Iraq et l'État abbasside (132/750–334/945)* (Damascus, 2009).

Tillier, Mathieu, *Histoire des cadis Égyptiens* (Cairo, 2012).

Tillier, Mathieu, 'Un traité politique du IIe/VIIIe siècle: l'épître de ʿUbayd Allāh b. al-Ḥasan al-ʿAnbarī au calife al-Mahdī', *AI*, 40 (2006), 139–70.

Tillier, Mathieu, 'Prisons et autorités urbaines sous les Abbassides', *Arabica*, 55 (2008), 387–408.

Tillier, Mathieu, 'La société abbasside au miroir du tribunal. Égalité juridique et hiérarchie sociale', *AI*, 42 (2008), 157–86.

Tillier, Mathieu, 'Qadis and the Political Use of the Maẓālim Jurisdiction under the Abbasids', in *Public Violence in Islamic Societies*, ed. Christian Lange and Maribel Fierro (Edinburgh, 2009), 42–67.

Tillier, Mathieu, 'Le statut et la conservation des archives judiciaires dans l'Orient abbasside (IIe/VIIIe–IVe/Xe siècle): un réexamen', in *L'autorité de l'écrit au Moyen Âge (Orient–Occident)* (Paris, 2009), 263–77.

Tillier, Mathieu, 'Vivre en prison à l'époque abbasside', *JESHO*, 52 (2009), 635–59.

Tillier, Mathieu, 'Women before the Qāḍī under the Abbasids', *ILS*, 16 (2009), 280–301.

Tillier, Mathieu, 'The Qāḍīs of Fusṭāṭ-Miṣr under the Tulunids and the Ikhshidids: The Judiciary and Egyptian Autonomy', *JAOS*, 131 (2011), 207–22.

Tillier, Mathieu, 'Les "premiers" cadis de Fusṭāṭ et les dynamiques régionales de l'innovation judiciaire (750–833)', *AI*, 45 (2011), 213–42.

Tillier, Mathieu, 'Scribes et enquêteurs. Note sur le personnel judiciaire en Égypte aux quatre premiers siècles de l'hégire', *JESHO*, 54 (2011), 370–404.

Tillier, Mathieu, 'Du pagarque au cadi: ruptures et continuités dans l'administration judiciaire de la Haute-Égypte (Ier–IIIe/VIIe–IXe siècle)', *Médiévales*, 64 (2013), 19–36.

Tillier, Mathieu, 'Legal Knowledge and Local Practices under the Early Abbasids', in *History and Identity in the Late Antique Near East*, ed. Philip Wood (Oxford, 2013), 187–204.

Tillier, Mathieu, 'Califes, émirs et cadis: le droit califal et l'articulation de l'autorité judiciaire à l'époque umayyade', *BEO*, LXIII (2014), 147–90.

Tillier, Mathieu, 'Judicial Authority and Qāḍīs' Autonomy under the Abbasids', *Al-Masaq*, 26 (2014), 119–31.

Tillier, Mathieu, 'The Qāḍī before the Judge: The Social Use of Eschatology in Muslim Courts', in *The Divine Courtroom in Comparative Perspective*, ed. Ari Mermelstein and Shalom E. Holtz (Leiden, 2014), 260–76.

Tillier, Mathieu, 'Dispensing Justice in a Minority Context: The Judicial Administration of Upper Egypt under Muslim Rule in the Early Eighth Century', in *The Late Antique World of Early Islam: Muslims among Christians and Jews in the East Mediterranean*, ed. Robert G. Hoyland (Princeton, 2015), 133–57.

Tillier, Mathieu, 'The Maẓālim in Historiography', in *The Oxford Handbook of Islamic Law*, ed. Anver M. Emon and Rumee Ahmed (Oxford, 2015).

Tillier, Mathieu, 'The Qāḍī's Justice according to Papyrological Sources (Seventh–Tenth Centuries CE)', in *Legal Documents as Sources for the History of Muslim Societies, Studies in Honour of Rudolph Peters*, ed. Maaike van Berkel and others (Leiden, 2017), 39–60.

Tillier, Mathieu, 'Qāḍīs and Their Social Networks: Defining the Judge's Neutrality in Abbasid Iraq', *Journal of Abbasid Studies*, 4 (2017), 123–41.

Trombley, Frank R., 'Sawīrus ibn al-Muqaffaʿ and the Christians of Umayyad Egypt', in *Papyrology and the History of Early Islamic Egypt*, ed. Petra M. Sijpesteijn and Lennart Sundelin (Leiden, 2004), 163–199.

Trombley, Frank R., 'Fiscal Documents from the Muslim Conquest of Egypt', *Revue des études byzantines*, 71 (2013), 5–38.

Tsafrir, Nurit, *The History of an Islamic School of Law. The Early Spread of Hanafism*, (Cambridge, MA, 2004).

Tsafrir, Nurit, 'The ʿĀqila in Ḥanafī Law: Preliminary Notes', in *The Islamic Scholarly Tradition, Studies in History, Law, and Thought in Honor of Professor Michael Allan Cook*, ed. Asad Q. Ahmed and others (Leiden, 2011), 239–65.

Tyan, Emile, *Histoire de l'organisation judiciaire en pays d'Islam* (Leiden, 1960).

Udfuwī, Kamāl al-Dīn Jaʿfar, *Al-Ṭāliʿ al-Ṣaʿīd*, ed. Saʿd Muḥammad Ḥasan (Cairo, 1966).

Udovitch, Abraham M., 'Merchants and Amīrs: Government and Trade in Eleventh-Century Egypt', The Medieval Levant. Studies in Memory of Eliyahu Ashtor (1914–1984), *Asian and African Studies* (Haifa), 22 (1988), 53–73.

Udovitch, Abraham M., 'Fatimid Cairo: Crossroads of World Trade – From Spain to India', in *L'Égypte fatimide son art et son histoire*, ed. Marianne Barrucand (Paris, 1999), 681–93.

Udovitch, Abraham M., 'International Trade and the Medieval Egyptian Countryside', in *Agriculture in Egypt from Pharaonic to Modern Times*, ed. Alan K. Bowman and Eugene Rogan (Oxford, 1999), 267–87.

'Umar al-Kindī, Ibn Muḥammad ibn Yūsuf al-Kindī, *Faḍā'il Miṣr*, ed. Ibrāhīm Aḥmad al-'Adawī and 'Alī Muḥammad 'Umar (Cairo, 1971).

Vliet, Jacques van der, 'Coptic Documentary Papyri after the Arab Conquest', *JJP*, XLIII (2013), 187–208.

Wakī', Muḥammad ibn Khalf ibn Ḥayyān, *Akhbār al-Quḍāt*, ed. 'Abd al-'Azīz Muṣṭafā al-Marāghī (Cairo, 1947–50), 3 vols.

Wakin, Jeanette A., *The Function of Documents in Islamic Law. The Chapters on Sale from Ṭaḥāwīs Kitāb al-Shurūṭ al-Kabīr* (Albany, 1972).

Walker, Paul E., 'Another Family of Fatimid Chief Qāḍīs: The al-Fāriqīs', *Journal of Druze Studies*, 1 (2000), 49–69, reprinted in Walker, *Fatimid History and Ismā'īlī Doctrine* (Aldershot, 2008).

Walker, Paul E., 'The Relationship between the Chief Qāḍī and Chief Dā'ī under the Fatimids', in *Speaking for Islam. Religious Authority in Muslim Societies*, ed. Gurdun Krämer and Sabine Schmidtke (Leiden, 2006), 70–95.

Webb, Peter, *Imagining the Arabs. Arab Identity and the Rise of Islam* (Edinburgh, 2016).

Weber, Max, *Economy and Society*, ed. Guenther Roth and Claus Wittich, many translators (Berkeley and Los Angeles, 1978), 2 vols.

Whitcomb, Donald, 'An Umayyad Legacy for the Early Islamic City: Fusṭāṭ and the Experience of Egypt', in *Umayyad Legacies. Medieval Memories from Syria to Spain*, ed. Antoine Borrut and Paul Cobb (Leiden, 2010), 403–16.

Worp, K. A., 'Hegira Years in Greek, Greek-Coptic and Greek-Arabic Papyri', *Aegyptus*, 65 (1985), 107–15.

Yanagihashi, Hiroyuki, *A History of the Early Islamic Law of Property. Reconstructing the Legal Development, 7th–9th Centuries* (Leiden, 2004).

Yanagihashi, Hiroyuki, 'The Doctrinal Development of "Maraḍ al-Mawt" in the Formative Period of Islamic Law', *ILS*, 5 (1998), 326–58.

Ya'qūbī, Aḥmad ibn Abū, *Ta'rīkh al-Ya'qūbī* (Beirut, 1960), 2 vols.

Yāqūt, al-Ḥamawī al-Rūmī, *Mu'jam al-Udabā'*, ed. Iḥsān 'Abbās (Beirut, 1993), vol. VI.

Young, Michael J. L., 'Abū l-'Arab al-Qayrawānī and his Biographical

Dictionary of the Scholars of Qayrawān and Tunis', *Al-Masaq*, 6 (1993), 57–75.

Zaman, Muhammad Qasim, *Religion and Politics under the Early Abbasids* (Leiden, 1997).

Zaman, Muhammad Qasim, 'The Caliphs, the "Ulamā", and the Law: Defining the Role and Function of the Caliph in the Early Abbasid Period', *ILS*, 4 (1997), 1–36.

Zaman, Muhammad Qasim, 'Death, Funeral Processions, and the Articulation of Religious authority in Early Islam', *SI*, 93 (2001), 27–58.

Zarinebaf, Fariba, *Crime and Punishment in Istanbul, 1700–1800* (Berkeley and Los Angeles, 2010).

Ziadeh, Farhat J. 'Adab al-Qāḍī and the Protections of Rights at Court', in *Studies in Islamic and Judaic Traditions*, ed. Stephen David Ricks and William M. Brinner (Denver, 1986), 143–50.

Zimmermann, Martin, 'Violence in Late Antiquity Reconsidered', in *Violence in Late Antiquity: Perceptions and Practices*, ed. H. A. Drake (Aldershot, 2006), 344–57.

Zinger, Oded, '"She Aims to Harass Him": Jewish Women in Muslim Legal Venues in Medieval Egypt', *AJS Review*, 42 (2018), 159–92.

Index

Abbott, Nabia, 16
ʿAbd al-ʿAzīz, governor
  policies, 14
ʿAbd al-ʿAzīz ibn Muḥammad ibn al-Nuʿmān, cadi
  judicial and administrative responsibilities, 133–4
  judicial appointments, 134–5
  teaching of Ismailism, 134
ʿAbd al-Malik, caliph
  policies, 8, 11, 14
ʿAbd al-Raḥmān ibn Muʿāwiya, cadi
  supervision of orphans, 52–3
Abū ḥajjāj Yūsuf, cadi
  judicial and administrative responsibilities, 155–6, 262
Abū Zurʿa, cadi
  judicial and administrative responsibilities, 88
  status, 88–9
Abū Zurʿa, historian, 45, 103
Ackerman-Lieberman, Philip I, 240–1, 249, 258
Afḍal, military vizier
  assassination, 150
  judicial policies in Alexandria, 146–7
  seizure of inheritances, 147, 148
ʿAlī ibn Qāḍī al-Nuʿmān, cadi
  early career, 123
  imposition of Ismāʿīlī law, 126
  judicial and administrative responsibilities, 124–5, 127
ʿAmr ibn al-ʿĀṣ, governor
  policies, 14, 16–17, 20, 26, 46, 48
amwāl al-yatāmā (orphans' money), 52, 53–4
  abuse, 130–1, 243
  proper management, 54–5
Anṭākī, historian, 173, 174, 175
ʿ*aqib*, 105
ʿ*āqila*, 49
ʿ*aql*, 51

Badr al-Jamālī, military vizier
  early career, 146
  judicial policies, 147, 150
  seizure of power, 146
Bakkār ibn Qutayba, cadi
  education, 108
  relations with Aḥmad ibn Ṭūlūn, 83, 85
  rulings, 83–4, 86, 106
  salary, 83, 85
  writings, 108, 109
Balawī, historian/biographer, 84, 162
Baldwin, James E., 259
Battle of Ṣiffīn, 17, 32, 51
Ben-Sasson, Menahem, 247
Booth, Phil, 16
Bouderbala, Sobhi, 61
Brett, Michael, 111
Brockopp, Jonathan E., 105
Bruning, Jelle, 9, 10, 47, 96, 98, 255

cadi
  appointment, 2, 23, 41, 70–1, 88–9, 91–2, 103, 124, 152, 153, 156
  coercive powers, 77–8
  education, 101
  executive powers, 212–13, 262
  extra-judicial powers, 91–4
  in Alexandria, 96, 128, 134, 137, 146–7
  in provincial towns, 10, 23, 90–1, 95, 96, 97, 116, 124, 125, 127, 134, 137, 139, 144, 156
  involvement in criminal cases, 5–6, 91–2
  involvement in tax collection, 153–4
  jail, 78

salaries, 73–4, 85, 86, 93
social background, 69–71
supervision of *waqfs*, 63–4, 65, 80, 86–7, 91, 93, 121, 134, 136, 137, 260
see also orphans, *qāḍī*
Canbakal, Hülya, 39
chief of police, 52, 64, 96, 126, 127, 162, 164, 167, 169, 170, 172, 173, 175, 176, 178, 180, 181; *see also ṣāḥib al-shurṭa*
Cohen, Mark R., 192, 236, 252
Copts
identity, 254, 255
in Byzantine Egypt, 253–4
in Muslim courts, 256, 257
Cornu, Georgette, 95
Coulson, Noel J., 100, 105
court witnesses, 65–9, 78, 129, 137, 149
crime
against religion, 77
apostasy, 173–4, 175
looting, 166, 176, 178, 181
murder, 169, 172, 180, 211
robbery, 170–1, 172
sexual, 48, 169
theft, 170, 171
Crone, Patricia, 100, 162, 185

Dachraoui, Farhat, 111
den Heijer, Johannes, 175
Dhuhlī, cadi
career under the Fatimids, 120–1, 123, 124, 261
early career, 94–5
old age and retirement, 125–6
rulings, 79–80, 122
dīwān (military payroll), 18–20, 49
cadi's archive, 71–2, 126, 137, 149
Donner, Fred M., 11, 161
Dutton, Yasin, 99

Ebstein, Michael, 161

famine
famine of 1024–5, 191–7
typology of famines in Egypt, 187–9, 190
Fāriqī, cadi
early appointments, 132
execution, 136
judicial and administrative responsibilities, 134–6
Foss, Clive, 13, 28
Foster, Benjamin R., 185
Frantz-Murphy, Gladys, 28, 34, 98, 256
Frenkel, Miriam, 239
Friedman, Mordechai Akiva, 34

Garel, Eshter, 254
Gascou, Jean, 25, 29
Gerber, Haim, 241
Gil, Moshe, 241, 242
Gimaret, Daniel, 197
Gleave, Robert, 98–9
Goitein, S. D., 170, 177, 232, 239, 241, 242, 258
Goldberg, Jessica L., 34
Gottheil, Richard J. H., 111

ḥabs, 177
in the palace, 177
run by cadi, 77–8
run by chief of police, 163, 170, 171, 177
ḥadd/ḥudūd, 2, 5, 162, 164
ḥajj, 15
Ḥākim, caliph
chiefs of police, 164–5, 166–7
generosity, 131
judicial appointments, 132–3
persecution of non-Muslims, 173, 223, 232
policies, 164–5, 203–4, 215, 227, 244
reign of terror, 227
ḥākim
in the towns of the Delta, 95, 96, 98
Hallaq, Wael B., 72, 104, 108
Halm, Heinz, 111
Ḥārith ibn Miskīn, cadi
appointments made by, 97
confrontation with the caliph, 43, 44–5
involvement in a *waqf* case, 61, 106
Hennigan, Peter C., 58
Hinds, Martin, 100
ḥisba (manuals) 1, 185–6, 189, 199, 263
institution of the, 3, 4, 197–8, 199–200
religious underpinnings, 185–6, 187, 201, 263
Hoyland, Robert, 13
Ḥusayn ibn ʿAlī ibn al-Nuʿmān, cadi
execution, 133
judicial and administrative responsibilities, 132
judicial appointments, 132–3
remuneration, 131
teaching of Ismailism, 132
weekly schedule, 138

Ibn ʿAbd al-Ḥakam, historian, 20, 45, 47
Ibn Abī l-ʿAwwām, cadi
early appointments, 132, 136
judicial and administrative responsibilities, 137–8, 139–40
natural death, 138
social background, 136
weekly schedule, 137
Ibn Abī Thawbān, cadi
incompetence, 121–2, 150
Ibn Dawwās, Yaʿqūb, *muḥtasib*
policies during the famine of 1024–5, 192–7
Ibn Durbās, cadi
judicial and administrative responsibilities, 156–7
nomination of Sunnī cadis, 152–3
Ibn Ḥabḥāb, governor
policies, 27
Ibn Ḥabīb, historian, 8, 48
Ibn Ḥajar, historian, 51, 86, 105, 108, 112, 121, 127, 138, 156, 175, 246
Ibn Ḥarb, cadi
financial dealings, 87
judicial and administrative responsibilities, 86–7
personality, 87–8, 261
salary, 86
Ibn Ḥawqal, geographer
description of the Delta, 10, 95–7, 247–8
Ibn Isḥāq, historian, 16
Ibn Khallikān, cadi
judicial and administrative responsibilities, 157, 260
Ibn al-Khayyāt, historian, 45
Ibn Killis, Yaʿqūb, vizier
involvement in judicial affairs, 122, 126–7, 128, 129–30, 144, 180
policies, 123–4
Ibn Muyassar, historian, 148
Ibn Saʿd, biographer, 17
Ibn al-Ṣayrafī, historian, 180
Ibn Taghrī Birdī, historian, 251
Ibn Ṭūlūn, Aḥmad, ruler of Egypt
cadis, 83–4, 85, 86
charities, 78–9
involvement in Abbasid politics, 85, 88
secret police, 74–5
social background of , 22
Ibn al-Ṭuwayr, historian, 198
Ibn Yūnus, biographer, 30, 32, 64
Ibn Zubayr, rebel, 14, 20, 101
Ibn Zūlāq, historian, 86, 121, 130, 164, 176, 260
author of *Faḍāʾil Miṣr*, 25, 33–4
Ibrāhīm ibn Isḥāq, cadi
criticism of authorities, 42–3
Idrīs ʿImād al-Dīn, historian, 113, 116, 117–18, 122
irtidād, 173, 174, 175
Ismāʿīl ibn Alīsa, cadi
nullification of *waqfs*, 59, 104
ʿIyād ibn ʿUbayd Allāh, cadi
consultations with the caliph, 50–1

jail *see ḥabs*
Jany, János, 4, 5
Jews/Jewish
court, 232, 233, 234, 237, 242, 244–5, 249
identity, 252, 258, 264
in Muslim courts, 243, 245–7, 248–9, 250, 251–2
in pre-Fatimid Egypt, 231–2
leaders and communal officials, 234, 235, 236–7, 239, 240, 241–2, 242, 244–5
orphans, 242, 243–4
see also waqf
John, Bishop of Nikiu, historian, 26
Jokish, Benjamin, 55
Judd, Steven, 91

Kaʾb ibn Ḍinna, cadi
in Arab paganism and early Islam, 46, 47–8
Kaegi, Walter E., 25
Kāfūr, ruler of Egypt, 23, 94–5, 261
support of jurists, 108
Khan, Geoffrey, 29, 109, 154, 155, 221, 225
Kindī, historian, 17, 18, 46, 47, 62, 63, 69, 73, 100, 101, 102, 104, 105, 106, 107, 246, 256
Knost, Stefan, 39
Krakowski, Eve, 214, 252

Lalani, Arzina B., 37
Lecker, Michael, 16, 161
Legendre, Marie, 9, 11
Libson, Gideon, 233

Madelung, Wilferd, 115
madhhab, 99, 104, 105, 106, 108
majlis al-ḥukm/taḥakkum, 97, 210, 211, 212

Ma᾿mūn, caliph
in Egypt, 41, 43
policies, 22, 43–4, 107
Manṣūr, caliph
policies, 18, 53–4, 103
political concepts, 41–2
Maqrīzī, historian, 70, 108, 121, 131, 138, 147, 148, 149, 153, 165, 167, 176, 190, 191, 199, 200, 202, 203
Marmer, David, 40
Marsham, Andrew, 16, 17
Marwarrudhī, cadi
in Kairouan, 113–15
masākīn wa-l-fuqarā᾿, 29, 58
Maslama ibn Mukhallad, governor
policies, 13, 52
Māwardī, jurist
author of *Aḥkām al-Sulṭāniyya*, 2
on the legal system, 2–7, 39–40, 201
al-mawārīth al-ḥashriyya, 63
mawlā/mawālī, 19, 49, 50, 70
maẓālim, 1, 111, 123
in Fatimid Egypt, 203–4
institution and court, 4, 5, 78, 86, 92, 105, 127, 132, 134, 153, 155 263
institutional characteristics, 204–5, 227, 228, 263
miḥna, 43, 44, 70, 81, 106, 107
Mikhail, Maged S., A. 9, 98, 233, 254
Morton, Alexander H., 185
Motzkin, Areyh Leo, 244
Mu῾āwiya, caliph, 12–13
naval policies, 31–2
policies, 13, 15, 16–17, 20, 31, 32, 51–2
titles, 12
Muḥammad ibn Masrūq, cadi
confrontation with the caliph, 76
Muḥammad ibn al-Qāḍī al-Nu῾mān, cadi
embezzlement of the orphan's money, 130–1, 243
judicial and administrative responsibilities, 128–9
rulings of 175
teaching of Ismailisim, 130
Muḥammad ibn Ṭughj al-Ikhshīd, ruler of Egypt
social background, 23
muḥtasib, 1
congruous terms, 184–5
duties, 186–7, 190, 197, 199–200, 249, 250
see also Ibn Dawwās
Musabbiḥī, historian, 130, 131, 138, 139, 143, 144, 154, 164, 168, 171, 172, 173, 174, 177, 178, 260
on the famine of 1024–5, 191–7
Mu῾taḍid, caliph
policies, 33
Mu῾taṣim, caliph
policies, 20, 21, 22, 106, 107
Mutawakkil, caliph
policies, 32–3, 44–5, 107

Nagy, Gyula Káldy, 38
naqīb/niqāba, 6, 156
Novak, Maria, 254

Oberauer, Norbert, 57
Olszowy-Schlanger, Judith, 244, 245
orphans
abuse of orphans' money, 53, 54, 130–1, 243
cadis' supervision, 52–3, 54, 55, 130–1, 261
see also Jews/Jewish

Palme, Bernhard, 253, 255
Papaconstantinou, Arietta, 255
Peirce, Lesile, 39
Peters, Frank E., 8
petitions
personal requests, 210, 211–12, 220–1, 221–2
submitted against cadis, 209
submitted against officials, 208
submitted by Christians, 223–4
submitted by Jews, 217, 218, 220–1, 224–5, 234–5
submitted by monks, 205–6, 207–8, 223–4
submitted to cadis, 209–10, 212–13, 215–16
pious endowment *see waqf*
police *see shurṭa*
Powers, David S., 39
Powers, Paul R., 106
prison *see ḥabs*

qāḍī
as a title, 151, 217; *see also* cadi
concept, 37, 38, 40, 248
in the towns of the Delta, 95–7
Qāḍī al-Fāḍil, administrator
early career, 151
letters of appointment written by, 152, 198

Qāḍī al-Nuʿmān, cadi
appointments in Ifrīqiya, 116–17, 118
life in Egypt, 138, 142
writings, 99, 112–13, 115, 117–18, 123, 130, 133, 134, 147
qāḍī al-quḍāt
in the Abbasid caliphate, 88, 89, 90, 103, 104
in the Fatimid state, 113, 116, 124, 133, 134–5, 138–44, 145, 149, 150, 151, 154, 155, 157, 209–10, 260
under Saladin, 152–3, 156–7
Qalqashandī, historian, 198
qaṣaṣ/qāṣṣ, 51–2
Quḍāʿī, historian, 51, 90, 144
Qurra ibn Sharīk, governor
letters, 32, 98, 206, 255
policies, 14, 26, 28–9

Rāġib, Yūsuf, 47
raʾy, 99, 101, 104
Rebstock, Ulrich, 78
Reinfandt, Lucian, 9, 10, 98
Richter, Tonio Sebastian, 254
Russell, Josiah C., 25
Rustow, Marina, 214, 215, 149

ṣadaqāt (charities), 21, 22, 26, 57, 58
alms tax, 29
ṣāḥib al-shurṭa, 1
responsibilities, 162, 163, 165–6, 180, 200
social background, 164–5, 166, 167
see also chief of police
Saladin, sultan, 15
cadis, 152, 153, 156–7
petitions submitted to, 218–19
seizure of power in Egypt, 152–3
Sarī ibn al-Ḥakam, governor
interference in judicial affairs, 43
Sayyid, Ayman Fuʾād, 111, 163
Schacht, Joseph, 2, 37, 57, 100, 262, 263, 264
Schneider, Irene, 79
Serjeant, R. S., 185
shurṭa, 1, 250
in Cairo, 163
in Fatimid Fusṭāṭ, 164, 168–76, 178,179, 180, 181, 183
in Ifrīqiya, 165
in pre-Fatimid Fusṭāṭ, 162
origins, 161–2, 263
terminological shift, 163–4
shurūt (formularies), 83, 108, 109
Sībawayhi, 'holy fool'
dislike of the *ḥisba*, 187
imprisonment, 76–7
Sijpesteijn, Petra M., 9, 28, 29, 98
Stern, Samuel M., 120, 207, 223, 224, 225
Stewart, Devin, 99
Stilt, Kristen, 201
Sulaym ibn ʿItr, cadi, 48, 49, 51–2
recording of rulings, 71–2, 80
rulings, 49
supreme cadi *see qāḍī al-quḍāt*
sulṭān
authority, 64, 84, 142
in the context of the Delta, 96, 247–8
in the Jewish context, 247, 250

Tawba ibn Namir, cadi, 42, 50
supervision of *waqfs*, 58–9, 61, 71–2
testimony (in court), 65–6, 67–8, 69–70
Tillier, Mathieu, 9, 10, 37, 38, 46, 68, 81, 89, 91, 96, 98, 100, 103, 105, 202, 209, 254
ṭirāz, 27, 125
Ṭurṭūshī, jurist
confrontation with the vizier, 147–9
in Alexandria, 119
Tyan, Emile, 3, 4, 5, 201, 202

Udovitch, Abraham L., 34
ʿUmar ibn ʿAbd al-ʿAzīz (ʿUmar II), caliph
involvement in judicial cases, 49, 50–1, 100–1, 102, 103
policies, 20, 21
ʿUmar ibn al-Khaṭṭāb (ʿUmar I), caliph
creation of a *waqf*, 56–7
creation of the judicial system, 45–6, 48
instructions to cadis, 41
policies, 19, 26–7
titles, 12, 26
ʿUmar al-Kindī, historian
author of *Faḍāʾil Miṣr*, 25–6, 33–4
uṣūl al-fiqh, 99

van der Vliet, Jacques, 254

wafd, 17, 18
Wakī, biographer, 65–6, 67
Wakin, Jeanette A., 108
walī ʿahd al-muslimīn, 12
Walīd I, caliph
policies, 32

waqf
  cadis' control, 58, 59, 63–4, 71, 80, 260, 261
  Christian, 176, 173, 207, 223, 224
  creation, 60–1, 62–3, 64, 65
  decline, 215
  disputes concerning, 92, 105–6
  Jewish, 241–2
  maintenance, 61–2, 260
  nullification, 59, 84
  origins, 55–8
  seizure by the Fatimids, 123–4
Weber, Max
  Kadijustiz concept, 38, 39, 101–2
Weiss, Bernard, 104
Weiss, Gershon, 238, 239
wuqūf, 13

Yaʿqūbī, historian, 15
Yāqūt, biographer, 261
Yāzūrī, vizier
  administrative and judicial responsibilities, 145
  execution, 145
  social background, 144–5

zakāt, 29, 58, 67
Zinger, Oded, 245, 247

EU representative:
Easy Access System Europe
Mustamäe tee 50, 10621 Tallinn, Estonia
Gpsr.requests@easproject.com

www.ingramcontent.com/pod-product-compliance
Lightning Source LLC
Chambersburg PA
CBHW050207240426
43671CB00013B/2249
* 9 7 8 1 4 7 4 4 5 9 2 4 2 *